TERRA
MAXIMA

The records of humankind

Wolfgang Kunth, editor

FIREFLY BOOKS

*For Nicolai
and Calvin*

A FIREFLY BOOK

Published in English by
Firefly Books Ltd. 2013

Copyright © 2012 Verlag Wolfgang Kunth
GmbH & Co KG, Munich

First printing

**Publisher Cataloging-in-Publication
Data (U.S.)**
A CIP record for this book is available from
Library of Congress

**Library and Archives Canada
Cataloguing in Publication**
A CIP record for this book is available from
Library and Archives Canada

Published in the United States by
Firefly Books (U.S.) Inc.
P.O. Box 1338, Ellicott Station
Buffalo, New York 14205

Published in Canada by
Firefly Books Ltd.
50 Staples Avenue, Unit 1
Richmond Hill, Ontario L4B 0A7

Printed in China

All the facts have been checked to the best
of our knowledge and with the greatest
possible care. The editors and the publisher
cannot however guarantee that the information is absolutely correct, complete and
up to date. The publishers are always grate-
ful for any information and suggestions for
improvements.

Shanghai has many faces. Here it
presents its futurist side: the business
and hi-tech district of Pudong.
Construction of this modern district
east of the Huangpu River only began
in 1990.

TERRA
MAXIMA
The records of humankind

INTRODUCTION

Sophisticated technology and the human enquiring mind have long allowed humans to conquer space. The "Voyager" space probe, sent into space in 1977, is considered one of NASA's greatest successes (small picture), and it still transmits data to Earth today. Large picture: the surface of Jupiter with one of its moons.

Humans have admired and studied the most outstanding products of civilization since time immemorial. Likewise, the ways that these records of achievement symbolize the cultures they represent never cease to captivate the human mind. In this book, the most important records of humankind have been brought together in one beautiful, useful compendium.

From the most widely used languages and scripts in the world and the greatest national and religious communities to giant structures and the technological successes of the modern age — this volume offers a fascinating overview of the great record achievements of humankind, presenting them in their entirety and diversity.

With a wealth of outstanding images by top photographers of international renown TERRA MAXIMA presents the greatest religious structures that have been built around the world. The book showcases the magnificent residences that secular rulers have had erected over the centuries as a symbol of their power, as well as the soaring monuments of contemporary architecture and the superb feats of modern engineering. Also explored are the economic developments and population growth in our planet's megacities as well as the pioneering work done in science and technology. Further sections cover innovations in the construction of museums, theaters, libraries and sports venues. Numerous ranking lists provide an at-a-glance overview, while concise descriptions supply useful background information on every topic.

—Wolfgang Kunth

In the wide plain of San Agustin in New Mexico, 27 radio telescopes are aiming their dishes at space. The Very Large Array is an interferometer intended for astronomic observations.

CONTENTS

The Golden Gate Bridge at the entrance to San Francisco Bay. The steel suspension bridge has been the city's emblem since its completion in 1937.

CONTENTS

St. Peter's Basilica in Rome, with its Michelangelo-designed dome, is not only the focal point for Christendom but also the largest of all Christian churches.

CONTENTS

COUNTRIES AND NATIONS

The political geography of Earth is subject to constant change. In the short period of time between the end of World War II and the start of the new

The UN has 193 member states

millennium alone important empires like the British Empire and the Soviet Union have vanished. New states have formed. The UN, which counted 51 member states when it was founded, today comprises 193 nations. The plurality of nations in the modern world contrasts with a trend for increasing international cooperation. Ever more countries forge alliances or treaties of collaboration. The member states of the European Union have even transferred some of their sovereign rights to supranational institutions.

THE LARGEST COUNTRIES IN THE WORLD (area)

① **Russia**
6,593,000 sq ml (17,075,800 sq km)
② **Canada**
3,855,101 sq ml (9,984,670 sq km)
③ **PR China**
3,722,340 sq ml (9,640,821 sq km)
④ **USA**
3,717,811 sq ml (9,629,091 sq km)
⑤ **Brazil**
3,286,487 sq ml (8,511,965 sq km)
⑥ **Australia**
2,967,908 sq ml (7,686,850 sq km)
⑦ **India**
1,269,219 sq ml (3,287,263 sq km)
⑧ **Argentina**
1,068,302 sq ml (2,766,890 sq km)
⑩ **Algeria**
919,595 sq ml (2,381,740 sq km)
⑪ **DR Congo**
905,567 sq ml (2,345,410 sq km)
⑫ **Mexico**
758,449 sq ml (1,964,375 sq km)
⑬ **Saudi Arabia**
756,985 sq ml (1,960,582 sq km)
⑭ **Indonesia**
741,100 sq ml (1,919,440 sq km)
⑮ **Sudan**
718,723 sq ml (1,861,484 sq km)
⑯ **Libya**
679,308 sq ml (1,759,400 sq km)
⑰ **Chad**
495,755 sq ml (1,284,000 sq km)

THE LARGEST COUNTRIES IN THE WORLD
(population)   (reference year 2010)

① PR China	1.35 billion
② India	1.21 billion
③ USA	317.2 million
④ Indonesia	237.6 million
⑤ Brazil	192.3 million
⑥ Pakistan	179 million
⑦ Nigeria	162.5 million
⑧ Russia	143 million
⑨ Bangladesh	142.3 million
⑩ Japan	127.8 million
⑪ Mexico	112.3 million
⑫ Philippines	92.3 million
⑬ Ethiopia	84.3 million
⑭ Germany	81.8 million
⑮ Egypt	81.7 million
⑯ Turkey	74.8 million

The globe in front of the Palace of Nations in Geneva. From 1933 until its dissolution in 1946 this building served as the headquarters of the League of Nations. Today it houses the "United Nations Office at Geneva," the second most important building of the community of states after its New York headquarters. The Office of the UN High Commissioner for Human Rights is also based here.

THE LARGEST COUNTRIES IN THE WORLD (AREA/POPULATION)

In the course of the voyages of exploration of the 15th and 16th centuries, vast areas on Earth were colonized by Europeans. After World War II most colonies achieved their independence, and the number of countries has multiplied.

Including the Vatican City State, which enjoys a special political status, at present 194 sovereign countries are recognized by the UN and are member states of the global community. The five largest of these by area, namely Russia, Canada, the USA, China and Brazil, cover around one-third of our planet's land mass, whereas the next five — Australia, India, Argentina, Kazakhstan and the Sudan — cover just under 15 percent. Nor is the world's population equally distributed on Earth: all the continents have vast regions that are virtually inaccessible and therefore only thinly populated. The vast majority of today's 7 billion people live in the coastal regions and along the large rivers. Almost 90 percent of the people of the People's Republic of China, for example, the most populous country on Earth, are crowded in the coastal areas of the country's southeastern regions. Here the population density is high, whereas in its mountainous west it is extremely low. In the People's Republic, just like in the populous countries of Southern Asia, Africa and Latin America, ever more people are drawn to the large conurbations. The

THE LARGEST COUNTRIES IN EUROPE

AREA
❶	Russia, Europe	3,952,800 sq km
❷	Ukraine	603,700 sq km
❸	France	547,030 sq km
❹	Spain	504,851 sq km
❺	Sweden	449,964 sq km
❻	Germany	357,021 sq km

POPULATION (reference year 2010)
❶	Russia, Europe	104 million
❷	Germany	81.8 million
❸	France	65.3 million
❹	Great Britain	62.3 million
❺	Italy	60.8 million
❻	Spain	47.2 million

THE LARGEST COUNTRIES IN ASIA

AREA
❶	Russia, Asia	13,123,400 sq km
❷	PR China	9,640,821 sq km
❸	India	3,287,263 sq km
❹	Kazakhstan	2,724,927 sq km
❺	Saudi Arabia	1,960,582 sq km
❻	Indonesia	1,919,440 sq km

POPULATION (reference year 2010)
❶	PR China	1.3 billion
❷	India	1.2 billion
❸	Indonesia	237.6 million
❹	Pakistan	179 million
❺	Bangladesh	142.3 million
❻	Japan	127.8 million

THE LARGEST COUNTRIES IN OCEANIA

AREA
❶	Australia	7,686,850 sq km
❷	Papua New Guinea	462,840 sq km
❸	New Zealand	268,680 sq km
❹	Solomon Islands	28,450 sq km
❺	Fiji	18,280 sq km
❻	Vanuatu	12,200 sq km

POPULATION (reference year 2010)
❶	Australia	22.9 million
❷	Papua New Guinea	7 million
❸	New Zealand	4.5 million
❹	Fiji	0.7 million
❺	Solomon Islands	0.5 million
❻	Vanuatu	0.2 million

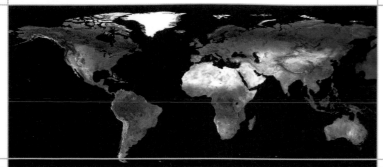

urban conglomerations of the Indian subcontinent, Indonesia and Brazil are bursting at the seams. According to estimates by UN experts, some 50 percent of the world's population lived in cities in 2007, and by the year 2050 this figure is expected to reach as much as 70 percent. At this point in time about 7 billion people live on Earth, by 2025 we are set to number about 8 billion.

This satellite image of Earth is composed of many hundreds of individual images. Most humans are crowded in the green zones of our planet (left).

THE LARGEST COUNTRIES IN AFRICA

AREA

❶	Algeria	2,381,740 sq km
❷	Congo	2,345,410 sq km
❸	Sudan	1,861,484 sq km
❹	Libya	1,759,400 sq km
❺	Chad	1,284,000 sq km
❻	Niger	1,267,000 sq km

POPULATION (reference year 2010)

❶	Nigeria	162.5 million
❷	Ethiopia	84.3 million
❸	Egypt	81.7 million
❹	DR Congo	67.8 million
❺	South Africa	50.6 million
❻	Tanzania	43.2 million

THE LARGEST COUNTRIES IN NORTH AND CENTRAL AMERICA

AREA

❶	Canada	9,984,670 sq km
❷	USA	9,629,091 sq km
❸	Mexico	1,964,375 sq km
❹	Nicaragua	130,773 sq km
❺	Honduras	112,492 sq km
❻	Cuba	109,886 sq km

POPULATION (reference year 2010)

❶	USA	317.2 million
❷	Mexico	112.3 million
❸	Canada	34.7 million
❹	Guatemala	14.7 million
❺	Cuba	11.2 million
❻	Haiti	10.1 million

THE LARGEST COUNTRIES IN SOUTH AMERICA

❶	Brazil	8,511,965 sq km
❷	Argentina	2,766,890 sq km
❸	Peru	1,285,220 sq km
❹	Colombia	1,138,910 sq km
❺	Bolivia	1,098,580 sq km
❻	Venezuela	912,050 sq km

POPULATION (reference year 2010)

❶	Brazil	192.3 million
❷	Colombia	46.4 million
❸	Argentina	40.1 million
❹	Peru	29.8 million
❺	Venezuela	27.1 million
❻	Chile	17.2 million

RUSSIA
THE LARGEST COUNTRY IN THE WORLD (AREA)

With a depth of 5,387 feet (1,642 m) Lake Baikal in Siberia is the deepest lake in the world and at the same time the single largest freshwater reserve on the planet. Its catchment area is four times the size of Germany (large picture).

Covering an area of 6,593,000 sq ml (17,075,800 sq km) the Russian Federation is the largest country on Earth. Its territory spans two continents, covering the entire north of Asia as well as large parts of the East European plains. It extends from the Baltic Sea in the west across some 5,600 miles (9,000 km) to the Pacific Ocean in the east, and a distance of about 2,500 miles (4,000 km) from the arctic regions in the north to its southern borders. Although the European part of Russia comprises only barely more than one-fourth of its entire territory, 104 million of its 143 million people live here. The land beyond the Ural Mountains, which form the border between Europe and Asia, is only thinly populated in contrast. Siberia, as the Asian part of Russia is called, covers an area of 5,066,970 sq ml (13,123,400 sq km), making it as large as China and India combined. Thirty-eight million people live there. The Russian taiga, which forms a section of the world's boreal forest, is the largest expanse of contiguous forest on Earth.

Moscow, the capital of Russia, is one of the most populous cities in Europe, with more than 11 million people crowded together in a small area (left).

The legendary port city of Shanghai is the most important economic hub in China. The boom attracts people from all areas of the People's Republic. The conurbation of Shanghai now boasts 25 million people (large picture).

With its 1.35 billion people the People's Republic of China is the most populous country in the world. It is also a multiethnic country where different ethnic groups live together. The Han Chinese, counting 1.189 billion people, make up the vast majority of the population. Some 6.2 percent, or 106 million people, belong to one of 55 ethnic minorities.

Although they were granted a limited degree of political autonomy and their languages have been recognized as official languages, independence movements have sprung up in many places in recent years. The protests of Tibetans and Uyghurs especially have attracted worldwide attention as well as provoking a crackdown by the Beijing central government. Most of the

ethnic minorities live in the inaccessible deserts and mountain regions of the west. More than 90 percent of the people live east of an imaginary line extending from the city of Heihe in the north to the county of Tengchong in the south, a line first drawn in 1935 by the geographer Hu Huangyong in order to illustrate the uneven distribution of the population in China.

Although the Chinese government encourages economic development in the thinly populated regions, ever more people are drawn to the economic boom area in the east. China's population is constantly growing and will probably count some 1.6 billion people by the year 2040.

About 39,000 people per square mile (15,000 people per sq km) are crowded together in Shanghai, the largest city in the People's Republic of China (left).

THE SMALLEST COUNTRIES IN THE WORLD (AREA/POPULATION)

Monaco is a European microstate and at the same time one of the most densely populated corners on the planet: more than 41,440 people per square mile live crowded together here (16,000 people per sq km) (large picture).

Tuvalu, Nauru, Palau and the Marshall Islands in the South Pacific, the European microstates of Vatican City, Monaco, San Marino and Liechtenstein, as well as the Caribbean islands of St. Kitts & Nevis and Dominica top the list of the smallest countries in the world. Although they only have a combined population figure of about 325,000 and thus have no more people than the average medium-sized European city, they are full and equal members of the international community of states. Except for Vatican City, which is represented by the Holy See, they all enjoy full voting rights at the UN General Assembly. Completely independent both internally and externally, they entertain diplomatic relations with many other countries around the world. However, most of them have transferred the defense of their countries to other states. Only the Vatican City State and San Marino maintain their own small armies; however, the Vatican's famous Swiss Guards and San Marino's armed forces have largely ceremonial functions. The euro is the official currency in the European microstates, whereas the

THE SMALLEST COUNTRIES IN EUROPE

AREA
❶	Vatican	0.44 sq km
❷	Monaco	2.02 sq km
❸	San Marino	61 sq km
❹	Liechtenstein	160 sq km
❺	Malta	316 sq km
❻	Andorra	468 sq km

POPULATION
❶	Vatican	800 pop.
❷	San Marino	32,250 pop.
❸	Monaco	35,880 pop.
❹	Liechtenstein	36,150 pop.
❺	Andorra	85,000 pop.
❻	Iceland	319,570 pop.

THE SMALLEST COUNTRIES IN ASIA

AREA
❶	Maldives	300 sq km
❷	Bahrain	665 sq km
❸	Singapore	704 sq km
❹	Brunei	5,770 sq km
❺	Lebanon	10,452 sq km
❻	Qatar	11,437 sq km

POPULATION
❶	Maldives	317,280 pop.
❷	Brunei	422,700 pop.
❸	Bhutan	708,260 pop.
❹	East Timor	1,066,000 pop.
❺	Bahrain	1,234,570 pop.
❻	Qatar	1,699,000 pop.

THE SMALLEST COUNTRIES IN OCEANIA

AREA
❶	Nauru	21 sq km
❷	Tuvalu	26 sq km
❸	Marshall Islands	181 sq km
❹	Palau	458 sq km
❺	Micronesia	702 sq km
❻	Tonga	748 sq km

POPULATION
❶	Tuvalu	10,000 pop.
❷	Nauru	10,000 pop.
❸	Palau	21,000 pop.
❹	Marshall Islands	54,300 pop.
❺	Kiribati	101,000 pop.
❻	Micronesia	102,600 pop.

U.S. or the Australian dollars are used on the islands of the South Pacific. Dominica and St. Kitts & Nevis are members of the Eastern Caribbean Currency Union, with the Eastern Caribbean Dollar, linked to the U.S. dollar, as official currency. All the microstates have their own telephone country codes and top-level Internet domains.

The European microstate of San Marino, although entirely surrounded by Italian territory, has been independent for many centuries (left).

THE SMALLEST COUNTRIES IN AFRICA

AREA
1. Seychelles — 455 sq km
2. São Tomé & Príncipe — 1,001 sq km
3. Comoros — 1,862 sq km
4. Mauritius — 2,040 sq km
5. The Gambia — 11,300 sq km
6. Swaziland — 17,363 sq km

POPULATION
1. Seychelles — 91,000 pop.
2. S. Tomé & Príncipe — 169,000 pop.
3. Cape Verde — 492,000 pop.
4. Equatorial Guinea — 720,000 pop.
5. Comoros — 754,000 pop.
6. Djibouti — 906,000 pop.

THE SMALLEST COUNTRIES IN NORTH/CENTRAL AMERICA

AREA
1. St. Kitts & Nevis — 261 sq km
2. Grenada — 344 sq km
3. St. Vincent & the Grenadines — 389 sq km
4. Antigua & Barbuda — 442 sq km
5. St. Lucia — 539 sq km

POPULATION
1. St. Kitts & Nevis — 51,970 pop.
2. Dominica — 71,680 pop.
3. Antigua & Barbuda — 89,140 pop.
4. St. Vincent & the Grenadines — 100,890 pop.
5. Grenada — 110,820 pop.

THE SMALLEST COUNTRIES IN SOUTH AMERICA

AREA
1. Suriname — 163,270 sq km
2. Uruguay — 176,220 sq km
3. Guyana — 214,970 sq km
4. Ecuador — 283,560 sq km
5. Paraguay — 406,750 sq km
6. Chile — 756,950 sq km

POPULATION
1. Surinam — 529,000 pop.
2. Guyana — 784,900 pop.
3. Uruguay — 3,203,800 pop.
4. Paraguay — 6,337,100 pop.
5. Bolivia — 10,426,200 pop.
6. Ecuador — 14,483,500 pop.

VATICAN CITY
THE SMALLEST COUNTRY IN THE WORLD

St. Peter's Basilica is the emblem and the center of Vatican City. In the immediate vicinity of the cathedral stands the Apostolic Palace, the official residence of the Pope, head of the Vatican City State (large picture).

Covering an area of 0.17 sq ml (0.44 sq km) and counting around 800 people, the Vatican City State is the smallest country in the world. Although it is no more than a tiny enclave within the Italian capital Rome, the Lateran Treaty of 1929 signed with Italy, then still a kingdom, grants complete territorial and political sovereignty to the Vatican.

The Pope, elected for life by the College of Cardinals, is the sovereign, uniting all legislative, executive and judicial powers in his hands. The worldly power of the Pope may not extend beyond the limits of the Vatican City State, yet in political terms his powers extend much further than a mere microstate. As the head of the Catholic Church he represents,

together with the Catholic Church in Rome, the "Holy See" — a religious authority that should not be confused with the Vatican City State, yet which nevertheless represents it in all external affairs and is recognized as subject to international law. As a sovereign country, the Vatican City State naturally has its own flag, its own coat of arms, its own national

holiday and, last but not least, its own armed forces. The smallest army in the world, the famous Swiss Guards, are responsible for the safety of the Pope and guard his residences. Vatican City is more than just St. Peter's Basilica and St. Peter's Square: important museums, libraries and gardens are also located within the country's borders.

St. Peter's Square, in front of the St. Peter's Basilica, covers a ground plan of 379,966 sq ft (35,300 sq m), which amounts to nearly one-tenth of the entire territory of the Vatican City State (left).

In a festive ceremony in 1990, the so-called "cold war" was officially declared over by NATO and the Warsaw Pact. However, countries around the world still continue to massively increase their military capabilities. According

U.S. Navy ships

to calculations by the Stockholm International Peace Research Institute (SIPRI), the worldwide expenditure for military purposes in 2010 amounted to 1.6 billion U.S. dollars, 1.3 percent more than in the previous year. The defense budget of the USA alone, by far the largest on the planet, increased by more than 20 billion to 687 billion U.S. dollars. In second place follows the People's Republic of China, with a budget of 114.3 billion dollars. In many countries the extent of military expenditure is kept a secret. The figures below are therefore not entirely reliable.

THE MOST POWERFUL COUNTRIES IN THE WORLD
(military budget for 2010 in U.S. dollars)

①	USA	687 billion
②	China	114.3 billion
③	France	61.28 billion
④	Great Britain	57.42 billion
⑤	Russia	52.58 billion
⑥	Japan	51.42 billion
⑦	Germany	46.84 billion
⑧	Saudi Arabia	42.91 billion
⑨	Italy	38.19 billion
⑩	India	34.81 billion
⑪	Brazil	28.09 billion

THE MOST POWERFUL COUNTRIES IN EUROPE
(military budget for 2010 in U.S. dollars)

①	France	61.28 billion
②	Great Britain	57.42 billion
③	Russia	52.58 billion
④	Germany	46.84 billion
⑤	Italy	38.19 billion
⑥	Spain	15.8 billion
⑦	Netherlands	11.6 billion
⑧	Greece	9.36 billion
⑨	Poland	8.38 billion
⑩	Norway	6.32 billion
⑪	Belgium	5.38 billion

THE MOST POWERFUL COUNTRIES IN ASIA
(military budget for 2010 in U.S. dollars)

①	China	114.3 billion
②	Japan	51.42 billion
③	Saudi Arabia	42.91 billion
④	India	34.81 billion
⑤	South Korea	24.27 billion
⑥	UAE	15.75 billion
⑦	Turkey	15.64 billion
⑧	Israel	13 billion
⑨	China (Taiwan)	8.53 billion
⑩	Singapore	7.65 billion

THE MOST POWERFUL COUNTRIES IN AUSTRALIA/OCEANIA
(military budget for 2010 in U.S. dollars)

①	Australia	19.79 billion
②	New Zealand	1.35 billion

THE MOST POWERFUL COUNTRIES IN AFRICA
(military budget for 2010 in U.S. dollars)

①	Algeria	5.59 billion
②	Egypt	3.91 billion
③	Angola	3.77 billion
④	South Africa	3.74 billion
⑤	Morocco	3.25 billion
⑥	Sudan	1.99 billion
⑦	Nigeria	1.72 billion
⑧	Libya	1.1 billion
⑨	Kenya	594 million
⑩	Tunisia	548 million
⑪	Eritrea	469 million

THE MOST POWERFUL COUNTRIES IN THE AMERICAS
(military budget for 2010 in U.S. dollars)

❶	USA	687 billion
❷	Brazil	28.06 billion
❸	Canada	20.16 billion
❹	Colombia	9.19 billion
❺	Chile	6.19 billion
❻	Mexico	4.85 billion
❼	Argentina	3.17 billion
❽	Venezuela	3.1 billion
❾	Peru	1.99 billion
❿	Uruguay	491 million
⓫	Dom. Republic	322 million

Soldiers of the Chinese People's Liberation Army, the largest army in the world with an estimated 2.1 million active soldiers. Its remit is to protect the territory of the People's Republic of China from attack. Like other states, China also seeks to reduce the size of its army. Today Chinese military leaders also focus on mobile and well-equipped small units rather than numerous troops.

THE UNITED STATES OF AMERICA
THE LARGEST MILITARY POWER IN THE WORLD

U.S. soldiers survey the horizon during their deployment in Iraq. The USA and its allies invaded the country in 2003. The last military advisors left Iraq in December 2011 (large picture).

Thanks to its vast arsenal of continuously developed high-tech weaponry and a sophisticated logistics system, permitting the mobilization of large troop contingents and their deployment to all corners of the world at lightning speed, the armed forces of the USA are by far the largest military power on the planet. Currently the Army, Navy and Air Force boast a combined total of more than 1.5 million active soldiers. The 662,000 optimally equipped members of the Army have at their disposal more than 19,000 armored personnel carriers, 5,850 battle tanks, 300 jets, 4,000 helicopters and all kinds of antimissile and antitank weapons systems. The ten fleets of the U.S. Navy, boasting a total of 71 U-boats, 11 aircraft carriers, 22 cruisers, 56 destroyers, 21 frigates, 16 coastguard vessels and 9 minesweepers as well as 300 amphibious assault ships, operate on all the world's oceans. The U.S. Air Force has at its disposal about 3,500 combat aircraft. This giant military force, operating with conventional weapons, is complemented by strategic weapons systems equipped with nuclear warheads. The United States Strategic

Command controls 500 intercontinental rockets, 95 B-52 and B-2 bombers as well as 750 nuclear submarines. Another part of the strategic weapons program is its early-warning satellite systems. Because of the wars that have been fought by the USA since 9/11, expenditure for the maintenance of the armed forces rose to 687 billion dollars in 2010.

Thirty Navy ships, including the destroyers pictured here, took part in the U.S. military war game Valiant Shield in 2006 (left).

NATO — THE LARGEST MILITARY ALLIANCE IN THE WORLD

Currently counting 28 member states, all of which have under their command armies equipped with the latest weapons technology, NATO is the largest military alliance in the world. Its beginnings date back to the start of the east–west conflict after World War II, when the countries of western Europe began to feel threatened by the military presence of the Soviet Union in Central Europe and sought to create a counterbalance. In the North Atlantic Treaty signed in Washington in 1949, the initially twelve signatory states (Belgium, Canada, Denmark, France, Italy, Iceland, Luxembourg, Netherlands, Norway, Portugal, UK, USA) undertook to assist one another in all cases when the safety and independence of a co-signatory would be threatened, including by military means if required. This commitment to mutual aid and assistance, based on the principle of collective self-defense, required the establishment of an organization that would secure

The destroyer "USS Roosevelt" is refueled during a NATO exercise.

NATO currently counts 28 members.

communication between the allies at times of peace as well, and coordinate the deployment of national forces in case the "mutual defense clause" was invoked. NATO, joined by Turkey, Greece and West Germany in the 1950s, was born. Twice a year the foreign ministers of its member states confer in its most important political committee, the North Atlantic Council, founded in 1949. These consultations are complemented by regular weekly meetings of the "permanent representatives" of the national governments.

PENTAGON
THE LARGEST OFFICE BUILDING IN THE WORLD

The Pentagon, a giant five-sided office building, is the headquarters of the U.S. Department of Defense. It is located on the Potomac River in Arlington (Virginia), a few miles south of the capital Washington.

With a total usable floor space of about 6,500,000 sq ft (600,000 sq m) and an effective office space of 3,660,000 sq ft (340,000 sq m), the Pentagon is the largest office building in the world by area. Boasting a volume of about 70,629,320 cu ft (2 million cu m), it is also one of the 10 or 15 largest office buildings in the world overall (depending on how this is calculated).

The outer walls of the five-sided building each measure 918 feet (280 m) long, and the overall diameter is almost 1,640 feet (500 m). The structure consists of five ring structures arranged around a central plaza, linked by corridors. The wings are all five stories high. An important reason for the structure of the complex is the fact that from any one point in the building it is possible to reach any other point in less than seven minutes. Thus, each area can be reached within a short time although the combined length of all the corridors amounts to almost 19 miles (30 km).

Around 23,000 personnel are today employed in the complex, which was inaugurated in 1943 — after a construction period of only 16 months. Some 14,000 builders and 1,000 architects

worked in three shifts around the clock to build it. The Pentagon was one of the targets of the terror attacks on September 11, 2001, during which nearly 200 people died there alone. At the time the complex had been in the process of a major renovation (since 1994). Because of the attack, renovation was not finished until 2011, since some structural parts had to be completely rebuilt.

Left and large picture: The Pentagon, situated not far from Washington D.C., is easy to identify from the air. Its name comes from the Greek word for a five-sided geometrical shape.

THE GREATEST ECONOMIC POWERS
IN THE WORLD (GDP)

The heads of government of the leading economic powers in the world have been meeting once a year since 1976 to discuss the state of the global economy. Aside from Russia, which was admitted to the select circle in 1998, the composition of this round of G7 or G8 has not changed until today. Now as then only the classic industrial nations USA, Canada, Japan, Great Britain, France, Italy and Germany, as well as Russia, take part in the meetings. Although these countries still produce 60 percent of the world's economic output, according to many observers the composition of

THE GREATEST
ECONOMIC POWERS
IN THE WORLD
(GDP in million U.S. dollars 2010)

①	USA	15,064,816
②	China	6,988,470
③	Japan	5,855,383
④	Germany	3,628,623
⑤	France	2,808,265
⑥	Brazil	2,517,927
⑦	Great Britain	2,480,978
⑧	Russia	1,884,903
⑨	India	1,843,382
⑩	Canada	1,758,680
⑪	Spain	1,536,479
⑫	Australia	1,507,402
⑬	Mexico	1,185,215

the round no longer reflects the actual economic balance of power in the world. By 2009 the Republic of China had advanced to rank No. 2 of countries with the greatest gross domestic product. In 2010 Brazil overtook Great Britain, and India overtook Canada. Experts estimate that this trend will continue in the future. Thus, according to the forecast of the International Monetary Fund, India should displace Japan from rank No. 3 of the world's leading economic nations in the near future.

Oil refinery at Grangemouth, Scotland: the chimneys are still smoking but economic power is shifting away from the old world.

Large picture: Aluminum factory in Yichuan in the eastern Chinese province of Henan. Since the reforms introduced in 1978 under Deng Xiaoping the economic power of the People's Republic has shown a tremendously dynamic growth. Whereas in 1980 its gross domestic product still amounted to 309.3 billion U.S. dollars, it already reached nearly 7 trillion U.S. dollars by 2010. In many areas of industrial production China today occupies a leading position.

UNITED STATES OF AMERICA
THE GREATEST ECONOMIC POWER IN THE WORLD

Although it is now in competition with the euro, the U.S. dollar is still the most important leading currency in the world: 60 percent of the world's currency reserves are held in dollars (large picture).

Despite the unprecedented collapse experienced by the U.S. national economy during the financial and economic crisis of 2008–9 it is today still by far the most productive economy in the world. In 2011 the 317 million Americans generated a gross domestic product of more than 14 trillion U.S. dollars, thus producing one-fifth of the world economic output. Because of this economic strength, the USA exercises a great influence on the global economy. U.S. enterprises operate in every corner of the world. The dollar is the leading currency on the planet. There are many reasons for the success of the U.S. economy: the country is rich in natural resources and boasts fertile soils and water supplies. The Americans themselves are known for their passion for innovation. Many of the technological inventions that have revolutionized the working and living conditions for people during the 20th century originated in the USA. After World War II the massive demand for consumer goods, the arms race and the space program encouraged its economic growth.

Wall Street in New York's Financial District has become synonymous with international finance and capitalism. Many major banks and the world's most important stock exchange are based here (left).

PIONEERS OF THE INFORMATION AGE

Like no other companies, Microsoft and Apple represent the innovative force of the U.S. economy. Since the end of the 1970s the two software giants have revolutionized people's lives. Today not only large companies but also small and micro-enterprises work with computers running a version of Windows, the operating system developed by Microsoft, and its associated applications. The company founded in 1975 has frequently been criticized because of its dominant position in the market. Apple, its greatest competitor, sells hardware and a purpose-made operating system as well as the associated software. Apple is today one of the most valuable brands in the world, enjoying something of a cult status.

Microsoft founder Bill Gates

Apple founder, the late Steve Jobs

THE GREATEST EXPORT NATIONS IN THE WORLD

The (unofficial) title of "export world champion" is awarded to the national economy boasting the greatest volume of exports in a year. The balance of imports versus exports is not taken into account. Thus the USA's balance of trade is in chronic deficit because of its very high imports, yet the country features in a top position in the ranking of exporting nations.

THE GREATEST EXPORT NATIONS IN THE WORLD
(export volume in 2010 in U.S. dollars)

❶	China	1.897 trillion
❷	Germany	1.543 trillion
❸	USA	1.511 trillion
❹	Japan	800.8 billion
❺	France	578.4 billion
❻	Netherlands	576.9 billion
❼	South Korea	558.8 billion
❽	Italy	508.9 billion
❾	Russia	498.6 billion

CHINA – THE GREATEST EXPORT NATION IN THE WORLD

Trading activity in Hong Kong greatly contributes to Chinese economic growth.

GERMANY — THE SECOND LARGEST EXPORT NATION IN THE WORLD

Although Germany had to relinquish its title as "export world champion," which it had held between 2003 and 2008, to the People's Republic of China, it still occupies a top position in the ranking of exporting nations: in 2010 the country exported goods to the value of 959.5 billion euros. Although the USA were the second biggest export nation in 2011, economists forecast that in 2012 Germany would again advance to second place. More than 60 percent of its exports are to other European Union countries, only 6.8 percent go to the USA and 5.9 percent to China. Cars are the export goods in greatest demand.

Three German export hits: BMW …

… Porsche …

… Mercedes.

With an annual economic growth rate of 7 to 9 percent on average, the People's Republic of China has developed as one of the most dynamic economies in the world, usurping Japan from rank No. 2 of the world's greatest national economies. In 2009 China overtook Germany as "export world champion." During that year the country exported goods to the value of 840 billion dollars to other countries whereas the Federal Republic only had exports to the value of 816 billion U.S. dollars. China, for a long time considered the "workbench of the world," now also exports top-end electronics and IT products.

Chinese export hits: wire…

… textiles …

… plush toys.

The Port of Hamburg is one of Europe's highest turnover harbors and Germany's gateway to the world. The products of German industry are shipped from there to the entire world.

The gross domestic product as well as the per capita income are considered by economists to be a good indicator of a country's wealth. It denotes

Three symbols of wealth: gold ...

... luxury cars ...

...luxury yachts.

the total value of goods and services produced or provided by a country. When calculating the per capita income, the gross domestic product of a country is divided by the number of its citizens.

THE RICHEST COUNTRIES IN THE WORLD
(Human Development Index 2010)

❶	Norway	0.943
❷	Australia	0.929
❸	Netherlands	0.910
❹	USA	0.910
❺	New Zealand	0.908
❻	Canada	0.908
❼	Ireland	0.908
❽	Liechtenstein	0.905
❾	Germany	0.905
❿	Sweden	0.904

THE RICHEST COUNTRIES IN THE WORLD
(GDP per capita, adjusted for purchasing power, in 2010)

❶	Qatar	$102,891
❷	Luxembourg	$84,829
❸	Singapore	$59,937
❹	Norway	$53,370
❺	Brunei	$49,518
❻	Hong Kong	$49,342
❼	UAE	$48,590
❽	USA	$48,140
❾	Switzerland	$43,509
❿	Netherlands	$42,331

NORWAY — THE RICHEST COUNTRY IN THE WORLD

Whereas institutions like the World Bank measure the wealth of a country exclusively with the help of economic data, the UN's Human Development Index also includes factors such as life expectancy and level of education. For many years now Norway has topped the list of countries with the highest Human Development Index. The Scandinavian state is among the countries with the highest per capita income and also boasts an exemplary health and education system.

Oslo, the capital of Norway, is considered one of the world's best cities to live in.

Norway derives its wealth from its vast offshore oil deposits.

The Pearl Oyster Monument in Doha, capital of Qatar, recalls the local tradition of pearl diving, once a main source of income for the people on the Persian Gulf. Today it is the extraction of oil that has made Qatar the richest country in the world. No other state has a per capita gross domestic product (adjusted for purchasing power) as high as the Emirate.

Economists talk about different forms of poverty. In the highly developed industrial nations one is only considered poor if one's income falls considerably short of the country's average income. The World Bank's International Development Association however denotes

Slum dweller in Bihar, India

A Zambian mother suffering from AIDS

those as poor who have less than $1.25 to spend per day. These people are not able to feed themselves adequately, and they have no access to medical care. Experts at the World Bank estimate that around one-sixth of humankind live below this absolute poverty line.

THE POOREST COUNTRIES IN THE WORLD
(Human Development Index 2010)

1	DR Congo	0.286
2	Niger	0.295
3	Mozambique	0.322
4	Chad	0.328
5	Liberia	0.329
6	Burkina Faso	0.331
7	Sierra Leone	0.336
8	Central African Republic	0.343
9	Guinea	0.344
10	Guinea-Bissau	0.353

THE POOREST COUNTRIES IN THE WORLD
(GDP per capita, adjusted for purchasing power, in 2010)

1	DR Congo	$348
2	Liberia	$417
3	Burundi	$430
4	Zimbabwe	$472
5	Eritrea	$732
6	Central African Republic	$775
7	Niger	$795
8	Sierra Leone	$847
9	Malawi	$853
10	Togo	$893

A young girl in a slum in Antananarivo, capital of Madagascar. The island state off Africa's eastern shores is one of the poorest countries in the world. More than half the population live below the absolute poverty line, with less than $1.25 a day at their disposal. About 50 percent of the people have no access to clean drinking water or medical care. An extremely high percentage of the population are illiterate.

With a total of 193 members the UN is today the largest intergovernmental organization in the world. With the exception of the Vatican City state, which enjoys observer status, and some countries whose status

The UN headquarters in New York (left)

The UN Security Council in session

The UN flag

is problematic according to international law, all sovereign nations on Earth today belong to the organization. The United Nations was founded by 51 countries as the successor to the League of Nations in San Francisco in 1945, at the instigation of the allied forces victorious in World War II. The UN's aims and responsibilities were defined in the Charter adopted on June 20, 1945: to secure peace and international cooperation as well as economic, social and cultural development in all parts of the world.

The General Assembly of the United Nations is composed of delegations from all member states. It meets at least once a year at the organization's New York headquarters and its task is to debate the problems of world politics. The resolutions it adopts are, however, not binding for anyone.

The European Union is unique in the world as a league of sovereign states that have committed themselves to act in a collective and coordinated manner in all policy areas. It

The EU building flying European flags

developed in stages out of the communities created in the 1950s (ECSC, EEC, EAEC) and was finally founded in 1992 with the signing of the "Treaty on European Union," which became known as the Maastricht Treaty. This treaty created the European Monetary Union as well as putting the collaboration between the members of the European Union on a new footing.

The European Parliament buildings in Strasbourg. Although their competences were extended by the "Lisbon Treaty," the representatives at the European Parliament still have less influence than their colleagues in the national parliaments. They are elected for a period of five years by the citizens of the EU's 27 member states.

The European Parliament Building in Brussels

For a long time the location of the seat of the European Parliament was controversial. France insisted the meeting place should be in Strasbourg whereas Belgium campaigned for Brussels. It was not until 1992 that the EU's heads of state agreed on Strasbourg as the official seat of the European Parliament. However, the meetings of the political groups and committees as well as six plenary sessions every year take place in Brussels. The General Secretariat is based in Luxembourg.

The spoken and the written word are fundamental to human cultural development, and they exist in numerous manifestations. Academics estimate that, currently, more than 6,000 natural languages are actively used around the world. Whereas some, like English, are used around the globe, others, like the languages of the Amazonian tribes, are spoken by only a few people. New languages have emerged time and again in the history of humankind but others have disappeared. Languages develop, change and encroach upon one another.

Speakers' Corner in Hyde Park, London

Employees at a meeting

THE MOST WIDELY SPOKEN LANGUAGES IN THE WORLD
(mother tongue)

❶	Chinese	845 million
❷	Hindi	370 million
❸	English	340 million
❹	Spanish	340 million
❺	Arabic	320 million
❻	Bengal	215 million
❼	Portuguese	210 million
❽	Russian	200 million
❾	Japanese	127 million
❿	German	90 million
⓫	French	85 million
⓬	Italian	70 million

·try (lăng′...

British act...

r with Edwar...

uage (lăng...

s of voice so...

sounds, in c...

Since the work of Ferdinand de Saussure, language has been regarded as a complex system of agreed signs that are used to designate facts and to exchange information and ideas. All the words in a language, that is its vocabulary, are called the lexicon in linguistics.

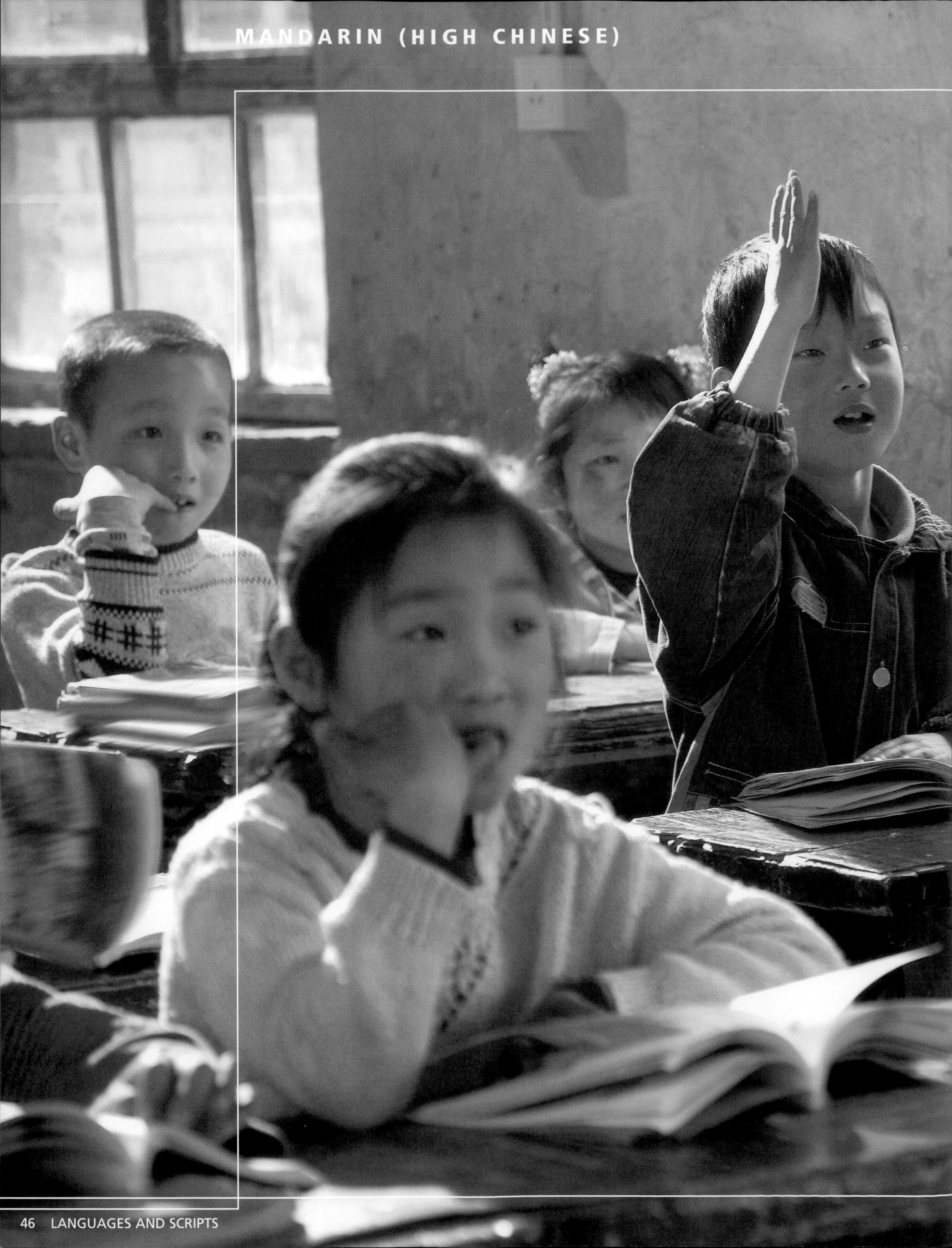

Chinese characters

Chinese advertising brochures

Since the end of the Chinese Empire, High Chinese, which is based on northern Chinese dialects, has become the most widely spoken language in the world. Today nearly 845 million people call it their first language. Mandarin, as it is also known in reference to the language spoken at the imperial court, is widely spoken not only in the People's Republic and on Taiwan, but also in South-East Asia. In Singapore it is the official language, together with Malay, Tamil and English. However, High Chinese earned its No. 1 place in the language ranking not only because of the massive population growth in the Middle Kingdom — it achieved this dominance also due to the efforts in the early 20th century of Chinese linguists who postulated a single, generally understood language for a nation that was fragmented into many linguistic communities, and who suggested binding standards of pronunciation. Although today all children learn Putong huà or Guóyu — as the high language is known in the People's Republic and Taiwan respectively — the preservation of the various languages and dialects of China is promoted by the state at primary school.

To hold their own in daily life Chinese students have to learn around 5,000 of the 87,000 Chinese characters.

HINDI — URDU (HINDUSTANI)

Among the more than 100 languages spoken on the Indian subcontinent, Hindi stands out especially, the language widely spoken in northern and central India. The first language of around 370 million people, it is the second most widely spoken first language on the planet after High Chinese. In India it is the only supraregional official language along with English, and it is also used as the official language by twelve Indian states. Like Urdu, the official language in Pakistan and six Indian states, Hindi evolved from Hindustani, a lingua franca that has been in use all over northern India since the days of the Mughal Empire and only developed into a separate

श्रद्धा गंगा

गाये ककचड़ान फेंके, यह घाट

मां गंगा सेवी ना

Posters with the text in Devanagari script

language during the course of the division of the subcontinent. Urdu emerged from a variant of Hindustani spoken at court during the Mughal Empire and is today the language of the Muslim minority in India. Although Hindustani is not an official language anywhere in India it is still used in everyday life today and spoken by 570 million people.

In India today more than 100 different languages are in use as well as at least ten different writing systems. One of the most important is Devanagari, a syllabary that emerged from classic Brahmi script and has been in use since the 11th century. Today it is mainly Hindi and Marathi that are written in Devanagari script.

the leaf fish is carried along

[until it comes near a smaller fi

Due largely to America's prominence on the world stage, the English language has since developed as the lingua franca of the entire planet, overtaking

Children learn English …

… everywhere on Earth.

all others. No one wanting to be successful in the globalized world of business, in international politics or in the sciences today can get by without English. Experts estimate that up to 1.5 billion people now possess some knowledge of English. After all, some 500 million people consider English their mother tongue, and it is the official language in more than 50 countries.

Since the beginning of the information age and the development of the Internet numerous expressions have trickled from English into other languages. Expressions such as "download," "service point" or "hotline" have become a firm constituent of everyday language in many countries, or belong to the technical vocabulary of business and specialist languages. Scientists assume that this development will continue despite the protests of language purists and that English will become the universal language of the future.

the currents

Large picture: Chinese youths during
their English lesson. English is the most
important lingua franca on Earth and is
today taught nearly everywhere in the
world. The language is comparatively
easy to learn and is understood by a large
number of people on all continents.

The invention of a writing system is perhaps the most important cultural achievement of humankind. Without these graphic signs, inscribed onto tablets, painted, written, printed or digitalized, communication across longer periods of time and greater distances would not be possible, nor would the storage and transmission of knowledge. Scripts were invented in many places on Earth, developing into very disparate sign systems such as the alphabetic systems and the syllabaries. Whereas Arabic script runs from right to left and Latin script in reverse, from left to right, Chinese characters have to be read from top to bottom. Many writing systems are used in a single country only, whereas the Latin alphabet is widely used around the world.

For more than 5,000 years information has been stored in its fixed written form. Until late into the 19th century writing was laborious and slow, then it speeded up considerably with the invention of the mechanical typewriter. Today this technology has been overtaken and replaced by electronic storage media.

THE MOST WIDELY USED SCRIPTS IN THE WORLD

❶ Latin script
Both Americas, Europe, West, Central and South Africa, Australia, South-East Asia
❷ Chinese script
People's Republic of China, Republic of China (Taiwan)
❸ Arabic script
North Africa, Near and Middle East, Afghanistan, Pakistan
❹ Cyrillic script
Russia, Belarus, Ukraine, Bulgaria, Serbia, Macedonia, Central Asia
❺ Devanagari
North India, Nepal
❻ Bengal script
Bangladesh, Indian states of Assam, Tripura and Manipur

LATIN — THE MOST WIDELY USED SCRIPT IN THE WORLD

Medieval Christian manuscript

The Latin script is the most widely used writing system in the world, not least because of its simplicity. It consists of only 26 characters, making it easier to learn than other writing systems. In the course of the Christianization of Europe it was disseminated across the entire continent, way beyond the borders of the Roman Empire. In the age of colonialism it continued its triumph around the world. Today the Latin or Roman alphabet is the only writing system used in Europe, America, Australia, South-East Asia and large parts of Africa.

CHINESE — THE SECOND MOST WIDELY USED SCRIPT IN THE WORLD

Chinese newspapers

The Chinese script, the most widely used writing system on Earth after the Latin alphabet, consists of around 87,000 different characters. Unlike letter-based writing systems it does not reflect the sound of the spoken language but the meaning of syllables and words.

ARABIC — THE THIRD MOST WIDELY USED SCRIPT IN THE WORLD

Arabic manuscript

With the triumph of Islam the Arabic script spread across all of North Africa and Asia Minor and as far as India. It is not only Arabic texts that are written using this script, but also Persian, Kurdish and Urdu texts. The Arabic script is a letter-based writing system like Latin, comprising 28 different characters. Unlike Latin however, it runs from right to left.

CYRILLIC — THE FOURTH MOST WIDELY USED SCRIPT IN THE WORLD

Russian newspapers

Aside from the Baltic countries the Cyrillic script is used as the only writing system by all the states of the former Soviet Union as well as some countries on the Balkan peninsula. Researchers believe that it developed in Bulgaria in the middle of the 10th century and spread from there across Eastern Europe. Recent research proves that it was not created by Cyril, whose name it took.

FAITH AND RELIGION

Religions have helped shape human history for thousands of years. Religion as the awareness of dependency on a supernatural power, an absolute, bestows meaning and dignity on the lives of believers, and it also inspires extraordinary achievements. Thus humans have built some of the most splendid and fascinating structures for religious purposes: cathedrals, synagogues, mosques, pagodas, temples and shrines. Soaring into the sky, the sacred buildings of Christianity, Judaism, Islam, Hinduism, Buddhism, Taoism, Jainism and Shintoism are the impressive embodiments of the spiritual yearning of the faithful.

Hinduism: a child made up as Shiva

THE GREATEST RELIGIONS IN THE WORLD

❶ Christendom	2200 million
❷ Islam	1400 million
❸ Hinduisms	875 million
❹ Buddhism	385 million
❺ Sikhism	23 million
❻ Judaism	15 million
❼ Jainism	5 million

Colorful wall paintings and giant Buddha statues are concealed in the Mogao Caves near Dunhuang in the Chinese province of Gansu. From the fourth to the 14th centuries an extensive network of around 1,000 caves was laid out along the old Silk Route in order to protect one of the greatest treasures of Buddhist art from the conquerors.

FAITH AND RELIGION

Pope Benedict XVI with Roman Catholic dignitaries

Priests of the Ethiopian Orthodox Church in the Lalibela rock church

The Ecumenical Patriarch of Constantinople, Bartholomew I, during Easter celebrations

THE LARGEST FAITH COMMUNITY IN THE WORLD

With around 2.2 billion followers, Christianity is the largest of the three monotheistic world religions. Emerging around 2,000 years ago in Palestine as a renewal movement within Judaism, it soon split away from the latter and in the fourth century became the official state religion in the Roman Empire. Missionaries spread Christianity to Asia, Europe, America and Africa.
Christians believe in Jesus of Nazareth, regarding the preacher and faith healer as the Messiah and the Son of God, as prophesied in the Old Testament — Father, Son and Holy Spirit form the blessed Trinity. The Bible with its Old and New Testaments is the holy book of Christians.
The word "church" not only designates a place of worship but also the Christian faith community. From the fourth century monasteries were founded where the faithful lived together as religious and economic communities. In the cities magnificent cathedrals were built in the architectural style predominant at the time. However, Christianity is divided. The Eastern Church seceded from the Catholic Church, the largest denomination, in 1054, forming the Russian Orthodox and the Greek Orthodox Churches. The Reformation in the 16th century brought about the Protestant Church as well as other Protestant groups.

CHRISTIANITY

THE LARGEST DENOMINATIONS

1. Catholics — 1.2 billion
2. Protestants — 700 million
3. Orthodox Churches — 260 million
4. Old Oriental Churches — 80 million
5. Anglican Church — 80 million
6. Non-Trinitarian Communities (Jehovah's Witnesses, Mormons) — 35 million

Procession in honor of the Blessed Virgin Mary in front of Notre Dame Cathedral in Paris. Christianity drew its strength to a not insignificant degree from popular beliefs, and also incorporated non-Christian traditions. These include for example the great veneration for Mary, the Mother of Jesus, by Roman Catholic believers.

GUADALUPE, MEXICO

On December 9, 1531, Our Lady of Guadalupe appeared to the farmer Juan Diego on Tepeyac Hill in present-day Mexico City. Surrounded by light she asked

him to build a chapel in her honor. Today "La Morenita" is venerated as the national saint. Every year around 20 million pilgrims, often arriving on December 9, make their way to the Marian shrine, which holds images of the Virgin and of the old and new basilicas imprinted on a cloak.

FATIMA, PORTUGAL

On May 13, 1917, the Madonna appeared in Fatima to three children who were guarding sheep and told them the three secrets of Fatima. To commemorate the apparition a chapel was built on the site, which holds the statue of Our Lady of Fatima and attracts around four million pilgrims each year. Today it stands at the center of the vast square in front of the church, flanked by the Basilica of Our Lady of Fatima (1928–1953) and the rotunda church of the Most Holy Trinity (2007).

The Sacred Heart of Jesus Statue standing in the middle of the pilgrimage site in Fatima.

CHURCH OF THE HOLY SEPULCHER, JERUSALEM

The burial church on Golgatha, the Hill of Calvary, in Jerusalem stands on the place identified as the site of both the crucifixion and the burial of Jesus Christ. The complex of chapels built on top and adjacent to each other and belonging to six Christian denominations (Roman Catholic, Greek Orthodox, Armenian Apostolic, Syrian Orthodox, Ethiopian Orthodox Churches, Copts) is considered one of the holiest places in Christianity. It is believed the body of Christ was anointed at the Stone of Unction next to the entrance. On the right, stairs rise to the Rock of Golgatha, the site of Christ's crucifixion. The rotunda on the left holds the Aedicule, the chapel with the Holy Sepulcher.

ST. PETER'S BASILICA, ROME

"I tell you that you are Peter, and it is on this rock that I will build my Church" — these are the words in the Gospel of Matthew from

which St. Peter's Basilica, the burial site of St. Peter, the first bishop of Rome, derives its outstanding significance for Christianity. The popes are the successors of St. Peter, dispensing their urbi et orbi blessing from the central balcony of St. Peter's Basilica at Easter and Christmas. On average about 20,000 faithful visit this site every day — in order to experience its aura, the papal tombs, the pope or his art-historical treasures.

ST. PAUL OUTSIDE THE WALLS, ROME

St. Paul Outside the Walls — so called because it is situated outside the Aurelian city fortifications — is, just like St. Peter's Basilica,

a papal basilica and the burial church of an apostle, in this case of St. Paul. His grave became a site of worship soon after his death, and many pilgrims still flock there today. The columned basilica was rebuilt in 1854 in the neoclassical style, after an early-Christian structure had burned down. The grave of the Apostle is crowned with a ciborium by Arnolfo di Cambio.

SANTIAGO DE COMPOSTELA, SPAIN

Pious Christians are believed to have rescued the bones of the Apostle St. James (the Elder) from the Saracens in the eighth century and taken them from St. Catherine's Monastery on the Sinai Peninsula to Galicia in northwestern Spain. There they were buried in a specially built cathedral, and the city of Santiago de Compostela developed around it. St. James became the patron saint of the Christians and Santiago developed into an important pilgrimage site, visited each year by thousands of pilgrims (150,000 to 300,000), arriving often on foot on the Way of St. James. The cathedral has a late-Gothic façade. Especially valuable is the "Portico of Glory" of 1188 by Master Mateo, featuring a Romanesque ensemble of statues.

LOURDES, FRANCE

Lourdes, visited each year by up to 6 million pilgrims, owes its fame to a vision of the Virgin Mary, this time appearing to Bernadette Soubirous in 1858. On the request of the "Lady," as Bernadette called her, a crypt was built in 1862 above the Grotto of Massabielle and the healing waters of a spring that rises here. In 1864 and 1883 the Basilica of the Immaculate Conception and the Rosary Basilica (Upper and Lower Church respectively) were added. The latter, in a historical style following Romanesque Byzantine architectural traditions, is richly appointed with mosaics.

CZESTOCHOWA, POLAND

Up to 4 million pilgrims a year flock to the pilgrimage site of the Luminous Mount, a monastery in Czestochowa, in order to venerate the most important Marian shrine in Central and Eastern Europe. Taken there by Pauline monks from Hungary, the miraculous image of the Black Madonna with the Child Jesus in her arm is of Byzantine origin. After its destruction it was repainted in the 15th century. When the Luminous Mount survived a Swedish siege in 1655, the image became a national shrine and a symbol for the liberation struggles of Poland.

Competing in their worship of God, churches of gigantic dimensions have been built over the course of the centuries. Most of these are Roman Catholic churches. Emblematic of all monumental churches is the Gothic cathedral. However only a few of these actually feature among the

St. Peter's Square with obelisk and St. Peter's Basilica

largest churches in the world, yet surprisingly many of these date from the 20th and 21st centuries.

The size of a church can be measured in terms of its capacity (number of people it can hold), its enclosed volume or the surface area over which it is built — the different methods yield different rankings. For the churches in the following lists, the built-over surface area was used as a basis (without courtyards and forecourts).

THE LARGEST CHURCHES IN THE WORLD
(built-over surface area)

1. St. Peter's Basilica, Rome
163,180 sq ft (15,160 sq m)
2. Mosque–Cathedral of Cordoba
161,460 sq ft (15,000 sq m)
3. Church of the Most Holy Trinity, Fatima
132,400 sq ft (12,300 sq m)
4. Basilica of the National Shrine of Our Lady of Aparecida
129,170 sq ft (12,000 sq m)
5. Milan Cathedral
125,940 sq ft (11,700 sq m)
6. Seville Cathedral
123,780 sq ft (11,500 sq m)
7. Cathedral Church of St. John the Divine, New York
120,560 sq ft (11,200 sq m)
8. St. Isaac's Cathedral, St. Petersburg
116,250 sq ft (10,800 sq m)
9. Basilica of Our Lady of Lichen
108,720 sq ft (10,100 sq m)
10. Liverpool Cathedral
104,410 sq ft (9,700 sq m)
11. Basilica of Our Lady of the Pillar, Zaragoza
89,340 sq ft (8,300 sq m)
12. Basilica of the Sacred Heart, Brussels
86,110 sq ft (8,000 sq m)
13. Basilica of Our Lady of Guadalupe, Mexico City
86,110 sq ft (8,000 sq m)
14. Basilica of Our Lady of Peace of Yamoussoukro
86,110 sq ft (8,000 sq m)
15. Cologne Cathedral
85,030 sq ft (7,900 sq m)
16. St. Paul's Cathedral, London
84,770 sq ft (7,875 sq m)

Underneath the dome of St. Peter's Basilica rises the Papal High Altar with the bronze baldachin by Gian Lorenzo Bernini. With its powerful turned columns the baldachin, measuring just under 100 feet (30 m) high, is the largest bronze work of art in the world. The grave of the Apostle St. Peter is said to be underneath the altar.

ST. PETER'S BASILICA
Rome   163,180 sq ft (15,160 sq m)

Above the roofs of Rome rises St. Peter's Basilica, the center of Christianity. Originally built under Emperor Constantine the Great around 324, it was a five-aisled basilica church above the presumed grave of the Apostle St. Peter. The foundation stone of the present church, begun under Pope Julius II, was laid in 1506. Planned initially by the first construction manager, Donato

St. Peter's Square with its two semicircular colonnades was designed by Gian Lorenzo Bernini.

Bramante, as a central structure in the shape of a Greek cross, after Bramante's death St. Peter's Basilica was however built as a longitudinal structure in the shape of the Latin cross with a central dome above the crossing, through which light entered the church. The dome designed by Michelangelo is the largest self-supporting brick structure in the world. The dimensions of St. Peter's Basilica are enormous: with its narthex it is 692 feet (211 m) long, boasting a height of 433 feet (132 m) and a dome of 138 feet (42 m) diameter. The built-over surface area of 163,180 sq ft (15,160 sq m) accommodates around 60,000 faithful.

The best Renaissance and Baroque artists of the day were involved in the planning and the design of St. Peter's Basilica, including along with Bramante and Michelangelo also Raphael and Bernini. Under the dome, directly above the grave of St. Peter, stands the Papal High Altar crowned in 1623 with a Baroque bronze canopy by Bernini.

A view of St. Peter's Basilica's central nave clearly illustrates the vast dimensions of this church. The interior of the Papal basilica is structured by 800 columns, an enormous main dome, eight smaller side cupolas and 45 altars. In front of the apse the outline of Bernini's bronze baldacchino with the Papal altar can be made out.

MOSQUE–CATHEDRAL
Cordoba   161,460 sq ft (15,000 sq m)

Mosque–Cathedral, Roman Bridge

Dating from the Moorish period and at a length of 587 feet (179 m) and a width of 440 feet (134 m) one of the largest religious buildings in the world, the Mosque–Cathedral is a hybrid in terms of religious history and architecture. Built as a mosque in 785 and extended several times, the complex is divided into a forecourt with washroom, haram (prayer room)

The dome above the mihrab

View across the choir altar to the ceiling

and mihrab (prayer niche). The artistic highlight is the mihrab, an octagonal room with a shell-shaped vault and decorated with mosaics depicting calligraphic and ornamental elements. Inside the visitor is overwhelmed by a veritable forest of columns with red and white striped double arches in horseshoe shapes. After the Reconquest the mosque was dedicated as a Christian church in 1236. From 1523 the columns in the central area had to make way for the interior design of a Roman Catholic cathedral. The Mosque–Cathedral was declared a UNESCO World Cultural Heritage site in 1999.

THE SECOND LARGEST CHURCH
IN THE WORLD

From the outside, the Mosque–Cathedral looks rather plain but inside it impresses with its veritable forest of 860 columns made from jasper, onyx, marble and granite, arranged in twin arcades and supporting bicolor horseshoe arches.

THE LARGEST CHURCHES IN THE WORLD

CHURCH OF THE MOST HOLY TRINITY
Fatima, Portugal
132,400 sq ft (12,300 sq m)

Not only is Fatima one of the most famous pilgrimage sites on Earth, but since the completion of the Church of the Most Holy Trinity in 2007 it has also become the location of one of the largest churches in the world.

In 1928, eleven years after the apparition of Mary, the Sanctuary of Our Lady of Fatima was built in the Portuguese village of Fatima in the neoclassical style, flanked by mighty colonnades. The 61 bells in the church tower, completed in 1953, chime every hour with the song of Fatima. Inside visitors can listen to the sounds of an organ, which has 12,000 pipes making it one of the largest in Europe.

In order to cope with the rush of pilgrims the new Holy Trinity Church was built immediately opposite and dedicated in 2007. The oval church designed by the Greek architect Alexandros Tombazis features a strapless flat roof and has a diameter of almost 427 feet (130 m), accommodating 9,000 faithful. This makes it the largest church built so far in the 21st century. Together the two sacred buildings flank the largest church forecourt in the world, at 2,460 feet (750 m) long and 656 feet (200 m) wide.

BASILICA OF THE NATIONAL SHRINE OF OUR LADY OF APARECIDA, BRAZIL
Aparecida, Brazil
129,170 sq ft (12,000 sq m)

The Basilica of Aparecida in the Brazilian federal state of São Paulo owes its existence to a miraculous statue of Mary, which was pulled out of the water by three fishermen in 1717 and brought them a rich catch of fish. The statue of Mary was initially worshipped in a small chapel, but in 1834 a basilica was built to house it. Our

Outside view of the cruciform structure

Lady of Aparecida received its present look as Madonna of Mercy in 1888 when Princess Isabella of Brazil gave the statue a blue cape and a crown.

When the dark statue of Mary was

Pilgrims in a confetti shower

declared a patron saint of Brazil in 1929, the old basilica was no longer fit to deal with the flood of pilgrims, and thus construction of the modern basilica was begun in 1955 to the plans of Benedito Calixto. Built in the shape of a Greek cross, the church's crossing is overarched by a 230 feet (70 m) high dome, while a 328 feet (100 m) tall tower stands guard on the side. The remaining measurements of this, the largest Marian shrine in the world, are equally impressive: 568 feet (173 m) long, 551 feet (168 m) wide, holding 45,000 faithful. Accommodating the throng of around 8 million pilgrims each year is a parking lot that covers an area nearly 74 acres (30 ha) and offers space for about 4,000 buses and 6,000 cars.

The Church of the Most Holy Trinity is designed to cope with the thronging masses of thousands of pilgrims. Thus it features 13 entrances (far left). The main altar is relatively plain; above it towers a giant crucifix (left).

Despite its vast dimensions the façade of Milan Cathedral has a filigree appearance with its dozens of steeples and statues (left). In the foreground the equestrian statue of Giuseppe Garibaldi

MILAN CATHEDRAL
Milan, Italy
125,940 sq ft (11,700 sq m)

"What a wonder it is! So grand, so solemn, so vast! And yet so delicate, so airy, so graceful! A very world of solid weight, and yet it seems … a delusion of frostwork that might vanish with a breath!" So wrote the amazed American writer Mark Twain in 1867, and it explains why Milan Cathedral is one of the best-known structures in Italy. The five-naved cathedral with its three-aisled tran-

Main nave of Milan Cathedral looking toward the altar

sept and a polygonal choir, mighty buttresses and cross-rib vaulting above pointed arches borrows from — but adapts — the language of Gothic shapes from north of the Alps. Because of its long construction period, from 1386 to final completion in 1858, however, many other forms were also integrated into the structure. Thus the façade combines neo-Gothic and neobaroque details. Nevertheless the light marble structure, punctuated outside by buttresses with countless pinnacles and around 4,000 statues, looks harmonious and unified.

CATHEDRAL OF ST. MARY OF THE SEE
Seville   123,780 sq ft (11,500 sq m)

When the decision was made in 1401 in Seville to build a cathedral where the Great Mosque still stood from the 12th century, the following phrase was supposedly uttered: "Let us build a church so beautiful and so great that those who see it built will think we were mad." The result was a 377 foot (115 m) long, 249 foot (76 m) wide and 138 foot (42 m) tall church, one of the largest anywhere and the largest Gothic church in the world. The minaret of the Moorish structure was raised to become a bell tower and integrated into the church complex. It is still the emblem of Seville today, known as Giralda. The cathedral was completed in 1519. It has five aisles — in part covered by reticulated vaulting

The choir and its superb ebony choir stalls

View of the choir wall

— and boasts an impressive forest of columns and two rows of chapels. The altarpiece of the main chapel is a masterpiece of Gothic wood carving in Spain.

One of the two organs

THE LARGEST GOTHIC CHURCH IN THE WORLD

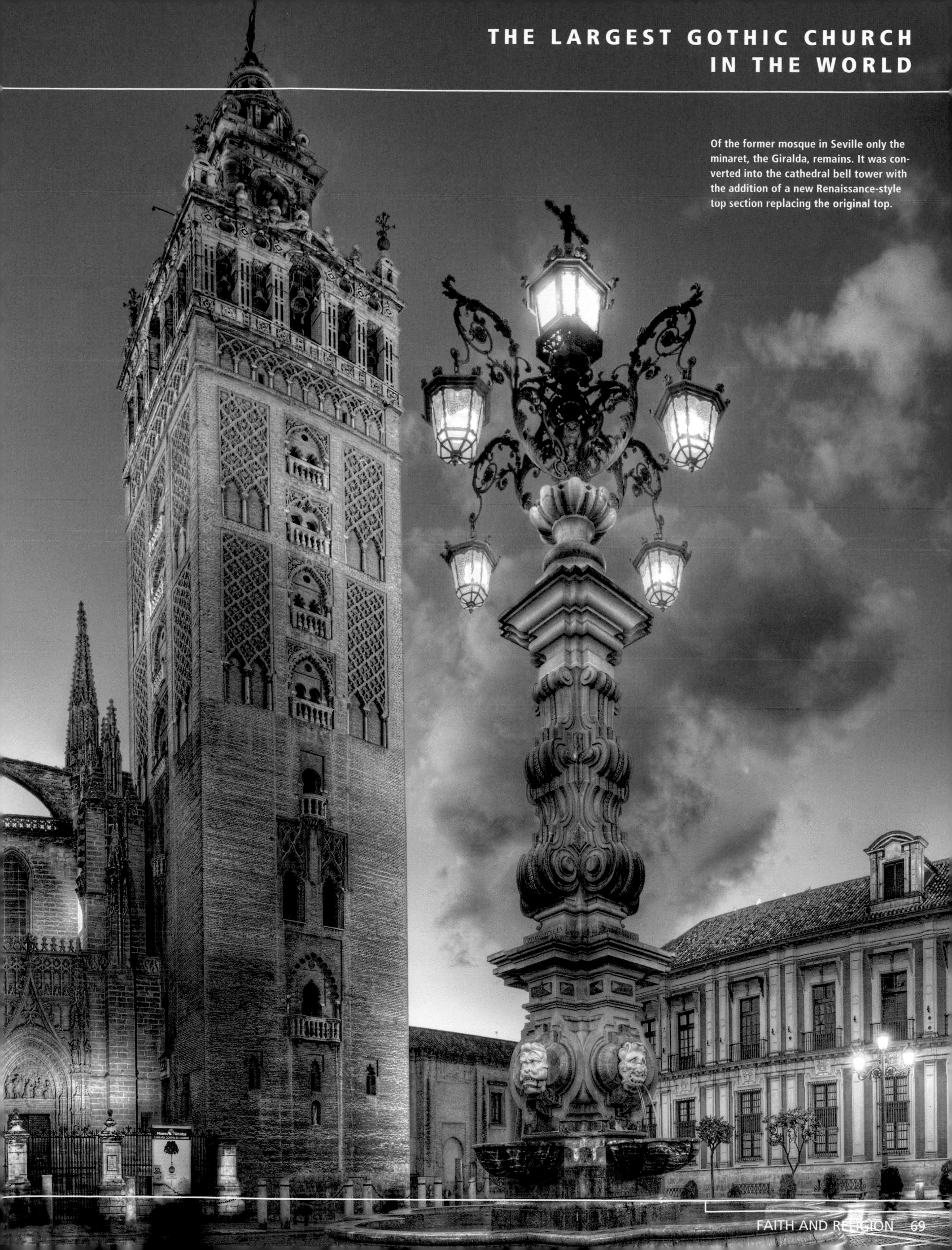

Of the former mosque in Seville only the minaret, the Giralda, remains. It was converted into the cathedral bell tower with the addition of a new Renaissance-style top section replacing the original top.

Even secular New York has a church of superlatives to be admired despite the fact that it was only two-thirds completed: the Anglican Cathedral of St. John the Divine.

ST. ISAAC'S CATHEDRAL
St. Petersburg, Russia
116,250 sq ft (10,800 sq m)

The St. Isaac's Cathedral is probably the most magnificent church in St. Petersburg, as well as one of the largest religious domed structures in the world. After his victory over

The mighty dome of St. Isaac's Cathedral

A magnificent iconostasis

View into the dome from below

Napoleon, Czar Alexander I commissioned the cathedral in the place of an earlier structure and had it converted into a national monument. Designed by the neoclassical architect Auguste de Montferrand it was built between 1818 and 1858. Splendidly fashioned in red granite and gray marble, the cathedral features a monumental gilded central dome (height: 331 feet / 101 m; diameter: 85 feet / 26 m) as well as four massive columned porticos, whose tympanums depict scenes from the life of St. Isaac and the history of salvation. Inside, the church is adorned with different types of marble, precious stones and mosaics (75,350 sq ft / 7,000 sq m) — a "museum of Russian geology."

CATHEDRAL OF ST. JOHN THE DIVINE
New York, USA   120,560 sq ft (11,200 sq m)

The foundation stone for St. John the Divine was laid in Manhattan's Upper West Side in 1892. Originally designed in the Byzantine Romanesque style, the church was built in the neo-Gothic style, using elements of the French High Gothic. The seven chapels are radially arranged around the ambulatory and dedicated to the national saints of the main immigrant nations. One of the altars was designed by Keith Haring.

St. John the Divine, 597 feet (182 m) long and 230 feet (70 m) wide, is the Anglican Church's largest religious building. Work on the church was repeatedly interrupted for years at a time. Because of a fire in the northern transept in 2001 the original plan — to build the second largest church in the world — was postponed and provisionally shelved. The serious damage it caused was only made good in 2008, after seven years of restoration work.

BASILICA OF OUR LADY OF LICHEN

Lichen Stary, Poland
108,720 sq ft (10,100 sq m)

The Basilica of Our Lady in Poland's second-most important pilgrimage site of Lichen Stary holds several national records: the largest church, it has the tallest steeple, the largest bell and the largest organ in the country. The

Basilica of Our Lady of Lichen and bell tower

monumental cruciform structure with a central dome was not built until 1994 to 2004, based on an early-Christian style. It houses the around 200-year-old image of Our Lady of Lichen, which is the destination for some 1.5 million pilgrims each year.

LIVERPOOL CATHEDRAL

Liverpool, Great Britain
104,410 sq ft (9,700 sq m)

Along with St. John the Divine in New York, Liverpool Cathedral is the largest Anglican church. Built in the neo-Gothic style to the plans of Giles Gilbert Scott, it, too, looks back on a long period of construction — the foundation stone was laid in 1904 but it was not completed until 1978. With a length of 620 feet (189 m) Liverpool Cathedral is one of the longest churches anywhere and its steeple is the tallest of its kind in the world.

Liverpool Cathedral and its massive central tower

BASILICA OF OUR LADY OF THE PILLAR
Zaragoza, Spain
89,340 sq ft (8,300 sq m)

The Basilica of Our Lady of the Pillar in Zaragoza, one of the largest churches in the world and Spain's largest baroque church, stands in the place where according to legend the Virgin Mary appeared on top of a column to the Apostle St. James the Elder. With its total of eleven domes and four corner towers, the majestic church, built in the 15th century and remodeled between 1681 and 1754, looks almost Byzantine. A masterpiece of baroque art is the Holy Chapel built on a curved plan. This "pavilion" was designed to look like an Oriental canopy within the church and houses the main object of veneration: a late-Gothic statue of the Madonna on a jasper column — the Madonna of the Pillar.

Basilica of Our Lady of the Pillar in Zaragoza, here reflected in the Ebro River, forms an imposing ensemble with a total of four towers and eleven domes. With its dimensions of 427 feet (130 m) long, 249 feet (76 m) wide and a 262 foot (80 m) high dome, it can accommodate thousands of faithful who come to venerate the statue of the Madonna of the Pillar that is kept there.

The central altar in the Basilica of Our Lady of the Pillar

BASILICA OF OUR LADY OF GUADALUPE
Mexico City, Mexico
ca. 86,110 sq ft (8,000 sq m)

Next to the Old Basilica of Guadalupe, the famous Marian shrine in Mexico City, the new basilica was erected in 1974 to the plans of the Mexican architect Pedro Ramirez Vazquez. The modern rotunda has a diameter of 328 feet (100 m) and carries a tent-shaped roof, which symbolizes the cape of the Virgin Mary. The church holds up to 20,000 people who come here to venerate the miraculous image of Our Lady of Guadalupe.

BASILICA OF THE SACRED HEART
Brussels, Belgium
c. 86,110 sq ft (8,000 sq m)

Built in the Art Deco style, which is rarely found in a church, the national Basilica of the Sacred Heart stands proud in Brussels' Koekelberg district. The 463 foot (141 m) long and 351 foot (107 m) wide church is the largest Art Deco structure in the world. Built from 1905 to 1970 on the plan of a Greek cross, the external appearance of the church is dominated by a mighty central dome and two very slender towers. From a platform at the base of the dome superb panoramic views over the Belgian capital can be enjoyed.

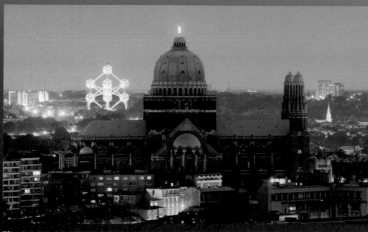

The Art Deco Basilica of the Sacred Heart with its central dome; in the background left the Atomium

Pilgrims from around the world in Guadalupe

Catholicism is but a minority religion in the Ivory Coast and the country's economic potential is very limited, yet is has been home to one of the largest churches in the world since 1988.

BASILICA OF OUR LADY OF PEACE
Yamoussoukro, Ivory Coast   **86,110 sq ft (8,000 sq m)**

Including its external elements (colonnades, vicarage), the Basilica of Our Lady of Peace has a surface area of 322,920 sq ft (30,000 sq m), making it the largest Christian church. In terms of length, width and height, the entire complex, which is clearly based on St. Peter's Basilica, outstrips its model; however, the actual church itself, with a capacity for 18,000 people and a surface area of 86,110 sq ft (8,000 sq m), is smaller. The 518 foot (158 m) tall domed building was commissioned by President Félix Houphouët-Boigny and built between 1985 and 1988 in Yamoussoukro, the new capital of the Ivory Coast. The basilica was built from Italian marble and fitted with 75,350 sq ft (7,000 sq m) of stained-glass windows made in France. The monumental structure was controversial owing to its overall construction cost of 250 million euros, officially paid out of the president's private pockets.

SAN PETRONIO
Bologna, Itay
83,960 sq ft (7,800 sq m)

Construction of the Gothic Basilica di San Petronio — incidentally financed not by the bishopric but by the citizens of Bologna — began in 1390. The lack of uniformity in its façade reveals that it was not completed then: only the bottom part is clad in marble; the naked brick walls are visible above. Many masters of their art worked on the plans (e.g. Baldassare Peruzzi and Andrea Palladio), the main portal was designed by Jacopo della Quercia. The organ, dating from about 1470, is the oldest of its kind still in use today. A special attraction is the 217 foot (66 m) long meridian by Cassini that was recessed into the floor.

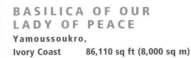

The massive incomplete façade of San Petronio dominates the Piazza Maggiore in Bologna

COLOGNE CATHEDRAL
Cologne, Germany
85,030 sq ft (7,900 sq m)

Cologne Cathedral of St. Peter and St. Mary is Germany's largest church and one of the largest churches built in the Gothic style, and its bell tower is the fifth tallest in the world. The five-naved basilica completed in 1880 was modeled on French cathedrals. Its main treasures are the Shrine of the Three Kings by Nicholas of Verdun, the altarpiece by Stephan Lochner and the Romanesque Gero Crucifix.

Views of Cologne Cathedral: eastern façade (right), mass at the High Altar

The giant complex of the Basilica of Our Lady of Peace of Yamoussoukro, the capital of the Ivory Coast, has an almost unreal appearance (far left). The vast central hall can accommodate up to 18,000 faithful.

ST. PAUL'S CATHEDRAL
London, Great Britain
84,770 sq ft (7,875 sq m)

The magnificent dome of St. Paul's Cathedral — after Liverpool Cathedral the second largest church in the United Kingdom — sits proudly and conspicuously enthroned in the middle of the city, London's financial district. The foundation stone for the present English baroque church on a cruciform plan and its 364 foot (111 m) high cathedral dome was laid in 1677, when an earlier structure had burned down. It was built to the plans of Sir Christopher Wren.

St. Paul's Cathedral: a massive domed structure with a baroque interior

TEMPLE OF ST. SAVA
Belgrade, Serbia
37,670 sq ft (3,500 sq m)

On top of Vra ar Hill in present-day Belgrade, the construction of a church was begun in 1935 to be dedicated to the founder of the Serbian Orthodox

Semi-domes inside the St. Sava Temple

Church, St. Sava, whose earthly remains had been burned here during Ottoman rule 340 years earlier. After a decade-long interruption, the largest church in southeastern Europe was not completed until recent times — however, most of the interior fittings are still missing. The marble-clad central dome built in the Serbian Byzantine style holds around 12,000 faithful.

THE LARGEST ORTHODOX CHURCH IN THE WORLD

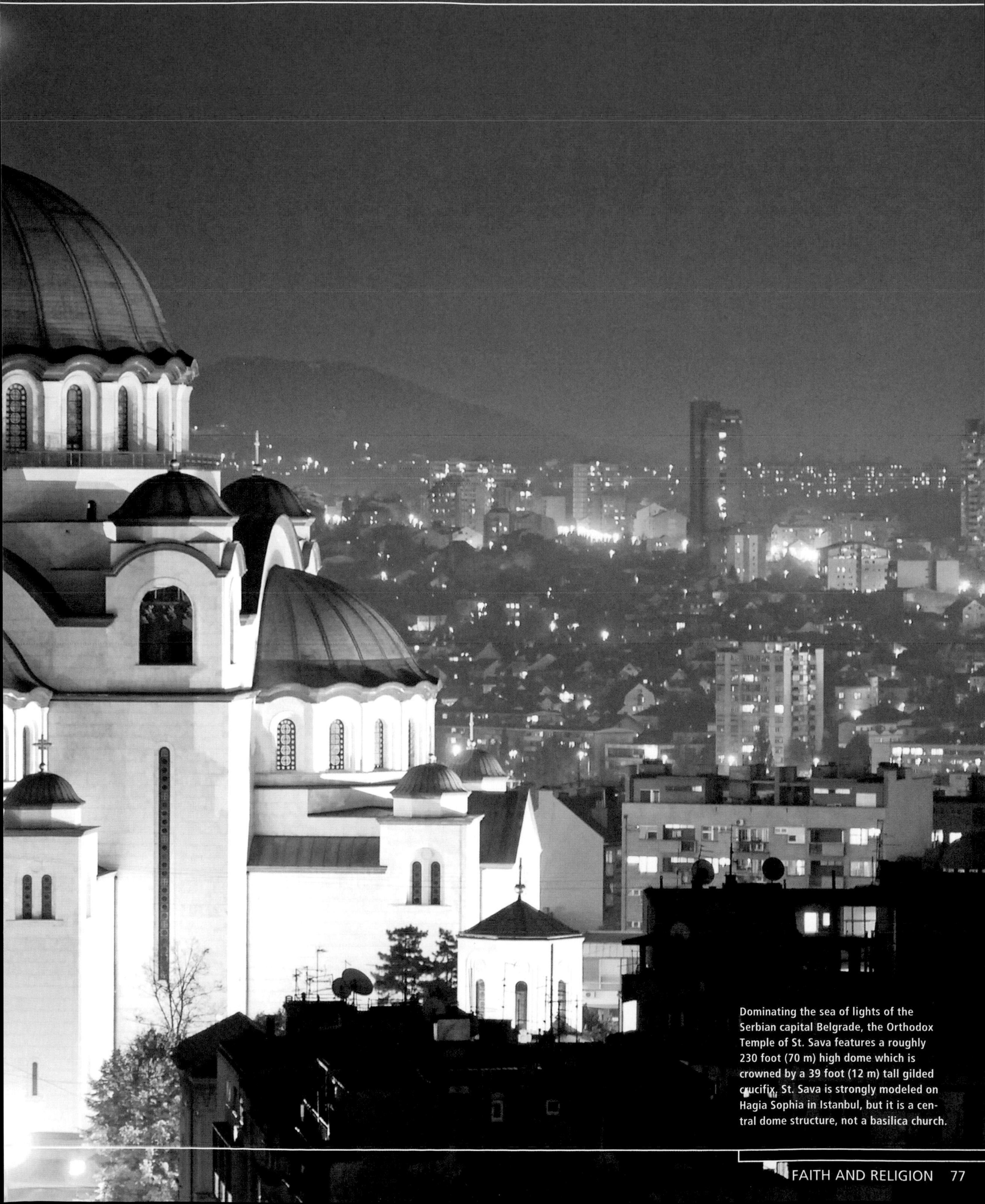

Dominating the sea of lights of the Serbian capital Belgrade, the Orthodox Temple of St. Sava features a roughly 230 foot (70 m) high dome which is crowned by a 39 foot (12 m) tall gilded crucifix. St. Sava is strongly modeled on Hagia Sophia in Istanbul, but it is a central dome structure, not a basilica church.

SALT LAKE TEMPLE
Salt Lake City
21,530 sq ft (2,000 sq m)

The largest structure of the Church of Jesus Christ of Latter-day Saints, commonly known as the Mormons, is located in Salt Lake City. Along with the Bible, the Mormons see the "Book of Mormon," named after the Prophet Mormon, as their sacred text. They believe them-selves to be Christians who have preserved their original Christianity. Their image of God is characterized by the essential differences between God, Jesus Christ and the Holy Spirit.

In 1846/47 Brigham Young,

The eastern façade of the Salt Lake Temple

the successor of Joseph Smith Jr., the religion's founder, led the Mormon Trail to the Great Salt Lake where later the state of Utah was founded. The foundation stone for the Salt Lake Temple was laid in the capital, Salt Lake City, in 1853 and it was dedicated in 1893. In the middle of Temple Square, which covers 430,560 sq ft (40,000 sq m), a roughly 197 foot (60 m) long and 98 foot (30 m) wide church was built from granite-like monzonite, its façade marked by its six towers, up to 210 feet (64 m) tall. The building's architecture, which borrowed from the style of the neo-Gothic, is rich in symbolism: thus the twelve façade turrets on each of the three

eastern towers represent the twelve Apostles, those of the three western towers the High Council. Each tower has stones featuring astronomical figures, including 52 suns, 34 earths and 104 stars.

The inside of the Salt Lake Temple is not to be imagined as a conventional church with nave and transept: it is in fact divided into se-veral stories and hundreds of rooms.

Immediately adjacent to the temple stands the Tabernacle, which boasts one of the largest organs in the world (11,623 pipes) and a conference center seating 21,000, the largest auditorium in the world used for religious purposes.

Dominating the center of Salt Lake City: the Mormon temple surrounded by gardens

The adjacent Salt Lake Tabernacle, home to one of the largest organs in the world

The figure of Christ stands in the visitors' center in Temple Square, in front of a diorama showing the stars, planets and other celestial bodies. Early Mormon prophets taught that the stars and planets are inhabited and that God lives near a star called Kolob.

THE TALLEST CHURCHES IN THE WORLD

Unlike the size of a church, which may be determined using different kinds of criteria, the height is clearly identifiable — namely by the height of the church tower. It is independent of the overall size of the church, and thus the list of the tallest churches in the world also includes some comparatively small buildings. Nevertheless the heavenward thrust is restricted by the laws of physics: over the course of the centuries some very

Cologne Cathedral and Hohenzollern Bridge

Strasbourg Cathedral, western façade

tall church towers — like those of Lincoln Cathedral, St. Olaf's Church in Tallinn or St. Mary's Church in Stralsund, for example — partly collapsed and had to be reduced in height during rebuilding. The present record holder has been the 528 foot (161 m) tall Ulm Minster since 1890.

ULM MINSTER — THE TALLEST CHURCH IN THE WORLD

Ulm Minster is the largest Protestant church in the world, and also boasts another record: its 528 foot (161 m) high church tower is the tallest in the world. This unusually large five-aisled basilica, which accommodates 30,000 people, was begun in the 14th century. In the subsequent 200 years it was extended under the direction of a number of master-builders in the styles of

Ulm Minster tower

the Prague and the Strasbourg High Gothic. During the time of the Reformation the citizens of Ulm converted to Protestant beliefs. After a lengthy period of inactivity the "citizens' cathedral" was finally completed in 1890. Highlights of its interior are the late-Gothic works by artists from the Ulm School, for example the choir stalls by Jörg Syrlin the Elder and Michel Erhart.

THE TALLEST CHURCHES IN THE WORLD

1. **Ulm Minster, Germany**
   528 feet (161 m)
2. **Basilica of Our Lady of Peace, Yamoussoukro, Ivory Coast**
   518 feet (158 m)
3. **Cologne Cathedral, Germany**
   515 feet (157 m)
4. **Rouen Cathedral, France**
   495 feet (151 m)
5. **St. Nicholas' Church, Hamburg, Germany**
   486 feet (148 m)
6. **Strasbourg Cathedral, France**
   466 feet (142 m)
7. **Basilica of Our Lady of Lichen, Poland**
   463 feet (141 m)
8. **St. Stephen's Cathedral, Vienna, Austria**
   446 feet (136 m)
9. **New Cathedral, Linz, Austria**
   443 feet (135 m)
10. **St. Peter's Cathedral, Rome, Italy**
    436 feet (133 m)
11. **St. Peter's Church, Hamburg, Germany**
    433 feet (132 m)
12. **St. Michael's Church, Hamburg, Germany**
    433 feet (132 m)

The Gothic St. Stephen's Cathedral with its steep saddle roof, the 446 foot (136 m) tall south tower and the surviving two Roman Towers on the west façade, is the emblem of Vienna. In the foreground the baroque dome of St. Peter's Church.

ST. MARTIN'S CHURCH, LANDSHUT — THE TALLEST BRICK CHURCH TOWER IN THE WORLD

With its slender, tall tower, St. Martin's Church dominates the cityscape of Landshut. The three-aisled brick hall church built in 1389 is one of the most important religious buildings of the late-Gothic style in southern Germany. The steeple was completed around 1500. Its shape, tapering toward the top and changing on plan from square to octagonal, gives it an elegant appearance. With its height of 427 feet (130 m) it was one of the ten tallest church steeples anywhere in the world when it was built.

Tower of St. Martin's Church in Landshut

THE LARGEST CHRISTIAN STATUES IN THE WORLD

Anyone contemplating colossal Christian statues will automatically think of the statue of Christ on the Corcovado Mountain high above Rio de Janeiro. It is however by far not the largest of its kind. The Christian record — the colossal Buddha statues are considerably taller in comparison — is held by Christ the King in the Portuguese city of Almada (total height including base) as well as the statue of St. Rita of Cassia in Santa Cruz in the Brazilian state of Rio Grande do Norte (height of the statue without base). Depending on whether the base is measured or the height of the statue alone, a different ranking emerges. The most common subject of monumental Christian statues is Jesus Christ, followed by Mary.

Our Lady of the Sacred Heart, France

THE TALLEST CHRISTIAN STATUES IN THE WORLD: WITHOUT BASE

1. St. Rita of Cassia, Santa Cruz, Brazil
   164 feet (50 m)
2. Statue of Christ the King, Swiebodzin, Poland
   118 feet (36 m)
3. Christ of Peace, Cochabamba, Bolivia
   112 feet (34 m)
4. Our Lady of the Sacred Heart, Le Mas-Rillier, France
   108 feet (33 m)
5. Christ the Redeemer, Rio de Janeiro, Brazil
   98 feet (30 m)

WITH BASE

1. Christ the King, Almada, Portugal
   338 feet (103 m)
2. St. Rita of Cassia, Santa Cruz, Brazil
   184 feet (56 m)
3. Our Lady of the Sacred Heart, Le Mas-Rillier, France
   174 feet (53 m)
4. Christ the King, Swiebodzin, Poland
   171 feet (52 m)
5. Christ Blessing, Indonesia
   164 feet (50 m)

SWIEBODZIN, POLAND: THE SECOND LARGEST CHRIST STATUE IN THE WORLD

Christ the King during its assembly

Christ the King in full splendor

Since 2010 the second largest Christ statue in the world (without base but including the 10 ft / 3 m tall gilded crown: 118 ft / 36 m) has been "Christ the King," in the Polish town of Wiebodzin. The base is unusual: an artificial stone pile a good 49 feet (15 m) high. When the 16.5 short ton (15 tonne) head was to be fitted (total weight of the figure: 485 short ton / 440 tonne) a crane fell over.

ALMADA, PORTUGAL: THE TALLEST CHRIST STATUE IN THE WORLD WITH BASE

Guarding the Tejo Valley on top of a giant base: Christ the King in Almada near Lisbon

The world record regarding the height of the base is held by Christ the King in Almada, completed in 1959: the statue of Christ stands on a 246 feet (75 m) base, making it seem small in comparison although it nevertheless measures an impressive 92 feet (28 m). From the viewing platform superb views of the Tejo River, the 25th of April Bridge and the city of Lisbon opposite can be enjoyed.

COCHABAMBA, BOLIVIA: THE THIRD LARGEST CHRIST STATUE IN THE WORLD

The statue of Christ of Peace in the Bolivian town of Cochabamba, with its 112 foot (34 m) height (without base), held the record until 2010 and today is still the Christ statue at the highest altitude. At 9,320 feet (2,840 m) above sea level the top of the Cerro San Pedro summit can be reached by lift, car or — assuming a sufficient degree of fitness — on foot via about 1,400 steps. On Sundays the monument itself can also be climbed. Built between 1987 and 1994 in steel and concrete, it was based on the famous model in Rio de Janeiro; from the top there are magnificent views of the Cochabamba Valley.

Christ of Peace in Cochabamba

VALLEY OF THE FALLEN, SPAIN: THE TALLEST MONUMENTAL CRUCIFIX IN THE WORLD

The concrete cross on the National Monument of the Holy Cross of the Valley of the Fallen near Madrid is some 492 feet (150 m) tall and 130 feet (40 m) wide. The "Valley of the Fallen" is a gargantuan complex with an underground basilica (at a length of 863 feet / 263 m the longest in the world), which houses the graves of the Spanish dictator Franco and of the founder of the fascist Falange movement, Primo de Rivera, as well as the bones of 30,000 of Franco's soldiers. The mausoleum — one of the largest in the world — was built by 20,000 forced laborers and is a highly controversial symbolic place for the Spanish right.

Underneath the world's largest crucifix: the mausoleum of the Spanish dictator Franco

RIO DE JANEIRO, BRAZIL: THE MOST FAMOUS CHRIST STATUE IN THE WORLD

A grand panorama: Christ the Redeemer with Sugarloaf Mountain and Guanabara Bay

Not the tallest but with about one million visitors each year by far the most popular of all Christ statues and the archetype for many copies is Christ the Redeemer on top of Rio de Janeiro's Corcovado Mountain. With its arms extended (92 feet / 28 m span) the 100 foot (30 m) tall statue (without base) looks toward Sugarloaf Mountain and Guanabara Bay. The armored concrete Jesus was built between 1922 and 1931, the precast parts being dragged up the hill by an electric train. Guglielmo Marconi, the pioneer of wireless transmission, started up the illumination by remote control from Italy.

Standing on top of the roughly 2,300 foot (700 m) high Corcovado Mountain south of Rio de Janeiro, Christ the Redeemer extends his arms protectively over the city and its millions of inhabitants. For those pilgrims who are not able to walk, the most famous Christ statue in the world can also be reached by car, cog train, elevator and moving stairway.

FAITH AND RELIGION

THE FIRST MONO-THEISTIC RELIGION IN THE WORLD

Although Judaism, with seven million followers around the world, is a comparatively small faith community, it has been of paramount importance in the historical development of religions. Two of the great world religions, namely Christianity and Islam, both arose from Judaism and share many of its convictions. Belief in the one and only God, the hope for eternal life and the idea that a divine judgment at the end of all days will adjudicate over the living as well as the dead, are all of Jewish origin. The lives of the faithful are determined by laws based on the Torah, the holy scriptures of the Jews, comprising the five books of Moses. The tradition of interpreting the Torah probably developed around the time it was written down, around 200 BC; over time it gained in canonic importance and became known as the Talmud. The Talmud contains a host of teachings, commentaries and annotations to the Torah and deduces from it legal rulings that are binding for devout Jews.

View of the Western Wall from the west, with the Temple Mount and the Dome of the Rock in the evening twilight

THE WESTERN (OR WAILING) WALL — THE HOLIEST SITE FOR THE JEWISH WORLD

The most important religious site for Jews is the only remaining section of the Second Temple in Jerusalem, which was destroyed by Titus in 70 AD, in the course of the brutal suppression of the Jewish rebellion against the Romans. This defeat marked a turning point in Jewish history: the Jews were expelled from Jerusalem, and the remains of their temple became the holiest pilgrimage destination. After the division of Jerusalem following the Arab–Israeli War in 1948 the Jews no longer had access to the Western Wall. It has only been accessible to them since the end of the Six-Day War in 1967.

Orthodox Jews in Jerusalem

Jews with prayer shawls

A Jewish man holding a shofar

Jews praying in front of the Western Wall, also known as the Wailing Wall. A section of only 197 feet (60 m) of this holiest of all Jewish religious sites is above ground. The greater part was built on after the temple's destruction in 70 AD and is now accessible only via a 1,585 foot (483 m) long tunnel from the forecourt.

A Jewish house of God is not only a place for prayer but also a meeting point where the entire community can meet up and discuss their affairs. Most synagogues have meeting rooms and libraries for the study of the Holy Scriptures. The prayer hall is mostly used for religious services. During the celebrations at the start of Sabbath, following age-old traditions, the Torah scrolls are taken out of their shrine and placed on top of a platform known as bimah. The prayer leader then reads out a different section of the Torah for each week of the Jewish calendar year.

THE BELZ GREAT SYNAGOGUE, JERUSALEM — THE LARGEST SYNAGOGUE IN THE WORLD

The Belz Great Synagogue in Jerusalem

This vast place of worship was built on the initiative of Rabbi Yissachar Dov Rokeach, the descendent of a Hassidic dynasty of rabbis from Belz in the Ukraine, and was dedicated in 2000. It is modeled on the first synagogue of Belz, which was destroyed by the Nazis, and like the latter was intended to be a place of Jewish scholarship. The entire complex comprises not only several prayer rooms but also libraries, reading and meeting rooms. The large central prayer hall alone accommodates 6,000 faithful. The shrine in which the Torah scrolls are kept is 59 feet (18 m) tall and weighs several tons (tonnes). The lectern of Rabbi Aharon Rokeach, the uncle of Yissachar Dov Rokeach who managed to flee to Palestine in 1944, is kept in a display case in his memory.

TEMPLE EMANU-EL, NEW YORK — THE SECOND LARGEST SYNAGOGUE IN THE WORLD

The main portal of the Temple Emanu-El

In New York's Upper East Side, in a famous location on the corner of Fifth Avenue/65th Street, stands one of the largest synagogues in the world: the Temple Emanu-El, built in 1928–9 and offering room for 2,500 faithful. Plain yet impressive from the outside, the synagogue is the headquarters of the oldest liberal Jewish community in New York, which was founded in 1845. Built from limestone, the massive religious building successfully combines neoromanesque and neobyzantine style elements with Moorish and Art Deco ornamentation. The Torah shrine is adorned with mosaics worked in magnificent detail. The synagogue, which also houses a museum, hosts lectures, concerts, symposia, exhibitions as well as other cultural events along with traditional services and religious celebrations.

The magnificent prayer hall of the Budapest Great Synagogue boasts impressive dimensions. The seating benches in the hall are reserved for men, whereas women are accommodated in the two side-galleries.

GREAT SYNAGOGUE, BUDAPEST

The Great or Dohány Street Synagogue was built by the Viennese master-builder Ludwig Förster in collaboration with two Hungarian architects, Frigyes Feszl and József Hild, in Budapest's Erzsébetváros district between 1854 and 1859. The Moorish-Oriental structure has a white and red brick façade and two 144 foot (44 m) tall onion towers. Its exuberantly appointed interior, featuring two magnificent chandeliers as well as beautifully adorned wooden galleries on both sides, extends over two stories and boasts a total of 3,000 seats.

Prayer room in the Dohány Street Synagogue, Budapest

GREAT SYNAGOGUE, PILSEN (PLZEN)

The onion domes of the Great Synagogue

The second largest Sephardic synagogue in Europe was dedicated in 1893. Its appearance is the result of a compromise agreed by the Jewish community of Plzeň. Originally it was designed to have 213 foot (65 m) high Gothic towers. After protests by the Plzeň magistrate, which feared that the synagogue might eclipse the Christian cathedral, the architects decided on a combination of Romanesque and Renaissance styles. The towers were crowned by onion domes and their height was reduced by 66 feet (20 m). The structure escaped the fury of the Nazis because it was used as a storage depot during the war. After 1945 it fell into disrepair, but was restored in the 1990s.

Interior with mosaic-adorned domes

Muslims at the breaking of the fast each evening during Ramadan in front of the Prophet's Mosque in Medina. In the fasting month believers are required not to eat or drink during the day. At the onset of dusk the fast is traditionally broken by a large communal meal.

ISLAM

THE SECOND LARGEST FAITH COMMUNITY IN THE WORLD

With about 1.2 billion believers, Islam is the second largest and also the youngest religion in the

Dome of the Rock in Jerusalem

world, regarding itself as the final revelation of the monotheisms of Judaism and Christianity. Of its followers it demands absolute compliance — and the term "Islam" means exactly that — with the will of God. In 610 AD, on top of Mount Hira, none other than the Archangel Gabriel is believed to have commanded the Prophet Mohammed from Mecca, the founder of Islam, to convert the people of his homeland to the belief in God as the sole ruler of the world and to recognize him as the sole judge over all the living and all the dead. Although initially the inhabitants of Mecca strongly resisted Mohammed's missionary efforts and the Prophet had to flee to Medina in 622 AD, the new teachings had spread across the entire western part of the Arabian peninsula by the time of his death. The Prophet created a strong religious community, highly motivated by the conviction that they represented the only true faith. During the campaigns of conquest by his successors, the caliphs, his teachings spread westward across North Africa into Spain and eastward across the Levant (eastern Mediterranean), Mesopotamia and Persia, and as far as India. Today Islam is the state religion in many countries of Africa and Asia.

Islam comprises two major branches that formed after the death of Mohammed in the course of a dispute over his succession. Whereas Sunni Muslims believe that their leader could be elected by the faithful, the Shi'ites only grant this privilege to an actual descendant of the Prophet. The smaller denominations have emerged from these two larger branches.

THE MOST IMPORTANT ISLAMIC SCHOOLS/ BRANCHES

❶ Sunnis	1, 2 billion
❷ Shi'ites	300 million
❸ Alevites*	20 million
❹ Ismailism*	18 million
❺ Ahmadiyya	10 million
❻ Ibadi	2 million

(*branches of Shia Islam)

Muslims during the circumambulation of the Kaaba, the building inside the Al-Masjid al-Haram Mosque in Mecca. It is wrapped in a black cloth worked with gold brocade. The Kaaba is the most sacred and central site of Islam, visited each year by 2.5 million pilgrims. The Qur'an prescribes that pilgrims walk seven times around the Kaaba and while doing so kiss or at the very least touch the "Black Stone" on its eastern corner.

MECCA, SAUDI ARABIA — THE MOST IMPORTANT PILGRIMAGE DESTINATIONS IN ISLAM

The birthplace of the Prophet Mohammed is the most sacred pilgrimage destination for the Islamic world. The Hajj, as the pilgrimage to Mecca is called, is one of the Five Pillars of Islam, and every believing Muslim should undertake the journey there at least once during his life. Despite the Meccans' initial reservations against the new religion, Mohammed himself made the pilgrimage from Medina to his hometown in 629, together with many thousand followers, and conquered it in the process. In pre-Islamic times the Kaaba was dedicated to deities of nature; the pilgrimage site was converted into a Muslim sanctuary by Mohammed.

The Kaaba in the courtyard of the Al-Masjid al-Haram Mosque

Moulay Idriss, Morocco

Aside from Mecca, Islam recognizes two further pilgrimage sites that are linked with the life of the religion's founder and therefore sacred to all Muslims: the grave of Mohammed in the Prophet's Mosque at Medina is visited by hundreds of thousands of believers each year. And the place of his "ascension to heaven" on Temple Mount in Jerusalem is a Pan-Islamic holy site. At the pilgrimage places in Iraq and Iran the imams are venerated, who are — according to the beliefs of the Shi'ite Muslims — the direct descendants of the Prophet and thus his only rightful successors. The pilgrimage sites in North Africa are dedicated to outstanding personalities who helped spread Islam.

The Shrine of Fatimah al-Masumah in Qom. The sister of the eighth imam, Fatima is venerated by Shi'ite Muslims as a holy woman. She died in 818 AD, probably as a result of poisoning. The mausoleum was built 50 years later.

MEDINA, SAUDI ARABIA

The Prophet's Mosque in Medina

Medina, the place where Mohammed founded the first Muslim faith community in 622 and where he also died, is the holiest city of Islam after Mecca. Each year nearly one million faithful make the pilgrimage there and visit the grave of the Prophet in the Al-Masjid al-Nabawi Mosque. Access to the holy sites is strictly barred to non-Muslims.

JERUSALEM, ISRAEL/PALESTINE

The Dome of the Rock in Jerusalem

The Dome of the Rock on Temple Mount in Jerusalem, one of the oldest Islamic religious buildings, is also one of the most important holy sites for Muslims. It was built as a shrine around 690 AD, exactly above the rock from which Mohammed is believed to have ascended to Heaven on the back of his horse Al-Buraq. The magnificent structure is a masterpiece of the early Umayyad style.

KAIROUAN, TUNISIA

Inside the Sidi Oqba Mosque

The fourth holiest city in Islam was founded in 670 AD during the Arab conquest of North Africa. Home to the Sidi Oqba Mosque it houses the oldest Islamic place of worship in Africa. Until the 11th century Kairouan was a center of Arabic Islamic culture. Outside the Old Town stands the Mosque of Sidi Saheb or the Barber's Mosque, an important pilgrimage destination that is believed to hold the grave of a friend of Mohammed's.

SANLIURFA, TURKEY

The sacred sites of Sanliurfa

The birthplace of Abraham, the progenitor of both Israel and the Arabs, this town is the fifth hollest place In Islam.

MOULAY IDRISS, MOROCCO

This place is one of the most important pilgrimage destinations in Islam and also the holiest town in Morocco. It is said that seven pilgrimages to the grave of the founder of the city, Moulay Idriss, count as much as one journey to Mecca. Moulay Idriss (r. 788–761 AD) was a descendant of the Caliph Ali ibn Abi Talib who introduced Islam to Morocco.

QOM, IRAQ

The shrine of Fatima bint Musa

This town is an important Shi'ite pilgrimage site. It is home to the grave of Fatima al-Masumah, the sister of the eighth imam and thus a direct descendant of Mohammed. Shia Islam admits only natural descendants of the Prophet to his succession.

KARBALA, IRAQ

Imam Hussein Shrine

This town is home to the grave of Imam Hussein ibn Ali, one of Mohammed's grandsons, who fell in 680 AD during the famous Battle of Karbala and has since been venerated as a martyr by Shi'ite Muslims. They were defeated in the battle by Sunni Muslims, their hopes of transferring the caliphate to a direct descendant of Mohammed shattered.

MASHHAD, IRAN

Imam Reza Shrine

The town is the most important pilgrimage place in Iran. Every year some 12 million believers make the pilgrimage to the grave of Imam Reza. The godly man is venerated as a martyr by Shi'ite Muslims. According to tradition he was poisoned by a Sunni opponent of the Shia in 818, during disputes about the rightful succession of the Prophet, which still divide the Muslim community until this day.

During its history, Islamic religious architecture has brought forth a wealth of forms and styles. Yet Muslim houses of worship largely resemble each other in their essential structure. A mosque always possesses a central prayer room where the faithful assemble to worship. Along one wall of the

Goharshad Mosque in Mashhad

hall the prayer niche points in the direction of Mecca, thus indicating the Qibla, or prayer direction. The pulpit is used by the imam for his sermons. Most mosques also have fountains and washbasins for ritual cleansing.

THE LARGEST MOSQUES IN THE WORLD
(by visitor capacity)

1 Al-*H*aram Mosque
Mecca, Saudi Arabia 820,000
2 Imam Reza Shrine
Mashhad, Iran 700,000
3 Prophet's Mosque
Medina, Saudi Arabia 600,000
4 Taj-ul-Masjid
Bhopal, India 175,000
5 Istiqlal Mosque
Jakarta, Indonesia 120,000
6 Hassan II Mosque
Casablanca, Morocco 120,000
7 Badshahi Mosque
Lahore, Pakistan 100,000
8 Friday Mosque (Jama Masjid),
Old Delhi, India 85,000
9 Faisal Mosque
Islamabad, Pakistan 74,000
10 Sheikh Zayed Mosque
Abu Dhabi 40,000

The large prayer hall of the Prophet's Mosque in Medina during the Friday prayers. The house of worship is one of the largest mosques in the world, capable of accommodating many thousands of faithful. It was built during the lifetime of Mohammed, near his residence and has repeatedly been extended and embellished.

AL-*H*ARAM MOSQUE

Mecca   820,000 people

The Al-*H*aram Mosque houses the Kaaba (Arabic "cube"), the most sacred shrine in Islam. It is the largest and most important Mosque in the Muslim world. The 36 foot (11 m) high Kaaba,

The Kaaba is surrounded by pilgrims …

… not only during the Hajj

around which all the believers walk seven times, is customarily clad in a black cloth but is cloaked in white during the pilgrimage (Hajj). The Qur'an requires all Muslims who are able to make the Hajj to Mecca at least once in their lifetime. In 630 AD Mohammed had all the pre-Islamic idols and symbols removed and a hypostyle mosque built around the Kaaba. After several enlargements the house of worship received its present look and size (3,840,560 sq ft / 356,800 sq m) in 1577. Its colonnaded arcades are surmounted by white cupolas. Currently the mosque is surrounded by nine minarets.

The Al-Haram Mosque (Masjid al-Haram) in Mecca is the guardian of the holiest Islamic shrine, the Kaaba. The cuboid building cloaked in black cloth was once in pre-Islamic days a sanctuary dedicated to gods of nature. The famous Black Stone, which is attached to the eastern corner of the Kaaba, dates from this period. It has not been possible even until today to confirm the belief that the lump is a meteorite.

IMAM REZA SHRINE
Mashhad   700,000 people

The final resting place of Ali ibn Musa-ar-Rida in the eastern Iranian city of Mashhad is probably the most important pilgrimage site of Shi'ite Islam,

The old courtyard at the Imam Reza Shrine

and is visited each year by millions of believers. Shi'ite Muslims venerate the imam as the rightful successor of the Prophet, appointed by God himself, and as a martyr, who allegedly was poisoned by

One of 21 vestibules of the burial chamber

Caliph al-Ma'mum in 818 AD. What is considered certain however is that the caliph had the imam buried there, in the mausoleum of his father, Harun al-Rashid. The tomb soon developed as an important shrine and was

repeatedly enlarged over the centuries. It is surrounded by several courtyards that are fringed by arcades and accessible via an iwan, open to the skies and magnificently decorated with mosaics. The complex covers an area of no less than 82 acres (33 hectare) and comprises further tombs, madrassas and two mosques. The 15th-century Gowharshad Mosque stands out with its double-skinned dome, a gem of Persian Timurid architecture in turquoise and cobalt blue. It is surrounded by a walled courtyard, which is accessible on each side via open iwans. The caravansaries of the shrine today house important museums. The Imam Reza Shrine compound is surrounded by open lawns and a ring road that keeps the worldly buildings of the city at a distance from the sanctuary.

Shi'ite believers during evening prayer in the courtyard of the Gowharshad Mosque at the Imam Reza Shrine. Visible in the picture background is the dome above the mausoleum where the eight imam lies buried. The courtyards around the central sanctum are accessible via iwans. These halls, open on one side, are typical of classic Persian and Central Asian Islamic architecture.

THE PROPHET'S MOSQUE
Medina   600,000 people

The Prophet's Mosque
(Al-Masjid al-Nabawi) is after the
Al-Haram-Mosque in Mecca one
of the most important Islamic
houses of worship in the world.
At one time the house of the
Prophet Mohammed stood in the
place where the Mosque stands
today. This is where his family
lived and the Muslim community
congregated, prayed, dispensed
justice and legislated. The mosque
was built during the life of the
Prophet and became a model for
Muslim houses of prayer anywhere
in the world. It was repeatedly
converted over the centuries: the
green dome above the Prophet's
tomb dates from the time of Sultan
Qalawun (r. 1279–1290).

Prayer room in the Prophet's Mosque

THE THIRD LARGEST MOSQUE IN THE WORLD

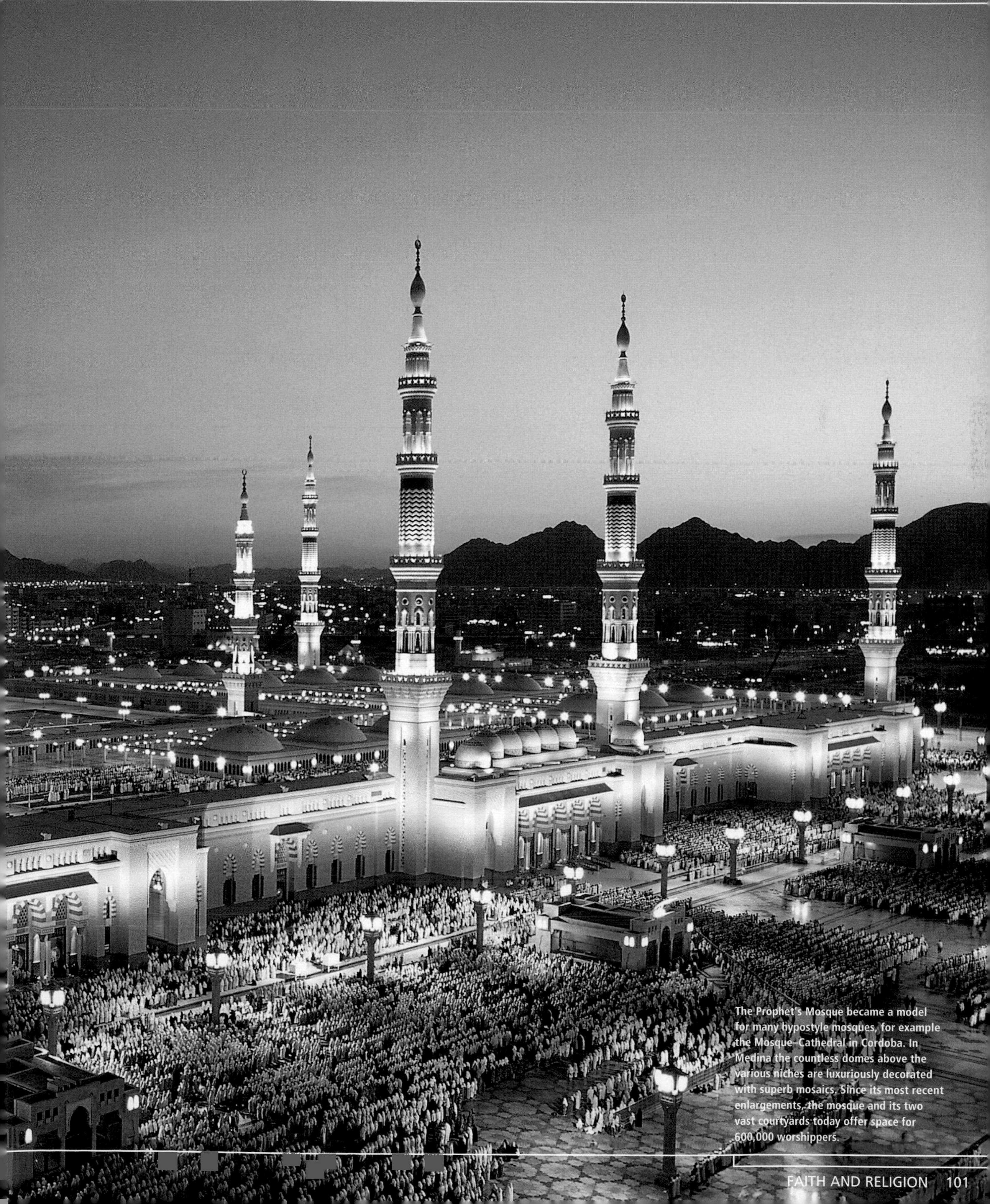

The Prophet's Mosque became a model for many hypostyle mosques, for example the Mosque–Cathedral in Cordoba. In Medina the countless domes above the various niches are luxuriously decorated with superb mosaics. Since its most recent enlargements, the mosque and its two vast courtyards today offer space for 600,000 worshippers.

Minarets have been a part of every mosque since the early days of Islam. In many cities of the Islamic world these tall slender towers still dominate the skyline. Until recently, the muezzin still called the faithful for prayer five times a day from his place in the upper

Koutoubia Mosque, Marrakech

part of the minaret. Today his call is mostly transmitted by loudspeakers, yet the minarets have remained as distinctive features of the mosques. No Islamic house of prayer is permitted to have more minarets than the mosque in Mecca.

DIE HÖCHSTEN MINARETTE DER WELT

① **Hassan II Mosque**
   Casablanca, Morocco
   690 ft (210 m)
② **Abdul Aziz Mosque**
   Shah Alam, Malaysia
   460 ft (140 m)
③ **Putra Mosque**
   Putrajaya, Malaysia
   380 ft (116 m)
④ **Sheikh Zayed Mosque**
   Abu Dhabi, UAE
   350 ft (107 m)
⑤ **Prophet's Mosque**
   Medina, Saudi Arabia
   344 ft (105 m)
⑥ **Sabanci Central Mosque**
   Adana, Turkey
   325 ft (99 m)
⑦ **Faisal Mosque**
   Islamabad, Pakistan
   295 ft (90 m)
⑧ **Al-Haram Mosque**
   Mecca, Saudi Arabia
   292 ft (89 m)

HASSAN II MOSQUE — THE TALLEST MINARET IN THE WORLD

With a height of 690 feet (210 m) this minaret surpasses the tallest church tower in the world, that of Ulm Minster in Germany, by nearly 165 feet (50 m). It is currently the tallest religious sacred building on Earth. During the minaret's construction, like the mosque designed by the French architect Michel Pinseau, the most up-to-date technologies were combined with traditional Islamic architecture. An elevator takes visitors up to the viewing platform, and after nightfall a laser beam from the top of the tower points out the direction of Mecca. Each side of the square minaret is 82 feet (25 m) long, its façades are clad in the finest marble and richly ornamented in the Moorish style. The structure is crowned by three enormous golden balls, together weighing 4 short tons (3,700 kg), with the largest of them boasting a diameter of almost 13 feet (4 m). The Hassan II Mosque was inaugurated in 1993.

The Blue Mosque of Shah Alam in Malaysia

The Sheikh Zayed Mosque in Abu Dhabi

The Putra Mosque of Putrajaya in Malaysia

The Sabanci Central Mosque of Adana in Turkey

The Mosque of Muhammad Ali in Cairo

Visible from afar the minarets indicate the presence of a mosque. Like no other type of building they are a symbol of Islam and Islamic architecture, which has brought about a multitude of minaret forms over the course of its history. There are round minarets as well as those with a square or polygonal ground plan. Most rise into the sky as overly slender, graceful towers. Some reach a height of more than 328 feet (100 m).

The largest mud brick religious building in the world is the Great Mosque of Djenné. The emblem of the West African

"Fête de crépissage" — the re-rendering festival

state of Mali, it stands in the Old Town of Djenné that has been a UNESCO World Heritage site since 1988. Its roots date back far into the 12th century, the present building however

was only built between 1907 and 1909, after an earlier structure was destroyed in 1834. The mud bricks, which are dried in the air, and the mud render suffer during the rainy season and have to be repaired on a regular basis. Once a year the citizens meet up for the "fête de crépissage," a large communal festivity when all the sustained damage is repaired. The trunks of palm trees are used as ladders that have been set into the walls to stabilize the mud brick structure. However, this restoration work alone is not always sufficient: at the end of 2009, after particularly heavy rains, one of the towers collapsed.

THE LARGEST MUD BRICK BUILDING IN THE WORLD

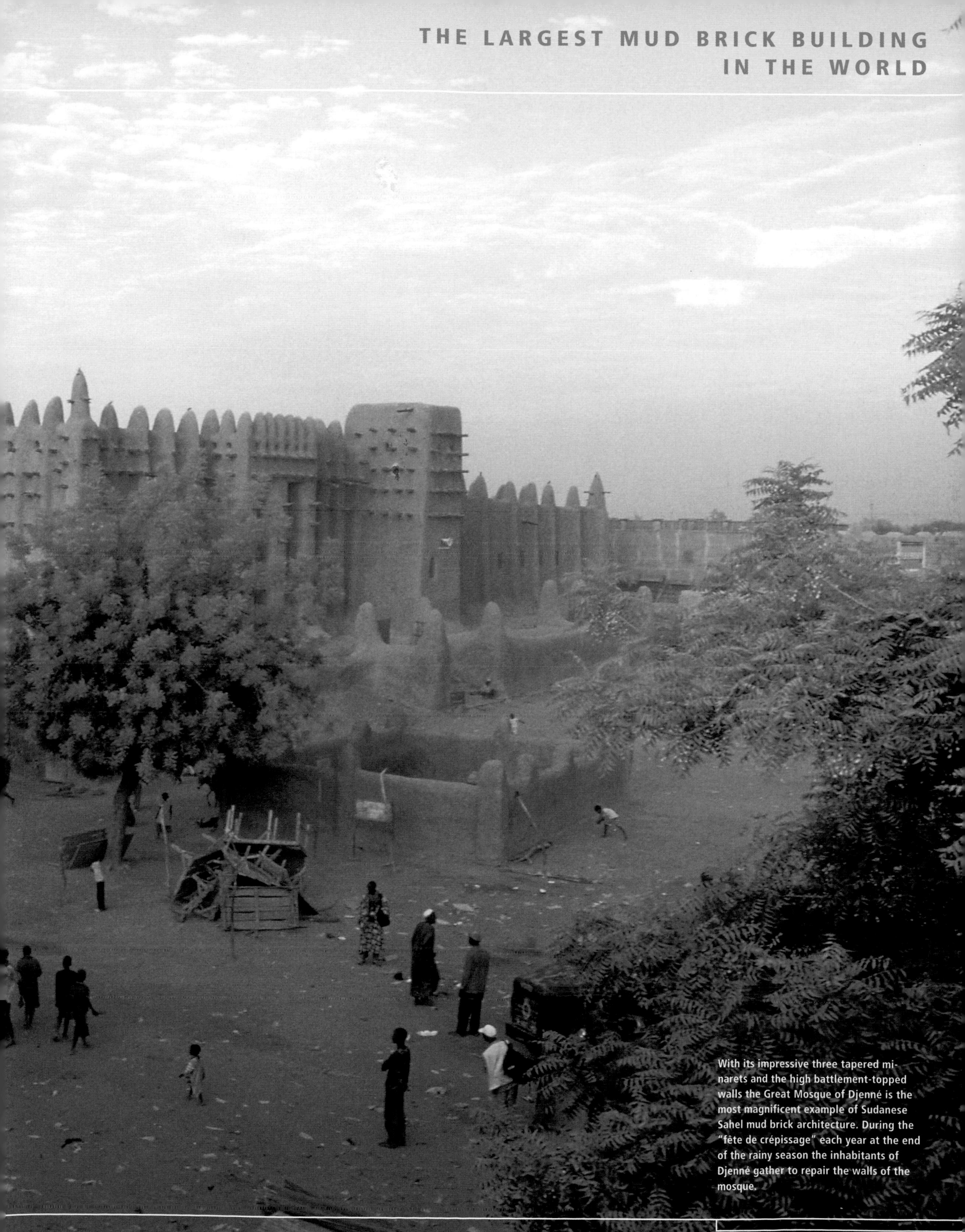

With its impressive three tapered minarets and the high battlement-topped walls the Great Mosque of Djenné is the most magnificent example of Sudanese Sahel mud brick architecture. During the "fête de crépissage" each year at the end of the rainy season the inhabitants of Djenné gather to repair the walls of the mosque.

Registan Square, in the Uzbek city of Samarkand, is surrounded by three unique madrassas, which earned it

Sherdor Madrassa

a place as a UNESCO World Heritage site. The Ulugbek Madrassa, one of the oldest in the region, was built in the Timurid style in the

15th century and a giant 115 foot (35 m) tall entrance portal was added. It was one of the best universities of the Orient. Very distinctive are the patterns of the mosaics on its façade, made from colored tiles in gold and blue. Like a mirror image, the Sherdor Madrassa was built opposite in the 17th century, following Bucharic models. Framed by these two madrassas is the Tilla-Kori Madrassa, built around 1650 AD; its shiny golden interior also served as a Friday mosque. Rather unusual for an Islamic building is the tiger decoration with a sun and a human face on the portal of the Sherdor Madrassa.

Interior of the Tilla-Kori Madrassa

Prayer niche in the Tilla-Kori Madrassa

The richly ornamented vaulted ceiling of the Tilla-Kori Madrassa

Three madrassas, one more opulent
than the next, form the magnificent
Registan ensemble in Samarkand:
Ulugbek, Tilla-Kori and Sherdor
(from left to right).

With the white marble tomb (UNESCO World Cultural Heritage) he built in the Indian town of Agra for his wife Mumtaz Mahal, who had died in 1631, the Mughal Emperor Shah Jahan brought this type of structure, originally developed for Humayun's Tomb, to the highest perfection. At the end

The Yamuna River with the Taj Mahal

of a terraced garden animated by fountains the perfectly symmetrical mausoleum rises from a square base. The central dome, sitting atop a high tambour in the Persian style, is joined by domed pavilions; the Persian-style façades face all four points of the compass. Four minarets accentuate the corners of the white marble terrace. The strong Persian influence probably goes back to the first master-builder, Isa Afandi, from Shiraz; artists and artisans from all over Asia Minor and Central Asia also contributed.

THE MOST BEAUTIFUL ISLAMIC TOMB IN THE WORLD

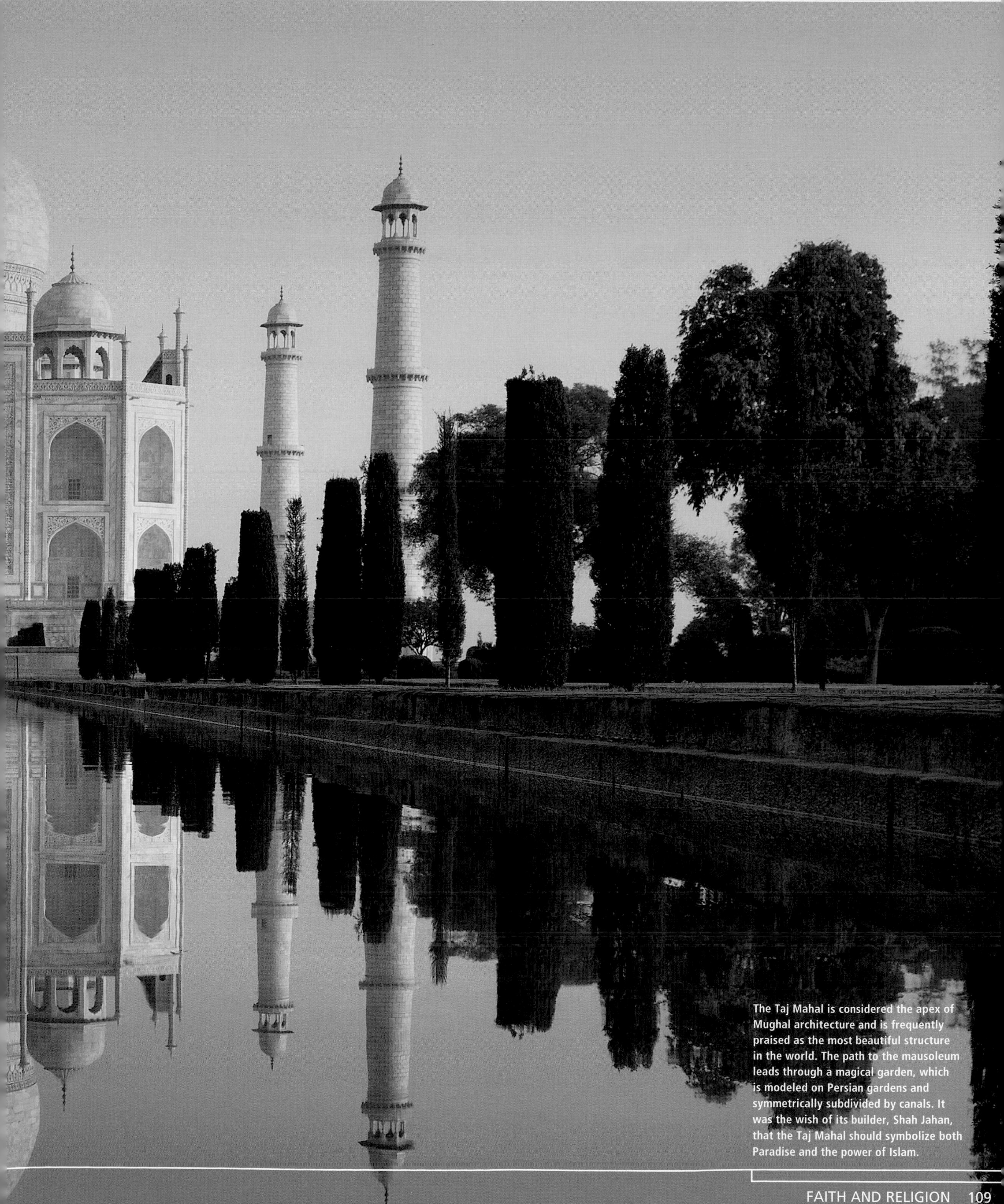

The Taj Mahal is considered the apex of Mughal architecture and is frequently praised as the most beautiful structure in the world. The path to the mausoleum leads through a magical garden, which is modeled on Persian gardens and symmetrically subdivided by canals. It was the wish of its builder, Shah Jahan, that the Taj Mahal should symbolize both Paradise and the power of Islam.

FAITH AND RELIGION

THE THIRD LARGEST FAITH COMMUNITY IN THE WORLD

With about 900 million followers Hinduism is the world's third largest religion. In its geographical distribution it is still largely confined to its land of origin, India, yet it is very popular around the world, especially in South-East Asia, Brazil, North America and Europe. Hinduism looks back on

a long history and has absorbed the most diverse traditions during its development. It encompasses thousands of deities and countless cults. More than a single religion

Krishna, an incarnation of Vishnu

it presents itself as a diversity of faiths of which two stand out: Vaishnavism sees Vishnu as the most important god, the creator and preserver of the world, whereas Shivaism foregrounds Shiva the destroyer. Together with Brahma, the gods form a trinity called trimurti, which unites in itself the basic aspects of divine intervention in the world — creation, preservation, and destruction. Despite its confusing diversity there are a few things that all Hindu cults share in common. They all believe in a hierarchy in the order of the world, which ranges from inanimate and animate nature via humankind to the gods. The infamous caste system also belongs to this order, known as dharma, and is considered to be god-given. Closely connected with the idea of dharma is the belief that, before final salvation, every creature must live through a series of reincarnations. For Hindu believers, humans are born with a shape and into a caste as a reward or punishment for their demeanor

in a previous life. This result of earlier actions is known as karma. However, a Hindu's true aim in life is not to be endowed with a better karma in the new incarnation, but to be released from the cycle of reincarnations and from one's individual existence. The philosophy of reincarnation was first formulated around 600 BC in the *Upanishads*, the most recent collection of *Vedas*. Together with the older Vedic texts they are the holy scriptures of India. No less important in the development of Hinduism are the great epics

Ramayana and *Mahabharata*, which were written around 400 BC. In these, Vishnu and Shiva push the older Vedic deities into the background.

A sadhu (ascetic wandering monk) during the 2007 Kumbh Mela pilgrimage in Allahabad. Several million believers take part in this, the largest Hindu festivity, which happens once every three years in alternating towns.

Hindu religions recognize numerous holy places to which believers make their pilgrimages. In many, local deities are venerated; others

Varanasi, pilgrim boat on the Ganges River

are linked with the names of the supreme gods like Shiva, Vishnu and Krishna. The most important ones are found at distinctive places along the course of the River Ganges, whose waters are attributed with beneficial divine powers. Every believer should therefore take a spiritually cleansing bath in the floods of the holy river at least once during his or her lifetime.

Ritual cleansing in one of India's holy rivers is an integral part of Hindu religious practices. A bath is considered to be especially beneficial if it is taken during the Kumbh Mela, the largest Hindu festival, which takes place every three years, alternating between the cities of Allahabad, Haridwar, Ujjain and Nashik. The picture shows a sadhu during the Kumbh Mela of 2007 in Allahabad, at the confluence of the Ganges and Yamuna rivers.

RISHIKESH

This town is located only a few miles north of the place where the Ganges River leaves the Himalayas. For Hindu believers it is the starting point for pilgrimages to the sources of the holy river. The city's many ashrams and temples are also visited by pilgrims from western countries.

Temple in Rishikesh

Ganga Aarti ceremony in Rishikesh

HARIDWAR

This town is located in the spot where the Ganges reaches the plains that are named after the river. It is one of the Hindus' seven holy cities, attracting millions of pilgrims each year. Many hundreds of faithful congregate every day for a ritual bath in the floods of the river at the Har ki Pauri ghat. During the Ganga Aarti ceremony thousands of lights are floated down the Ganges River each day at nightfall. Haridwar is the venue for the Kumbh Mela once every

The Kumbh Mela in Haridwar in 2010

twelve years. The town takes it turns with Allahabad, Ujjain and Nashik as the host of the largest religious festival in the country, which happens every three years. Many million pilgrims gather to take part in the festivities.

VARANASI

This metropolitan city with its millions of inhabitants stands out among India's holy cities. A pilgrimage to Varanasi, on the middle reaches of the Ganges River, is every Hindu's dream. Believers have made the pilgrimage there for hundreds of years in order to bathe in the holy river, cleansing themselves of all the river. People throng here from the early morning to sundown in order to perform ritual ablutions, meditation and prayers. During the Ganga Aarti ceremony, thousands of lights are set to float down the river each night. Some of the ghats are reserved exclusively for the cremation of the dead whose ashes are then sprinkled into the Ganges.

Varanasi, Ganga Aarti ceremony

The ghats of Varanasi

sins. Many bring relatives who are close to death. People believe that whoever dies in Varanasi and is cremated by the Ganges, has a greater chance of being freed from the circle of death and rebirth. On the west bank of the Ganges some 80 different stone staircases are set into the embankments, the so-called ghats, leading down to

A pilgrim during ritual ablutions

VRINDAVAN

According to Hindu belief, Krishna, one of the incarnations of Vishnu, was raised by cowherds in a forest near the present city of Vrindavan. His relationship with local girl Radha is significant in Hinduism. Every year Hindus and followers of Krishna from around the world come to visit the holy place.

A pilgrim in Vrindavan

Vrindavan, Sri Bhagwan Bhajan Ashram

THE MOST IMPORTANT PILGRIMAGE DESTINATIONS IN HINDUISM

BADRINATH TEMPLE
Badrinath, India

This sanctuary in the Himalayas is located along two popular Hindu pilgrimage routes and is visited each year by many thousands of believers. The temple dedicated to Vishnu was founded in the eighth century by the famous philosopher Shankara. It stands right on the banks of the Alaknanda River, one of the two main

The Vishnu Temple in Badrinath

headstreams of the Ganges. A pilgrimage to the origins of the holy river is a virtual must for devout Hindus.

DWARAKADHEESH TEMPLE
Dwarka, India

The temple is dedicated to Krishna and is one of the holiest shrines of Hindu India. The national epic *Mahabharata* tells that Krishna himself founded Dwarka and lived there. Each year in August believers from all parts of India travel there for the celebrations of Krishna's birthday. Dwarka is also a staging post on the famous Char Dham pilgrimage route.

Dwarka, the temple dedicated to Krishna

The Jagannath Temple in Puri in the east Indian state of Odisha is an important site of Hindu pilgrimages and also the starting point each year in the summer of the Ratha Yatra, a procession during which statues of the god Jagannath and his brother and sister that are normally kept in the temple are driven through the streets on enormous chariots.

RAMANATHASWAMY TEMPLE
Rameswaram, India

The Ramanathaswamy Temple

The Indian national epic *Ramayana* tells how Rama once saved his wife Sita from the demon king Ravana, stopping off in Rameswaram in order to pray to Shiva. The Ramanathaswamy Temple was built on the site of this mythical event. One of the twelve holiest Shiva temples in India, it is also one of the most important sites for Hindu pilgrimages in the country. Each believer should visit it once during their lifetime.

JAGANNATH TEMPLE
Puri, India

Jagannath, to whom this pilgrimage site is dedicated, is venerated by Hindus as "Lord of the Universe"

The Jagannath Temple in Puri

and as an incarnation of Vishnu. Statues of the god and his brother and sister are kept in the temple. Countless priests guard the three deities and dress them in new clothes each day for the ceremonies. Every year in the summer the statues are carried through the city on three processional chariots and accompanied by thousands of believers.

AKSHARDHAM TEMPLE —
THE LARGEST HINDU TEMPLE IN THE WORLD

The Akshardham Temple is the most recent attraction in India's capital New Delhi. Currently the largest Hindu temple in the world, it was entered into the _Guinness Book of Records_ in 2007.

The world's largest Hindu temple was inaugurated in November 2005 and has since attracted not only Hindu believers but also countless tourists. More than just a house of worship it is also a historical museum and a theme park. Films, slide shows and other media inform visitors about all aspects of Indian culture. During a 12-minute boat ride many thousands of years of the subcontinent's history is summarized. The "Hall of Values" offers an introduction to the Hindu lifestyle, in particularly that of the Swaminarayan sect. The extensive park surrounding the central shrine is home to bronze statues of major personalities from all periods of Indian history. The vast temple in the center of the complex is considered a veritable miracle of architecture. Traditional Hindu building styles from all the regions of India were married here with elements of Mughal and Jain architecture as a harmonious ensemble. The temple was built entirely from red sandstone and white

marble, symbols of devotion to god and purity. It is adorned all over with sculptures of Indian deities, and is crowned by nine domes. Thousands of artists and artisans were occupied for over five years with the construction of the building that was initiated by Pramukh Swami Maharaj, leader of the Swaminarayan sect.

Brightly illuminated, the Akshardham Temple is a grand spectacle at night (left).

Although the Hindu art of temple construction has brought about a multitude of styles during the course of its history, its temples largely resemble one another in terms of ground plan and layout. Conception and construction are based on certain principles and these have not changed for nearly 2,000

Shiva decoration on a façade

years. Hindu temples are always also the residence of the god to whom they are dedicated. In their middle is the inner sanctum with its idol. This cella is surrounded by a promenade for the ambulation ritual and crowned by a tower (sikhara), symbolizing the holy mountain, Meru. The larger temples also possess courtyards, terraces and other rooms. In South India, the entrance to the temple district is often guarded by giant gateway structures, known as gopurams. Often hundreds of priests work in a Hindu temple. During the puja the cult image in the inner sanctum is dressed anew each day and provided with sacrificial offerings.

THE MOST IMPORTANT TEMPLE COMPOUNDS IN HINDUISM

1. **Akshardham**
   India, New Delhi
   247 acres (100 ha)
2. **Sri Ranganathaswamy**
   India, Srirangam
   148 acres (60 ha)
3. **Nataraja Temple**
   India, Chidambaram
   37 acres (15 ha)
4. **Arunachaleswarar Temple**
   India, Thiruvannamalai
   25 acres (10 ha)
5. **Meenakshi Sundareswarar Temple**
   India, Madurai
   15 acres (6 ha)
6. **Jagannath Temple**
   India, Puri
   9 acres (3.7 ha)
7. **Brihadishvara Temple**
   India, Thanjavur
   7.2 acres (2.9 ha)
8. **Kumbeshvarar Temple**
   India, Kumbakonam
   6.9 acres (2.8 ha)
9. **Lingaraj Temple**
   India, Bhubaneswar
   5.4 acres (2.2 ha)

The Meenakshi Sundareswarar Temple built in the 17th century is one of the most magnificent buildings of Indian religious architecture. The vast complex covers an area of no less than 15 acres (6 ha) and comprises numerous temples, shrines and columned halls. Sundareswarar and Meenakshi are the main temples, dedicated to manifestations of Shiva and his wife Parvati. The large picture shows one of the richly decorated ambulatories in the sanctuary.

THE MOST IMPORTANT TEMPLES IN HINDUISM

Hindu religious architecture has developed an impressive range of forms and styles. During the course of the centuries the temples became ever larger, the decoration of the façades ever more sophisticated.

KHAJURAHO
Madhya Pradesh, India

Located in Madhya Pradesh, the Khajuraho Group of Monuments became famous thanks to its 20 or so preserved temples dating from the heyday of the Chandelas, a dynasty of Indian rulers who reigned over parts of India between the 9th and 13th centuries. The temple façades are richly decorated with unique sculptures and reliefs. One recurring theme are scenes of sexual union symbolizing fertility and the perpetual renewal of the world. All temples are built according to similar principles and are orientated from east to west, with an entrance hall, adjoining vestibule, a main hall and a cella, where the cult image is kept.

The shikharas, the tower-sized roofs of the temple, symbolize Meru, the World Mountain and residence of the gods. The largest temple, the Kandariya Mahadeva Temple, probably built in the first half of the 11th century, is considered the apex of Hindu religious architecture during the Middle Ages. The temple district is a UNESCO World Heritage site.

HAMPI
Karnataka, India

Near Hampi, a small town in the South Indian state of Karnataka, are the ruins of Vijayanagara, the capital of the eponymous Hindu empire that controlled the south of the subcontinent between the 14th and 16th centuries. The former trading town, one of the most important cities in South India during the heyday of the Vijayanagara Empire, looks like an open-air museum of South Indian architecture. Surrounded by a ring of fortifications, it is home to palaces and temples belonging to the Dravidian princes. The Vittala Temple, built as late as the first half of the 16th century but never completed, boasts numerous impressive and masterly crafted sculptures as well as a 26 foot (8 m) tall temple chariot in the courtyard. The highlight of the Virupaksha Temple, along with its wealth of figures, is the more than 164 foot (50 m) tall gopuram — the monumental tower typical of South Indian Hindu temples. The temple is dedicated to Shiva, and the ruined city is a UNESCO World Cultural Heritage site.

The gopuram of the Virupaksha Temple rises 164 feet (50 m) into the sky (top right), the Vittala Temple chariot is 26 feet (8 m) tall (below right).

BELUR
Karnataka, India

The Chennakesava Temple in Belur is the largest of three preserved temples from the Hoysala Empire era. Built in the 12th century, the complex comprises one main and several lesser temples, dedicated to Chennakeshava, an incarnation of Vishnu. The buildings are richly decorated with sculptures both inside and out. The complex is the only Hoysala Temple that is still in use today.

The Chennakesava Temple recalls the medieval period when the Hoysala dynasty ruled in South India.

Between the eighth and 13th centuries, probably some 80 Hindu and Jain temples were erected within the vast grounds of the unique temple city of Khajuraho. Twenty of these are still remarkably well preserved today.

THIRUVANANTHAPURAM
Kerala, India

The beginnings of the Padmanabhaswamy Temple in Thiruvananthapuram (Trivandrum) date back to the 12th century, although it did not receive its present look until the 18th century, during the reign of the Travancore royal family in South India. Until 2011 it was the property of the royal family; after ownership had been transferred to the federal state of Kerala, a precious treasure of jewels was discovered inside the temple.

The Padmanabhaswamy Temple is one of the most impressive Hindu sanctuaries in South India.

SRIVILLIPUTHUR
Tamil Nadu, India

Among Hindu temples, the Andal Temple of Srivilliputhur is particularly remarkable. One of the holy sites of Tamil Vaishnavism, it is dedicated to Andal, a female incarnation of the deity. It is said that as a young girl Andal devoted her life to the service of Vishnu. The 190 foot (58 m) tall gopuram in her temple today adorns the coat of arms of the federal state of Tamil Nadu.

A colorful columned walkway in the Andal Temple of Srivilliputhur.

SUCHINDRAM
Tamil Nadu, India

The Thanumalayan Temple of Suchindram is considered an architectural gem, even within South Indian temple architecture, which boasts many masterpieces indeed. The sanctuary, which is dedicated to the trinity of Vishnu, Shiva and Brahma, was built between the 13th and 18th centuries. The gopuram boasts a wealth of superbly crafted sculptural decorations. The magnificent ceiling of the dance hall is supported by 1,035 splendidly worked columns.

The Thanumalayan Temple with its 130 foot (40 m) tall gopuram (on the right in the picture).

The gopurams of the Meenakshi Sundareswarar Temple are completely covered with brightly colored sculptural decorations. Every single one of the small statues is a masterpiece of the art of sculpting.

MADURAI
Tamil Nadu, India

The beginnings of the giant temple complex in the South Indian state of Tamil Nadu probably date back to the first century BC, but the complex only received its present appearance in the 16th and 17th centuries, during the rule of the Nayak Dynasty of Madurai.

The main shrines are dedicated to Sundareswarar and Meenakshi, who are worshipped as manifestations of Shiva and his wife Parvati. The complex is surrounded by a tall wall and covers a surface area of about 15 acres (6 ha). Aside from the two central sanctuaries there are many smaller shrines, columned halls and walkways to be found in the grounds as well as a 164 foot (50 m) long cleansing basin. The entire complex boasts 12 gopurams, whose façades are adorned with colorful sculptures of deities and demons all over. The gopurams on the four sides of the outer fortifications boast a height of about 164 feet (50 m), while those inside the complex are smaller.

Colossal gopurams, visible from afar, tower over the temple compound of Madurai. The gate towers are a characteristic feature of South Indian Hindu temples (left).

SRIRANGAM
Tamil Nadu, India

The Sri Ranganathaswamy Temple of Srirangam in the South Indian state of Tamil Nadu is one of the largest Hindu temples in the world. Built on an island in the Kaveri River, it extends over a total area of about 150 acres (60 ha). The

The temple's gopurams

Façade decoration of the temple

Detail of the façade's decorations

extraordinary proportionality of the complex has been admired since time immemorial. Seven concentric walls surround the temple, which comprises about 50 shrines, dozens of pavilions and a vast hall with 1,000 columns. The inner sanctum is dedicated to Vishnu in the form of Ranganatha. No fewer than 21 gopurams of up to 230 feet (70 m) tall mark the entrances to the temple grounds. The beginnings of the temple date back to the 10th century. Repeatedly enlarged and extended until the present day, it is nevertheless considered an outstanding example of medieval Hindu temple architecture.

The topmost steps of one of the 21 mighty, upwardly tapered gopurams at the entrances to the Sri Ranganathaswamy Temple in Srirangam. The exuberant colorful sculptural decoration on its façade is a characteristic feature of Indian temple architecture. The sculptures represent deities and demons from Indian mythology.

THE MOST IMPORTANT TEMPLES IN HINDUISM

With a height of 39 feet (12 m) and a width of 108 feet (33 m), the bas-relief "The Descent of the Ganges" in Mamallapuram is one of the largest in the world. The recess in its middle symbolizes India's holiest river.

THANJAVUR
Tamil Nadu, India

From the ninth to the 12th centuries, South India was under the rule of the Chola dynasty. Thanjavur, about 220 miles (350 km) south of Chennai, was the royal city of residence from 907 until the beginning of the 11th century, and the Chola kings had it built in the South Indian style, based on the style used by the Pallava princes in Mamallapuram. One of the most monumental constructions of Vimana architecture of the time is the Brihadishvara Temple of Thanjavur, commissioned by King Rajaraja and completed in 1010. The temple is located in expansive grounds and comprises several columned halls and shrines. The tower above the cella was built in granite and covered with a large finial stone. It measures nearly 200 feet (60 m) high and boasts no less than 13 stories, tapering toward the top. The complex is dedicated to Shiva, which is evidenced by the wealth of phallic symbols, images of Shiva and representations of the bull Nandi, the deity's mount.

CHIDAMBARAM
Tamil Nadu, India

The Nataraja Temple in Chidambaram, dedicated to an incarnation of Shiva, is without doubt one of the most important Shiva temples in India. Probably constructed in the 13th century, it is considered an outstanding example of the Dravidian temple architecture in South India. The inner sanctum is surrounded by four walls that divide it into different areas.

The Shivaganga tank in the grounds of the Nataraja Temple (right)

KUMBAKONAM
Tamil Nadu, India

Among the more than 150 Hindu temples, to which Kumbakonam owes its title of "temple city," two stand out especially. The Kumbesvarar Temple in the heart of the city has three impressive gopurams that are richly adorned with colorful sculptures. Probably built during the 16th century, it is dedicated to Shiva. The Vishnaiva Sarangapani Temple also boasts exuberantly adorned façades. The shrine in the inner sanctum of this 15th-century structure has the form of a war chariot.

Left: The tower of the Brihadishvara Temple of Thanjavur is an architectural masterpiece, fashioned from monolithic blocks of stone weighing several tons each.

KANCHIPURAM
Tamil Nadu, India

The capital of the eponymous district in the South Indian state of Tamil Nadu is also known as the "city of a thousand temples." In the center of Kanchipuram alone stand more than 200 Hindu temples, of which the Kailasanatha Temple is the oldest, dating back to the seventh century and dedicated to Shiva. The wall frescoes from the time of its construction mark it as an example of early South Indian temple architecture.

Wall frescoes in the Kailasanatha Temple of Kanchiparum (right)

MAMALLAPURAM
Tamil Nadu, India

The temple district of Mamallapuram is one of India's most fascinating archeological sites and has been a UNESCO World Cultural Heritage site since 1984. The princes of the Pallava dynasty, who reigned over large parts of South India from the middle of the sixth to the end of the ninth centuries, had several temples built there that are considered outstanding examples of early South Indian architecture. The five Pancha Rathas, temples carved out of rock monoliths, and the bas-relief "Descent of the Ganges" are masterpieces of sculpture.

THIRUVANNAMALAI
Tamil Nadu, India

With its Arunachaleswarar Temple this town in the South Indian state of Tamil Nadu is home to one of the greatest shrines in India. The entire temple complex covers an area of 25 acres (10 ha) and is divided into three distinct areas by the three circular walls surrounding the inner sanctum. A gateway, crowned by a gopuram, is set on each side of each wall. The four outer gate-towers are impressive in their height. They were built between the 11th and 16th centuries.

THE MOST IMPORTANT TEMPLES IN HINDUISM

The Nagara style characteristic of medieval temples in North India developed in the eastern part of the country from the eighth century. The Lingaraj Temple is considered an early example, the complex in Konarak as a late masterpiece of this building style.

KONARAK
Orissa, India

The Temple of Konarak, dedicated to the sun god, is one of the most famous Hindu temples and a UNESCO World Cultural Heritage site. Construction was begun around 1240 AD but never completed. The temple's congregation hall is a replica in stone of the chariot used to ride across the sky each day by Surya, who was already venerated as the giver of life in Vedic times. It rises from a tall base that is adorned with reliefs depicting 24 wheels. Art historians believe that these symbolize the hours of the day. Its shikhara (tower) must have been an impressive structure, at a height of 230 feet (70 m), before it collapsed in the 19th century; even without it the temple itself still has gigantic proportions. The congregational hall alone covers an area of almost 14,000 sq ft (1,300 sq m), and the bricked-up inner sanctum of the temple is one of the largest ever built in classic Hindu temple architecture.

BHUBANESWAR "TEMPLE CITY" OF INDIA
Odisha, India

The capital of the Indian state of Odisha, Bhubaneswar is a center of Shiva worship. The Lingaraj Temple is one of the most important temples dedicated to this deity, the "Lord of the three worlds." Covering an area of more than 5 acres (2 ha), it is surrounded by 6.6 foot (2 m) thick fortifications. Non-Hindus are barred from entering this closed area. The center of the complex is formed by a 148 foot (45 m) high tower, which houses the inner sanctum and which is preceded by three halls. In addition, the temple grounds are also home to around 50 smaller sanctuaries. Historians believe that the beginnings of the temple date back to the sixth century, but it did not receive its present look until the 10th century. The Lingaraj Temple is considered a milestone in the development of North Indian temple architecture. The extension with the three halls was an innovation that was subsequently further developed. In the tower the architects referred back to earlier traditions. Its shape, tapered toward the top, as well as the clear segmentation of the outside walls by arrow-like projections are typical of the Nagara style.

A view of the well-preserved main temple of Koranak (far left in the picture), one of the 24 relief wheels that decorate the base (left in the picture).

With its sculptural decorations the Brahneswar Temple is one of the most important sanctuaries in the temple city of Bubaneshwar. Its beginnings date back to the ninth century, but its present look probably dates from the 11th century. The inner sanctum is vaulted by a shikhara, a characteristic feature of North Indian temples at the time.

SHIVA TEMPLE
Elephanta, India

The cave temple dedicated to Shiva and located on an island in the Bay of Mumbai has become famous mainly for its stonemasonry, representing Shiva in his

Over-life-size statues of Shiva

various manifestations. The sculptures date from the seventh century and are among the highlights of early Hindu art. The 20 foot (6 m) tall portrait of Shiva Mahadeva, especially, is monumental in its dimensions; it shows the god with three faces and a splendid headdress. Shiva, one of the most important deities in Hinduism together with Brahma and Vishnu, is venerated as the god of destruction as well as of new creation, and as the king of dance. Often he appears with an entourage of mythical creatures, which were all carved into the stone in Elephanta. His emblem, the lingam, is considered a phallic symbol. In Elephanta it is kept in the form of a stone in the inner sanctum.

The colossal portrait in the Shiva Shrine of Elephanta represents "Sadashiva," the Shiva of Mercy. The sculpture is impressive thanks to the vividness of its facial features. The god's face exudes a dignified serenity.

The Kailasa Temple with the mighty shikhara in the foreground

KAILASA TEMPLE
Ellora, India

Near the village of Ellora, northwest of Aurangabad, 34 Hindu, Buddhist and Jain temples were cut into the rock between the fifth and 11th centuries AD. Probably the most impressive sanctum in this area is the Kailasa Temple dedicated to Shiva and built from 757 to 773 AD. Unlike the other temples of Ellora it was not cut into the rock as a cave but worked from a freestanding and protruding outcrop. The mighty shikhara, the Nandi shrine dedicated to Shiva's mount, the mandapa (columned outdoor hall) and the entrance area with the gopuram are all freestanding. Only some side rooms and galleries surrounding the shrine were cut into the rock faces. With a length of 328 feet (100 m) and a width of 246 feet (75 m), the Kailasa Temple is the largest rock temple in India.

The temples of Prambanan near the city of Yogyakarta on Java indicate that during the Middle Ages the influence of Hindu culture extended far into South-East Asia. Historians believe that the Indianization of the region happened peacefully and was promoted by merchants. Hinduism was pushed back with the Muslim campaigns of conquest that began in the 15th century.

Visible from afar, the tall temple towers known as "prangs" dominate this complex, the construction of which was probably begun as early as the eighth century. The main temple, Lara Djonggrang, however, was probably not completed until about the year 915. It was dedicated to Shiva: here the Hindu deity is celebrated as a god uniting in himself the destructive, creative and preserving powers. This is also why his symbol, the lingam, is omnipresent. Brahma and Vishnu both have their own smaller temples south and north of the central main tower. The complex in its entirety is dedicated to the "trimurti" — the trinity of the main Hindu gods. During an earthquake in 1549 it was largely destroyed and not reconstructed until 1937. During a further serious earthquake in May 2006 the temples, which form a UNESCO World Heritage site, were again damaged but have been successfully rebuilt since.

The temple towers of Prambanan on Java in a surreal light

The temples of Prambanan were built during the reign of the Hindu Sanjaya dynasty, who ruled the Mataram Kingdom on Java between the eighth and tenth centuries. Although the houses of worship were probably planned as a Hindu answer to the Buddhist temples of Borobodur, the Sanjayas also promoted the Buddhist temples. Thus, for example, the Sewu Temple was enlarged during the reign of their King Rakaitan.

The Sewu Temple near Prambanan is the second largest Buddhist temple on Java, after the Borobodur Temple.

SHRI VENKATESWARA BALAJI HINDU TEMPLE
Great Britain, Tividale

The splendid temple complex, covering an area of about

12 acres (5 ha), was inaugurated in August 2006, in a festive ceremony lasting several days. Not only is it the largest Hindu temple in Europe, but also the first such temple on the continent, dedicated to Shri Venkateswara, an incarnation of Vishnu. The beginnings of

Pilgrims at the temple in Tividale

the construction project date back to the 1970s. Some 30 years elapsed between the first planning stages and final completion because the developers repeatedly encountered fierce opposition to the project from the inhabitants of Tividale, a small town with a population of about 11,000 near Birmingham. Today the temple is a much-visited pilgrimage destination and a tourist attraction.

The Shri Swaminarayan Mandir Temple in the London district of Brent is crowned by seven turrets with golden tips and five domes. Underneath each tower there is a shrine for a Hindu deity.

SHRI SWAMINARAYAN MANDIR HINDU TEMPLE
Great Britain, London

The second largest Hindu temple outside India stands in London. It was inaugurated in 1995, after only three years of construction, and has repeatedly attracted attention since. The sanctuary is truly a temple of superlatives. In its construction, 3,120 short tons (2,828 tonnes) of sandstone and 2,200 short tons (2,000 tonnes) of Italian marble were used. The material was worked into artful reliefs and sculptures by stonemasons in India. The temple interior and exterior resemble a traditional Hindu house of worship.

The Shri Swaminarayan Mandir Temple at night

The interior of the Shri Swaminarayan Mandir Temple features masterful stonemasonry, covering the columns, walls and ceilings. They were created in the traditional manner in India by more than 1,000 artisans and then shipped to London. The entire temple complex consists of the actual sanctum, a large cultural center and a permanent exhibition, which provides detailed information about Hinduism. The temple is used by Hindu believers as a place of devotion, prayer and meditation. Inside the sanctum the traditional ceremonies are performed on a daily basis, yet the temple is also open to non-Hindus.

A columned hall in the Shri Swaminarayan Mandir Temple

The Golden Temple of Amritsar is the central sanctuary of the Sikhs, a religious community that was founded in the 15th century in northwest India by Nanak Dev (1469–1539) and has around 23 million followers worldwide. The Sikhs, who venerate the founder of their religion as the first guru, combine the monotheism spread in India by the Muslim conquerors with the Hindu teachings of reincarnation. They reject the caste system, asceticism and religious rituals, believing instead that every human being can attain salvation through their actions in the world, independent of the caste they belong to. The last guru of the Sikhs, Gobind Singh (1666–1708), had no offspring to succeed him and therefore decreed that the *Adi Granth*, a collection of his ancestors' writings, should have canonical value. It is kept at the Golden Temple.

THE MOST IMPORTANT TEMPLE
IN SIKHISM

The Golden Temple of Amritsar is open to everyone

The Temple of Amritsar, entirely covered in gold leaf, has been reflected in the waters of Lake Amritsar for 400 years. The main sanctuary of the Sikhs, it was built under their fifth guru, Arjan Dev (1563–1606), and stands at the center of a vast palace compound.

Although the 4.4 million Jains are a religious minority of insignificant size, their degree of discipline always causes astonishment around the world. Like no other religion Jainism demands a rigorous asceticism of its followers. Jains are strictly forbidden to kill or harm any living creatures.

A statue of a Thirtankara

They reject the consumption of meat and all activities that are connected with the slaughter of animals. The strict asceticism is intended to help the soul break free from the cycle of reincarnations. Jainism was founded by Mahavira, who probably lived around 500 BC and was a contemporary of the Buddha. He was the last of the 24 Tirthankaras, who are venerated by the Jains as leaders toward salvation. Apart from Mahavira, all Tirthankaras are mythological creatures who together have attained an age of several million years.

Jain monks meditate at the feet of the 59 foot (18 m) tall Bahubali statue in Shravanabelagola, a Jain pilgrimage place in South India. The giant Bahubali is worshipped by the Jains as the son of the first Thirthankara.

BHANDASAR JAIN TEMPLE
Bikaner, India

This temple in Bikaner stands out thanks to its precious interior. The columned hall is abundantly decorated with murals, sculptures and floral ornaments. The house of prayer is dedicated to Sumtinatha, the fifth Tirthankara.

Temple entrance

Columned hall in the Bhandasar Jain Temple

DILWARA JAIN TEMPLES
Mount Abu, India

The five Jain temples on the plateau of Abu in Rajasthan are an important Jain pilgrimage destination. According to the calculations of archeologists they were built between the 11th and 15th centuries. The two older structures of the ensemble, the

Jain Temple on top of Mount Abu

Vimal Vasahi Temple built around 1040 and the Luna Vasahi Temple built some 200 years later, are particularly impressive: they are lavishly adorned with filigree stonemasonry, which abundantly covers the walls, ceilings and columns of the interior. The Vimal Vasahi Temple is dedicated to Rishabha, the first Tirthankara, and the Luna Vasahi Temple to Neminatha, the 22nd Tirthankara.

MALLINATH TEMPLE
Mount Girnar, India

The two major shrines for the Jaina on Mount Girnar, a mountain range in the Indian state of Gujarat rising to 3,100 feet (945 m), are among the most important temples of India. The older and larger of the two, the 12th-century Neminath Temple, is dedicated to the 22nd Tirthankara. It is impressive thanks to the artfully worked reliefs and sculptures inside. The Mallinath Temple dates back to the 13th century and is dedicated to the 19th Tirthankara. Important Hindu temples can also be found on top of Mount Girnar.

The Mallinath Temple on Mount Girnar

ADISHWAR TEMPLE
Mount Shatrunjaya, India

The main temple on the Jainas' holiest mountain, the nearly 2,300 foot (700 m) tall Mount Shatrunjaya in the Indian state of Gujarat, is dedicated to the first Tirthankara. The present temple was built around 1530 on the site of a 10th-century temple that had been destroyed

Jain temple on Mount Shatrunjaya

by Muslim conquerors. Like most Jaina temples it stands in a walled courtyard and is abundantly decorated inside with unique sculptures, reliefs and statues. Altogether there are said to be more than 850 Jain shrines on Mount Shatrunjaya's summit plateau.

CHAUMUKHA MANDIR TEMPLE
Ranakpur, India

The temple compounds of Ranakpur are among the most magnificent Jaina temples. The main shrine features light and airy columned halls. Built on a terrace, it is accessible from all sides via stairs.

The main entrance to the Chaumukha Temple

Inside the temple

FAITH AND RELIGION

At one time, the Drepung Monastery to the west of Lhasa was one of the largest and most influential Buddhist monasteries in Tibet, with more than 10,000 monks living there at times — some 600 monks still live there today.

BUDDHISM

With more than 400 million followers, Buddhism is one of the great world religions, shaping religious life in the entire eastern Asiatic region. "Buddha" is a Sanskrit word meaning

Buddhist monks at prayer

"the awakened one " or "the enlightened one." Designating human beings who have attained complete wisdom, it is the honorary name of Siddhartha Gautama, the founder of the religion. Although recently doubt has been cast on the biographical data of Siddhartha, said to have lived between 560 and 480 BC, it can be regarded as certain that he developed his philosophy in debate with the ancient Indian Brahman priesthood, and that he was also influenced by the Upanishads, one of India's holy scriptures. Like many of his contemporaries Siddhartha was convinced that only the rejection of worldly temptations could liberate humans from the eternal cycle of reincarnations and thus from life and death. Whereas the followers of Mahavira, the founder of Jainism, led a life of rigorous asceticism, Buddha found that a mental attitude that would limit the excesses of self-indulgence would lead to salvation. Everyone can reach this insight known as "enlightenment" if they follow certain ground rules. These principles, summarized by Buddha in his speech on the "Setting in Motion of the Wheel," have been incorporated into Buddhist teaching as the "Four Noble Truths." They can be read as successive guidelines, building on one other and giving the practical skills for dealing with life's challenges: the observation that life is sorrowful and that suffering is caused by greed has to be followed by the insight that only the elimination of cravings or at least their reigning in will lead to salvation from suffering and to liberation from the cycle of death and rebirth.

To obtain liberation, one must follow the "Noble Eightfold Path," observing a number of virtues, such as the right faith, right actions and right aspiration. Soon after his first sermon Siddhartha began to attract many followers. Like him they went around northern India as beggar monks and were supported by alms from a growing number of lay supporters and believers. The Buddhist order called Sangha was founded. Soon after the death of the Buddha, his teachings were canonized by several councils. A number of different schools and traditions developed.

THE MAIN BRANCHES OF BUDDHISM

In the centuries after the death of the Buddha two Buddhist schools emerged that still determine the religious life of Asia today. Theravada Buddhism, also known as Hinayana, meaning "the inferior vehicle," is based in South-East Asia. Its followers share the conviction that humans can only find salvation within and for themselves. The tradition of the Mahayana ("the great vehicle") on the other hand teaches that bodhisattvas, those who have already been enlightened, can show others the way to salvation. In this school, theological speculation developed at an early stage that interpreted the bodhisattvas as various incarnations of a divine being. Like Siddhartha Gautama they are believed to be mortal yet also a part of the supernatural world. All bodhisattvas attain nirvana together. Mahayana Buddhism is based in China, Korea and Japan. Tibetan Buddhism also emerged from this school. In India Buddhism was displaced by Hinduism and Islam.

LUMBINI
Nepal

Since archeologists rediscovered Siddartha Gautama Buddha's place of birth in 1895, ancient Lumbini has become the destination of countless pilgrimages. All the great Buddhist faith

Novices in Lumbini

traditions went on to build monasteries there, and a temple was built in the exact spot where Siddhartha was said to have been born. In the heart of ancient Lumbini stands a stone column of the Indian ruler Ashoka, which was found during the excavations in 1895. Ashoka's (269–232 BC) political

BODH GAYA
India

Bodh Gaya, the former Uruvela, is the place where Siddhartha became "enlightened" and found the path to delivery from all suffering, and so it became

Bodh Gaya, Mahabodhi Temple

one of the four most important Buddhist pilgrimage sites. From Buddhist texts we know that Buddha's "enlightenment" took place under a Bodhi tree (sacred fig) in 528 BC, after days of asceticism and meditation, causing him to abandon the ascetic movement. It is not permanent self-mortification that frees humans from suffering — thus Siddhartha's insight after his "awakening"

work contributed significantly to the spread of Buddhism in India. The Buddha was probably born around 560 BC, the son of a noble member of the warrior caste. From traditional texts we can deduce that he enjoyed a carefree childhood in the lap of luxury and married his cousin Yahodvera

Lumbini: an altar in a Tibetan temple

when he was 16 years old. When he began to have doubts in the stability of the world in which he lived, he left his family and joined the northern Indian ascetics. Siddhartha was then 29 years old.

A praying monk in front of the Bodhi tree

— rather it is their attitude, which renounces the indulgence of their desire. As early as the third century BC Ashoka had a sanctuary built in the place of Buddha's "enlightenment." The beginnings of the Mahabodhi Temple date back to the sixth century. A famous Bodhi tree stands in the temple's garden, said to be a scion of the sacred fig underneath which Buddha was enlightened.

SARNATH
India

The site where Siddhartha Gautama preached his first sermon after his "awakening" is also the place where the Buddhist movement started. Here Buddha assembled a group of followers around him, which quickly grew and spread the new teachings across the whole of North India. Sarnath became a center of the Buddhist order founded by Siddhartha, attracting monks from all over North India. The Chinese pilgrim Xuan Zang, who traveled the country in the seventh century, reported that more than 1,000 monks lived in the large monasteries of Sarnath. In the 12th century the village was destroyed by Muslim conquerors and remained forgotten for a long time. But since the ancient places were rediscovered by archeologists in 1835, it has once more become one of the major Buddhist pilgrimage destinations. Communities especially from East and South-East Asia built

Stupa in Sarnath.

monasteries and temples in Sarnath based on the styles of their own countries. The ruins of ancient stupas and monasteries, especially, as well as an Ashoka Column, recall the great era of Buddhism in India.

KUSHINAGAR
India

Siddhartha Gautama Buddha died and is said to have achieved the final nirvana, or parinirvana, at this North Indian town on the border with Nepal, it is now the most

Ramabhar Stupa

important Buddhist pilgrimage site — along with Sarnath, Bodh Gaya and Lumbini. Buddhist communities from all over East and South-East Asia have built new sanctuaries there in recent years. For a long time the place where the Buddha died had been forgotten. It was not until the middle of the 19th century that it was rediscovered during the course of archeological excavations. English researchers found the remains of ancient monasteries and a stupa (burial mound), which was painstakingly restored, as well as the statue of a reclining Buddha, probably dating from the fifth century. The stupa became known as Mahaparinirwana

Kushinagar, a woman presenting sacrificial offerings

Stupa. It is believed to be the place where the Buddha achieved parinirvana. The ruins of the Ramabhar Stupa mark the site of his cremation.

The gilded statue of the meditating Buddha in the Mahabodhi Temple of Bodh Gaya in the Indian state of Bihar. The place where, according to tradition, Siddhartha Gautama "awakened" and found a path of deliverance from suffering is visited each year by thousands of pilgrims from around the world.

Bayon differs from the other temples in Angkor above all because of its face-towers. Thirty-seven towers remain today and on their sides are carved into the stone 200 faces, up to 16 feet (5 m) tall, of the smiling Avalokiteshvara, "ruler of the world" in Buddhist beliefs.

TEMPLES OF ANGKOR
Angkor

Angkor, the largest temple city in the world, is situated near the town of Siem Reap in Cambodia. Once it was a residential and temple complex, covering an area of approximately 77 sq mi (200 sq km) and belonging to the legendary Khmer Empire (9th to 15th centuries). The latter was characterized by Indian tribes that had immigrated to South-East Asia. In its heyday, Angkor was the largest town in the world (with 100,000 inhabitants), and vast temples were built within its limits. In the beginning of the 13th century the Khmer rulers were still oriented toward Hinduism, later they turned to Buddhism. As after the death of a god-king, his temple also became his burial place, each Khmer king had to have a new sanctuary built for himself, and

Banteay Srei Temple in Angkor

The most famous and the largest temple complex in the Khmer Empire: Angkor Wat with its striking towers

Angkor Wat: once a center of the Khmer Empire, today overgrown by tropical vegetation

The Angkor Wat temple complex

The Bayon temple complex with its unusual face-towers

thus the number of temples in Angkor continued to grow. Today some 1,000 temples have been uncovered. The largest temple complex is Angkor Wat, which was built for Suryavarman II (r. 1113–1150). Lotus flower-shaped towers, symbolizing Mount Meru, the mountain of the gods, rise on three levels. With the moats and fortifications surrounding it, the complex covers an area of 1,420 by 1,640 yards / 0.8 by 0.9 miles (1.3 by 1.5 km). The Bayon Temple of Angkor Thom is a sign of the change in religion. During the reign of Jayavarman VII (r. 1181–1218) no fewer than 54 towers were built there, featuring up to 16 feet (5 m) tall monumental faces of the bodhisattva Avalokiteshvara looking into the four directions of the compass.

This giant temple city is located in the heart of Myanmar, on the eastern banks of the Irrawaddy River. No fewer than 2,000 Buddhist religious structures are found there in an area of 14 sq ml (36 sq km). Bagan was established between the 11th and 13th centuries by the

Stupas in Bagan

A Buddha statue in a temple

Burmese King Anawrahta (r. 1044–1077) and his successors. The monumental splendor of the monasteries, temples and pagodas still astounds visitors today. King Anawrahta is considered the founder of the First Burmese Kingdom. He conquered vast tracts of Myanmar, which was then fragmented into various local principalities, thus creating an important empire. He was converted to Buddhism by a monk and became a major promoter of the new religion. King Kyanzittha, who violently usurped Anawrahta from the throne, continued his predecessor's work. Buddhist culture flourished during his and his successors' reigns, and this is attested to by the splendid buildings of Bagan. In 1287 Anawratha's empire was conquered by Kublai Khan.

Historians believe that there were around 10,000 Buddhist religious buildings in the capital alone during the heyday of the empire of Bagan, between the 11th and 13th centuries. Today more than 2,000 monasteries, temples and stupas can still be visited. The temple city is located in an extensive, steppe-like plain. It is a designated archeological zone and nominated to become a UNESCO World Cultural Heritage site.

POTALA PALACE
Lhasa, Tibet/China

A unique politico-religious culture is manifested in this grand structure (UNESCO World Cultural Heritage site), rising 360 feet (110 m) above the Lhasa Valley. With its windowless base, the palace is first and foremost intended to

Potala Palace

be a defensive structure. Its main part, the 1,050 foot (320 m) long White Palace, was built in the 17th century under the fifth Dalai Lama, the supreme spiritual leader of Tibetan Buddhism, who also exercised political power. He had chosen the Red Mountain, on top of which Tibet's first king, Songtsen Gampo, had built his residence in the seventh century. After the death of the Dalai Lama the Red Palace was built to house the most important treasures within the palace complex, and later it was covered with golden roofs. Altogether the majestic structure comprises about 1,000 rooms on a ground plan of nearly 1,399,300 sq ft (130,000 sq m).

Dharma wheel on the roof of the Jokhang Temple

Buddha statue inside the Jokhang Temple

Frescoes in the Jokhang Temple

JOKHANG TEMPLE
Lhasa, Tibet/China

This temple in the heart of Lhasa is the most important shrine of Tibetan Buddhism and also the oldest building in town. Its beginnings date back to the Tibetan King Songsten Gampo, who probably had it built around 642 as a repository for the Buddha statues brought into the marriage by his Nepalese and his Chinese wives. Allegedly this abundant dowry included the famous Jowo Rinpoche, a 5 foot (1.5 m) tall gilded Buddha statue kept in the Jokhang Temple. Originally, the temple must have been quite small, but over the centuries it was repeatedly enlarged and expanded as a giant complex of numerous buildings and chapels. The entire complex, which became known under the name of Lhasa Tsuglagkhang, covers grounds of no less than 242,190 sq ft (22,500 sq m). Together with the Potala Palace, the Jokhang Temple is listed by UNESCO as a World Cultural Heritage site.

Up to the country's occupation by troops from the People's Republic of China and the Dalai Lama's escape in 1959, the Potala Palace in Lhasa was the seat of the Tibetan government. In recent times it has again become the residence of monks.

BOROBUDUR TEMPLE

The Borobudur Temple Compounds erected during the eighth century on the main Indonesian island of Java are the most important ancient Buddhist shrine outside of India. The temple, a copy of the world mountain Mount Meru, is divided into three spheres following Buddhist concepts: the first sphere comprises the world of the human being

Relief on the Borobudur Temple

as a sensual creature. In the Borobudur Temple this is symbolized by the bottommost square platform. The five square terraces that rise above it correspond to the sphere into which human beings enter after their deliverance from all desire. The three uppermost round terraces finally represent the world of the divine and of the awakening. The large stupa at the top of the building is framed by 72 small stupas with Buddha statues.

The Borobudur on the island of Java is probably the largest Buddhist temple anywhere. Consisting of several superimposed terraces as well as a large stupa at its top, it rises some 130 feet (40 m) into the sky. Its sides are each 394 feet (120 m) long at the base. Altogether two million blocks of stone were used in its construction.

A meditating Buddha on one of the upper terraces of the Borobudur Temple

The Borobudur Temple is impressive not only thanks to its dimensions: the exuberant wealth which with each of the terraces is adorned by masterly worked reliefs and Buddha statues is just as unique. A total of 72 statues of the meditating Buddha have been discovered inside the small stupas on the upper three terraces of the Borobudur. The reliefs are found on the inside walls of the lowest five terraces, totaling more than 3 miles (5 km) in length. They depict scenes from the life of Siddhartha Gautama.

THE MOST IMPORTANT TEMPLES OF BUDDHISM

BOUDHANATH STUPA
Kathmandu, Nepal

Boudhanath is the most important Buddhist shrine in the Kathmandu Valley (UNESCO World Cultural Heritage site) as well as the center of Tibetan Buddhism in Nepal. The stupa is, at a height of 130 feet

Prayer flags at the Boudhanath Stupa

(40 m), the largest religious structure of its kind in the entire region. The Cini Lama, the third most important dignitary of the Tibetans after the Dalai Lama and the Penchen Lama, resides in a monastery in the valley. According to a story the Boudhanath Stupa was built by one of the king's mistresses — she had asked him for as much land as she could stake out with a cowhide. But she cut the hide into narrow strips, thus obtained as a gift large enough grounds for her temple. The structure of the stupa resembles a mandala — a mythical circular or polygonal image symbolizing in its concentric layout the universe, the realm of the gods or psychological aspects. Thousands of prayer wheels have been set into the walls that surround the stupa.

The stupa of Boudhanath in the Kathmandu Valley is visited by many thousands of pilgrims each year. The custom to adorn the stupa with prayer flags is based on an age-old tradition. Prayer flags flutter in the wind at many places in the Himalayas; they are designed to direct the prayers of the faithful toward heaven.

Although since the 10th century Buddhism has been replaced in its country of origin, India, by Hinduism and Islam, the north of the country boasts some of the most important Buddhist sanctuaries.

RUMTEK MONASTERY
Sikkim, India

More than 500 monks and novices live today at the Rumtek Monastery, which with its numerous outbuildings is one of the largest monasteries in the Indian state of Sikkim. The headquarters of Karma Kagyü School, a sect founded in Tibet in the 12th century and steeped in traditions, which is also known under the name of "Black Hats," Rumtek is one of the most important Buddhist sites in India. During the course of the Chinese invasion of Tibet, the 16th Karmapa, the spiritual head of the Karma Kagyü School, fled to Sikkim in 1959, where he built a new religious center for his sect on the land of a long dilapidated monastery. The compound was laid out like its model, the Tibetan mother monastery in Tsurphu, and was inaugurated in 1966. The bones of its founder are kept in a stupa in the monastery's grounds. The complex also houses an Institute of Buddhist Studies.

HEMIS MONASTERY
Ladakh, India

The beginnings of the monastery are shrouded in mystery but probably date back to the third century BC. Buddhist sources only report that it was newly

Buddha statue in the Hemis Monastery

built around 1630 by Sengge Namygal, who ruled over the Ladakh Kingdom between 1616 and 1642. It is one of the oldest and wealthiest Buddhist monasteries in the Himalayas. Among the monastery's treasures are numerous valuable statues of the Buddha.

MAHABODHI TEMPLE
Bodh Gaya, India

The first empire in the early history of India was founded by King Ashoka (r. 273–231 BC). He

Bodh Gaya, the Mahabodhi Temple

turned toward Buddhism and had a temple built in the spot where the Buddha found enlightenment (or "bodhi") under a Bodhi tree. A later structure, the famous Mahabodhi Temple (UNESCO World Cultural Heritage site), was built under the Gupta Dynasty (320–540 AD). It is one of the four main Buddhist pilgrimage sites.

The Rumtek Monastery was laid out on terraces (left). The monastery's prayer hall is decorated in impressively bright colors (right).

AJANTA CAVES
Ajanta, India

This Buddhist monastery, hidden in the deep gorges of the Waghora River, has been a UNESCO World Cultural Heritage site since 1983. Over the course of 800 years, Buddhist monks have cut 29 caves into the virtually perpendicular rock faces. The early construction period spans the time from the second century BC to the second century AD; the subsequent phase happened during the Gupta era (4th–6th centuries). Eight of the Ajanta Caves wall paintings have been preserved; they are outstanding in their narrative richness and their

Wall paintings from the early days of the temple

Fresco with a scene from a *Jataka* tale

artistic execution. The murals depict episodes from the life of the Buddha and from the Jataka Tales, which recount the earlier lives of the founder of the religion. Whereas figures in the caves dating from pre-Christian times are mostly shaded in red and brown and characterized by strongly drawn contours, the figures in the caves that were built after the fifth century look more realistic.

The masterly reliefs and wall paintings in the caves of Ajanta, created between the second pre-Christian and the sixth post-Christian centuries, reflect 800 years of Buddhist art history in India.

Although Buddhism has long since disappeared from India, it still dominates religious life in Sri Lanka today. Indian missionaries spread the religion to the island as early as the third century BC.

GOLDEN TEMPLE
Dambulla, Sri Lanka

The beginnings of the five cave temples of Dambulla in the heart of Sri Lanka date back to the early days of Buddhism on the island. The first of three reliably proven

Dambulla, Buddha statue in the temple

creative periods on the slopes of the "Rock of Dambulla" began at the start of the first century BC under King Vattagamani Abhaya, who had fled from Anuradhapura before the second great Tamil invasion and found shelter in these granite rocks during his 14-year exile. Later the sanctuary fell into oblivion and was not rediscovered until the 12th century. The third period happened during the reign of King Kirti Sri Rajasinha (1747 to 1782). In the first cave, the "Cave of the Divine King" (Devaraja Vihara), is a fascinating 46 foot (14 m) long statue of the reclining Buddha. The largest cave is the "Cave of the Great King" (Maharaja Vihara); it boasts an astonishing number of expressive Buddha statues.

Statue of a seated Buddha in the cave temples of Dambulla

ANURADHAPURA
Sri Lanka

The temple city has important shrines from the early period of Buddhism in Sri Lanka. Mahavihara is probably the oldest Buddhist temple on the island. It was built in the third century BC under King Devanampiya Tissa (250–210 BC), who had been converted to Buddhism by the monk Mahinda, a son of the Indian ruler Ashoka. The temple is still an important pilgrimage location today because the sacred bo-tree grows there. The tree is said to be a scion of the sacred fig under which Siddhartha Gautama was enlightened; allegedly it was brought to Sri Lanka by Sanghamitta, one of Mahinda's sisters. The Isurumuniya Temple is another important pilgrimage place — according to tradition it was founded in the third century BC by laypeople who had touched the bo-tree and became ordained as monks. The impressive Ruvanveli Dagoba, whose semi-sphere is 360 feet (110 m) high, was built in the second century BC.

The "Reclining Buddha" in the Isurumuniya Temple probably dates from the seventh or eighth century

TEMPLE OF THE TOOTH
Kandy, Sri Lanka

The magnificent Temple of the Tooth (UNESCO World Cultural Heritage site) was built in Kandy between 1687 and 1782. Seen from the outside, the octagonal tower stands out. The main complex is laid out on three stories. The third story houses the Golden Shrine. At its center is a chamber in which a tooth of the Buddha is kept underneath a golden dagoba. According to legend, four teeth and a clavicle were saved when the body of Siddhartha Gautama, the founder of the religion, was cremated around the year 480 BC. Many myths are

Guards at the reliquary chamber

The famous dagoba in the Temple of the Tooth

woven around the subsequent odyssey of these relics. Thus, the tooth kept in Kandy was allegedly taken to Sri Lanka hidden in the hair of a Buddhist nun. The veneration of the tooth is based on the idea that it has the spiritual power of the Buddha — the powers of a rainmaker are attributed to the tooth.

SHWEZIGON PAGODA
Bagan, Myanmar

Begun during the reign of King Anawrahta (1014–1077) and completed in 1090 under his successor Kyanzittha (1041–1113), this temple is

Shrines at the Shwezigon Pagoda

probably the best-known structure in the historic temple city of Bagan. The large stupa in its center is completely covered in gold leaf and surrounded by many smaller shrines and stupas. Four entrances in the fortification wall give access to the sanctuary, which is said to house a shrine with a tooth and a bone of the Buddha, making it the destination of countless pilgrimages. One of the most important Buddhist temples in Myanmar, it was the model for the construction of many other religious shrines in the country, for example the famous Shwedagon Pagoda of Yangon.

ANANDA PAHTO TEMPLE
Bagan, Myanmar

Completed around 1105, this Buddhist sanctuary is one of the 11 largest structures in the temple city of Bagan. With its more than 2,000 preserved temples dating from the 11th to the 13th centuries, the city is today the most important archeological excavation site in all of South-East Asia. The exterior and interior of this temple, influenced by Indian architecture, are masterpieces of Buddhist temple architecture: built on a perfect cruciform plan, several terraces lead up to the gilded top.

The center has a cuboid shape. At each corner stands a 33 foot (10 m) tall golden Buddha statue, in niches and facing into the four directions of the compass. The sandstone reliefs in the base of the structure depict episodes from the life of Gautama Buddha. In the entrance hall on the western side, a footprint of the Buddha is imbedded in the marble floor.

Gilded Buddha in the Ananda Temple

The majestic Shwezigon Pagoda is the most famous sanctuary in the temple city of Bagan in Myanmar. The gold leaf covered stupa rises via three rectangular terraces, reaching a height of about 165 feet (50 m), making it visible from afar.

SUKHOTHAI TEMPLE COMPLEX
Sukhothai, Thailand

The ruins of the capital of the kingdom of Sukhothai, which existed in what is now Thailand from the 13th to 14th centuries, attest to a high degree of sophistication in Buddhist art and architecture. Whereas the early structures in the complex still reveal the influence of the Khmer, the temples from the heyday of the empire show that Sukothai developed its own unique forms of artistic and architectural expression. The Wat Mahathat Temple, for example, completed in the middle of the 14th century, is an impressively large complex. Once encircled by a wall, the temple complex covers an area of 10 acres

Colossal Buddha in the Wat Si Chum Temple

(4 ha), on which stood hundreds of buildings. The colossal Buddha in the Wat Si Chum Temple is an outstanding example of the elegant Sukothai style. The ruined city of Sukhothai has been made into a historical park and was declared a UNESCO World Heritage site in 1991.

KAMPHAENG PHET TEMPLE RUINS
Kamphaeng Phet, Thailand

The Historical Park of Kamphaeng Phet belongs to a UNESCO World Cultural Heritage site, together with Si Satchanalai and Sukhothai. The town on the Ping River was founded by King Liu Thai in 1347 as an outpost of the Sukhothai Empire. After the latter's fall it remained a major garrison town, where further important temples were built. Toward the end of the 16th century the Burmese raided the city. Along with remains of the city walls, the ruins of the Wat Phra Kaeo, of the Wat Phra That and of the Wat Phra Si Iriyaboth temples as well as other shrines have been preserved from this

Buddha statues in the Wat Phra Si Iriyaboth Temple

heyday of Kamphaeng Phets. The Kamphaeng Phet National Museum exhibits Buddha statues that were found within the confines of the historic city. The Emerald Buddha of the Wat Phra Kaeo Temple of Kamphaeng Phet is today kept at the Wat Phra Kaeo in Bangkok.

AYUTTHAYA TEMPLE RUINS

Ayutthaya, Thailand

The capital of the second Thai Empire was founded around 1350. It is an open-air museum of Buddhist high culture. Many temples, monasteries, palaces and monumental sculptures still attest today to the former splendor of the city, located on an island in the river. "The indomitable one," as the name "Ayutthaya" translates, was a city of millions at its peak, boasting 375 monasteries and temples, around 100 city gates and 29 fortresses. However, the much-praised city proved not entirely indomitable: in 1767 it succumbed to the Burmese onslaught and was destroyed. The residence of 33 kings, Ayutthaya was for more than 400 years the political and cultural focus of a large empire that comprised the entre South-East Asian mainland. The most significant monuments, including the temple ruins of Wat Phra Si Sanphet, Wat Mahathat and Wat Rajaburana, stand in the historical center of the ruined city.

Ayutthaya, Wat Phra Si Sanphet

Inside the Wat Mahathat Temple

A view of the ruins of the Wat Mahathat Temple of Sukothai. The vast temple compound was the holiest Buddhist shrine in the first Thai kingdom, built during the reign of Si Intharathit (1240–1270) and enlarged by his successors. In its heyday, the Wat Mahathat comprised many hundred chedis (stupas), temples and other religious buildings.

WAT PHRA KAEO TEMPLE
Bangkok, Thailand

In the historic heart of Bangkok, in the grounds of the Grand Palace, stands the Wat Phra Kaeo, the most important temple complex in Thailand. Consisting of more than

Temples and stupas of the Wat Phra Kaeo

100 richly decorated temples, pagodas and statues, it was commissioned in 1782 by King Rama I on the occasion of the founding of Bangkok, but it was not completed until 100 years later. Unlike other Buddhist shrines, the complex has no residential quarters for monks, but is exclusively reserved for devotions. Its center is the phra ubosot, the holiest prayer room, where the national shrine of Thailand is kept, the famous Emerald Buddha. This 30 inch (75 cm) tall figure of green jade, whose ownership even led to the outbreak of a war, is exhibited in a glass case high above the heads of the visitors.

Interior of Wat Phra Kaeo

An entrance to the Phra Mondop, a library in the grounds of the Wat Phra Kaeo, where sacred Buddhist scriptures are kept. The tower-like structure was built under King Rama I (1737–1809) on the site of an earlier building that had been destroyed by a fire. The two entrances of the library are guarded by demons. The statues are regarded as masterpieces of the Rattanakosin style.

WAT ARUN TEMPLE
Bangkok, Thailand

Thanks to its location on the west bank of the Chao Phraya River, the Wat Arun, or Temple of Dawn, has become the emblem of Bangkok. The temple was first named Wat Makok and was built during the Ayutthaya era (1351–1767). The Emerald Buddha was held here from 1778 to 1784. When King Rama I moved his residence to the

The central prang of the Wat Arun

opposite bank of the river and took the national shrine along with him, the temple initially lost its importance. It was however restored under Rama II and endowed with a monumental prang (tower). The king also named the temple Wat Arun. The center of the compound is formed by a roughly 260 foot (80 m) tall pagoda, covered with a mosaic of porcelain and shells, which is also reverently known as "central prang." At its four corners stand smaller prangs, dedicated to the wind deity, Phra Phai.

Buddha statue of the Wat Doi Suthep

WAT DOI SUTHEP
Chiang Mai, Thailand

This 14th-century temple is an important pilgrimage destination, because a relic of the Buddha, allegedly a bone splinter, is kept in the gilded 52 foot (16 m) tall chedi. It is said it was found by a monk, and originally it was intended to be kept in the Wat Suan Dok, another important Buddhist temple in Chiang Mai. When, miraculously, the relic split into two, a dignified place of storage for the second piece was sought and it was decided to fasten it, enclosed in a small altar, to the back of a white elephant, which was then released. The Wat Doi Suthep was built in the spot where the animal first settled down.

The gilded chedi of the Wat Doi Suthep, located on the slopes of a 3,490 foot (1,063 m) high mountain, is surrounded by temples richly decorated in the Thai style as well as Buddha statues and small altars. Every year thousands of Buddhist believers from around the world bring their sacrificial offerings here.

Impressive cave temples dating from the fifth century are proof that Buddhism had early followers in the Middle Kingdom.

MOGAO CAVES
Dunhuang, China

For more than a millennium merchants, generals, widows and monks expressed their entreaties or their gratitude and their hopes for deliverance to supernatural powers in the prosperous oasis of Dunhuang: they cut grottoes into the stone of a nearby rock outcrop and had them adorned with scenes from the life of Gautama Buddha, with depictions of paradise, scenes from this life as well as splendid ornaments. The legendary grottoes became known as the Caves of Dunhuang. Around 1900, in the Mogao Caves that form a part of this complex, a monk discovered a bricked up library containing more than 50,000 manuscripts dating from the fourth to 10th centuries. The roughly 1,000 caves extend along a cliff in several lines on top of one another over a length of 5,250 feet (1,600 m). Frescoes measuring 484,380 sq ft (45,000 sq m) in total and 2,400 colored clay figures are still preserved today. The caves have been included in the list of UNESCO World Cultural Heritage sites since 1987.

YUNGANG GROTTOES
Wuzhou Mountains, China

The emperors of the Wei dynasty had raised the status of Buddhism to that of the state religion. Yet suddenly in 446 Emperor Tai Wudi forbade Buddhism — and soon after

Over-lifesize Buddha statue

Statue of a seated Buddha

he died unexpectedly. His grandson Wen Chengdi interpreted this as a sign from heaven. To make amends for the sacrilege he had the Yungang Grottoes cut into the rock of the Wuzhou Mountains. To do so the monk Yunyao recruited more than 10,000 workers who began building the giant structure in 460. By 465, the first five grottoes in the honor of the five Wei rulers had been completed. The remaining grottoes were cut from the rock within the next 30 to 40 years, until the time the Wei capital was moved to Longmen. The Buddha sculptures in the grottoes of Yungang are 0.8 inches (2 cm) to 56 feet (17 m) high. The ear of the largest seated Buddha measures 10 feet (3.1 m), his feet 15 feet (4.6 m). It eventually became a UNESCO World Heritage site, in 2001.

This mural in one of the Mogao caves depicts Amitabha, an otherworldly incarnation of the Buddha that is highly revered in eastern Asia

LONGMEN GROTTOES
Luoyang, China

These grottoes are the largest cave complex ever carved by humans anywhere in China. They are located on a 1/2 mile (1 km) long cliff along the Yi River, only a few miles south

Cave of the Thousand Buddhas

of Luoyang in Henan Province. More than 2,000 grottoes and niches are strung together on the steep slope of the Longmenshan or Dragon Mountains above the river. The caves contain valuable inscriptions and around 10,000 stone statues as well as rich sculptural ceiling and wall decorations. The first grottoes were established toward the end of the fifth century. Preserved from this early time are the Guyang Cave as well as the Binyang Cave. In the "Longmen style," a distinctive Chinese Buddhist art of sculpting developed between the fifth and ninth centuries. The Longmen Grottoes have been included on the UNESCO list of World Cultural Heritage sites since 2000.

Over-lifesize Buddha statues in the main grottoes of Longmen

THE MOST IMPORTANT TEMPLES OF BUDDHISM (CHINA)

MOUNT EMEI
Sichuan, China

The sacred Mount Emei (UNESCO World Cultural Heritage site) in the Chinese province of Sichuan has been a refuge valued by hermits since the Later Han (or (Eastern Han) dynasty (25–220

Temple on the summit of Mount Emei

AD). Soon the first Buddhist temples and monasteries were built there. Over the course of time, more than 200 monasteries and hermitages were built on Mount Emei, and the stream of pilgrims grew ever wider. Among the 20 preserved sanctuaries (many became victims of the Cultural Revolution), some closely hug the side of the rock, and others were built on top of the summit. Some shrines date back to the Sui dynasty (581–618 AD), but the buildings that still stand there today are predominantly from the 17th century. According to legend, Samantabhadra, the bodhisattva of universal virtue and the mountain's patron saint, once taught on Mount Emei. He is remembered by an over 26 foot (8m) tall statue in a mountain temple.

The gilded Buddha statue on Mount Emei depicts the bodhisattva Samantabhadra, the embodiment of universal virtues. He is believed to have flown to the top of the mountain on a three-headed elephant. The statue is 157 feet (48 m) tall and conceals a temple inside.

MOUNT WUTAI
Shanxi, China

The first Buddhist monks trekked to Mount Wutai 2,000 years ago in order to find enlightenment there. Over time more than 100 monasteries were built on and near the holy mountain. Even the emperors of the Ming dynasty traveled there to seek the counsel of the monks. Visitors today can admire the diversity of Chinese Buddhist temple architecture: the Foguang Temple, built around 900, is one of the oldest and tallest wooden structures in China. The Nanchan Temple is famous for

Xiantong Temple on Mount Wutai

its elaborately designed Great Buddha Hall, and the Shuxiang Temple holds 12 colorful statues telling the story of Manjushri: Manjushri was one of the Buddha's students who is revered as a bodhisattva and the protector of scholars; he resides on Mount Wutai.

MOUNT JIUHUA
Anhui, China

Mount Jiuhua in the Chinese province of Anhui is one of the four holy mountains of Chinese Buddhism. Visitors will find dozens of monasteries and temples in the mountain region, of which more than 90 are accessible today. Most of these places of worship are dedicated to the bodhisattva Ksitigarbha, who is still very popular in China today. He has been venerated on Mount Jiuhua since the eighth century, when monks thought they saw in Prince

Qiyuan Temple on Mount Jiuhua

Kim Qiaoque a reincarnation of the bodhisattva. Among the most important sites are the Huacheng and Roushen Baodian monasteries, whose roots can be followed back to the beginnings of Ksitigarbha worship. The present buildings, however, were built a few centuries later.

MOUNT PUTUO
Zhejiang, China

On the island of Mount Putuo, off the shores of China's Zhejiang Province, rises the eponymous peak, one of the four holiest mountains in Chinese Buddhism. Avalokiteshvara, the bodhisattva

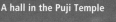

A hall in the Puji Temple

of universal compassion, who is revered in China in his female manifestation as Guanyin, is believed to have awakened in this mountain region. With its around 20 temples, Mount Putuo is an outstanding pilgrimage destination. The buildings date back to the early tenth century, when Japanese monks built a statue of the enlightened one there. With a total of nine halls, the Puji Temple is the most impressive complex.

THE MOST IMPORTANT TEMPLES OF BUDDHISM (JAPAN)

TODAI-JI
Nara, Japan

This vast temple complex in the ancient imperial city of Nara is one of the most important Buddhist sanctuaries in all of Japan. With the Daibutsu-Den, the Great Buddha Hall,

Statue of the Great Buddha

it comprises the largest wooden temple and with the Daibutsu the largest bronze Buddha statue in the world. The complex was built in the middle of the eight century on the orders of Shomu Tenno, as the main temple of an entire network of Buddhist sanctuaries. The emperor, an ardent follower of the Buddha, wanted to use it to encourage a final breakthrough for the new faith that had reached Japan around the middle of the sixth century. As well as the Daibutsu, the Todai-ji also boasts the Shoso-in, a treasure house, and the Nandaimon Gate, dating from 1199 and holding two impressive figures of guardians. The oldest structure in the grounds is the Sangatsu Hall, built in 733 and housing many invaluable Buddhist works of art.

THE GREAT BUDDHA OF TODAI-JI — THE LARGEST BRONZE BUDDHA IN THE WORLD

The 52 foot (16 m) tall and approximately 500 short tons (450 tonnes) heavy Buddha statue in the Todai-ji was, like the building of the temple itself, commissioned by Shomu Tenno in 743. Historians believe that the project was meant to unite the nation and at the same time strengthen the standing of Japan in the entire Buddhist world. Building the colossus was a challenge for the country and it took almost ten years to complete. The statue was finally inaugurated in 752, in the presence of about 10,000 guests, including Buddhist monks from China and India. It depicts a Buddha Vairocana.

THE GREAT BUDDHA HALL — THE LARGEST WOODEN TEMPLE IN THE WORLD

The Great Buddha Hall in the grounds of the Todaj-ji Temple

The present Daibutsu-Den, as the Great Buddha Hall in the grounds of the Todai-ji temple complex is known in Japanese, was built at the beginning of the 18th century. Although at a height of 157 feet (48 m) and a width of 164 feet (50 m) as well as a length of 187 feet (57 m) it is noticeably smaller than earlier structures, it is nevertheless the largest wooden temple in the world. Over the course of the nearly 1,300 years of their history, both the hall and the Buddha statue were repeatedly badly damaged by fires and earthquakes and had to be restored. The most recent such damage occurred in 1692.

Construction of the monumental Buddha figure in the Todai-ji complex is today praised as a logistical masterstroke. More than 80,000 artisans participated in its execution. The statue depicts a Buddha Vairocana, who is venerated as a cosmic, all-knowing Adibuddha, and who made his first appearance in theological deliberations by Chinese Buddhists during the fifth century.

HIGASHI-HONGANJI (EASTERN TEMPLE OF THE ORIGINAL VOW)
Kyoto, Japan

The Higashi-Honganji temple compound is located in the middle of the ancient imperial city of Kyoto. Together with other holy places it has been a UNESCO World Cultural Heritage site since 1994. With the Nishi-Honganji (Western Temple of the Original Vow) it is the spiritual center of the Jodo Shinshu, the second largest faith community in Japanese Buddhism today. Built in 1602, the Higashi-Honganji consists of a large Founder's Hall and a smaller Buddha Hall with a statue of the Buddha Amitabha.

Nishi-Honganji is the largest wooden structure in Kyoto

ENRYAKU-JI
Kyoto, Japan

The Enryaku-ji temple compound, which comprises about 130 buildings, rises impressively on the summit of the 2,780 foot (848 m)

Pagoda of the Enryaku-ji

high Mount Hiei near Kyoto. Founded in 788 by the monk Saicho, the monastery was the headquarters of the Buddhist Tendai School. During the attempt in 1571 to bring the Buddhist Ikko Monks under his control, the Oda Nobunaga Shogun destroyed large parts of the compound, but today these have been restored.

The eastern pagoda and the Amida Hall, which is dedicated to the Buddha Amitabha, in the Enryaku-ji, one of the most important Buddhist temple and monastery compounds in Japan. The vast Enryaku-ji district once comprised around 3,000 buildings; today 130 temples and pagodas still exist within its grounds.

MOUNT KOYA
Koya, Japan

In the dense woods around Mount Koya to the south of Nara are located the 154 shrines of the temple city of Koya-san, which together with other cult sites and pilgrimage treks in the Kii Mountains was added to the list of UNESCO World Cultural Heritage sites in 2004.

The beginnings of Koya-san go back to Kukai, the founder of Shingon Buddhism. The monk withdrew into the mountain region probably around 816 and there founded a sanctuary for the order that he had created.

Shingon Buddhism represents a synthesis of Japanese Shinto and Buddhism, which had been adopted from Korea and China in the sixth century. Counting around five million followers in Japan, the sect's main temple is the Kongobu-ji. The Okunoin mausoleum holds the earthly remains of Kukai, the founder of the temple. His monumental tomb is surrounded by the largest and most important cemetery in all of Japan. The Konpon Daito Pagoda is another of the attractions on the monastic mountain.

The central temple district of Koya-san in the northeastern part of Wakayama

FUSHIMI SHRINE
Kyoto, Japan

This shrine, standing in the southeast of the old Japanese imperial city of Kyoto, is dedicated to Inari, the goddess of fertility, and is one of the most popular Shinto sanctuaries anywhere in Japan. Consisting

Torii at the Fushimi Shrine

of five individual shrines, it is spread across the wooded slopes of Mount Inari. Its beginnings date back to the ninth century, but the main shrine visible today was built in 1594. Miles of corridors with flaming red torii, donated by pilgrims, lead up to the shrine. Unlike other Shinto shrines, the inner sanctum is open and freely accessible to all. The splendid Fushimi Shrine is the main shrine out of more than 30,000 Inari sanctuaries in Japan.

Veritable forests of torii, donated by pilgrims, point the way to the Fushimi Shrine on top of the Inari, a wooded hill in Kyoto. These gates, often painted vermillion, stand symbolically at the entrance to each Shinto shrine as the passageway between the secular and the holy worlds. The two crossbeams linking the posts, or lying on top of them, are their distinctive feature.

ISE GRAND SHRINE – THE MOST IMPORTANT SHINTO SHRINE
Ise, Japan

The Ise Shrine, the ancestral shrine of the imperial family, is the most important Shinto sanctuary. Every

A bridge in the grounds of the Ise Shrine

goddess of the sun, Amaterasu, is venerated at the naiku; she Is considered the ancestral mother of

Meditation hall in the Ise Shrine

year some six million pilgrims come here. The shrine was founded in the third century and is subdivided into an inner (naiku) and an outer (geku) district. The naiku comprises 91, the geku 32 lesser shrines. According to an age-old tradition the buildings are completely dismantled and rebuilt according to the original plans every 20 years. While the geku is dedicated to the goddess of food, clothes and housing, the

the Japanese imperial household. A mirror is kept inside a brocade bag in the inner sanctum of this shrine. It is one of the imperial regalia in Japan and a symbol of the goddess of the sun. With its help, the other deities are said to have lured Amaterasu from a cave where she had escaped after her brother had murdered a servant girl, thus returning the light of the sun to the world.

ITSUKUSHIMA SHRINE
Miyajima, Japan

The shrine complex on the island of Miyajima, located in the Seto Inland Sea not far from Hiroshima, one of the most attractive spots along the Japanese coast,

paint has maintained the style of the Heian period (eighth to 12th centuries), when it was first built in a similar form. Eight larger and several smaller buildings were

Torii, entrance to the Itsukushima-Shrine

A hall in the Itsukushima Shrine

is probably the best-known sanctuary in Japan. With great perfection it embodies the worship of divine nature in the Shinto religion. According to legend, the shrine, dedicated to the three daughters of the god of storms, was built in 593. Miyajima Island, or Itsukushima, has been a holy district since the earliest days and until the 11th century only priests were permitted to enter. Today there is still no cemetery here so that the purity of the cult site could be preserved. Even though the main structure dates from the years 1556 to 1571, the overall complex with its bright red

erected on stilts in the shallow water and linked by galleries; other buildings on land form the "outer shrine." In 1875 the 52 foot (16 m) tall torii was added, the "entrance gate" to the holy district. This eighth red gate in the Shrine of Itsukushima, standing 574 feet (175 m) offshore in the sea, completes the scene and perfects the great harmony it exudes. The Itsukushima Shrine has been a UNESCO World Cultural Heritage site since 1996. Miyajima Island houses more than 3,000 temple complexes and Shinto shrines in total.

The stupa is one of the most important religious structures in Buddhism. It developed from ancient Indian burial mounds and was very widespread in India even in the early days of Buddhism. Inside the stupa, relics of Buddha or famous Buddhist monks are kept.

Kathmandu, Swayambhunath Stupa

A stupa consists of a base above which rises a domed structure. The shrine with the relics sits enthroned on top of the building and is protected by a stone parasol. Each stupa is surrounded by an ambulatory and a wall that is often decorated with reliefs and usually has four entrance gates. From this basic type developed the chedi in Thailand, the dagoba in Sri Lanka and the pagoda in Myanmar.

PHRA PATHOM CHEDI
Nakhom Pathom, Thailand   417 ft (127 m)

The tallest stupa in the world is at the same time the oldest Buddhist structure in Thailand. Archeological finds confirm that

Entrance of the Phra Pathom Chedi

a chedi was probably built on the site of the sanctuary that can be seen today as early as the third century AD. Between the ninth and 12th centuries, large parts of Thailand were occupied by the Khmer; in subsequent centuries it was overgrown by the jungle. King Rama IV rediscovered the ruins in the 19th century and had a magnificent new shrine built above them.

MAHASEYA DAGOBA
Mihintale, Sri Lanka   c. 330 ft (100 m)

Visible from afar, this stupa sits enthroned on a hill in Mihintale, one of the most important Buddhist pilgrimage destinations

Ambasthale and Mahaseya Dagoba

The Mahaseya Dagoba

in Sri Lanka. It was built in the first century AD under King Mahadathika Mahanaga and is said to hold one of Buddha's hairs. The beginnings of the temple of Mihintale date back to the third century BC. King Devanampiya Tissa is said to have encountered the monk Mahinda here who converted him to Buddhism.

พื้นที่บริเวณรอบองค์พระปฐมเจดีย์ เขตพุทธาวาส
ห้ามมิให้พ่อค้า-แม่ค้า หาบเร่ แผงลอย เข้ามา
ทำการค้าขาย หรือกระทำการอย่างใดอย่างหนึ่ง
อันเป็นการรบกวนบุคคลอื่น
หากฝ่าฝืน! ทางวัดจะดำเนินการ ตามกฎหมาย
คณะกรรมการวัดพระปฐมเจดีย์

GLOBAL VIPASSANA PAGODA

Mumbai, India   **315 ft (96m)**

The dome of this shrine which was dedicated in 2009 is one of the tallest in the world. Reaching a height of almost 98 feet (30 m), it arches over a vast hall, where some 8,000 people are able to

The golden dome of the Global Vipassana Pagoda

meditate together. The entire temple complex was modeled on the Shwedagon Pagoda of Yangon in Myanmar. Unlike that famous example, however, only the tip of the pagoda was covered in genuine gold leaf — all other parts of the structure were painted gold. The relics of the Buddha, which came from one of the stupas in Sanchi, are kept in the finial stone of the sanctuary.

JETAVANA DAGOBA

Anuradhapura, Sri Lanka
233 ft /71 m (367 ft/112 m)

This shrine, belonging to the Jetavana Monastery in the historical Singhalese capital of Anuradhapura, is the tallest historical stupa in the world. Its height from the base to the tip

The historical Jetavana Dagoba

measures 400 feet (122 m), and the base is 577 feet (176 m) long. Around 90 million bricks were used to build it. The Singhalese King Mahasena (r. 274–301 AD) had the monumental stupa built as a sign of his support for a group of monks who had been expelled from the Mahavihara Monastery. A part of the holy city of Anuradhapura, it is a UNESCO World Heritage site.

OG MIN OGYEN MINDROLLING

Dehra Dhun, India   **187 ft (57 m)**

This stupa is impressive not only because of its size but also because of its elegant architectural shape. Based on the stupa of the Tibetan Mindrolling Monastery, it was built on the initiative of monks who had fled

A modern stupa in Dehra Dun

to India after the annexation of Tibet by China in 1959. The stupa was inaugurated in 2002, and the new monastery is the largest Buddhist meditation center in the world.

Covered with shiny orange-red bricks, the Phra Pathom Chedi is one of the most important Buddhist pilgrimage sites in Thailand. A large, wide flight of stairs leads up to the southern entrance of the shrine. At the top of the 12.5 foot (3.8 m) tall statue of the enthroned Buddha awaits the faithful, the "Phra Puttha Narachet."

This incredibly famous temple is an emblem of Myanmar and a symbol for the intense spirituality of its people. Only the most precious of materials were used in the construction and decoration of the stupa. It rises on a vast marble platform 328 feet (100 m) in height and is surrounded by dozens of smaller stupas. Like the Burmese stupas in general, it consists of a terraced lower structure, on which sit two upper structures, the "bell" and the so-called "upturned alms bowl." The elements at the top of the stupa's dome are known as "lotus petals" and "banana bud." Whereas the lower and upper structures of the stupa are covered with gold leaf, "lotus petals" and "banana bud" are covered in gold plating with a total weight of 66 short tons (60 tonnes). The

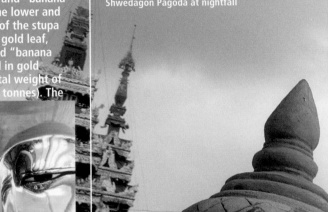

Shwedagon Pagoda at nightfall

The golden Buddha

stupa's iron parasol and its flag are studded with thousands of diamonds and rubies. The diamond at the tip alone is 76 carat.

The central stupa of the Shwedagon Pagoda in Yangon is completely covered in gold. The sanctuary is the emblem of the capital of Myanmar and of the entire country, and at the same time a major pilgrimage site. The giant 645,830 sq ft (60,000 sq m) large marble platform, from which rise the stupa as well as numerous smaller shrines and temples, is attended by thousands of followers every day.

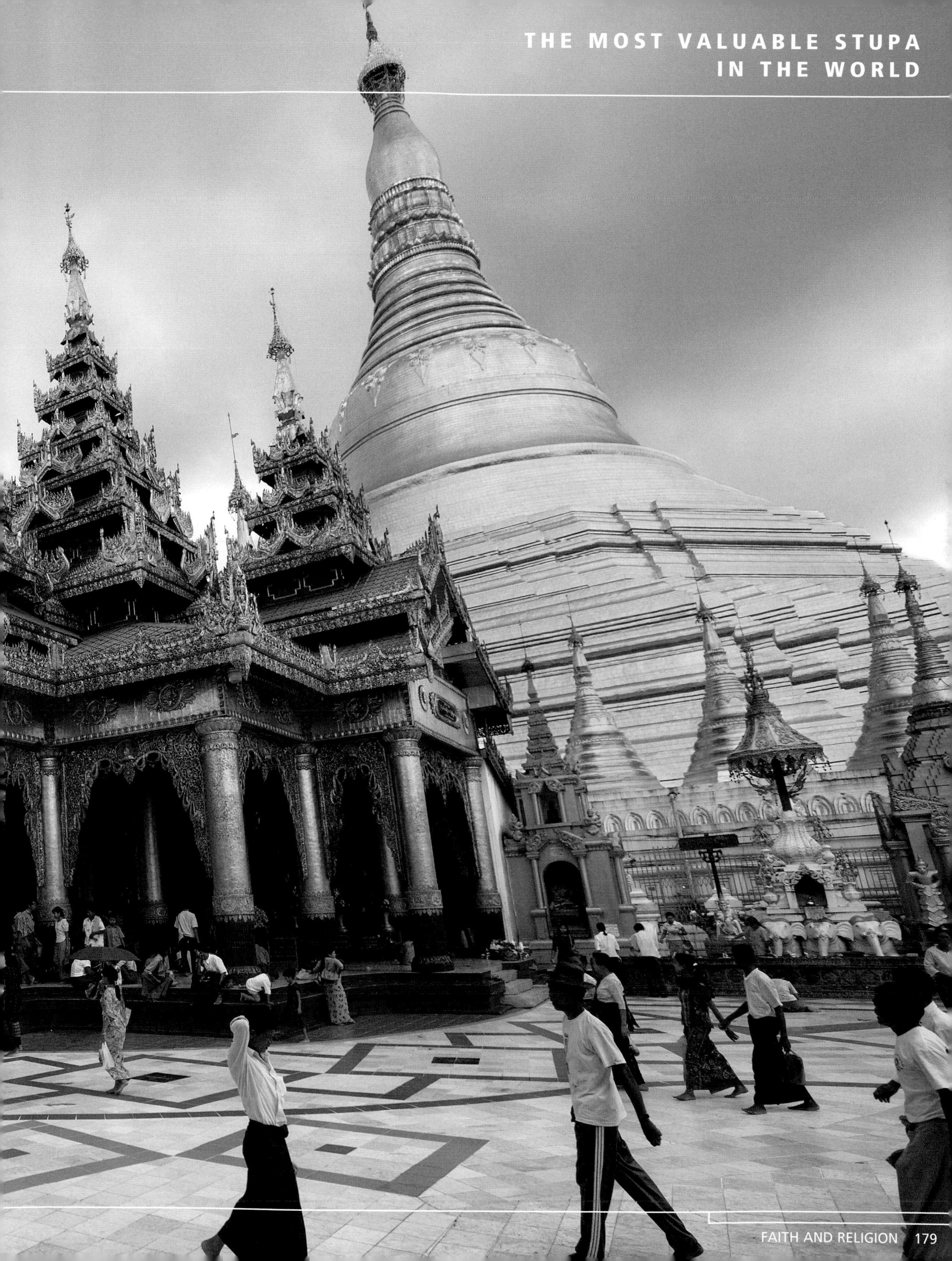

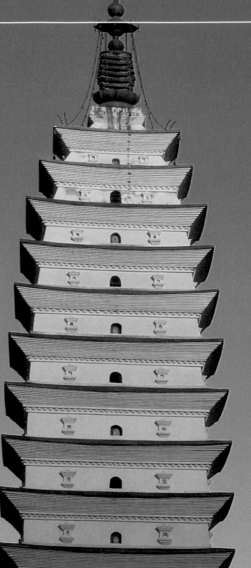

TIANNING PAGODA – THE TALLEST PAGODA IN THE WORLD

Changzhou, China   505 ft (154 m)

Tianning Pagoda and Buddha Maitreya

At 505 feet (154 m) tall, this pagoda surpasses the Cheops Pyramid by about 66 feet (20 m). The sanctuary was inaugurated in 2007 and is said to have cost almost 39 million dollars to build. Its tip and the decoration of the roofs are pure gold. Valuable timber that had to be imported from Myanmar and New Guinea was used as building material. The pagoda belongs to a temple whose beginnings date back to the Tang dynasty (617–907 AD). Through the centuries it was repeatedly destroyed and rebuilt. The newly built pagoda is an indication of the renaissance that Buddhism is experiencing in the People's Republic China.

The Qianxun Pagoda rises about 230 feet (70 m) up into the sky. The shrine is the tallest of the three pagodas in the grounds of the Chongshan Monastery near Dali in southwestern China. The graceful pagoda in the picture background only reaches a height of 148 feet (45 m).

LIAODI PAGODA

Dingzhou, China   276 ft (84 m)

This structure is the tallest ancient Chinese pagoda and at the same time the tallest brick pagoda in the world. It was built at the time of the Song dynasty and completed in 1077. The Kaiyuan Temple, which it forms a part of, was destroyed. Buddhist scriptures were kept inside the pagoda, but it was also used as a watchtower.

BEISI PAGODA

Suzhou, China   249 ft (76 m)

The Beisi or North Temple Pagoda

The Beisi or North Temple Pagoda dates from the 12th century. In 1570 it was badly damaged by a fire and had to be rebuilt. The walls of the tower, which rise above an octagonal base, were built from stone, the eaves and the balustrade of the galleries running around it are made from timber.

QIANXUN PAGODA

Dali, China   230 ft (70 m)

The three pagodas of the Chongsheng Temple

This pagoda is the oldest and at the same time the tallest of three slender tower structures in the grounds of the Chongsheng Temple near Dali in southwestern China. It was built a hundred years earlier than her two sister structures, during the time of the Tang dynasty in the first half of the ninth century. On all 16 stories there is a shrine with a seated Buddha at each of the four sides.

YONGYOUSI PAGODA

Chengde, China   220 ft (67 m)

Yongyousi Pagoda

The nine-story pagoda in the grounds of the imperial summer residence of Chengde (UNESCO World Cultural Heritage site) triumphs with its beautifully balanced proportions.

Built under the Qing Emperor Qianlong during the second half of the 18th century, it was modeled on the much-praised, Porcelain Tower of Nanjing, which dates back to the early 15th century but was destroyed in the 19th century.

The pagoda is a regular feature of Buddhist religious buildings in eastern Asia, and like the Indian stupas it is used as a repository for a relic or an image of the Buddha. In the course of the spread of Buddhism in the Middle Kingdom it developed out of the traditional Chinese

Xi'an, Giant Wild Goose Pagoda

tower and now is generally constructed of three or five stories, tapered toward the top. On each level the central core of the structure is surrounded by freely accessible, walkable and roofed galleries. The roofs are turned up at the corners and often have bells attached.

THE TALLEST PAGODAS IN THE WORLD

1. **Tianning-Pagode**
   Changzhou, China
   505 ft (154 m)
2. **Liaodi Pagoda**
   Dingzhou, China
   276 ft (84 m)
3. **Beisi Pagoda**
   Suzhou, China
   249 ft (76 m)
4. **Qianxun Pagoda**
   Dali, China
   230 ft (70 m)
5. **Yongyousi Pagoda**
   Chengde, China
   220 ft (67 m)
6. **Fogong Temple Pagoda**
   Ying, China
   220 ft (67 m)
7. **Giant Wild Goose Pagoda**
   Xi'an, China
   210 ft (64 m)
8. **Kaifeng Iron Pagoda**
   Kaifeng, China
   194 ft (59 m)
9. **To-ji Pagoda**
   Kyoto, Japan
   187 ft (57 m)
10. **Xumi Pagoda**
    Chengde, China
    157 ft (48 m)

THE LARGEST BUDDHA STATUES IN THE WORLD (STANDING)

SPRING TEMPLE BUDDHA — THE TALLEST BUDDHA STATUE IN THE WORLD

Lushan, China   420 ft (128 m)

The base of the Spring Temple Buddha houses a monastery.

This Buddha statue, together with the base on which it stands, reaches a height of 502 feet (153 m), making it nearly as tall as the towers of Cologne Cathedral. It was erected at the beginning of 2001 and inaugurated in 2002, in memory of the destruction of the Buddha statues of Bamiyan by the Taliban. The colossus is assembled from copper parts and weighs 1,100 short tons (1,000 tonnes).

This gilded Buddha statue stands in Wat Muang, a Buddhist temple dating from the 17th century in the Thai province of Ang Thong, and only rediscovered in the 1980s. The colossus is 305 feet (93 m) tall and at knee height 203 feet (62 m) wide. After a 16-year construction period it was inaugurated in 2007. The Buddha's right hand points downward, symbolizing his victory over the Demon Mara, who embodies suffering and death.

LAYKYUN SETKYAR
Monywa, Myanmar   380 ft (116 m)

The giant Buddha statue of Monywa

This giant Buddha figure was built in the city of Monya in the north of Myanmar, together with the statue of a reclining Buddha. After 12 years of construction it was inaugurated in February 2008. The colossus is currently the tallest Buddha statue after the Spring Temple Buddha. From top to bottom it measures 380 feet (116 m). Standing on a 44 foot (13.5 m) high base, it reaches a total height of 425 feet (129.5 m). Monya is a center of Buddhism in Myanmar. In the city's environs a whole string of shrines attest to the deep spirituality of the Burmese. More than 87 percent of the population are followers of the teaching of Buddha.

In the early time of Buddhism, the Buddha was depicted via means of certain symbols that signified individual phases of his life. The tradition of Buddha statues, still unbroken until this day, developed during the course of the refinement of the teaching about bodhisvattvas as the worldly incarnation of a transcendent

Female Buddha Guanyin, Sanya

Adibuddha in Mahayana Buddhism. The Buddha statues built in China and Japan following this tradition often allegorize this transcendent Buddha. In the countries of Theravada Buddhism, however, it is mostly the Buddha Siddharta Gautama who is the object of the work of art.

THE TALLEST BUDDHA STATUES IN THE WORLD
(total height)

❶ **Spring Temple Buddha**
Lushan, China
502 ft (153 m)

❷ **Laykyun Sethyar**
Monywa, Myanmar
423 ft (129 m)

❸ **Ushihu Daibutsu**
Ushihu, Japan
394 ft (120 m)

❹ **Guanyin**
Sanya, China
354 ft (108 m)

❺ **Sendai Dai Kannon**
Sendai, Japan
328 ft (100 m)

❻ **Sekai Heiwa**
Awaji-shima, Japan
328 ft (100 m)

❼ **Guishan Guanyin**
Weishan, China
325 ft (99 m)

❽ **Buddha von Ang Thong**
Wat Muang, Thailand
305 ft (93 m)

❾ **Buddha am Lingshan**
Wuxi, China
305 ft (93 m)

THE LARGEST BUDDHA STATUES IN THE WORLD (RECLINING)

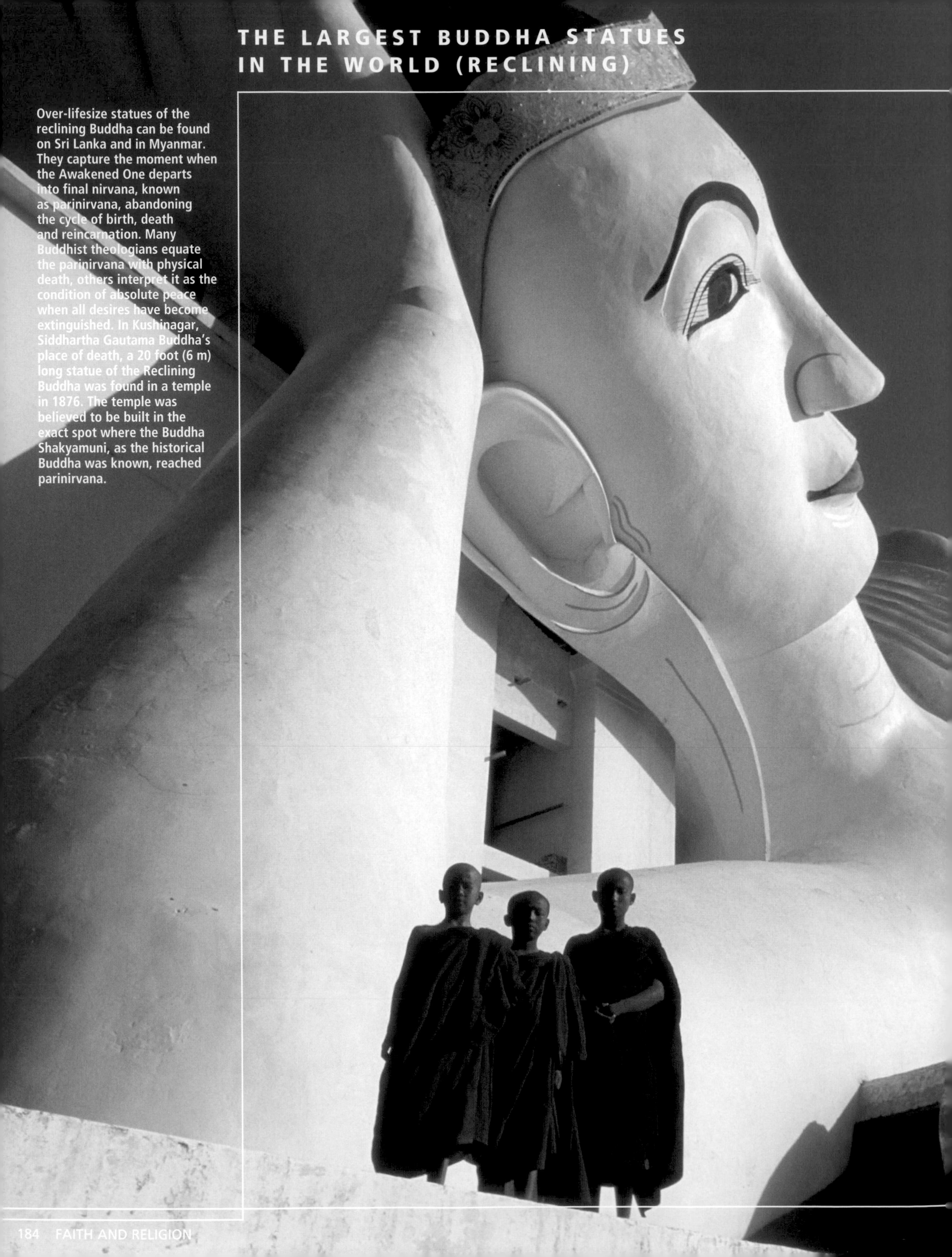

Over-lifesize statues of the reclining Buddha can be found on Sri Lanka and in Myanmar. They capture the moment when the Awakened One departs into final nirvana, known as parinirvana, abandoning the cycle of birth, death and reincarnation. Many Buddhist theologians equate the parinirvana with physical death, others interpret it as the condition of absolute peace when all desires have become extinguished. In Kushinagar, Siddhartha Gautama Buddha's place of death, a 20 foot (6 m) long statue of the Reclining Buddha was found in a temple in 1876. The temple was believed to be built in the exact spot where the Buddha Shakyamuni, as the historical Buddha was known, reached parinirvana.

ZINATHUKHA YAN AUNG CHANTHA BUDDHA — THE LONGEST RECLINING BUDDHA IN THE WORLD
Mudon, Myanmar   590 ft (180 m)

The largest statue in the world of a reclining Buddha was built in the small village of Mudon, situated near the town of Mawlamyaing in the south of Myanmar between 1991 and 2008. The colossus clocks in at an amazing 590 feet (180 m) long and 98 feet (30 m) high. Inside it has 182 rooms displaying an exhibition of a wealth of works of art and other visual materials that tell of the teachings of the Buddha, the history of Buddhism and its significance for Myanmar. One of the rooms housing a shrine is used as a devotional hall.

It took 17 years to build the largest statue of a reclining Buddha

ALANTAYAR BUDDHA
Monywa, Myanmar   449 ft (137 m)

This Buddha statue was built immediately before the statue of the Laykyun Setkyar, in the city of Monywa in the north of Myanmar. It is 312 feet (95 m) long and 66 feet (20 m) high. Up to the completion of the Zinathukha Yan Aung Chantha it was the largest Buddha statue of its kind in the world. The inside is accessible and is said to house 9,000 statues of the Siddhartha Gautama Buddha. Construction of the two colossuses of Monywa cost several million dollars and was financed by donations from wealthy followers of the Buddha.

The Alantayar Buddha of Monywa is the second largest reclining Buddha in the world

Until completion of the Zinathukha Yan Aung Chantha Buddha, the Alantayar Buddha of Monywa was the largest statue of the reclining Buddha in the world. The statue's face exudes serene tranquility and equanimity. Like all reclining Buddhas it captures the moment when Buddha attained the final nirvana.

SANCTUARY OF TRUTH

This giant structure is unique in every respect. It impresses not only with its sheer size, but also with its sweeping shape and lavish decoration. Begun in 1981 and still not completed today, the structure consists entirely of precious teak timber, based on traditional Thai architecture. Every square inch is covered in artistic woodcarvings. With the Sanctuary of Truth, its builders wanted to emphasize the importance of the eastern teachings of wisdom for the modern world. The vast interior is dedicated to the great Far Eastern religions and cultural spheres. The tops of the outer towers are adorned with sculptures that symbolize life, religion and philosophy as well as peace. The middle and the tallest tower are crowned by a figure of the Buddha bodhisattva.

The Sanctuary of Truth is covered all over with woodcarvings

The building is based on traditional Far Eastern architectural shapes

The Sanctuary of Truth was built in the vicinity of Pattaya directly by the sea. The enormous complex covers an area of 34,440 sq ft (3,200 sq m) and attains a height of 344 feet (105 m). Although construction was begun in 1981, it has not yet been possible to complete it. The structure is made entirely from teak wood and is prone to decay and therefore has to be constantly renewed.

Wooden Buddhas adorn the temple's roof

CITIES AND METROPOLISES

Up to the 19th century only few towns had more than one million inhabitants. Since then, however, the situation has changed drastically. The number of large cities has grown rapidly in the past 100 years, and so has the number of their inhabitants. The growth of the larger metropolises will probably become one of the greatest problems for humankind in the 21st century, for linked with the growing number of city dwellers, for whom an adequate infrastructure needs to be created, are the global increases in air pollution by industry and automobile exhaust fumes as well as ever-greater volumes of refuse. According to UN estimates more than half the world's population will live in cities in ten years time. In the developing countries, more than three-fourths of all people will have moved into the metropolises by 2015, attracted by the promise of prosperity. But this influx mostly leads to overcrowding.

THE LARGEST METROPOLISES (conurbations) IN THE WORLD

① Tokyo
Japan — 35 million

② Mexico City
Mexico — 20–25 million

③ Seoul
South Korea — 20–25 million

④ New York
USA — 19–25 million

⑤ São Paulo
Brazil — 15–25 million

⑥ Mumbai
India — 15–25 million

⑦ Metro Manila
Philippines — 15–25 million

⑧ Hong Kong -Shenzhen
China — 15–25 million

⑨ Jakarta
Indonesia — 15–25 million

⑩ Delhi
India — 15–25 million

⑪ Istanbul
Turkey — 15–25 million

⑫ Cairo
Egypt — 15–20 million

⑬ Shanghai
China — 15–20 million

⑭ Kansai
Japan — 15–20 million

⑮ Kolkata
India — 10–20 million

⑯ Dhaka
Bangladesh — 10–20 million

The sea of skyscrapers in Manhattan, one of New York's five districts or boroughs, symbolizes the face of the modern city like nowhere else on Earth. Now as then the glamorous metropolis on the Hudson River is seen as the de facto capital of the world and as the urban jungle par excellence.

TOKYO/YOKOHAMA
THE LARGEST METROPOLITAN REGION IN THE WORLD

Like in many eastern Asian metropolises, the nighttime cityscape of Tokyo resembles that of the large cities of North America. Large parts of the city were destroyed by the Great Kanto Earthquake of 1923 and rebuilt in the style of western cities.

The largest metropolitan area on the planet comprises not only the Japanese capital, but the three further megacities of Kawasaki, Saitama and Yokohama as well as 20 municipalities counting more than 200,000 inhabitants each. In total, some 35 million people live in the conurbation of Tokyo, which covers an area of more than 5,200 sq mls (13,500 sq km). The political, cultural and economic heart of the third largest national economy in the world beats in Greater Tokyo. Around one-third of the Japanese gross domestic product is generated here, and 44 percent of all Japanese enterprises and numerous international companies have their headquarters in Tokyo. The two international airports are among the largest in the world. The ingenious local transportation system is state of the art technology; high-speed trains link the region's large cities. The core is formed by Tokyo City itself, which was dissolved as an administrative unit and divided into in 23 autonomous wards in 1943. The megalopolis was already one of the largest cities in the world in the days of the Shogun, who ruled Japan between 1603 and 1868.

Shinjuku city ward boasts the highest density of skyscrapers in the Greater Tokyo Area.

The Tokyo skyline with the eye-catching Tokyo Tower (left, picture center). Shibuya ward in the southwest of the center is a luxury shopping paradise (below).

THE LARGEST METROPOLITAN REGIONS IN EUROPE

Europe's most populous metropolises are located on the very edge of the continent. Due to enormous economic growth the number of inhabitants in the Moscow metropolitan area and in Istanbul climb continuously.

ISTANBUL
Turkey   **15–22 million**

The legendary metropolis at the interface of Asia and Europe is one of the world's rapidly growing megacities. In 1955 the number of inhabitants was still 2.5 million, but today the metropolitan region has far exceeded the 15-million mark. Istanbul acts like a magnet, especially for the people from rural parts of Turkey — 84 percent of the population has moved there from the Anatolian provinces in search of a job and a higher quality of life. For a long time Istanbul was thought of as a Third World metropolis, yet in the course of Turkey's economic liberalization since the 1980s it has developed as one of Europe's most dynamic cities. Almost 30 percent of Turkey's economic output is generated in the boomtown on the Bosporus. Modern technology and service industries are springing up like mushrooms. The historic sights of the 2,600-year-old city attract millions of tourists every year.

MOSCOW
Russia   **10–20 million**

Within the last decade, this, the most populous city in Europe after Istanbul, has developed into one of the most expensive metropolises in the world. It is now considered a shopping paradise for millionaires, attracting customers with its array of luxury shops. Whereas the population of Russia is on the decline overall, the number who live in Moscow grows steadily. The above-average wages lure many people from the impoverished regions of the vast country. The country is registering high economic growth rates; the unemployment rate officially stands at one percent. The vibrant metropolis is not only the political and economic, but also the cultural center of Russia, and it boasts an extremely diverse range of museums and theaters.

The Kremlin is the official residence of the Russian president (right).

LONDON
Great Britain   **10–20 million**

The Greater London Area, created as an administrative unit in 1965, comprises the City of London and 32 other boroughs. Although the number of inhabitants has declined slightly since the end of the 1930s, the metropolitan region is still the most populous one within the European Union. As a trade and finance center London plays an outstanding role in the global economy. In the lists of the most important metropolises in the world compiled by the "Globalization and World Cities Research Network," the capital of the United Kingdom is regularly at No. 2 after New York. In the cultural realm, too, London time and again sets new standards. London's artists and fashion designers are considered especially innovative.

St. Paul's Cathedral and modern bank buildings in the City (right)

The famous Galata Bridge spans the Golden Horn where it flows into the Bosporus. The New Mosque dates from the 17th century (left).

The metropolitan regions of Central Europe may seem rather small in terms of their population in a worldwide comparison, yet they are among the best-performing economic regions of the planet.

ILE-DE-FRANCE (PARIS)

France　　　　10–15 million

The capital of France is the undisputed political, administrative and cultural center of the country and forms the heart of a booming economic region. One-third of the French gross domestic product is generated in the agglomeration around Paris, the Ile-de-France. The most important French enterprises and large international companies are based here; many international organizations have their headquarters in Paris. The metropolis is the world's capital of fashion and in addition acts as an inspiration for cultural developments around the globe. Many artistic revolutions emanated from here and still do so today. Paris has some of the most important museums and theaters in the world. Although the city still attracts people from around the world, the number of inhabitants in its core area has been in decline. Due to the high cost of living many people are drawn to the surrounding countryside.

RHINE–RUHR (COLOGNE, DÜSSELDORF, ESSEN, DORTMUND)

Germany　　　　10–15 million

This urban agglomeration area comprises the entire Ruhr region as well as the Rhine Valley down to Bonn. It is one of Europe's largest metropolitan regions and the most populous region of Germany. Rhine–Ruhr does not have an urban center, but rather consists of a dense accumulation of cities and municipalities that are all linked with each other by a densely woven network of transportation routes. Despite structural changes in the coal and steel industries, which particularly affected the Ruhr area, this region has remained one of the economically most-performing areas of Europe. Around 15 percent of the German gross domestic product is generated here.

Cologne is the largest city in the Rhine–Ruhr metropolitan region (right).

A port of Düsseldorf

RANDSTAD (AMSTERDAM, ROTTERDAM)

Netherlands　　　　6–8 million

This conurbation in the west of the Netherlands extends from Amsterdam in the north to Rotterdam in the south. It also comprises several other cities, which together with the two metropolises form an urban belt around a rural center, the green heart of Randstad. Some 50 percent of all Dutch people live in the region. It is not only one of the most populated metropolitan regions of Europe, but also the economically most powerful after London, Paris, Rhine–Ruhr and Milan. With the Port of Rotterdam it boasts the largest seaport, and with Schiphol Airport in Amsterdam the fourth largest airport on the continent.

Amsterdam has the greatest population density in the Randstad metropolitan region (right).

Notre Dame Cathedral on the Ile de la Cité, built between 1162 and 1345, is one of the landmarks of the French capital.

A coking plant in the Ruhr area, Germany's former industrial heartland

The port city of Rotterdam has many splendid hypermodern buildings.

Thanks to changes in the prevailing political conditions, Madrid, Barcelona, St. Petersburg and Berlin have once more developed as world-class metropolises. Manchester and Liverpool, too, have recovered from economic decline.

MADRID
Spain   **5–10 million**

The largest metropolitan area in southern Europe includes the capital of Spain as well as more than 40 municipalities in its environs. It forms the undisputed cultural and economic center of the country, generating 18 percent of the Spanish gross domestic product. Up to the beginning of the world economic crisis of 2008 it was one of the most dynamic regions within the European Union, but now the real estate crisis has stopped it in its tracks. Nevertheless, Madrid is still a finance center of international standing. The city looks back on a turbulent past and is blessed with magnificent palaces, churches and world-class museums. Although the metropolitan region registers an increase in population, the number of inhabitants in Madrid itself fell below the three million mark during the 1990s, but it has climbed again since the turn of the millennium. The continued economic growth has attracted migrants from all over Latin America.

MANCHESTER-LIVERPOOL
Great Britain   **4–6 million**

Although officially the two largest cities of the "North West England" region are the centers of separate metropolitan areas, they are frequently mentioned in the same breath. Located only 34 miles (54 km) apart from each other, they form an urban agglomeration where the industrial revolution began over 200 years ago. Via the Port of Liverpool, the industrial enterprises of Manchester were supplied with raw materials and the products of the English textile and later of the iron industries were exported around the world. After a period of decline following World War II the region experienced an upswing in the 1990s. It has become an attractive business location and a popular tourist destination.

Top: Salford Quays in Manchester
Bottom: port buildings in Liverpool

BARCELONA
Spain   **4–6 million**

Despite the current crisis the metropolitan region around the Catalan capital is one of the economically best performing in Europe. While Madrid is the financial center of Spain, Barcelona's industrial sector still fulfills an immensely important role in the economic development. Many car manufacturers are based in the region, and the implantation of hi-tech companies is promoted by the state. Barcelona's artists, fashion gurus and industrial designers act as trendsetters for the world. The city of Antoni Gaudi has a reputation as a mecca for young creatives and as the unconventional metropolis of the avant-garde. Barcelona is hip, one of many reasons that make it an attractive destination.

The Port of Barcelona is the largest in the western Mediterranean (right).

The Calle de Alcalá is one of Madrid's many boulevards. The Spanish capital boasts a wealth of magnificent buildings in different architectural styles (left).

ST. PETERSBURG
Russia   4–6 million

The second largest city in Russia after Moscow, St. Petersburg and its environs is an important industrial location and, thanks to its large commercial ports, Russia's gateway to the world. Currently the economy grows by about ten percent each year. Based here are not only the large Russian industrial companies but numerous international enterprises have also opened branches in St. Petersburg. From 1712 to 1918 the metropolis was the capital of the Russian Czar and his empire. The magnificent palaces and churches, extensive parks and squares that were built during that time attract tourists from around the world today. St. Petersburg has the Hermitage, a world-class museum, and a multifaceted theatrical landscape. Today the city features as one of the ten most popular travel destinations on the planet.

Nevsky Prospect, the best-known boulevard in St. Petersburg (left)

BERLIN/BRANDENBURG
Germany   4–6 million

The metropolitan region created in 2006 comprises not only the German capital and its environs but also the entire state of Brandenburg beyond, making it the largest metropolitan region by area within Germany. Whereas the areas of Brandenburg are largely rural in character, Berlin itself is one of the most populous metropolises in Europe. For a long time a divided city, Berlin is known as a center for the arts and sciences. Several universities and numerous research institutes as well as museums, theaters and orchestras of worldwide renown are all based here. The low cost of living attracts artists and young people from around the world. Not least thanks to its vibrant nightlife Berlin has become one of the most popular travel destinations in Europe.

Above: sculptures on the Kurfürstendamm
Below: Potsdamer Platz and the Sony-Center

THE LARGEST METROPOLITAN REGIONS IN ASIA

The metropolitan regions of the Asian emerging economies are still battling with a high population growth. From Seoul, a First World metropolis, however, people are increasingly drawn to the towns in the surrounding countryside.

SEOUL
South Korea   20–25 million

Since the end of the Korean War in 1951 the South Korean capital on the Hangang River has become one of the most populated and economically most dynamic metropolises in the world. Seoul Capital Area has long grown together with the port city of Incheon, situated 17 miles (28 km) farther to the west, and other cities in Gyeonggi Province to become a single urban agglomeration. Every second Korean lives in the metropolitan region, whose cities and municipalities are linked by a tightly woven network of roads and highways as well as a well-developed public transportation system. Seoul is the political, cultural and economic center of South Korea. Around one-fourth of the Korean gross domestic product is generated here. Seoul's cityscape of skyscrapers is an emblem of modern Korea, while many historic sights recall the turbulent history of the country. Seoul boasts a diverse array of cultural sights and events.

MUMBAI
India   15–25 million

The giant metropolis by the Arabian Sea symbolizes the economic upswing of the country like no other city in India. Undoubtedly, the economic heart of the nation beats in Mumbai, the city of millions. All the major Indian stock exchanges and banks as well as countless international companies are based there. Mumbai's movie industry became famous around the world under the name of "Bollywood." The share of tax revenue collected by the metropolitan region stands at 30 percent. Not only are there said to be more multimillionaires living in Mumbai than in Manhattan, but the city also has more slums than any other Indian city. Around 30 percent of the inhabitants still live in the shantytowns extending throughout the area.

At night Mumbai is transformed into a glamorous metropolis (right).

METRO MANILA
Philippines   15–25 million

As well as the Philippine capital, 16 other large and smaller towns belong to the metropolitan region of Metro Manila. Whereas Manila itself, with its currently 1.6 million inhabitants, is only a little larger than Munich, more than 20 million people now live in the entire agglomeration according to estimates by experts, making it one of the most populous in the world. With a recent gross domestic product of 74 billion U.S. dollars, the metropolitan region of Manila has gained itself a place among the top 50 in the PricewaterhouseCoopers ranking of the most prosperous and most-performing urban centers in the world. Only a small upper layer of society benefits from the economic success, however. The majority of the population live in slums.

Makati is one of the 17 cities forming Metro Manila (right).

With about 46,600 inhabitants per square mile (18,000 per sq km) the Korean capital Seoul is one of the most densely populated places in the world (left).

HONG KONG -SHENZHEN
China   **15–25 million**

Although the two sister cities on the Pearl River Delta do not form an administrative unit, they are mostly named together. Shenzhen is separated from Hong Kong only by two small streams and, like the former British crown colony, it too has the status of Special Economic Zone. Both towns profit from being neighbors. The involvement of investors from Hong Kong contributed to the development of a modern and competitive industry in Shenzhen. Not more than 30 years ago the city counted 30,000 inhabitants; today twelve million people live here. Hong Kong and Shenzhen are two of China's economically most-performing metropolises. Experts believe that in the near future both cities will merge with other towns of the region to form one gigantic economic area of 120 million inhabitants.

The financial metropolis of Hong Kong is one of the most expensive cities in the world (left).

JAKARTA
Indonesia   **15–25 million**

The capital of Indonesia, located on the island of Java, is one of the world's most explosively expanding megacities. Despite the government's efforts to stem the influx of people from the rural regions of Indonesia, Jakarta, as the economic center of South-East Asia's most populous country, continues to attract countless refugees from poverty. The metropolis has long grown together into a giant agglomeration with the neighboring cities of Bogor, Tangerang and Behasi. Like other megacities Jakarta fights against the problems of overpopulation. Large parts of the city area have become slums. Health care centers are insufficient and drinking water is often scarce. Due to the high density of traffic, the air pollution is unbearable.

The skyline of modern Jakarta is characterized by skyscrapers (left).

Whereas the number of inhabitants of the towns in the Kansai region shows only an insignificant increase, Shanghai and Delhi have to battle with the enormous growth of their populations.

DELHI
India   **15–25 million**

This metropolitan region, after Mumbai the largest in India, consists of the two communes Delhi and New Delhi. Whereas Delhi can look back to a centuries-old history, New Delhi is a comparatively young city that was systematically laid out by its British colonial rulers at the beginning of the 20th century, becoming the capital of independent India in 1947. Despite all the contrasts, the two towns form a single conurbation that attracts people from all parts of India. Delhi is not only the administrative and political center of the country but also an important industrial location. Although in the course of economic development a rapidly growing middle class is forming, 20 percent of all inhabitants still live in poverty. Like other metropolitan regions in the emerging and developing countries, Delhi too has to battle with fast population increase, an enormous traffic volume and serious environmental issues.

SHANGHAI
China   **15–20 million**

Like no other Chinese metropolis, this port city, located where the Yangtze River flows into the East China Seas, symbolizes the rapid change of the Middle Kingdom from a developing country to one of the most dynamic national economies on the planet. Within only 20 years the metropolitan region has become an economic center of global significance. Important industries, one of the world's most highly capitalized stock exchanges and large financial services providers are based here. The dynamism of the economy is obvious in its brisk construction activity. Futurist skyscrapers shoot out of the ground like mushrooms, changing the face of the city. Despite strict immigration controls the number of inhabitants grows apace.

The new town of Pudong, a symbol of modern Shanghai (right)

KANSAI (OSAKA/KOBE/ KYOTO)
Japan   **15–20 million**

The Kansai (or Kinki) metropolitan region is the most populous and economically most-performing in Japan after Tokyo. The gross domestic product that is generated in the conurbation around Osaka, Kyoto and Kobe every year approximates that of Australia. Although the three cities and their environs have now merged into a single urban agglomeration, each has preserved its distinctive features. The ancient imperial city of Kyoto scores with its rich historic heritage, and Osaka and Kobe are known as modern centers of trade and industry. In 2006 seven prefectures in the area joined forces in a purpose-made league with the intent to coordinate their administration.

Kobe is the site of an internationally important commercial port (right).

The old city of Delhi awaits visitors with its rich historical heritage. The grand mughals, who reigned in India for about three centuries, left behind magnificent mosques and palaces (left).

KOLKATA
India   10–20 million

Many hundreds of towns, municipalities and villages belong to India's most populous metropolitan region after Mumbai and Delhi. Calcutta or Kolkata, the undisputed center

Brücke über den Hugli bei Kolkata.

of this giant agglomeration, was for a long time notorious as the world's "poorhouse." Today, however, the megapolis is considered a boomtown. Even so, one-third of the inhabitants still live in slums, and a large percentage of the population work in the black economy.

DHAKA
Bangladesh   10–20 million

The capital of Bangladesh is one of the uncontrollably growing giant cities in the world. There is probably no other metropolitan region in Asia that has to cope with a similar population explosion. Every year hundreds of thousands of refugees from poverty migrate from the rural areas to the overpopulated capital. Between 1990 and 2005 alone, according to expert estimates, the number of inhabitants rose from 6.5 to 12.5 million. Nobody knows exactly quite how many people live in the metropolitan region today. Between 30 and 40 percent of the population are slum dwellers. The living conditions there stand in sharp contrast to the luxury in the modern business center of Dhaka.

TEHRAN
Iran   **10–20 million**

Iran's capital is by far the largest city in the Middle East, and in a ranking of the most populous megacities in the world it occupies the No. 19 slot. The metropolitan region registers an enormous increase in its population. Although many people had to leave the country in the course of the Islamic Revolution and the Iran–Iraq War between 1980 and 1988, the number of inhabitants in Tehran tripled within the last three decades. Excellent educational facilities and job opportunities led and still lead today to an influx of hundreds of thousands of young Iranians from all parts of the country. Many of these settle in the rapidly growing towns in the surroundings of the capital city.

KARACHI
Pakistan   **10–20 million**

Until the country's independence, the port city on the Arabian Sea was a medium-sized city within the British Empire. After the division of the Subcontinent into Islamic Pakistan and Hindu India in 1947, hundreds of thousands of Muslim refugees settled there, leading to an explosion in the population figures. Karachi developed as one of the most populous metropolises in the South Asian region. Although it is no longer the capital of Pakistan, it is still the country's economic center today.

BEIJING
China   **10–20 million**

In the course of the reforms introduced under Deng Xiaoping at the end of the 1970s, the capital of the People's Republic of China developed into a bustling cosmopolitan city that stands up to comparison with metropolises like New York City or London. Beijing is not only the administrative and political center of a world power, it is also the location for many globally operating enterprises. From the early 1980s, the city limits have been systematically expanded through the incorporation of rural districts. The new districts are laid like rings around the city's center, together forming an administrative unit that is under the direct control of the Chinese government. The Beijing metropolitan area covers an area of about 6,180 sq mls (16,000 sq km) and is densely populated.

Beijing's business center, with the city's tallest building, the "China World Trade Center-Tower." The Chinese capital has transformed itself into a western-style metropolis within the last 20 years.

The three Australian metropolises offer a high quality of life. In a ranking of the best cities to live in they regularly occupy leading positions.

SYDNEY
Australia 4–6 million

Australia's largest city, with just under four million inhabitants, is certainly one of the world's smaller metropolises, but it nevertheless enjoys a phenomenal global standing and is placed on a par with cities like Singapore and Hong Kong by the "Globalization and World Cities Network." The economic heart of the continent beats in Sydney. It is here that 25 percent of the Australian gross domestic product is generated, and that the largest Australian and more than 500 international enterprises have their base. Sydney's museums and theaters enjoy an international reputation. The fast-paced development of the population numbers was caused not least by the large number of immigrants. In 1935 the number of inhabitants in the metropolitan region reached the one million mark, in 1962 there were already two million and by 2006 it had reached four million. Immigrants shaped the face of the city. Sydney is a multicultural metropolis, which is probably what makes it so cosmopolitan.

MELBOURNE
Australia 3–5 million

The capital of the south Australian state of Victoria is the second largest city on the continent. Today around four million people live in the metropolitan region, which is about twice as many as there were as recently as the 1950s. Of Melbourne's inhabitants, 36 percent were born outside Australia, and a sizeable number moved there from other Australian states. Thanks to a comparatively low cost of living and excellent leisure facilities, the quality of life is higher here than elsewhere in Australia. Melbourne was voted the best city in the world to live in most recently in 2011. It is the location of Australia's largest port, an important economic factor and Australia's gateway to the world.

At night Melbourne is transformed into a sea of lights (right).

BRISBANE
Australia 2 million

The capital of Queensland, Brisbane is the third largest city on the continent and the economic heart of northeast Australia. Numerous Australian and international companies have opened branches there. No other city between Sydney in the south and Singapore in the north boasts a comparable economic strength. The beginnings of Brisbane go back to a penal colony founded in 1824. In 1842 the area was ceded for free settlement and in 1859 Brisbane became the capital of the newly founded colony that had separated from the federal state of New South Wales. The present City of Brisbane emerged from the merger of 25 municipalities and shires in 1925. It is the heart of the South East Queensland metropolitan region.

Story Bridge, a famous landmark of Brisbane (right)

Sydney's modern skyline features such world-famous landmarks as the Sydney Harbour Bridge and the Sydney Opera House (left).

THE LARGEST METROPOLITAN REGIONS IN AFRICA

Population numbers in Africa's large metropolitan regions are growing explosively, due to high birthrates and an ever-greater rural exodus, the inevitable consequence of never-ending civil wars.

CAIRO
Egypt   **15–25 million**

The Egyptian capital has a reputation as an urban behemoth, and is often named in the same breath as Mexico City, Delhi and Jakarta and, indeed, Cairo suffers from an enormous growth in population. The high birthrate and an ongoing rural exodus have led to a doubling of the number of inhabitants within just 40 years. Today eight million people live within the limits of the city, which is comparatively small with a surface area of only 83 sq mls (214 sq km); according to estimates by experts the metropolitan region though houses 25 million people. A large number of them live in slums and provisional settlements such as the so-called City of the Dead, or Cairo Necropolis – a vast cemetery with mausoleums dating from all periods of Cairo's Islamic history that has been turned into a residential district. Despite immense social problems, the total gridlock threatening to happen every day and a serious degree of air pollution, Cairo is still a source of great fascination for people from around the world. The

LAGOS
Nigeria   **10–20 million**

The largest metropolitan region of Africa's most populous country grows at a faster pace than any other megacity of this world. In 1960 the number of inhabitants was still clocked at 700,000, yet by the year 2011 it had overstepped the ten million mark. It is expected to have doubled again by 2020. More than half the population live in the slums and shanty towns of Greater Lagos. The bustling modern center of the City extends across three islands in the Gulf of Guinea.

KINSHASA
DR Congo   **8–12 million**

Like many metropolises in the developing country, the capital of the Democratic Republic of the Congo also registers a rapid population growth. In 1960, the year of the Congo's independence, there were only 400,000 people in Kinshasa; today more than nine million live there. Although Kinshasa is the economic center of one of the richest African countries in raw materials, the economy lies in tatters due to the never-ending civil war and rampant corruption.

KHARTOUM
Sudan   **8–12 million**

The capital of the Republic of the Sudan counts only 2.6 million inhabitants, yet according to estimates the population figures in the metropolitan region have jumped to between eight and twelve million in the last few years, making Greater Khartoum one of the most populous agglomerations in Africa. Most people came as refugees from the crises areas in the Chad, Uganda, Darfur or Southern Sudan and quickly settled in the rapidly growing shantytowns outside the City.

JOHANNESBURG
South Africa   **9–12 million**

This metropolis may not be the political and cultural center of South Africa, but it is its economic hub, the skyscrapers of the Business District its emblem. Today nearly four million people live in Johannesburg, and more than nine million in the metropolitan region. The infamous townships were incorporated after the end of Apartheid, but a large part of the black population there still live in impoverished conditions.

Johannesburg is the economic center of South Africa (picture center).

Pyramids of Giza, as well as the more than 1,000-year-old Islamic Cairo with its many mosques and bustling bazaars each year attract millions of tourists. Many of the neoclassical buildings erected during the reign of Ismail Pasha (r. 1863–1879) stand in Downtown Cairo, whereas Modern Cairo boasts towering office blocks and hotels by the Nile.

The opera house inaugurated in 1867 is one of the neoclassical structures built under Ismail Pasha, which earned Cairo the epithet of "Paris on the Nile."

ABIDJAN

Ivory Coast **4–8 million**

The former capital of the Ivory Coast is the second largest city in West Africa after Lagos and an economic center for the entire region, boasting a relatively high density of industrial enterprises. In its center the city is characterized by modern multi-story buildings. The population figure rises at a faster than average rate, not least due to the refugees that poured into the city following the civil war. Whereas not more than 50,000 people lived in Abidjan in 1950, the number is today estimated to be more than four million.

IBADAN

Nigeria **4–8 million**

The capital city of Oyo State in western Nigeria is one of the great economic centers of the country as well as one of the most populous metropolitan regions in Africa. Because of the immense size of the city, which according to official data is said to cover an area of 1,190 sq mls (3,080 sq km), its population density is comparatively low. Ibadan is a university town and a center of trade as well as for the processing of agricultural produce.

ALGIERS

Algeria **5–10 million**

Algeria's capital, steeped in tradition, suffers from great overcrowding. Although many Algerians leave their country as economic migrants, the number of inhabitants in Algiers has risen threefold in the years since the country's independence in 1962. According to estimates, between five and ten million people live in the metropolitan region today. The economic heart of Algeria, people are drawn to the capital as if by a magnet.

Algiers has to cope with a rapidly growing population (left).

CAPE TOWN

South Africa **4–6 million**

South Africa's second largest city, Cape Town is the multicultural flagship of the rainbow nation, and people from different cultures have given the city its distinctive face. Some 20 years after the end of the Apartheid Regime the consequences of racial segregation can still be felt. Today still many black South Africans live in the townships on the city's margins. The agglomeration of Cape Town is one of the economically strongest in Africa.

Thanks to its location Cape Town is one of the most beautiful cities in the world (left).

Although the situation has calmed somewhat, the population of Mexico City grows much faster than that of the large U.S. cities. The metropolis still attracts economic migrants from all parts of Mexico.

MEXICO CITY
Mexico   **20–25 million**

The Mexican capital city regularly occupies a leading slot in the various ranking lists of the largest cities on the planet published by research institutes. The vast metropolis is still generally considered an uncontrollable behemoth that has to battle with a tremendous population explosion and serious environmental problems. In fact, however, the situation has marginally improved in recent years. The rate of increase in population numbers has slowed down, and, thanks to various measures taken by the Mexican government, the still-high air pollution is starting to abate. Although Mexico City is the economic heart of an emerging country and as such a financial and trading center of global importance, a large proportion of the population still live in poverty. First and Third Worlds meet here in the most confined of spaces. Despite the ever-present chaos, Mexico City is a lively metropolis with a diverse art and drama scene.

NEW YORK
USA   **19–25 million**

The metropolitan region comprises New York City and its catchment area. Although the number of inhabitants has not markedly increased in recent years, the giant agglomeration stills counts as one of the most populated in the world. New York City is still the "capital of the world." Not only is the city the most important trade and finance center on the planet as well as the base of the United Nations, but it also time and again sets new standards in the worlds of art, fashion and design. The skyscrapers in Manhattan, the most famous of New York's five city boroughs, became the model for town planners all over the world. Immigrants from nearly 200 nations have made New York a multicultural melting pot.

The sea of skyscrapers in Manhattan in the twilight (right)

LOS ANGELES
USA   **10–20 million**

The largest metropolitan area in the USA after the New York Metropolitan Area, Los Angeles is one of the world's most important urban economic centers. Large industrial groups, innovative IT companies and not least the leading enterprises of the American entertainment industry all have their headquarters there. The region is heavily fragmented. In an area of about 34,750 sq mls (90,000 sq km) are more than 50 cities, municipalities and small villages, all linked with each other by highways. Even Los Angeles, the metropolis of millions, in large tracts resembles a giant urban patchwork consisting of many individual suburbs. People from all nations and cultures call the "City of Angels" their home.

The skyscrapers of the Business District dominate the LA cityscape (right)

The sea of houses in Mexico City extends right up to the horizon (picture left). Liberty column with a Winged Victory on the main avenue, Paseo de la Reforma (picture right).

From Chicago via Toronto to Philadelphia and Boston: North American metropolises advertise themselves with their imposing skylines, which give each city a unique face.

CHICAGO
USA   **10 million**

"Chicagoland," as the agglomeration around the legendary city on the southwest banks of Lake Michigan, counting today some 2.7 million inhabitants, is also known, is one of the 30 largest and economically most-performing metropolitan regions in the world. A major location for industry, globally operating companies such as Motorola and McDonald's have taken up residence here. Well-known companies like Boeing and the largest commodity futures exchange of the USA are based in Chicago itself. Although the number of inhabitants in the city has been dropping since the 1990s, that of the metropolitan region continues to rise. The middle class especially is drawn to the suburbs and municipalities around the city. Chicago's population is multiethnic, made up of immigrants from almost every corner of Earth and their descendants. Despite liberalization, the effects of segregation are still noticeable in habitation trends of neighborhoods.

BALTIMORE–WASHINGTON
USA   **5–8 million**

The Baltimore–Washington Metropolitan Area includes Washington DC, the capital of the United States and its environs, as well as the conglomeration of Baltimore in the federal U.S. state of Maryland. In the statistics of the "Office of Management and Budget" it is listed as the most prosperous region in the United States. The standard of education of the local population also far exceeds that of other regions in the country.

The Capitol in Washington is the seat of the American Congress (right).

SAN FRANCISCO
USA   **4–7 million**

The San Francisco Bay Area is one of the most prosperous in the United States. In the south of the region is Silicon Valley, which has become a worldwide synonym for the digital revolution that started there. Giants of the information age like Apple, Google and Oracle are all based here. San Francisco is the mythical stronghold of the hippies, and the city also boasts a lively art scene.

Skyscrapers characterize the cityscape of downtown San Francisco (right).

DALLAS
USA   **5–10 million**

The Dallas metropolitan area in the northeast of Texas comprises, as well as Dallas, such important industries and enterprise locations as Irving, Plano, and Fort Worth and Arlington. In official statistics it is known as The Metroplex, as opposed to a metropolitan region consisting of several urban centers. Dallas is an economic center of global importance.

The Dallas skyline features many futuristic structures (right).

Chicago's skyscrapers are impressive in their architectural diversity, as can be seen here in the view of the piers and lake promenades on the banks of Lake Michigan.

TORONTO
Canada   **5–10 million**

Together with its environs, this city of millions on the northwest banks of Lake Ontario forms the most populated and at the same time economically most-performing metropolitan region in Canada. The share of Canada's gross domestic product generated in the Greater Toronto Area is around ten percent. Thanks to the business environment, the population grows faster here than anywhere else in the vast country.

Toronto's CN Tower dominates all other buildings in the city (left).

PHILADELPHIA
USA   **6 million**

The metropolitan area around the city of Philadelphia comprises several counties in the Delaware River estuary and is the largest metropolitan region on the United States east coast after the New York Metropolitan Area. American independence was declared in Philadelphia. Today the city is the base for renowned media enterprises and important universities.

Philadelphia, although steeped in tradition, also shines with a modern skyline (left).

BOSTON
USA   **5–8 million**

The region around the historic New England metropolis of Greater Boston is one of the economically most powerful in the United States as well as in the world. Major financial services and insurance companies have their headquarters there. Harvard University and the Massachusetts Institute of Technology in Cambridge are two of the world's best universities. The American Revolution, which led to the founding of the United States of America, began in Boston.

In Boston, too, monotonous multistory buildings determine the cityscape (left).

SÃO PAULO

Brazil **15–25 Million**

The agglomeration around the megalopolis of São Paulo is the most populous metropolitan region in the southern hemisphere and the sixth largest on the planet. Taking into account the cities in its immediate vicinity it is nearly as large as Tokyo. The enlarged Complexo Metropolitano Expandido already counts about 30 million inhabitants, and in the not-too-distant future its cities will have merged into what will probably be the world's largest urban conurbation. The heart of Brazilian industry beats in Greater São Paulo. The region's factories produce cars, textiles and pharmaceutical products and also process agricultural produce. Numerous international companies have opened production plants in Grande São Paulo. São Paulo itself, today a vast urban behemoth with about 11 million inhabitants, has transformed itself into a modern services center that represents the economic upswing in Brazil.

The sea of houses in São Paulo extends right up to the horizon.

The Avenida 9 de Julio in the middle of Buenos Aires is the widest avenue in the world, featuring seven lanes in each direction.

BUENOS AIRES

Argentina   **10–20 million**

The most populous metropolitan area in South America after Greater São Paulo, Greater Buenos Aires extends to the west, east and south far beyond the city limits of Buenos Aires. Whereas the capital of Argentina covers an area of only about 77 sq mls (200 sq km), Gran Buenos Aires now extends across a 1,500 sq mls (3,880 sq km) area that is densely built up and considered worldwide as a cautionary example of extreme housing sprawl. Although in the course of Argentina's economic recovery after its great crash of 2001, Greater Buenos Aires developed as one of the economically most dynamic metropolitan areas on the globe, one-fifth of the population still live in poverty. The economy, which generates around one-fourth of the Argentinean gross domestic product, is still largely industrial. Buenos Aires has always been regarded as the most European of all South American metropolises and is often compared with Paris. In its vibrant center neoclassical palaces and prestigious buildings from the Belle Epoque as well as wide boulevards and avenues from the period between 1880 and 1930 when Argentina experienced an economic boom still determine its distinctive cityscape.

A tightly woven network of highways and expressways traverses São Paulo's sea of houses, with dense traffic coursing along it always. Currently seven million passenger cars are registered in the city, and mile-long traffic jams are an everyday occurrence.

THE LARGEST METROPOLITAN REGIONS
IN SOUTH AMERICA

The expectation of better chances in life still lures many refugees from poverty into the South American metropolises, and outside their city centers the shanty towns expand ever farther. Only few profit from the growing prosperity.

RIO DE JANEIRO
Brazil   10–15 million

The most populous Brazilian metropolitan area after São Paulo, Rio de Janeiro extends over an area of about 1,930 sq mls (5,000 sq km) around Guanabara Bay. As well as the legendary city of millions it also comprises numerous other small and large towns. Greater Rio is the powerhouse of the Brazilian economy and the most important industrial base in the country after São Paulo. Many enterprises in the steel, textile, pharmaceutical and petrochemical industries have their headquarters here. Many international companies also have a presence in Rio de Janeiro, the indisputable center of the region.

Like other giant cities on the planet, this megalopolis also has many faces. The glittering façades of high-rise buildings in the pulsating center attest to the increase in prosperity, while the infamous favelas on the city margins are witnesses to the widespread poverty. Despite its large social problems the myth of the city still attracts millions of visitors each year.

BOGOTÁ
Colombia   7–10 million

Colombia's capital and its environs form an agglomeration that is growing at an uncontrollable rate. The Metropolitan Area of Bogota, the economic and administrative center of Colombia where most of the country's industrial enterprises are based, still attracts economic migrants from the rural parts. Between 2005 and 2010 alone the number of inhabitants rose by 33 percent.

Bogota is located on a high plain in the Andes Mountains, at an altitude of 8,660 feet (2,640 m) (right).

LIMA
Peru   7–10 million

Around one-third of the population of the Andes country live in the Lima Metropolitan Area, which comprises the Peruvian capital and the port city of Callao. For those who dwell in Peru's rural areas, Lima acts like a magnet. Much of Peruvian industry is located in the conurbation around the city, but 50 percent of Lima's inhabitants live in slums.

Lima is located at the end of the western Andes foothills (right).

BELO HORIZONTE
Brazil   5–10 million

The capital of the Brazilian federal state of Minas Gerais, Belo Horizonte is at the heart of the third largest metropolitan area in the country, after São Paulo and Rio de Janeiro. Into the 1990s the enterprises of the metalworking industry dominated the economic life here. Today 85 percent of the gross domestic product is produced in Greater Belo Horizonte's service industries.

Modern Belo Horizonte is a planned city, just like Brasilia (right).

SANTIAGO
Chile   5–10 million

The Santiago Metropolitan Region is one of Chile's 15 administrative districts. Around 40 percent of the Chilean population live there, generating almost half of the Chilean domestic gross product. The economic and cultural center of the region is of course Santiago de Chile. Since the end of the Pinochet dictatorship, the capital of the Andes country has developed as a modern and cosmopolitan metropolis. Despite robust economic growth, the contrast between rich and poor is getting ever greater: 50 percent of the population live in slums.

The view of Rio de Janeiro's glittering sea of houses, with Sugarloaf Mountain in the background, makes it easy almost to forget the city's social problems (left).

SALVADOR DA BAHIA
Brazil **3–5 Mio**

The former capital of the Portuguese colonial empire and the present capital of the Brazilian federal state of Bahia is the country's best-known city after Rio. The historic Old Town, a UNESCO World Cultural Heritage site, and its local culture which is characterized by Afro-Brazilian traditions, each year attract hundreds of thousands of visitors from around the world. Tourism makes a significant contribution to the economic development of the agglomeration.

View from the historic Old Town of Salvador toward the business center (left).

RECIFE
Brazil **3–5 million**

The metropolitan area around the capital of the Brazilian federal state of Pernambuco is an engine in the economic development of northeastern Brazil. Around 80,000 companies are based here. The 90 enterprises of the "Porto Digital," which is part of the IT sector, export their products to the whole world. Despite the economic growth in the area, almost 40 percent of Recife's inhabitants live in shantytowns.

The regional capital Recife is one of Brazil's economic powerhouses (left).

CARACAS
Venezuela **3–6 million**

Venezuela's capital owes its immense population growth to the country's oil wealth. The companies in the oil industry, which emerged in the 1930s, attract hundreds of thousands of people from all over South America wishing to escape poverty and soldiers of fortune from around the world. The city, located in a valley surrounded by mountains of 6,560 feet (2,000 m) height, is growing continually beyond its limits and up the mountain slopes. Large areas are slum-ridden.

Caracas is one of the fastest-growing cities in South America (right).

PORTO ALEGRE
Brazil **3–5 million**

The economic heart of the Brazilian state of Rio Grande do Sul beats in the metropolitan area around its capital region. Not least because of farsighted infrastructure policies the economy grows faster here than in other parts of the country. Greater Porto Alegre is one of the most important trade and industry centers of Brazil. Many companies process the agricultural produce of the region as quality finished products, thus contributing to economic development and prosperity. Social and welfare policies are renowned as exemplary.

CURITIBA
Brazil **3–5 million**

The capital of the southern Brazilian state of Parana is a model for other fast-growing metropolises in the emerging and developing countries. The city fathers of Curitibas have banked on sustainability since the 1970s. Numerous parks and green spaces run through the cityscape. The public transportation system is well developed. The dwellers of the favelas are able to exchange their garbage against foodstuffs or bus tickets and thus participate in the trash removal. The Curitiba Metropolitan Area is one of Brazil's most prosperous region.

URBAN MEGASTRUCTURES

For a good 100 years, America, with its cities Chicago and New York, was the global center of multistory architecture. The classic example is the Empire State Building in New York, which as early as 1931 reached a height of 1,250 feet (381 m) and held on to its record for more than 40 years. Subsequent record-holders were the World Trade Center in New York and the Willis Tower in Chicago. Since then, the competition for the "biggest one" has relocated to Asia where entire skyscraper cities have popped up in the booming metropolises like Hong Kong, Shanghai and Dubai and where the current record-holder, the Burj Khalifa, stands in Dubai with a height of 2,720 feet (828 m).

The elevation figures are based on the structural height, that is, spires are counted as part of the building's structure (even if they only serve to "artificially" increase the height of the building), but radio antennae are not counted.

THE MOST IMPRESSIVE SKYLINES IN THE WORLD

Cities with the greatest number of buildings taller than 656 feet (200 m)

❶	Dubai	109
❷	Hong Kong	87
❸	Shanghai	75
❹	New York City	68
❺	Chicago	49
❻	Tokyo	21

THE TALLEST SKYSCRAPERS IN THE WORLD
(structural height)

❶	Burj Khalifa, Dubai	828 m
❷	Makkah Clock Royal Tower Hotel, Mecca	601 m
❸	Taipei 101	508 m
❹	Shanghai World Financial Center	492 m
❺	International Commerce Centre, Hong Kong	484 m
❻	Petronas Towers, Kuala Lumpur	452 m
❼	Greenland Square Zifeng Tower, Nanjing	450 m
❽	Willis Tower, Chicago	442 m
❾	Kingkey 100, Shenzhen	442 m
❿	Guangzhou International Finance Center	438 m
⓫	Trump International Hotel & Tower, Chicago	423 m
⓬	Jin Mao Tower, Shanghai	421 m

SKYLINES AND SKYSCRAPERS

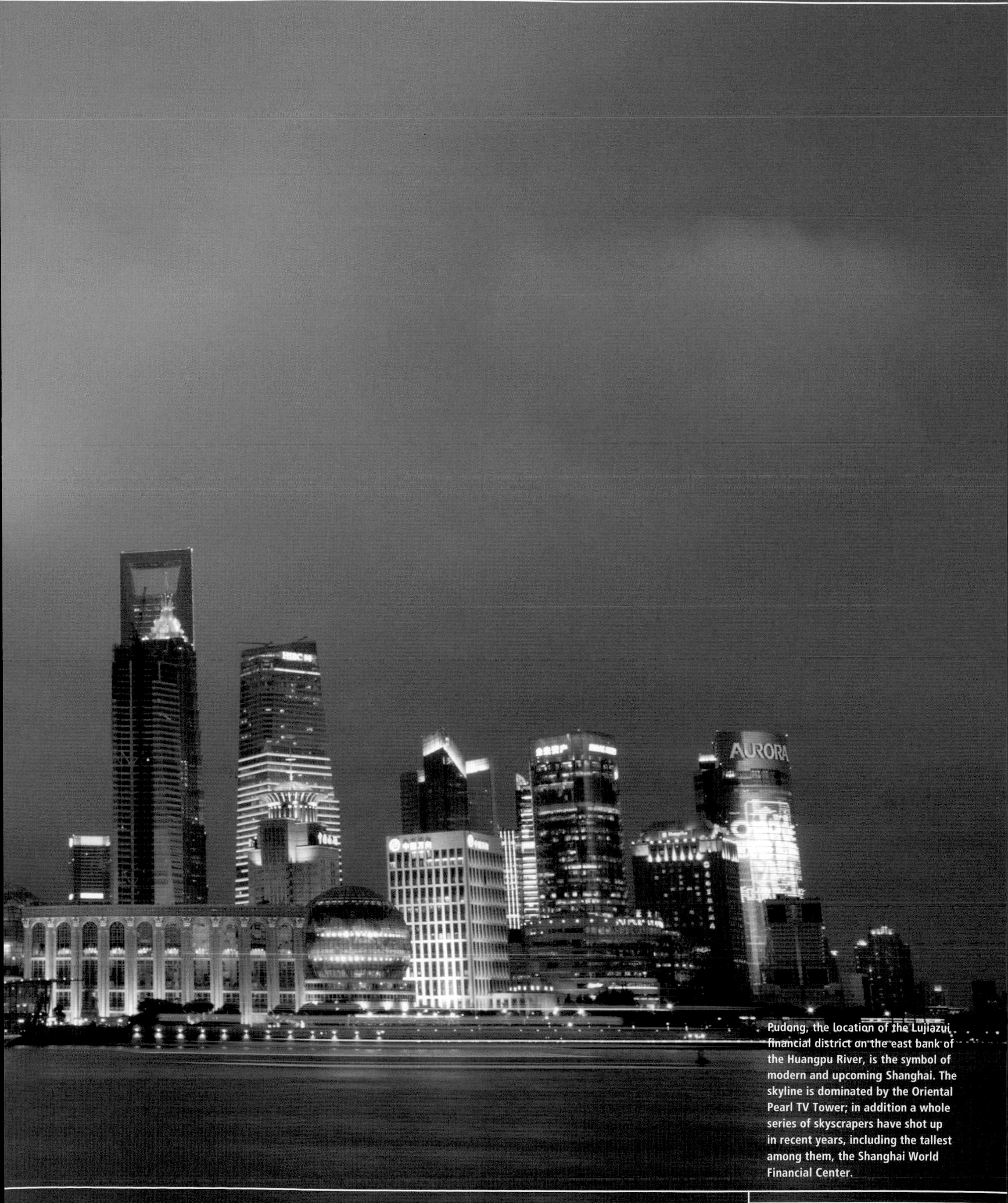

Pudong, the location of the Lujiazui financial district on the east bank of the Huangpu River, is the symbol of modern and upcoming Shanghai. The skyline is dominated by the Oriental Pearl TV Tower; in addition a whole series of skyscrapers have shot up in recent years, including the tallest among them, the Shanghai World Financial Center.

Dubai, the capital of the eponymous emirate in the UAE, is one of the fastest growing metropolises as well as the world's skyscraper capital.

Today more than 400 skyscrapers stand in Dubai City — a skyscraper generally being defined as a building that reaches more than 330 feet (100 m) in height. And soon there will be very many more of them. Most importantly, however, the world's tallest building, the Burj Khalifa, was completed in Dubai in 2010. At a height of 2,720 feet (828 m) it is also by far the tallest structure in the world, clearly rising above even the tallest TV towers and masts.

The first major skyscraper project in Dubai was the Burj Al-Arab. At its inauguration in 1999, this building, at a height of 1,053 feet (321 m), was the tallest high-rise building in the city, and until 2007 it also remained the tallest hotel in the world. It eventually had to cede this title to the Rose Tower (1,093 feet/333 m), also in Dubai, but the Burj Al-Arab nevertheless became Dubai's landmark thanks to its remarkable architecture: the elegant building stands on an artificial island and is shaped like a giant sail.

There are today many more tall buildings under construction in Dubai — including more than ten projects

that are set to rise more than 984 feet (300 m) into the sky — for example the Pentominium, designed as the world's tallest residential building with a height of 1,693 feet (516 m). Due to the financial crisis, which seriously affected the real estate market in Dubai, work on this as well as other skyscrapers has been put on hold for the time being.

Two different views of the skyline of Dubai City: on the left, the perspective from the Dubai Creek, with the Burj Khalifa on the left-hand edge of the picture, below a view of the parade of skyscrapers along Sheikh Zayed Road.

More than 2,300 skyscrapers stand in Hong Kong, all of them over 328 feet (100 m) tall. This makes Hong Kong the city with the greatest number of skyscrapers in the world. Fifteen of its multi-story buildings are more than 820 feet (250 m) tall.

The era of skyscrapers in Hong Kong began in 1935 with the completion of the 230 foot (70 m) tall headquarters of the Hong Kong & Shanghai Bank. Because of the confined space and the high cost of land in the city, the buildings shot upward into ever-greater heights. Hong Kong experienced its first skyscraper boom in the 1980s, when numerous smaller multi-story buildings were erected. It was only with the construction of the new Hong Kong International Airport in 1998 that further building restrictions were lifted, and this led to a new wave of tall building construction in the early 21st century, creating the current total of around 100 skyscrapers taller than 656 feet (200 m).

View of the Hong Kong skyline with the Two International Finance Centre skyscraper dominating the entire scene on the right in the picture

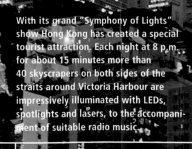

With its grand "Symphony of Lights" show Hong Kong has created a special tourist attraction. Each night at 8 p.m. for about 15 minutes more than 40 skyscrapers on both sides of the straits around Victoria Harbour are impressively illuminated with LEDs, spotlights and lasers, to the accompaniment of suitable radio music.

In total Shanghai has more than 400 skyscrapers, with most of these built after about 1990 in the new city district of Pudong. This is also the site of the Shanghai World Financial Center towers, at a height of 1,614 feet (492 m) the tallest building in the People's Republic of China. In its immediate vicinity stand the Jin Mao Tower (1,381 feet/421 m) and the Oriental Pearl Tower (223 feet/68 m). Currently, the Shanghai Tower is under construction in Pudong, which at a height of 2,073 feet (632 m) will be the tallest skyscraper in China. Its completion is planned for 2014.

The nighttime cityscape of Shanghai along the Bund waterfront area

View of the new area of Pudong on the east bank of the Huangpu River, with its many skyscrapers. The three tallest buildings can be clearly made out in the skyline (from left to right): Oriental Pearl Tower (1,535 feet/468 m), Jin Mao Tower (1,381 feet/421 m) and Shanghai World Financial Center (1,614 feet /492 m).

NEW YORK

At the end of the 19th century New York and Chicago were the first cities where skyscrapers were built. The preconditions for these architectural feats were the invention of the safety elevator, which prevented a sudden fall of the cab, and developments in steel construction which facilitated lightweight design and as such the erection of taller buildings. In 1894 the Manhattan Life Building (348 feet/106 m) was built, the first building of a height greater than 328 feet (100 m). With the completion of the Empire State Building (1,453 feet/443 m) in 1931 and the onset of the world Great Depression, the construction boom that had brought about such distinctive skyscrapers as the Chrysler Building (1,047 feet/319 m) in Manhattan ended. Taller structures were not built again until the late 1960s, for example the two towers of the World Trade Center (1,362/415 and 1,368 feet/417 m).

View of the sea of skyscrapers in Manhattan, New York. On the far left the outline of the Empire State Building, in the center of the picture the magnificent Chrysler Building, one of the most beautiful skyscrapers ever built, with its cleverly illuminated stainless steel Art Deco spire.

Manhattan's skyline, with the Empire State Building in the center of the picture and the Bank of America Tower (with a sloped roof) to its right

Chicago boasts more than 300 skyscrapers of more than 328 foot (100 m) height, with six of these reaching a height of over 984 feet (300 m). The metropolis on Lake Michigan is, together with New York, the birthplace of the construction of multistory buildings, and at the end of the 19th century the Chicago School emerged. Its proponents created the first skyscrapers, for example the pioneering Home Insurance Building of 1885. No longer in existence today, it had ten stories and was 138 feet (42 m) tall. Most of the skyscrapers are concentrated in the Chicago Loop community area in Downtown Chicago. The tallest skyscraper in the city and in the United States is the 1,450 foot (442 m) tall Willis Tower of 1974 (known as Sears Tower until 2009), once the tallest building in the world; the second tallest is the Trump International Hotel and Tower completed in 2009 (1,388 feet/423 m).

For a long time, the center of skyscraper construction was — along with New York — in Chicago. The multistory buildings in the city on Lake Michigan were among the tallest in the world right up to the end of the 20th century; they included, for example, the trapezoid John Hancock Building (bottom picture, left background) and the Willis Tower (top picture, far left).

TOKYO

Tokyo features more than 550 skyscrapers that are over 328 feet (100 m) tall. The tallest among these, however, is "only" 814 feet (248 m) tall: it is Tokyo Midtown, a complex of buildings, completed in 2007, in the Minato Ward of Tokyo. The Tokyo Midtown center comprises a total of six buildings with a maximum of 54 stories, built on a floor area of only 17 acres (7 ha).

The entire ensemble is considered one of the most successful tower complexes in city planning terms anywhere in the world, comparable with the Rockefeller Center in New York City. The city's second tallest skyscraper is the Tokyo Metropolitan Government Building (797 feet/243 m), the third tallest the NTT Docomo Yoyogi Building (787 feet/240 m), with its antenna (892 feet/272 m).

The history of skyscraper building in Tokyo does not date back as far as in Chicago or New York. Until the year 1963, the maximum building height was legally restricted to only 102 feet (31 m). It was forbidden to build any taller structures because of the dangers of earthquakes. In 1968 — after the annulment of the buildings restrictions — the Ka-sumigaseki Building (512 feet/156 m) was erected,

Tokyo's first skyscraper.

Taller still, however, are the TV towers in Tokyo: the Tokyo Sky Tree (2,080 feet/634 m), completed in 2012, is the second tallest structure and the tallest TV tower in the world, and the Tokyo Tower (1,093 feet/333 m), which remained the tallest TV tower in the world for several years after its construction in 1958.

The Shinjuku District boasts the greatest concentration of skyscrapers in the Japanese capital.

View of the Tokyo skyline at night. In the foreground the Rainbow Bridge, on the right next to the bridge pier the Tokyo Tower, a tourist attraction and a symbol of reconstruction in Japan after the end of World War II. It was modeled on the Eiffel Tower in Paris and is frequently used as a film set.

BURJ KHALIFA

The Burj Khalifa — known as the Burj Dubai up to the day of its inauguration — has been the tallest structure in the world since April 2008, that is just under two years before its completion, and it is also the tallest used for residential purposes. It exceeds every other tower in the world and also boasts the most stories of any building in the world (189). Construction was begun in 2004, in January 2009 a building height of 2,717 feet (828 m) was reached (the overall height comes to 2,723 feet/830 m when the signaling system is included), and one year later, on January 4, 2010, the ceremonial opening took place.

View from the entrance to the top

The stories of the Burj Khalifa are accessed by a total of 57 elevators and eight moving walkways. Two twin elevators take visitors up to the observation deck on the 124th floor, at 1,483 feet/452 m height. With a speed of 33 ft/sec = 22 mph (10 m/sec = 36 km/h) they are the fastest twin elevators in the world. In addition, the building has an elevator stop at the highest altitude anywhere in the world (2,093 feet/638 m). A total of 2,909 steps lead from the ground floor up to the 160th floor, at a height of 1,969 feet (600 m). The Burj was built as a reinforced concrete structure up to this height, whereas the remaining part of the central tower (more than 656 feet/200 m height) is a steel frame construction.

Where once there was an expanse of desert, today the Burj Khalifa rises in the middle of Dubai like the giant steeple of a gothic cathedral. On a clear day the tip of its tower can be seen from a distance of more than 62 miles (100 km). The exact height of the skyscraper as well as the total number of its floors was kept secret until its inauguration in January 2010.

The Burj Khalifa towering above all else in Downtown Dubai. On the right in the picture the main shopping street, the Sheikh Zayed Road

In terms of the height of its tallest buildings, Europe cannot keep up with Asia or North America. Among the world's 200 tallest skyscrapers only just over ten that reach a maximum height of more than 984 feet (300 m) are located in Europe. In recent years, Moscow has become Europe's skyscraper metropolis, with one high-rise tower after another springing up in the Moscow City district. In Germany only Frankfurt has a respectable skyline to offer — Messe Tower and Commerzbank Tower were the tallest buildings in Europe for a while, from 1991 to 1997 and 1997 to 2003 respectively.

THE TALLEST SKYSCRAPERS IN EUROPE

1. Mercury City Tower, Moscow
   1,089 ft (332 m)
2. Shard London Bridge, London
   1,017 ft (310 m)
3. Capital City Moscow Tower, Moscow
   991 ft (302 m)
4. Naberezhnaya Tower, Moscow
   879 ft (268 m)
5. Triumph Palace, Moscow
   866 ft (264 m)
6. Commerzbank Tower, Frankfurt
   850 ft (259 m)
7. Capital City St. Petersburg Tower, Moscow
   843 ft (257 m)
8. Messe Tower, Frankfurt
   843 ft (257 m)

Moscow is Europe's new skyscraper city. The panoramic shot shows old and new skyscrapers: the "Seven Sisters" and the Moscow International Business Center.

MERCURY CITY TOWER
Moscow   1,089 ft (332 m)

The Mercury City Tower in Moscow's skyscraper district, the Moscow International Business Center, also known as Moscow City, was completed in 2012. At 1,089 feet (332 m) high it is currently the tallest skyscraper in Europe. It is distinguished from its neighboring towers by its copper-red glass façade and rectangular-trapezoidal borders with tapering tops — the latter borrowing its style from Russian constructivism.

The copper-red glass front of the Mercury City Tower

NABEREZHNAYA TOWER C

Moscow 879 ft (268 m)

From 2007 to 2010 this 59-story office tower was the tallest building in Europe. It forms part of a complex of three buildings, which in addition comprises Tower A with 17 stories (279 feet/85 m) and Tower B with 27 stories (417 feet/127 m). Tower C, together with the two Capital City skyscrapers, is one of the skyscrapers that characterize the skyline of Moscow City.

CAPITAL CITY MOSCOW TOWER

Moscow 1,017 ft (302 m)

In 2010 the Capital City Moscow Tower, comprising 76 stories, replaced the Naberezhnaya Tower in its immediate vicinity as the tallest building in Europe. The high-rise building was at the same time the first structure on the continent to have reached a height of more than 984 feet (300 m). The skyscraper is a part of the Capital City complex of buildings, which also includes a slightly smaller office building, the Capital City St. Petersburg Tower (843 feet/257 m).

Capital City Moscow Tower (center)

TRIUMPH PALACE

Moscow 866 ft (264 m)

Competed in 2005, this skyscraper has 54 stories and is used exclusively as a residential building. With the construction of its spire in December 2003 it replaced the Commerzbank Tower in Frankfurt as Europe's tallest multistory building. Today, however, the Triumph Palace has only held on to the record of being Europe's tallest residential building. In its architectural style it is modeled on the monumental structures of the so-called "Seven Sisters" dating from the 1950s, and colloquially it is therefore also known as the "eighth sister."

The Triumph Palace, a structure in the "old Moscow style"

At a height of 1,017 feet (310 m) and 95 stories, the London multistory office tower known as the Shard London Bridge was for a short time in 2012 the tallest building in Europe (before being overtaken by the Mercury City Tower in Moscow). Built to the plans of Renzo

Shard London Bridge by the Thames

One of London's new landmarks since 2012: the Shard London Bridge skyscraper

Piano and completed in 2012, the tower is tapered sharply toward the top, creating associations with a glass splinter — hence the name. The building has 44 elevators, and a roofed plaza gives direct access to London Bridge station. A mixed use is desired; alongside a well-known

business consultancy company, which occupies a large part of the usable floor space, the building is planned to house a five-star hotel, restaurants, shops and luxury apartments. On the 73rd floor, at a height of 725 feet (221 m), there is a public viewing platform, from

which great views can be enjoyed thanks to about 602,780 sq ft (56,000 sq m) of specially coated glass walls. Above the viewing platform, from a height of 761 feet (232 m) onward, there are only technical installations, which are not accessible to the public.

The Shard: an elegant pyramidal skyscraper whose shape, however, was also associated by its name givers with broken glass. Likely no taller building will be constructed in London in the near future — the aviation authority, during the course of discussions about the building of this skyscraper, set the point at which the air space begins at 1,000 feet (305 m). The Shard measures 1,016 feet (just under 310 m).

THE TALLEST SKYSCRAPERS IN EUROPE

SAPPHIRE OF ISTANBUL

Istanbul   856 ft (261 m)

With its 66 stories, this skyscraper is currently (2012) the tallest building in Turkey. The complex houses luxury apartments as well as, at a height of 535 feet (163 m), a golf practice area with views of the Bosporus. Completed in 2011, the Sapphire of Istanbul is the first ecologically constructed skyscraper in Turkey, which is equipped with the most up to date energy-saving technology. Its special double-façade construction is supposed to bring an energy saving of at least 30 to 35 percent. In addition, a vertical garden was created on every third floor in order to improve air quality and protect from noise.

COMMERZBANK TOWER

Frankfurt   850 ft (259 m)

With its antenna the Commerzbank Tower attains an overall height of 984 feet (300 m), which means that it was the tallest building in Europe from 1997 to 2003. Just

The skyline of Frankfurt: Commerzbank Tower (center), Messe Tower (right)

under 20,950 short tons (19,000 tonnes) of steel were used to erect the 65-story building — about twice as much as for the Eiffel Tower. The design is by star architect Sir Norman Foster.

MESSE TOWER

Frankfurt   843 ft (257 m)

At the time of its completion in 1991, the office block was the tallest building in Europe. The pyramid-shaped tip alone, which makes the skyscraper look like a pencil, is 121 feet (37 m) high. Architecturally the design of the Messe Tower is oriented on the American Art Deco style of the 1930s skyscrapers, such as the Chrysler Building.

CAPITAL CITY ST. PETERSBURG TOWER

Moscow   843 ft (257 m)

This office tower forms a part of the Capital City complex of buildings, which also comprises the almost 164 feet (50 m) taller Capital City Moscow Tower. With a total of 65 stories and an overall height of 843 feet (257 m), the St. Petersburg Tower is nevertheless one of Europe's tallest skyscrapers. Its two towers, both in their names and in their distinctive, not continuously smooth façade, are meant to represent Russia's two main cities, St. Petersburg and Moscow, as a unit.

TORRE CAJA MADRID

Madrid   820 ft (250 m)

The 45-story office tower was
originally built as a part of the
Cuatro Torres Business Area,
which consists of four separate
skyscrapers. However, while still
under construction it was taken
over by the Spanish savings bank,
Caja Madrid — hence the name.
The skyscraper was completed
at the end of 2008. It is currently
the tallest building in Spain and
also one of the tallest in Europe.

The four towers of the Cuatro Torres
Business Area

TORRE DE CRISTAL

Madrid   817 ft (249 m)

The 52-story "Crystal Tower"
was built as a component part of
the Cuatro Torres Business Area
complex, just like the Torre Caja.
It is only marginally smaller than
the latter and as such currently
Spain's second tallest building.
Its name is derived from the
virtually continuous glass façade.
In addition, the Crystal Tower
has a very unusual shape: its
base is a rectangle, but higher
up the structure is transformed
into a hexagon via trapezoid and
tetrahedron-shaped sides.

The Commerzbank Tower in Frankfurt —
here seen in a panoramic view of the city
on the Main River — houses the headquarters of the Commerzbank, with its board
rooms on the 49th story. Thanks to the
high-quality architectural design as well
as innovative and sustainable construction
methods, the skyscraper was given the
Frankfurt "Green Building Award" in 2009.

THE TALLEST SKYSCRAPERS IN ASIA

MAKKAH CLOCK ROYAL TOWER
Mecca, Saudi Arabia
1,972 ft (601 m)

Since reaching its final height of 1,972 feet (601 m) in July 2011, this 120-story skyscraper has been the second tallest building in Asia and in the world. Architecturally the main tower of the Abraj Al-Bait Towers is reminiscent of the Big Ben clock tower in London. It is crowned by a long spire and a crescent, which can be walked on. In addition, the tower boasts the highest viewing platform in the world, at 1,831 feet (558 m) height. In the summer of 2010 a giant tower clock was installed, the largest of its kind in the world. The clock faces are 141 feet (43 m) long around the edge, the minute hands are 75 feet (23 m) long and 11 feet (3.5 m) wide.

The compact complex of buildings has more than 10,764,000 sq ft (1 million sq m) of floor space and was constructed to house as many Muslim pilgrims as possible visiting the holy sites of Mecca — more than 30,000 people are said to be accommodated in the hotels belonging to the complex.

Tradition and modernity in Mecca

A giant clock tower with a view of Mecca: the Abraj Al-Bait Towers skyscraper complex

The Taipei 101 skyscraper needs to be able to withstand enormous stresses for Taiwan is one of the most active earthquake regions in the world. Its supporting structure therefore functions in a way similar to a bamboo cane. In addition, a steel sphere 18 feet (5.5 m) in diameter and weighing 728 short tons (660 tonnes) is suspended between the 88th and the 92nd floor to counteract any movements in the structure by acting as a tuned mass damper.

TAIPEI 101

Taipei, Taiwan   1,670 ft (509 m)

From 2004 the Taipei 101 was the tallest building in the world, but in early 2008 it was superseded by the growing construction of the Burj Khalifa in Dubai (which was however not officially recognized as the new record-holder until its inauguration on January 4, 2010). At a height of 1,667 feet (508 m)

the Taipei 101 — so-named after its 101 stories — clearly rises above the city's skyline. As it is used exclusively as an office building, the Taipei 101 is, for the time being, the tallest office tower in the world. It also boasts the fastest elevators in the world — visitors are catapulted up to the 89th floor at a speed of 55 ft/sec (16.8 m/sec) or 37 mph (60 km/h).

The stepped glass front façade of the Taipei 101 tower

SHANGHAI WORLD FINANCIAL CENTER

Shanghai, China   1,614 ft (492 m)

The currently tallest building in the People's Republic of China as well as the fourth tallest in the world was opened on August 28, 2008. The sightseeing platform of this 101-story skyscraper is at a height of 1,555 feet (474 m) and thus the second highest in the world. The Sky Walk is a 180 foot (55 m) long corridor with a transparent glass floor.

Despite its asymmetric shape featuring concave and convex façades, the walls, structure and mechanical components of the building were designed as a modular system that repeats after 13 stories. Thanks to the simplified production and assembly of the structural elements and other components, the construction time was shorter and structural inefficiency was reduced.

Shanghai World Financial Center, surrounded by other skyscrapers in Pudong

The most distinctive feature of this tower is an about 164 foot (50 m) wide "portal" in the upper part of the structure, a structural masterstroke that is meant to reduce the enormous wind load on the top of the building. Colloquially the skyscraper is known as the "bottler opener," in reference to its unusual shape.

THE TALLEST SKYSCRAPERS IN ASIA

The International Commerce Centre — just like the Shanghai World Financial Center — was designed by the renowned international architectural practice of Kohn Pedersen Fox Associates, who specialize in high-rise buildings.

INTERNATIONAL COMMERCE CENTRE
Hong Kong, China   1,588 ft (484 m)

Built in the years 2002 to 2010 after a lengthy planning phase, the International Commerce Centre in Hong Kong with its 108 stories is the tallest building in the city, surpassing the previous local record-holder, the

Two International Finance Centre, which measured only 1,352 feet (412 m). Currently the fifth tallest building in the world, it also has the highest indoor swimming pool on the 116th floor as well as the highest hotel in the world on its top 15 stories. At a height of 1,270 feet (387 m) there is also a viewing platform, the highest in Hong Kong.

The skyscraper is clad almost in its entirety with a blue-shimmering glass façade. The load-bearing components of the external walls are predominantly made from steel, the massive inner core around the central service duct however is made from reinforced concrete. Guests are taken to the desired floor by one of 83 elevators.

PETRONAS TOWERS
Kuala Lumpur, Malaysia
1,483 ft (452 m)

Thanks to their structural height (1,483 feet/452 m, including the towers' spire) the two office towers in the Malaysian capital were considered the tallest building in the world from 1998 up to the completion of the Taipei 101 skyscraper in 2004 (1,667 feet/508 m). However, this classification was somewhat controversial because the roof was (1,240 feet/378 m) lower than that of rival skyscrapers (for example the Willis Tower, 1,450 feet/442 m).

The two towers are linked by a steel bridge, the Skybridge, at a height of 564 feet (172 m). It is 190 feet (58 m) long and weighs about 827 short tons (750 tonnes). The Skybridge rests on giant spherical bearings so that its vibrations would not damage the towers designed by the Argentinean architect César Pelli. It is the highest walkable connection between buildings in the world.

Petronas Towers and urban greenery …

… and the As Syakirin Mosque

GREENLAND SQUARE ZIFENG TOWER
Nanjing, China   1,476 ft (450 m)

Built to a design by Skidmore, Owings and Merrill, the skyscraper, which is also known as Nanjing Greenland Financial Center, has a

Nanjing's skyline, with the Greenland Square Zifeng Tower

height of 1,476 feet (450 m) (with the spire; height to the roof: 266 feet/81 m) and 89 stories, making it the third tallest building in China. There is a public observatory on the 72nd floor, at 889 feet (271 m) height.

KINGKEY 100

Shenzhen, China   1,450 ft (442 m)

With exactly 100 stories and a height of 1,450 feet (442 m), the Kingkey 100 tower has been the tallest building in Shenzhen and the fourth tallest in the People's Republic of China since its inauguration in 2011. The skyscraper houses numerous company offices and a hotel. On the topmost usable floor there is a restaurant and the Sky Garden (1,250 feet/381 m) — a publicly accessible viewing area over city and region.

Kingkey 100 tower in Shenzhen

GUANGZHOU WEST TOWER

Guangzhou, China   1,437 ft (438 m)

At a roof height of 1,437 feet (438 m) and boasting 103 stories, this skyscraper, which is also known as the Guangzhou International Finance

Guangzhou West Tower.

Center, is the tallest building in the 10-million-inhabitant metropolis (better known as Canton). The building was completed in 2009 and houses offices as well as a luxury hotel.

JIN MAO TOWER
Shanghai, China   1,381 ft (421 m)

From 1998 to 2008 the Jin Mao Tower was the tallest skyscraper in China, then it was surpassed by the Shanghai World Financial Center. The outer shape of this 88-story

Front façade of the Jin Mao Tower

tower building was inspired by traditional Chinese design, with the stepped façade, for example, modeled on a pagoda or a bamboo stalk. Responsible for the design was Adrian Smith, the architect of the Burj Khalifa.

A luxury hotel with the world's largest atrium is based in the top 38 floors of the Jin Mao Tower, which is tapered towards its top like a pagoda. The atrium extends from the 53rd to the 87th floor, measures 499 feet (152 m) in overall height and has a diameter of 89 feet (27 m). Additionally the hotel boasts the longest laundry chute in the world, reaching from the 52nd floor down into the basement.

THE TALLEST SKYSCRAPERS
IN ASIA

TWO INTERNATIONAL FINANCE CENTRE
Hong Kong, China   1,352 ft (412 m)

After three years of construction the 86-story office block (1,352 feet/412 m) was completed in 2003. Until 2010 it remained the tallest building in Hong Kong. From October to November 2003 the

Two International Finance Centre.

outside wall of the cigar-shaped tapered skyscraper carried a roughly 755 foot (230 m) tall advertising poster, stretching across some 50 stories. This was the hitherto largest advertising area displayed on a skyscraper.

PRINCESS TOWER
Dubai, United Arab Emirates
1,358 ft (414 m)

In 2012 the imposing parade of skyscrapers along Jumeirah Beach at the eastern end of Dubai Marina had a further tower added to its number. Although at a height of 1,358 feet (414 m) the

The Princess Tower with its domed top

Princess Tower is only half as tall as the Burj Khalifa, it is however the tallest residential building in the world.

AL HAMRA TOWER
Kuwait City, Kuwait   1,352 ft (412 m)

This elegant 77-story skyscraper is currently the tallest building in Kuwait. It was designed by the famous architectural office of Skidmore, Owings and Merrill from Chicago. Its façade features a twisted shape, finishing with a sloping roof structure. Completed in 2011 the tower building houses mainly offices as well as a restaurant with panoramic views.

The eye-catcher in the skyline of Kuwait City: the spectacular Al Hamra Tower

The Two International Finance Centre, which here dominates the skyline of Hong Kong, could be admired even before its inauguration in movies and on TV: in the film "Lara Croft: Tomb Raider," Angelina Jolie and her partner parachute from the still-unfinished top floor.

THE TALLEST SKYSCRAPERS IN AUSTRALIA

Australia is the home of the tallest skyscrapers south of the Equator, including some of the tallest purely residential buildings anywhere.

Q 1
Gold Coast   **1,060 ft (323 m)**

The Q1 Tower (Queensland Number One Tower), boasting an overall height of 1,060 feet (323 m), was opened on the Gold Coast in 2005. The 78-story tower is located in the Surfers Paradise district of Gold Coast City and is the tallest building in the southern hemisphere. In addition it also ranks among the top ten residential towers in the world. The tower was named in homage to Australia's eponymous Olympic rowing team of the 1920s.

On floors 77 and 78 there is an observation platform (755 feet/230 m), from which views of the entire Gold Coast can be enjoyed. A second viewpoint is an outside terrace located at a height of 590 feet (180 m). The building also features the Sky Garden, a miniature tropical rainforest extending from the 60th to the 70th floor. The tower's steel spire, one of the tallest in the world at a height of almost 322 feet (98 m), was installed on the 76th floor at a height of 738 feet (225 m) and rises 154 feet (47 m) above the actual roof.

EUREKA TOWER
Melbourne   **974 ft (297 m)**

Completed in 2006 the Eureka Tower is the tallest building in Melbourne and the second tallest in Australia. At 935 feet (285 m) height there is a public observation deck on the 88th floor known as Skydeck 88. Inside the building a further platform, the Edge, projects about 10 feet (3 m) horizontally out from the building and has frosted glass panes that become transparent at the press of a button.

Dominating all other buildings in Melbourne: the Eureka Tower (top)

120 COLLINS STREET
Melbourne   **866 ft (264 m)**

This skyscraper, in Melbourne's Collins Street — hence the name — was Australia's tallest building at a height of 866 feet (264 m) including the antenna (height to the roof: 722 feet/ 220 m) from its completion in 1991 to 2005. Today it still holds the record as "Australia's tallest office building." Of the 52 stories, the lower 50 are office levels where the headquarters of international companies are based. With its gray granite façade, buttresses and central mast it is somewhat reminiscent of the Empire State Building in New York.

101 COLLINS STREET
Melbourne   **853 ft (260 m)**

Melbourne's second skyscraper that has only its address as the name reaches an overall height of 853 feet (260 m); the roof height is 640 feet (195 m). On the roof of the multistory office tower that was completed in 1991 are seven communications platforms as well as a 213 feet (65 m) tall twin antennae. From 1991 until 2005 it was Australia's second tallest building. On all four sides glass lobbies protrude from the granite façades, which recede in a stepped fashion towards the top and are optically continued by the antennae structure on the roof.

RIALTO TOWERS
Melbourne   **823 ft (251 m)**

The Rialto Towers skyscraper complex — also known as Rialto Center — comprises 63 stories, and no fewer than 36 elevators are available to transport visitors to the desired floor level. The fully reflective glass façade of the office tower, constructed between 1982 and 1986, changes color depending on the daylight, ranging from deep blue to glistening gold. For a while the more than 1,200 steps to the top were the location of the Rialto Run-up stair race.

Right: the Rialto Towers skyscraper complex in Melbourne

Left: The Q1 Tower (on the right edge of the picture) is the most conspicuous skyscraper in the Surfers Paradise skyline of the Gold Coast in the federal state of Queensland, not only thanks to its size but also because its shape recalls that of a torch.

CENTRAL PARK
Perth   817 ft (249 m)

The 817 feet (249 m) tall skyscraper (including antenna; roof height: 741 feet/226 m) has 51 stories and is the tallest building in the West Australian city of Perth. Constructed from 1988 to 1992, the skyscraper stands out among the other tall buildings in Perth thanks to its interesting architectural design: a square central tower is flanked up to the half and three-quarter height respectively by two side wing additions that are triangular on plan.

Top: skyline of Perth with the local record-holder, the Central Park

CHIFLEY TOWER
Sydney   800 ft (244 m)

The second tallest skyscraper in Sydney after the Citigroup Centre, this tower has 53 stories and boasts a height of 800 feet (244 m) including antenna. Inaugurated in 1992, the building is mostly used as office space. In the upper part of the tower a steel pendulum weighing about 440 short tons (400 tonnes) is meant to counteract any movement caused by storms or earthquakes. In the entrance lobby stands a larger-than-life statue of Ben Chifley, the former Australian prime minister (1945–1949) after whom the building was named.

CARLTON CENTRE
Johannesburg, South Africa
732 ft (223 m)

After its completion in 1973, the Carlton Centre, at a height of 732 feet (223 m), was for a few years the tallest building in the southern hemisphere. Today it is still the tallest skyscraper in Africa and after the two telecoms towers Telkom Joburg Tower (883 feet/269 m) and Sentech Tower (778 feet/237 m), which also stand in Johannesburg, it is South Africa's third tallest structure. The viewing platform on the 50th story, the Top of Africa, provides superb panoramic views over the city of Johannesburg. Today the Carlton Centre houses the headquarters of South African Railways. The lower levels feature a shopping center with more than 180 individual stores and an ice rink.

PONTE CITY
Johannesburg, South Africa
568 ft (173 m)

The Ponte City skyscraper — once known as the Strydom Tower — is located in the Hillbrow neighborhood of Johannesburg. The 568 feet (173 m) tall residential tower has 54 stories and was built in 1975; it is currently the tallest purely residential building in Africa. The building is shaped like a cylinder and has an open interior space extending across all the stories and providing the apartments with additional daylight. The high-rise building was once a ritzy address thanks to the magnificent panoramic views of Johannesburg, but Hillbrow is now considered a problem neighborhood.

The Ponte City skyscraper with the Hillbrow Tower

The Carlton Centre complex of buildings (in the picture the tall building on the left) was once the home of the famous Carlton Hotel. Before its closure in 1997 it was a popular film set during the 1970s, and successful movies like "Flatfoot in Africa" with Bud Spencer in the lead were shot there.

WILLIS TOWER
Chicago, USA   1,450 ft (442 m)

America's tallest skyscraper is the 108-story Willis Tower, built between 1970 and 1974 and until 1998 the tallest building in the world. At the time it was still known under its earlier name of Sears Tower, but in 2009 the building was renamed Willis Tower. From the Skydeck viewing platform at a height of 1,352 feet (412 m) it is possible to see for up to 50 miles (80 km) across Lake Michigan on a clear day. Two elevators take visitors up to the platform within

Chicago's landmark skyscraper: the Willis Tower

45 seconds; they are among the fastest in the world.

The skyscraper has a distinctive shape — it consists of nine cuboid blocks, which end at different heights. Up to the 50th floor at 656 feet (200 m) height, the nine individual cubes form one large single block, but two of them end there, at opposite corners. At the level of the 66th floor (886 feet/270 m) two more corner blocks finish so that the building has a cruciform plan from there up to the 90th floor at 1,214 feet (370 m); in the upper stories it then takes on a rectangular shape.

The evening skyline of Chicago with the Willis Tower, crowned by two antennae

The Willis Tower (in the background right) has dominated the Chicago skyline for 40 years with its distinctive shape and the antennae soaring up to a height of 1,729 feet (527 m). The skyscraper has a glass façade but its load-bearing elements are almost exclusively made from steel.

TRUMP INTERNATIONAL HOTEL AND TOWER

Chicago, USA   1,388 ft (423 m)

The Trump Tower is a 98-story skyscraper in Chicago. Completed in 2009, it is currently the second tallest

Trump Tower and neighboring buildings

building in North America. The tower belongs to the well-known entrepreneur Donald Trump, who runs the five-star hotel inside the tower. The skyscraper is tapered toward the top via several recesses in the building; the terraces these create are available as open spaces to hotel guests.

An impressive view of the Trump Tower unfolds from the Chicago River. The roof of the building is at a height of 1,171 feet (357 m). A 217 foot (66 m) tall spire was installed on the roof, thereby giving the tower a structural height of 1,388 feet (423 m). At night the spire is illuminated by a colorful light show.

EMPIRE STATE BUILDING

New York City, USA 1,250 ft (381 m)

The Empire State Building is probably the best-known skyscraper in the world. For 40 years, from its completion in 1931 until 1972, it was also

The tallest tower in Midtown Manhattan

the world's tallest building. The Empire State Building's design has to be classed as somewhere between Art Deco and Modernism. The elegant shape of the high-rise tower was also influenced by the building code of the day, which prescribed that buildings had to be tapered towards the top so that they would not throw too large a shadow on adjacent structures.

THE TALLEST SKYSCRAPERS IN NORTH AMERICA

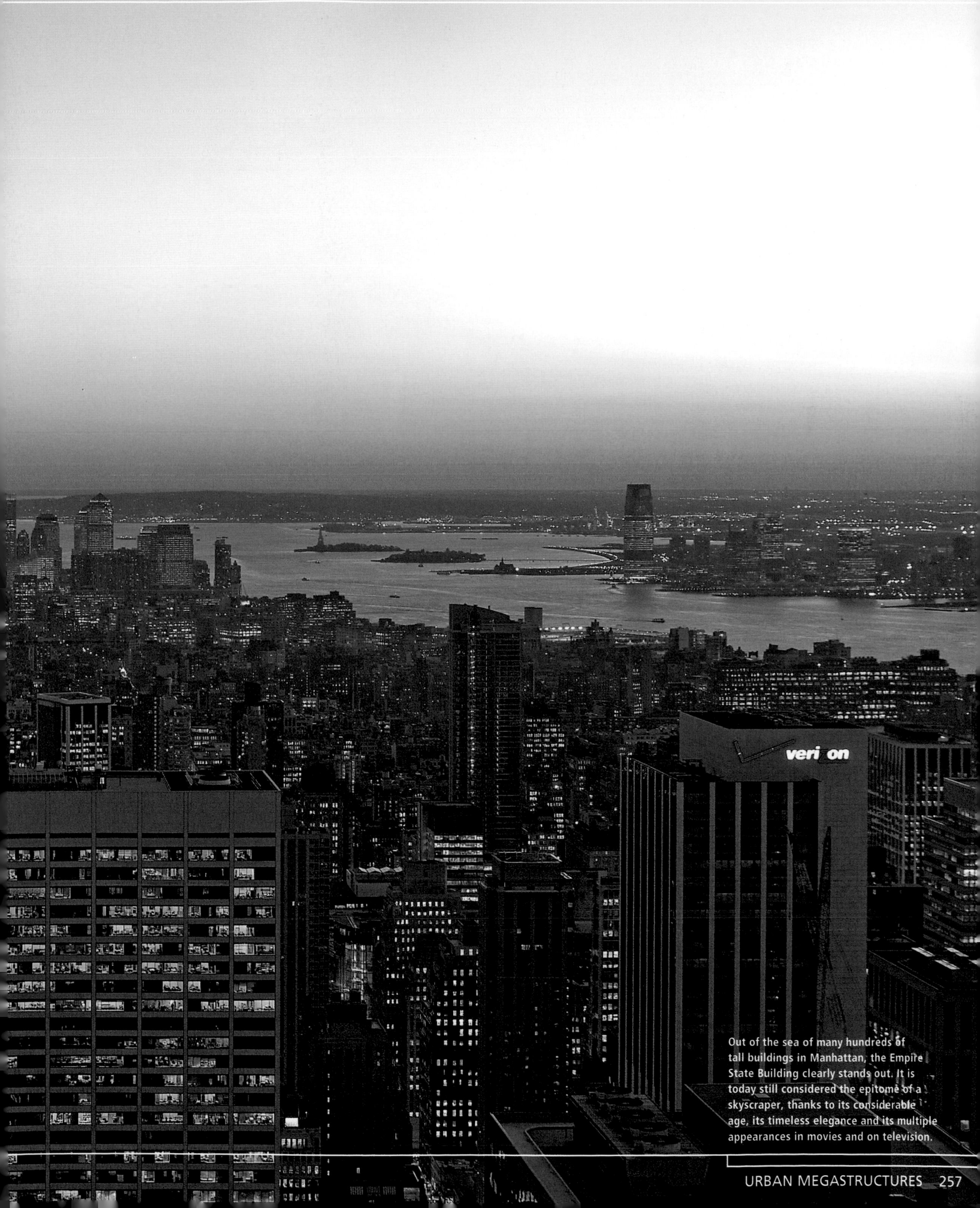

Out of the sea of many hundreds of tall buildings in Manhattan, the Empire State Building clearly stands out. It is today still considered the epitome of a skyscraper, thanks to its considerable age, its timeless elegance and its multiple appearances in movies and on television.

WORLD TRADE CENTER
New York City, USA
1,362/1,368 ft (415/417 m)

The World Trade Center (WTC) was a complex at the southern tip of Manhattan consisting of seven tower buildings. In the public perception

The twin towers up to 2001

The attack on September 11, 2001

Ground Zero after 9/11

the 110-story twin towers dominated. Opened in 1973, they were the tallest buildings in New York for almost 30 years, with structural heights of 1,368 feet (417 m) for the North Tower, including antenna 1,726 feet (526 m) and 1,362 feet (415 m) for the South Tower. The North Tower was for a while also the tallest building in the world. On September 11, 2001, during a terror attack, two commercial aircraft were flown into the towers and caused the buildings to collapse. Almost 3,000 people died, and the "War on Terror" as well as the wars in Iraq and Afghanistan ensued as a consequence of the attack.

On the site of Ground Zero a new complex of buildings is being constructed that, along with the National Memorial for the casualties of the terror attack, is set to comprise six new tower buildings. The centerpiece is to be the new One World Trade Center (under construction).

The One World Trade Center, here implanted into the Manhattan skyline in a simulation

ONE WORLD TRADE CENTER
New York City, USA
1,776 ft (541 m)

The One World Trade Center, which until 2009 operated under the name of Freedom Tower, is being built on Ground Zero, at exactly the site where the first World Trade Center had stood until it was destroyed by a terror attack on September 11, 2001. At its completion in 2013 the 1,776 foot (541 m) tall skyscraper will be America's tallest building.
The One World Trade Center was conceived by David Childs of the renowned architectural practice of Skidmore, Owings and Merrill (SOM), who had already realized other grand projects such as the Willis Tower and the Burj Khalifa. It was modeled on a design by Daniel Libeskind, who won the architectural competition in 2002; however, his plans were greatly changed, in particular the design of the tower's steeple was rejected, which was to recall the arm of the Statue of Liberty. The design of the structural shell was also modified. What remained unchanged, however, was the height of the building: 1,776 foot (541 m), a reference to the date of the United States' Declaration of Independence in 1776.

Statue of Liberty and One World Trade Center

The United States of America was the first center of skyscraper building, especially the cities of Chicago and New York. Until the end of the 20th century the tallest buildings in the world stood in these two cities.

BANK OF AMERICA
New York City, USA   1,200 ft (366 m)

Completed in 2009, this office tower in the New York borough of Manhattan belongs to the Bank of America, after which it is named. The 55-story skyscraper measures 945 feet (288 m) to its roof, and with the spire it reaches a structural height of 1,200 feet (366 m).

The skyscraper features a very unusual shape: the side walls are conceived with right angles in the lower part that transform themselves toward the top into triangular and trapezoid shapes, with "kinks" in the façade. Some of the slanted curtain walls rise beyond the actual roofline of the building, creating the impression of a building that is not rectangular on plan. The tower's spire is illuminated in changing colors at night.

In 2010 the skyscraper was awarded a prize for ecological skyscrapers, with the use of environment-friendly building materials being especially highly rated.

AON CENTER
Chicago, USA   1,135 ft (346 m)

This skyscraper is named after the Aon Corporation, which has its headquarters in the building. Completed in 1973 the office tower boasts a total of 83 stories. After its completion it was for a short time the tallest building in Chicago.

For just under 20 years the building was clad in Carrara marble. However, between 1990 and 1992 the elegant façade had to be renewed with white granite panels because of weather-induced damage.

JOHN HANCOCK CENTER
Chicago, USA   1,129 ft (344 m)

This skyscraper, counting 100 stories, was constructed from 1965 until 1969. At its completion it was the second highest building in the world after the Empire State Building. Characteristics of the iconic skyscraper are the X-bracings of the steel skeleton that are visible in the façade, its tapering trapezoid shape and the dark aluminum façade. The John Hancock Center is used mainly as a residential tower.

CHRYSLER BUILDING
New York City, USA   1,046 ft (319 m)

At its completion in 1930 the Chrysler Building was the tallest building in the world, with a height of 1,047 feet (319 m), yet as soon as 1931 it was overtaken by the Empire State Building; it remained the world's second tallest building until the inauguration of the 1,129 foot (344 m) high John Hancock Center in 1969. The skyscraper is a classic Art Deco building and considered one of the most beautiful towers ever built. Its distinctive roof structure is still a major landmark in the Manhattan skyline today.

Aon Center, Chicago

John Hancock Center, Chicago

New York Times Building

Left: The Bank of America Tower in New York stands out from the surrounding skyscrapers not only because of its height but also thanks to its distinctive triangular and trapezoid façades.

Bank of America Plaza, Atlanta

U.S. Bank Tower, Los Angeles

NEW YORK TIMES BUILDING
New York City, USA   1,047 ft (319 m)

This Manhattan skyscraper was completed in 2007. The 52-story building is currently the third tallest in New York, sharing this rank with the Chrysler Building. However, the tower only measures 745 feet (227 m) up to the roof, and a spire was installed on the roof that is part of its structure and allows the office block to reach the official height of 1,047 feet (319 m). The New York Times Company, publishers of the daily newspaper *The New York Times*, has its headquarters in the building.

BANK OF AMERICA PLAZA
Atlanta, USA   1,040 ft (317 m)

The 55-story skyscraper in central Atlanta was built between 1991 and 1993. It belongs to the Bank of America and is the tallest building in the United States outside the skyscraper cities of Chicago and New York.

The tower's architecture is a postmodern interpretation of the Art Deco buildings of the previous century. With its gilded spire it references the Chrysler Building in New York.

U.S. BANK TOWER
Los Angeles, USA   1,017 ft (310 m)

This 73-floor skyscraper is the tallest building on the west coast of the United States. Although it was built as early as the years 1987 to 1989, it still looks impressive in the Los Angeles cityscape. Particular attention was paid to the skyscraper's earthquake protection because the Los Angeles region is frequently afflicted by earthquakes — it was built to withstand a quake up to 8.3 on the Richter scale. On its roof is the highest helicopter pad situated on top of a building.

The Art Deco crown is what gives the Chrysler Building such a striking and unforgettable appearance in the Manhattan skyline. Made from stainless steel, the eye-catching roof construction measures 184 feet (56 m) tall but weighs a mere 33 short tons (30 tonnes) — it is a purely decorative building component.

PANAMA CITY —
THE TALLEST SKYLINE IN CENTRAL AMERICA

Panama City is the town with the greatest number of skyscrapers in Central America. Currently there are about 20 completed tower buildings with a height of 656 feet (200 m) or more, and of the ten tallest buildings in Central America several stand in Panama City.

Until the early 1990s all the skyscrapers in Panama City had fewer than 30 stories, but at the beginning of the new millennium a building boom began that was only slightly slowed down by the financial crisis of 2008. In 2012 the city already had about 150 skyscrapers under construction, and more tall buildings are planned.

Currently the tallest of the skyscrapers in Panama City is the Trump Ocean Club International Hotel, which was inaugurated in 2011. The tower has 70 stories and attains a height of 961 feet (293 m); in one part of the building is a luxury hotel, the remainder has apartments. Also a part of the complex of buildings are a casino, a spa, a conference center as well as a yachting marina. The outer shape of the tower is modeled on a sail.

Other tall buildings in Panama City include the residential tower The Point (873 feet/266 m), the office building Tower Financial Center (837 feet/255 m) and the apartment block Ocean Two (807 feet/246 m).

**THE TALLEST
SKYSCRAPERS
IN CENTRAL AMERICA**
(all in Panama City)

1. **Trump Ocean Club International Hotel & Tower**
   961 ft (293 m)
2. **The Point**
   873 ft (266 m)
3. **Tower Financial Center**
   837 ft (255 m)
4. **Ocean Two**
   807 ft (246 m)
5. **Pearl Tower**
   794 ft (242 m)
6. **Revolution Tower**
   764 ft (233 m)
7. **Torre Waters**
   761 ft (232 m)
8. **Megapolis Torre 1**
   755 ft (230 m)

Slightly twisted: the Revolution Tower

Large picture and left: the skyline of Panama City in the Punta Pacifica area of the Paitilla business district is characterized by a whole series of skyscrapers. In 2005 the tallest building was still just 577 feet (176 m) high but with the emergence of Panama as a financial center there were already around 20 skyscrapers here by the year 2012.

THE TALLEST SKYSCRAPERS IN SOUTH AMERICA

South America's "rascacielos" (as the skyscrapers are known in Spanish) are concentrated in only a few countries: Venezuela, Colombia and Chile. However, only three buildings surpass a height of 656 feet (200 m): the twin towers of the Parque Central Torres Oeste y Este (Central Park East and West Towers), built in 1979 and 1983 respectively, in Venezuela's capital city of Caracas (both with 56 stories each, 738 feet/225 m) and the record-holder for all of Latin America since its completion in 2012, the Gran Torre Santiago in the Chilean capital (70 stories, 984 feet/300 m). Just below the 656 feet (200 m) mark are the Torre Titanium La Portada (640 feet/195 m) in Santiago de Chile, the Torre Colpatria (630 feet/192 m) and the Centro de Comercio Internacional (623 feet/190 m) in Bogota as well as the Torre de Cali (600 feet/183 m) in Cali.

THE TALLEST SKYSCRAPERS IN SOUTH AMERICA

❶ **Gran Torre Santiago**
Santiago de Chile
984 ft (300 m)

❷ **Parque Central Torre Oeste,**
Caracas, Venezuela
738 ft (225 m)

❸ **Parque Central Torre Este**
Caracas, Venezuela
738 ft (225 m)

❹ **Torre Titanium La Portada**
Santiago de Chile
640 ft (195 m)

❺ **Torre Colpatria**
Bogota, Colombia
630 ft (192 m)

❻ **Centro de Comercio Internacional**
Bogota, Colombia
623 ft (190 m)

❼ **Torre de Cali**
Cali, Columbia
600 ft (183 m)

The skyline of Santiago de Chile, with the World Trade Center in the Las Condes district. Since 2012 the tallest building in South America has also stood in the Chilean capital, the Gran Torre Santiago.

GRAN TORRE SANTIAGO

Santiago de Chile   **984 ft (300 m)**

The Gran Torre Santiago (also called Gran Torre Costanera) with its 70 stories has been the tallest building in Latin America since 2012. Originally the skyscraper's completion date had been set for 2010, but the financial crisis in 2008 led to a lengthy interruption in the construction. The office tower was designed by César Pelli, who was also responsible for the Petronas Towers in Kuala Lumpur. Openly accessible viewing platforms on the two top levels provide superb views of the city and its environs.

Torre Colpatria, Bogota

Torre Titanium La Portada, Santiago

PUERTO MADERO — THE TALLEST SKYSCRAPERS IN ARGENTINA

Most of Argentina's skyscrapers are to be found in the capital Buenos Aires. The tallest among them also feature near the top of the continental ranking lists. The national record-holder since 2012, with 51 stories and a height of 564 feet (172 m), is the apartment tower Torre Renoir 2, which is located in the Puerto Madero port area, just like the twin residential towers of Torre El Faro I and II (each with 46 stories and a height of 558 feet/170 m). More than ten skyscrapers boasting a height of over 459 feet (140 m) form the port district's impressive skyline.

Parque Central Torre Oeste, Caracas

"Rascacielos" (skyscrapers) standing at attention in the Puerto Madero of Buenos Aires

MAKKAH CLOCK ROYAL TOWER HOTEL

Mecca   1,972 ft (601 m)

The Abraj Al-Bait Towers hotel compound in Mecca comprises seven skyscrapers. The 1,972 foot (601 m) tall main tower, Makkah Clock Royal Tower, with its distinctive crescent moon, leaves all the other towers of 787 to 853 feet (240 to 260 m) far behind in height.

The giant tower clock high above Mecca

ROSE RAYHAAN

Dubai   1,093 ft (333 m)

This hotel tower, opened in 2010, has 72 stories and is the third tallest hotel in the world. Its unconventional roof construction resembles the Art Deco top of the Chrysler Building. With its spire the building attains a height of 1,093 feet (333 m).

Hotel Rose Rayhaan in the Rose Tower

BURJ AL-ARAB

Dubai   1,093 ft (333 m)

The hotel skyscraper opened in 1999 on an artificial island in Dubai City off the coast. It is not only one of the tallest but also one of the most luxurious hotels in the world. New architectural standards were set in the hotel's construction: shaped like a sail it has become a landmark of the

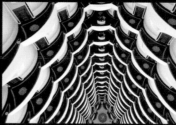

The atrium of the Burj Al-Arab

The most select materials were used to build the Burj Al-Arab

metropolis on the Persian Gulf. 459,090 cu ft (13,000 cu m) of Carrara marble was used in the building, and at a height of 689 feet (210 m) it has a helicopter pad with the hotel's own helicopter.

Built in Dubai City from 2006 to 2012, this complex of buildings located in the immediate vicinity of the Burj Khalifa comprises two 77-story twin towers. At the time of their completion they were the second tallest hotel building in the world.

JUMEIRAH EMIRATES TOWERS

Dubai   1,014 ft (309 m)

The Emirates Towers are twin towers that form an architectural unit. The slightly smaller tower houses the Jumeirah Emirates Towers Hotel on 54 levels.

Jumeirah Emirates twin towers

THE TALLEST HOTELS IN THE WORLD

❶ **Makkah Clock Royal Tower,** Mecca, Saudi Arabia
1,972 ft (601 m)

❷ **Emirates Park Towers,** Dubai, United Arab Emirates
1,165 ft (355 m)

❸ **Rose Rayhaan,** Dubai
1,093 ft (333 m)

❹ **Burj Al-Arab,** Dubai
1,053 ft (321 m)

❺ **Jumeirah Emirates Towers,** Dubai
1,014 ft (309 m)

❻ **Baiyoke Tower II,** Dubai
997 ft (304 m)

❼ **Hotel JAL Tower,** Dubai
883 ft (269 m)

❽ **Lan Kou Grand Hyatt Hotel,** Chongqing, China
846 ft (258 m)

On an artificial island off the coast of Dubai City stands the Burj Al-Arab Hotel (Tower of the Arabs). In the picture the circular platform of the helicopter pad can easily be made out (on the right of the building) as well as (on the left) the cantilevered panoramic restaurant at a height of about 656 feet (200 m).

THE LARGEST HOTELS
IN THE WORLD

Of the ten largest hotels in the world — when counting the number of their rooms — more than half stand in Las Vegas. The American desert metropolis with its themed mega-hotels and gaming casinos now has competition from Asia where, for example in Malaysia, Thailand and China, ever more gigantic hotel complexes are being created. Generally, these are hotel resorts with large shopping malls, gaming casinos, fitness spas and adjoining theme parks.

Lobby of the Venetian Hotel, Las Vegas

THE VENETIAN & THE PALAZZO
Las Vegas, USA   7,128 rooms

Since the opening in 2007 of its sister hotel, the "Palazzo," the "Venetian" has been the largest hotel complex in the world, with a total of 7,128 hotel rooms. The hotel, which also comprises almost 20 restaurants and a multitude of shops, is located on the Las Vegas Strip, the main stretch of road on which the premier casinos and hotels in Las Vegas are found. The "Venetian" is a so-called themed hotel: its specialty is the architectural reproduction of the sights of Venice such as the Rialto Bridge, the Campanile, St. Mark's Square and various canals with gondolas.

THE LARGEST HOTELS IN THE WORLD
(number of rooms)

1. Venetian & Palazzo Hotel, Las Vegas, USA — 7128
2. MGM Grand Hotel, Las Vegas, USA — 6853
3. First World Hotel, Genting, Malaysia — 6118
4. Sands Cotai Central, Macao, China — 6000
5. Wynn Las Vegas, Las Vegas, USA — 4750
6. The Luxor Hotel, Las Vegas, USA — 4408
7. Ambassador City Jomtien, Pattaya, Thailand — 4210
8. Excalibur Hotel, Las Vegas, USA — 4008
9. Aria Resort & Casino, Las Vegas, USA — 4004
10. Hotel Bellagio, Las Vegas, USA — 3933

MGM GRAND
Las Vegas, USA   6,853 rooms

The MGM Grand Hotel complex with all its annexes counts a total of 6,853 hotel rooms, making it the world's second largest hotel. As well as a casino covering an area of about 172,220 sq ft (16,000 sq m), the hotel also has the MGM Grand Garden Arena with a seating capacity of more than 15,000, a famous venue of boxing matches. The hotel is named after the Metro-Goldwyn-Mayer studio in Hollywood (casino and studio belong to the same majority shareholder), and this is also why the casino lobby is adorned by a valuable bronze lion — after the MGM lion logo. The ceremonial inauguration in 1993 also had a movie theme ("The Wizard of Oz").

FIRST WORLD HOTEL
Genting Highlands, Malaysia   6,118 rooms

The third largest hotel in the world is located a good 30 miles (50 km) outside the Malaysian capital of Kuala Lumpur, on a 5,900 foot (1,800 m) high mountain plateau. Featuring a colorful exterior it is incorporated into a large theme park (Genting Highlands) that boasts five further hotel complexes. The hotel rooms are in two towers with 28 stories each. Also in the grounds are a casino, various restaurants, shopping malls, indoor theme parks for adults and for children featuring an amazing free fall ride.

SANDS COTAI CENTRAL
Macao, China   6,000 rooms

The former Portuguese colony Macao is famous for its gaming casinos, luxury hotels and megaresorts. Today Macao is a special administrative region in the People's Republic of China, like Hong Kong, which lies about 30 miles (50 km) to its east. Visitors are attracted by casinos, shopping centers and luxury hotels with their shows on the so-called Cotai Strip, the reclaimed land between the offshore islands of Coloane and Taipa. In 2012 yet another luxury hotel compound was opened in Macao: the Sands Cotai Central. In this new hotel group, three separate hotels boast a total of 6,000 rooms, making the complex the fourth largest in the world. In addition it boasts about 20 restaurants, plus shopping malls with expensive shops and designer boutiques as well as two casinos.

With its reproductions of the Campanile, the Rialto Bridge and canals it may look a little like Venice, but is in fact a hotel with casinos and various other entertainment facilities in the desert state of Nevada: the Venetian in Las Vegas, the largest hotel in the world with more than 7,000 rooms.

A city resort is a hotel complex, whose facilities go way beyond those of a mere lodging operation. In a city resort, the resort guests usually also have at their disposal shopping malls, extensive fitness and spa facilities, gaming casinos, meeting and conference centers, golf courses, marinas and even entire resort theme parks. City resorts thus reflect the all-inclusive services that have become ever more popular since the 1990s. A guest finds all the leisure facilities on-site and therefore will not have to leave the resort.

The casino hotels of Las Vegas could also be classified as city resorts. For most of them, however, the lodging aspect predominates, and so they were listed as hotels in this volume. Only a very few, where the resort aspect plays a major role, are included below as city resorts. The world's largest city resorts (by floor space) are to be found in the Asian region and the Middle East, including the record-holder, which opened in Mecca in Saudi Arabia in 2012.

THE LARGEST CITY RESORTS IN THE WORLD
(floor space in sq ft/sq m)

1. Abraj Al-Bait Towers, Mecca, Saudi Arabia
   16,146,000 sq ft (1,500,000 sq m)
2. Central World, Bangkok, Thailand
   11,022,000 sq ft (1,024,000 sq m)
3. The Venetian Macao, Macao, China
   10,549,000 sq ft (980,000 sq m)
4. Berjaya Times Square, Kuala Lumpur, Malaysia
   7,535,000 sq ft (700,000 sq m)
5. Central Park, Jakarta, Indonesia
   7,050,000 sq ft (655,000 sq m)
6. The Palazzo, Las Vegas, USA
   6,943,000 sq ft (645,000 sq m)
7. Grand Indonesia, Jakarta, Indonesia
   6,889,000 sq ft (640,000 sq m)
8. Marina Bay Sands, Singapore
   6,254,000 sq ft (581,000 sq m)
9. Renaissance Center, Detroit, USA
   5,543,000 sq ft (515,000 sq m)

ABRAJ AL-BAIT TOWERS
Mecca, Saudi Arabia
16,146,000 sq ft (1,500,000 sq m)

With a floor space of a around 16.1 million sq ft (1.5 million sq m) the Abraj Al-Bait Towers group of buildings is the largest city resort in the world. The Makkah Clock Royal Tower five-star hotel based in the 1,972 foot (601 m) tall main tower of the hotel complex has 858 hotel rooms on offer. A vast prayer hall is said to accommodate up to 10,000 faithful.

CENTRAL WORLD
Bangkok, Thailand
11,022,000 sq ft (1,024,000 sq m)

Central World with Christmas lights

Central World Plaza Shopping Center

With a total floor space of more than 11 million sq ft (1 million sq m) this city resort ranks second in size in the world. The shopping mall alone, boasting a retail area of 5,920,000 sq ft (550,000 sq m), is one of the largest on the planet. The Centara Grand Hotel with its 565 hotel rooms is based in a 770 foot (235 m) tall skyscraper, offering fantastic views of the Thai capital.

THE VENETIAN MACAO
Macao, China
10,549,000 sq ft (980,000 sq m)

The lobby of the Venetian Macao

This resort hotel and casino was built from 2004 to 2007 and modeled on its namesake in Las Vegas. By floor space it is the third largest city resort in the world. The complex of buildings is dominated by the 738 foot (225 m) high hotel wing with 39 stories and a total of 3,000 hotel suites.

BERJAYA TIMES SQUARE
Kuala Lumpur, Malaysia
7,535,000 sq ft (700,000 sq m)

Berjaya Times Square Shopping Mall

This group of buildings is home to a vast shopping mall with more than 1,000 shops, the largest indoor theme park in Asia, an IMAX cinema, various restaurants and the Berjaya Times Square Hotel & Convention Center, which is based in the two 666 foot (203 m) tall multistory towers and features 900 luxurious hotel suites and conference rooms.

CENTRAL PARK JAKARTA
Jakarta, Indonesia
7,050,000 sq ft (655,000 sq m)

This complex of buildings in Jakarta has on offer a shopping mall with 2,024,000 sq ft (188,000 sq m) retail space, three apartment condominiums with 56 levels each, a 42-story office tower, a hotel with over 300 luxurious rooms, spa and fitness center as well as meeting rooms — plus parking for 6,000 vehicles.

THE PALAZZO
Las Vegas, USA
6,943,000 sq ft (645,000 sq m)

The Palazzo Resort Casino, Las Vegas

Built between 2004 and 2007 this city resort is part of the Venetian casino hotel. It offers a total of 3,068 luxurious hotel rooms and a casino with a total area of about 107,640 sq ft (10,000 sq m). In addition, the hotel is the tallest building in Las Vegas, with 53 levels and a height of 643 feet (196 m).

GRAND INDONESIA
Jakarta, Indonesia
6,889,000 sq ft (640,000 sq m)

This city resort comprises the Shopping Town mall with 1,399,000 sq ft (130,000 sq m)

Grand Indonesia Shopping Mall

retail space, a five-star hotel, and two skyscrapers of more than over 50 stories (one of these is an office tower). The city resort was built around the existing building of the Hotel "Indonesia" dating from 1962; it was the first five-star hotel in Indonesia and is now a protected monument.

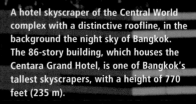

A hotel skyscraper of the Central World complex with a distinctive roofline, in the background the night sky of Bangkok. The 86-story building, which houses the Centara Grand Hotel, is one of Bangkok's tallest skyscrapers, with a height of 770 feet (235 m).

MARINA BAY SANDS

Singapore   6,254,000 sq ft (581,000 sq m)

City Resort Marina Bay Sands and its spectacular ArtScience Museum

The Marina Bay Sands complex consists of three hotel towers with 55 levels each and a total of 2,561 hotel rooms. The three towers are linked by a roof terrace, which gives the building an iconic appearance. This so-called SkyPark is located at a height of 623 feet (190 m) and offers stunning panoramic views over all of Singapore. Also on the viewing platform are restaurants, bars and an infinity swimming pool with a total length of 479 feet (146 m). The roof terrace can accommodate about 4,000 guests. The hotel towers' annexes also house a casino, theater and function rooms as well as an ArtScience Museum shaped like a lotus flower.

Marina Bay Sands with its spectacular roof terrace somewhat reminiscent of a flying saucer, to its left and also part of this building complex is the ArtScience Museum, modeled on a lotus flower. When the weather allows, laser shows take place there at night. The swimming pool on the cantilever roof terrace is one of the largest in its height category.

RENAISSANCE CENTER
Detroit, USA 5,543,000 sq ft (515,000 sq m)

Located on the Detroit River bank is the Renaissance Center with its five towers.

This complex of buildings was opened in 1977, but had to endure above-average vacancy rates as a consequence of Detroit's industrial decline. In 1996 it was taken over by the car manufacturer General Motors and completely renovated and modernized. Today it is the company headquarters of General Motors — the GM logo on the tallest tower in the complex is visible from afar.

The entire complex consists of seven skyscrapers. Housed in the tallest of these is a Marriott Hotel with an upscale restaurant at the top with views of the Canadian city of Windsor opposite. With a height of 728 feet (222 m) the hotel tower is one of the tallest buildings in Detroit. Other towers in the complex house restaurants, several banks, business consultancies, a museum and the GM University.

URBAN MEGASTRUCTURES

Towers look back on a long architectural history and tradition. For centuries defensive towers served to watch the enemy and to transmit messages, for example by lighting beacons, and also as orientation points. As if that wasn't enough, when people began to be interested in nature, viewing towers were built and climbed in the 18th and the 19th centuries; in the period of Romanticism old castle towers and ruins became popular spots to enjoy panoramic views of the newly discovered countryside. Today the world's tallest and most spectacular towers still serve to transmit information; the structures that are presented here broadcast television and radio signals and are at the same time popular viewpoints. Two construction types dominate: they are either reinforced concrete towers, like the Europa Tower in Frankfurt, or are steel lattice towers, like the Kiev TV Tower. In architectural terms towers and masts are not considered to be buildings, because they do not have a frame structure consisting of walls and floors.

THE TALLEST TOWERS IN THE WORLD

① **Tokyo Sky Tree**
Tokyo, Japan
2,080 ft (634 m)

② **Canton Tower**
Kanton, China
1,969 ft (600 m)

③ **CN Tower**
Toronto, Canada
1,814 ft (553 m)

④ **Ostankino Tower**
Moscow, Russia
1,772 ft (540 m)

⑤ **Oriental Pearl Tower**
Shanghai, China
1,535 ft (468 m)

⑥ **Milad Tower**
Teheran, Iran
1,427 ft (435 m)

⑦ **Menara Tower**
Kuala Lumpur, Malaysia
1,381 ft (421 m)

⑧ **Tianjin Radio TV Tower**
Tianjin, China
1,362 ft (415 m)

⑨ **China Central Radio TV Tower**
Beijing, China
1,329 ft (405 m)

⑩ **Kiev TV Tower**
Kiev, Ukraine
1,263 ft (385 m)

⑪ **Tashkent Television Tower**
Tashkent, Uzbekistan
1,230 ft (375 m)

⑫ **Riga Radio and TV Tower**
Riga, Lettland
1,211 ft (369 m)

猎德大桥

The extraordinary architecture of the
Canton Tower, an elliptical supporting
lattice framework, has as an advantage
the benefit of only minimal wind resistance. When it is illuminated its stunning
shape becomes particularly apparent. The
almost 2.5 mile (4 km) long Liede Bridge
crosses the Pearl River in the foreground.

TOKYO SKY TREE

Despite the danger of earthquakes in Japan's capital, the Tokyo Sky Tree was built between 2008 and 2012 and soars 2,080 feet (634 m) into the sky, making it the tallest TV tower in the world. Construction happened at a speedy pace — in some phases the tower grew by 23 feet (7 m) a week. On the one hand the tower improves the transmission of radio and TV signals for the city and its environs, and on the other hand it is an attraction for tourists, who can enjoy the view of the metropolis from its two observation decks (at 1,148 ft/350m and 1,476ft/450 m). The rush of interested visitors was already very

The TV tower has 13 elevators

great at its inauguration in May 2012. Construction of Tokyo's new landmark was hardly interrupted by the earthquake of March 2011, and thanks to advanced static and architectural measures the structure is able to withstand even the strongest earth tremors. Its modern, almost futuristic appearance is underlined by effective illumination. The tower stands in the Sumida ward, which has experienced a revival since its construction, and especially since its completion. The tower's height of 634 meter (2,080 feet) is a reference to the district's former name of "Musashi," which means: *mu* — 6, *sa* — 3, *shi* — 4.

Around the base of the Tokyo Sky Tree new buildings are springing up, including a large shopping mall. The new urban center has good transportation links with other hubs in Tokyo.

CANTON TOWER

During its inauguration ceremony in September 2010, the Canton Tower (previously known as Guang-zhou Tower) was, at 1,969 feet (600 m), the tallest TV tower in the world, but at the start of 2011 already it had to cede its top ranking to the Tokyo Sky Tree. The structure is planned for an annual visitor number of five million and boasts a stunning, heavily twisted shape resembling a

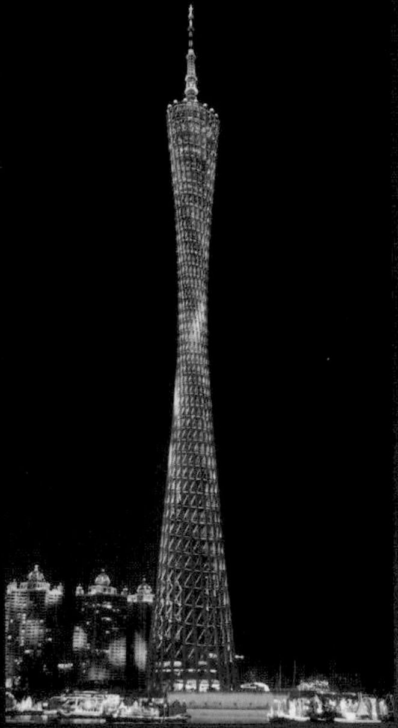

When illuminated the tower seems to be weightless.

very slender hourglass. From afar the elliptical lattice frame looks like a net; the Dutch architectural team Hemel/Knit called it a "female shape."

THE HIGHEST FERRIS WHEEL IN THE WORLD

On the highest of its three observation platforms, at 1,490 feet (454 m), the Canton Tower has a Ferris wheel. Comparable to a horizontal merry-go-round, 16 transparent passenger cabins travel on an inclined outer track along the oval open-air platform. During the slow journey visitors can enjoy views of the Chinese city of Guangzhou and of Guangdong Province. Entertainment is, however, also guaranteed at lower levels: revolving restaurants, cafés, teahouses and outdoor gardens offer plenty of distraction.

The view of the city from the glass bubbles is nothing short of spectacular, both by day and night.

Guangzhou, the metropolis on the Pearl River, is — like many Asian towns — a city of superlatives. Its landmark is the Canton Tower. For the opening ceremony of the Asian Games in 2010 the TV tower was beautifully illuminated.

Whether as showcases for the former eastern bloc countries or exclusively for its functionality as radio and television signal transmitters — Europe's tallest towers all soar more than 984 feet (300 m) into the skies and the Moscow TV tower even reaches a staggering 1,772 feet (540 m). These structures are esthetically beautiful, have special technological features, are built using very different construction methods, and often stand in unusual sites, such as on an island in a river. Some can be climbed and promise excellent panoramic views from their observation decks or from revolving restaurants.

Moscow's TV tower at night

Riga's slender tower in the Daugava River

OSTANKINO TOWER
Moscow, Russia   1,772 ft (540 m)

After its topping out in 1967 and until 1975, Moscow's TV tower was, at 1,772 feet (540 m), the tallest free-standing structure in the world. For years it was closed due to several fires and complex renovation work but it has been open to the public again since 2009.

KIEV TV TOWER
Kiev, Ukraine   1,263 ft (385 m)

Kiev's TV Tower is a lattice steel construction and the tallest of this kind in the world; as a special feature the tower has four roughly 328 foot (100 m) tall legs. These are also built in lattice steel constructions. There are no rivets anywhere in the tower — the structure has been entirely continuously welded.

RIGA RADIO AND TV TOWER
Riga, Latvia   1,211 ft (369 m)

In the middle of the Daugava, a river that flows into the Baltic Sea, on Zakusala Island stands Riga's tallest structure — the TV tower. During its planning and implementation flood and even earthquake protection were taken account of, although the tower does not stand in a particularly seismologically active area. In order to improve its resistance to serious storms, pendulums have been installed at a height of about 656 feet (200 m) to counterbalance any wind-induced movement. It stands on three pillars, the only tower in the world to do so. The elevators inside the pillars run on non-vertical rails.

GERBRANDY TOWER
Ijsselstein, Netherlands   1,204 ft (367 m)

The Gerbrandy Tower, standing near the town of Utrecht in the Netherlands, was named after the former Dutch prime minister, Pieter Gerbrandy. It is the tallest structure in the Netherlands. A guyed steel tube mast was mounted on top of the 328 foot (100 m) tall reinforced concrete tower. As the antenna had to be replaced several times the original overall height of 1,253 feet (382 m) was reduced to the present 1,204 feet (367 m).

The Tower of Europe has a revolving pod.

Framed by the domes of the cathedral: Berlin's TV tower

TV TOWER VINNYTSIA
Vinnytsia, Ukraine   1,161 ft (354 m)

Ukraine has one 1,161 foot (354 m) tall tower in Vinnytsia. The town is located in the country's interior, about 250 miles (400 km) north of Odessa. The tower was built during the Soviet era in 1961, purely as a radio and television transmission tower, and it cannot be climbed.

TOWER OF EUROPE
Frankfurt, Germany   1,109 ft (338 m)

The Europaturm is Germany's second tallest television tower. At the time of its completion in 1979 it was still the No. 1 in West Germany, but after the country's reunification it had a rival in the East German Berlin TV tower. At its base it measures 66 feet (20 m) in diameter and underneath the revolving six-story pod 36 feet (11 m). The pod has a diameter of 194 feet (59 m), making it the

BERLIN TV TOWER
Berlin, Germany   1,207 ft (368 m)

A popular sightseeing destination, the Berlin TV Tower (Fernsehturm), colloquially also known as "Alex" after the square on which it stands, Alexanderplatz, defines Berlin's cityscape. In the 1960s the East German government decided to build the tower, in part to demonstrate the competitiveness of Socialism. Its sphere was supposed to recall the Soviet satellite "Sputnik."

On a narrow concrete shaft sits the tower's pod with its rotating observation deck. The vertical line is continued above by the steel transmitter mast. During the Festival of Lights the television tower, built in the years 1965 to 1969, is strikingly illuminated. *Neues Deutschland*, the newspaper of the East German Socialist party's executive, called it "Telespargel," meaning TV asparagus spear. The tower did not start its career as a popular souvenir — as a baking mold, a pin or a motif on T-shirts — until after reunification.

EIFFEL TOWER

The Universal Exposition of 1889 was to be a unique event, celebrating its 100th anniversary in Paris. Work on the Eiffel Tower, the then tallest structure in the world, had begun in 1887. It was named after its engineer, Gustave Eiffel. In record time some 3,000 metal workers assembled the iron lattice using just under 20,000 industrially prefabricated individual components and around 2.5 million rivets. Skeptics were proved wrong: the tower was able to withstand any storm. Paris had a new landmark, then 1,024 feet (312 m) tall, and the world had gained the epitome of the capabilities of modern architecture.

Alexandre Gustave Eiffel owed the idea for the Eiffel Tower to his collaborators, Maurice Koechlin and Émile Nouguier. Using a tripartite division and round arches, architect Stephen Sauvestre imparted transparency to the structure and enthused Eiffel, who took on the design, management and execution. Originally the tower was set to be demolished after the Exposition, but it was left standing because it could be used as a radio tower. Once every seven years, the Eiffel Tower is refreshed with about 66 short tons (60 tonnes) of paint. It is at its most attractive when brightly lit and with its flashing beacon at night.

The Eiffel Tower, Paris's famous landmark

The over 984 feet (300 m) tall iron lattice construction was built within only 16 months under the management of the engineer Gustave Eiffel. The viewing platform is reached by elevator and is one of the city's greatest attractions.

ORIENTAL PEARL TOWER

Shanghai, China   1,535 ft (468 m)

The Oriental Pearl Tower soars in the Pudong district of Shanghai, directly opposite the famous strolling boulevard, the Bund. The tower boasts

The illuminated Oriental Pearl Tower

several records: it is the tallest structure in Shanghai and the second tallest in China, as well as the third tallest in all of Asia. Each year the tower with the distinctive pods of 164 feet (50 m) and 148 feet (45 m) respectively in diameter has more than two million visitors. There are several restaurants and the highest viewing platform is based in the topmost pod at a height of 1,122 feet (342 m). Above it there is a 387 foot (118 m) tall antenna.

THE TALLEST TOWERS IN ASIA

1. **Tokyo Sky Tree**
   Tokyo, Japan
   2,080 ft (634 m)
2. **Canton Tower**
   Canton, China
   1,969 ft (600 m)
3. **Oriental Pearl Tower**
   Shanghai, China
   1,535 ft (468 m)
4. **Milad Tower**
   Teheran, Iran
   1,427 ft (435 m)
5. **Menara Tower**
   Kuala Lumpur, Malaysia
   1,381 ft (421 m)
6. **Tianjin Radio TV Tower**
   Tianjin, China
   1,362 ft (415 m)
7. **China Central Radio TV Tower**
   Beijing, China
   1,329 ft (405 m)
8. **Tashkent Television Tower**
   Tashkent, Uzbekistan
   1,230 ft (375 m)

The skyline with the new Oriental Pearl Tower has become Shanghai's new landmark. Up until the 1990s, Pudong was just an area of swampland, but within little more than a decade a new town with hundreds of skyscrapers has been raised here. The magnetic levitation train, which links the city center with the international airport and the exhibition grounds of 2010, also serves this area.

MILAD TOWER
Teheran, Iran   **1,427 ft (435 m)**

The tallest tower in Iran, the Milad Tower has at its top, at a height of 820 to 1,033 feet (250 to 315 m), a large pod extending over 12 stories and featuring several observation decks. Specially treated glass, covering an area of 199,130 sq ft (18,500 sq m), was used to withstand extreme weather conditions.

The Milad Tower stands in the north of Tehran.

MENARA TOWER
Kuala Lumpur, Malaysia   **1,381 ft (421 m)**

The Menara or Kuala Lumpur Tower serves as a communications tower for the broadcasting of radio and television programs; it is also open to the public as a viewing tower. Visitors are transported to the top either by four rapid elevators or they can climb or race up the 2,058 steps. At a height of 906 feet (276 m) it has an eight-story pod with a diameter of about 165 feet (50 m). This houses a revolving restaurant, and on top of the pod's roof there is a station for the annual KL Tower Base Jump.

The Petronas twin towers can be seen from the Menara Tower

TIANJIN RADIO AND TV TOWER
Tianjin, China   **1,362 ft (415 m)**

China's third largest television tower stands in Tianjin, a metropolis of 12 million inhabitants and an important port city in the north of the country. The tower was inaugurated in 1991 and is open to the public. At heights of 830 and 843 feet (253 and 257 m) respectively are an observation platform and a revolving restaurant.

The television tower soars above Tianjin.

CHINA CENTRAL RADIO AND TV TOWER
Beijing, China   **1,329 ft (405 m)**

The signals of the Chinese state television station are transmitted via the China Central Television Tower (CCTV). The tower also houses a broadcasting center. Observation decks at 781 feet (238 m) and a restaurant provide stunning views of Beijing for visitors.

Beijing's Central Radio and TV Tower is located in the Haidian district.

TASHKENT TELEVISION TOWER
Tashkent, Uzbekistan   **1,230 ft (375 m)**

In its appearance the TV tower was meant to resemble a rocket on the launchpad. The lower of the two tower pods, with observation decks and restaurants, is open to visitors. The tower also houses a weather station.

Rocket-like: the Tashkent Television Tower

THE TALLEST TOWERS IN OCEANIA AND AFRICA

View of the Sky Tower from below

SYDNEY TOWER
Sydney, Australia   1001 ft (305 m)

The appearance of the Sydney Tower, or Sydney Tower Eye, is characterized by the 56 steel cables of 7.7 short tons (7 tonnes) weight each, which hold up the TV tower and its pod with an open-air observation deck at 820 feet (250 m) height. One of the levels holds a water tank with a capacity of more than 338,140 U.S. pints (160,000 l) of water. The tank also contributes to the tower's stability in strong winds. The tower was opened in 1981, after a seven-year construction period.

The Sydney Tower blends harmoniously into the modern cityscape.

SKY TOWER
Auckland, New Zealand
1,076 ft (328 m)

Visitors of the Sky Tower can enjoy views of Auckland from three different platforms. Thrills are provided by the glazed elevators and the glass floor in the lowest observation deck. From the entrance 1,267 steps lead up to the topmost platform, the Sky Deck. A German man holds the record for racing up — he had reached the top after four minutes and 53 seconds.

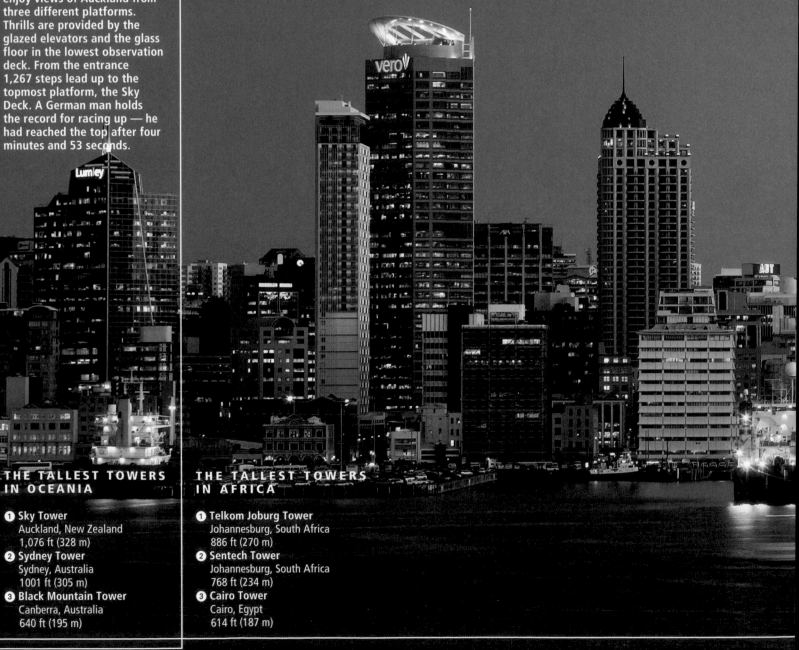

THE TALLEST TOWERS IN OCEANIA

❶ **Sky Tower**
Auckland, New Zealand
1,076 ft (328 m)
❷ **Sydney Tower**
Sydney, Australia
1001 ft (305 m)
❸ **Black Mountain Tower**
Canberra, Australia
640 ft (195 m)

THE TALLEST TOWERS IN AFRICA

❶ **Telkom Joburg Tower**
Johannesburg, South Africa
886 ft (270 m)
❷ **Sentech Tower**
Johannesburg, South Africa
768 ft (234 m)
❸ **Cairo Tower**
Cairo, Egypt
614 ft (187 m)

TELKOM JOBURG TOWER
Johannesburg, South Africa
886 ft (270 m)

Until 2005 Johannesburg's TV
tower was known under the name
of Hillbrow Tower, but then its
name was ceremoniously changed
to Telkom Joburg Tower. After a
construction time of three years
it became operational in 1971,
but after ten years, in 1981,
it was closed to the pubic for
security reasons. Today it is used
only for the broadcasting of radio
and television programs and for
telecommunications purposes.

Since its name change the tower has been lit at night

The skyline of tall buildings soaring
around harbor basin is now considered
Auckland's landmark. The main eye-
catcher is the 1,076 foot (328 m) tall
Sky Tower, on the right in the picture.
Superb panoramic views unfold from its
observation decks across the dynamic
cityscape and the cone-shaped mounds
of almost 50 inactive volcanoes at some
distance from the city.

CN TOWER
Toronto, Canada
1,814 ft (553 m)

At the end of the 1960s so many skyscrapers were built in Toronto that the reception of

Toronto's Tower is a magnet for visitors.

radio and TV signals noticeably deteriorated with the density and height of the buildings, and a new tower had to be built. Initially a mast with a height of at least 1,148 feet (350 m) was planned but this was soon increased: the conditions at its site in the southern inner city were so excellent that it was possible to build it to a height of 1,814 feet (553 m).

THE TALLEST TOWERS IN NORTH AMERICA

1 CN Tower
Toronto, Canada
1,814 ft (553 m)
2 Stratosphere Tower
Las Vegas, USA
1,148 ft (350 m)
3 Tower of the Americas
San Antonio, USA
751 ft (229 m)

THE TALLEST TOWERS IN SOUTH AMERICA

1 Torre Espacial
Buenos Aires, Argentina
748 ft (228 m)
2 Brasilia TV Tower
Brasilia, Brazil
735 ft (224 m)
3 Torre TV Bandeirantes
São Paulo, Brazil
696 ft (212 m)

STRATOSPHERE TOWER
Las Vegas, USA   1,148 ft (350 m)

Near the city center on the Las Vegas Strip stands "The Strat," a combined hotel, casino and observation tower. Visitors are agreed: a visit to the Stratosphere Tower, in the evening or at night to admire the city's blaze of light, is a must during a stay at Las Vegas.

Along with the views of Las Vegas, the main attractions for visitors are the rides located at the level of the observation decks at 886 feet (270 m) height. The "Big Shot" catapults visitors to the top of the tower. "X-Scream"

The mighty Stratosphere Tower looks particularly slender and elegant when lit by the moon.

maneuvers its passengers via a ramp up and beyond the tower, then drops back down at top speed. Those without fear of

The rides on the "The Strat"

vertigo try "Insanity," a sort of chair swing ride that goes beyond the edge of the platform at a height of almost 900 feet (270 m).

The TV tower of the Canadian National railroad company was completed in the year 1976. At that time it was still the tallest freestanding structure in the world. Its seven-story Main Pod, enthroned at a height of 1,152 feet (351 m), is home to a revolving restaurant. The brave can go even higher: four glazed external cabins float within 58 seconds to the 1,467 feet (447 m) high Sky Pod. In the picture to the left of the CN Tower is the Rogers Centre.

URBAN MEGASTRUCTURES

Magnificent residences or palaces have always existed, and even in ancient cultures the ruling circles had homes built for themselves that would express their social standing and their power status. In different forms this can be observed anywhere in the world, in the Tokyo Imperial Palace as in the Royal Palace of Madrid. These vast palace complexes are impressive not least because of their size. In addition, each group of buildings has its own special characteristics, which have made them famous around the world, like the splendid Palace of Versailles with its unique Hall of Mirrors. The suites of rooms in the Louvre seem almost monumental, whereas the palace inhabited by the Sultan of Brunei boasts almost unimaginable luxury. The vast extent and the layout of the Forbidden City are legendary, and the Winter Palace in St. Petersburg impresses visitors with its glorious interiors. Since the end of the 18th century certain public buildings have also been called palaces, such as "palaces of justice" or "palaces of parliament." These buildings also serve a representative function, and they are essential in a modern democracy.

THE LARGEST PALACES IN THE WORLD

① Louvre
Paris, France
2,260,420 sq ft (210,000 sq m)

② Istana Nurul Iman
Bandar Seri Begawan, Brunei
2,152,780 sq ft (200,000 sq m)

③ Winter Palace
St. Petersburg, Russia
1,978,620 sq ft (183,820 sq m)

④ Forbidden City
Beijing, China
1,614,590 sq ft (150,000 sq m)

⑤ Royal Palace
Madrid, Spain
1,453,130 sq ft (135,000 sq m)

⑥ Versailles
Versailles, France
1,184,030 sq ft (110,000 sq m)

⑦ Buckingham Palace
London, Great Britain
828,820 sq ft (77,000 sq m)

⑧ Royal Castle
Budapest, Hungary
699,650 sq ft (65,000 sq m)

⑨ Royal Palace
Stockholm, Sweden
658,750 sq ft (61,200 sq m)

For eight centuries the Louvre served as the residence of the French monarchs. However, the building has become famous around the world mainly thanks to the museum it houses today. The main entrance is marked by a glass pyramid designed by I. M. Pei and completed in 1989

VERSAILLES

Versailles is the epitome of a chateau and at the same time one of the largest grand buildings in Europe. The complex has four parts, of which the 1,903 foot (580 m) long palace building with its wings, gardens and halls is the most impressive. King Louis XIII first had a small hunting lodge built in the wooded and game-rich area near the village of Versailles, to the west of Paris. His son and heir to the throne, Louis XIV, also liked to spend time there and so he had the gardens enlarged in 1661 and commissioned the architect Louis Le Vau (1612–1670) with the systematic extension of the castle. Work began in 1668; however, Louis XIII's earlier

The garden side of the Palace of Versailles, with a statue of Neptune in the foreground

The garden architect André Le Nôtre developed a type of garden at Versailles that became known as a "French (formal) garden" and was soon copied at courts all over Europe. A characteristic feature are the topiary hedges along geometric sightlines.

building was not torn down but built around. Thus the main tract of the chateau was created, with Le Vau's successor Jules Hardouin-Mansart (1646–1708) responsible for the extension. Charles Le Brun (1619–1690) designed the interior. The construction of the chateau was done as magnificently as necessary but at the same time as inexpensively as possible. As a consequence fire did not draw properly in the chimney places, the rooms were so cold that the liquor would freeze, and the bathrooms had no water. During Louis XIV's time, a court retinue of 20,000 people lived there. Especially worth seeing along with the palace chapel and the throne room are the apartments of the queen and Louis XIV's bedchamber as well as the 240 feet (73 m) long and 36 feet (11 m) wide Hall of Mirrors with its 17 arcaded windows facing the park. The ultimate archetype of a royal residence for an absolutist king, the chateau became a model for many European residential palaces; the name "Versailles" came to symbolize the entire era of the courtly high and late baroque in Europe. From October 1682 until the Revolution of 1789, the chateau served as the residence of the French kings. A period of decay followed, then King Louis Philippe had the palace rebuilt as a national museum, containing a gallery of paintings, a collection of historical portraits and a sculpture and furniture exhibition.

LOUVRE

LOUVRE
Paris, France
2,260420 sq ft (210,000 sq m)

The oldest building of this French royal palace dates back to the 12th century. The fortress was built directly by the Seine River, as part of the first city walls. In the subsequent two centuries the fortress was transformed into a royal residence, and virtually every French ruler added to it until it had grown into a horseshoe shape. Napoleon I also commissioned further extensions, and these were completed under Napoleon III. In 1989 a new subterranean tract was added as well as the new entrance in the shape of a steel and glass pyramid which itself has become world-famous. The roughly 400,000 art treasures presented here in an exhibition space of about 656,600 sq ft (61,000 sq m) today attract more than five million visitors a year. The Louvre Museum was opened in 1793 and made the royal art collection, which had been declared a national treasure, accessible to the public. During the Napoleonic wars and through purchases the museum's collection was constantly enlarged and quickly became one of the most important art collections in the world.

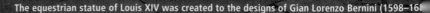

The equestrian statue of Louis XIV was created to the designs of Gian Lorenzo Bernini (1598–168

The Louvre's collections are divided into the following curatorial departments: Egyptian Antiquities; Near Eastern Antiquities; Islamic Art; Greek, Etruscan and Roman Antiquities; Decorative Arts; Sculptures; Paintings; Print and Drawings. Each department presents masterpieces of the highest quality, and yet there are certain works that everyone thinks of in connection with the palace museum, most of all Leonardo da Vinci's "Mona Lisa."

Large picture: "A museum for the people," was the motto of the revolutionary government, when the public was given access to the Louvre as a museum in 1793.

Napoleon III's living quarters can be visited at the Louvre.

THE LARGEST PALACES IN THE WORLD

Only a few of the world's largest palace complexes are today inhabited (for example Tokyo and Brunei), whereas most house art collections like the Louvre — or are themselves museums.

ISTANA NURUL IMAN
Sultanate of Brunei
c. 2,150,000 sq ft (200,000 sq m)

Thanks to its natural gas fields and oil deposits the Sultanate of Brunei on the island of Borneo is today considered the wealthiest country in South-East Asia. The Sultan Omar Ali Saifuddin Mosque and the vast Istana Nurul Iman Palace in the capital, Bandar Seri Begawan, attest to this wealth. The palace has been in use by the Sultan of Brunei as his official residence and the seat of the government since 1984. The sultan rules as an absolutist prince; there is no parliament and no political parties. The palace houses 1,780 rooms with a living space of 2,152,780 sq ft (200,000 sq m) as well as a garage for his collection of sports cars comprising 367 vehicles. Also in the grounds is his racetrack, located in a giant garden area. Since the Sultan of Brunei lives at his vast palace, the general public can only visit some parts and on very few days in the year, for example on the ruler's birthday and at the end of Ramadan. All the visitors are then invited to a feast and are personally greeted by the ruling

WINTER PALACE
St. Petersburg, Russia
1,978,620 sq ft (183,820 sq m)

One of the most important buildings of the Russian baroque, the Winter Palace was erected in 1754 by the Neva River as the residence of the Czar, to the plans of Bartolomeo Rastrelli. It is the largest component of the Hermitage complex, which also comprises the Small, the New and the Old Hermitages as well as the Hermitage Theater. The square in the front of the Winter Palace, where the statue of Alexander stands, was the scene of important historical events. In 1905, during an uprising, 1,000 demonstrators were murdered by Czarist soldiers, and in 1917 the Russian October Revolution began here when the Bolsheviks stormed the Winter Palace. Today it houses an archeological department and a collection of European art ranging from Michelangelo via Rembrandt to Picasso.

The Winter Palace belongs to the group of buildings that make up the Hermitage.

ROYAL PALACE
Madrid, Spain
1,453,130 sq ft (135,000 sq m)

A catastrophe beset the Royal Palace on a Christmas Eve of all days: a fire on December 24, 1734, destroyed many parts of the building. Felipe V planned a new structure that was to be the equal of other royal palaces in Europe, like Versailles. With its over 2,000 rooms the building was so colossal that it took 17 years to build. Phillip V had died in the meantime and did not see it completed. His son, Charles III was the first king to reside in the new palace. The interior is appointed with the finest materials. Rock crystals sparkle in the chandeliers of the throne room and the walls in the porcelain room are clad in Buen Retiro porcelain.

The Royal Palace in Madrid has immense proportions.

couple. The rooms are illuminated by 564 vast chandeliers, and 257 luxuriously appointed bathrooms, 44 stairwells and 18 elevators cater for every comfort. In addition, the palace's own mosque offers room for 1,500 faithful and the banqueting hall accommodates 4,000 diners. The costs of constructing the palace have been estimated at over 400 million U.S. dollars.

Sultan Hassanal Bolkiah Mu'izzaddin Waddaulah, the ruler in the Sultanate of Brunei, has lived since 1984 in the world's largest residential palace building (left), located near the capital city of Bandar Seri Begawan.

PALACE OF VERSAILLES
Versailles, France
1,184,030 sq ft (110,000 sq m)

Of the many magnificent halls and staterooms, the Hall of Mirrors is historically the most important. Part of a series of rooms that extend across the entire garden front they are the apex of the baroque art of decoration. The room, which intimidates visitors with its

The Palace of Versailles is a UNESCO World Cultural Heritage Site.

View of the Gallery of Battles

sheer size alone, is the venue where the German emperor had himself crowned in 1871 and

where the Versailles Treaty was signed in 1919. It owes its name to the 17 mirrors reflecting the light of the windows immediately opposite them. The mirrors thus exude an esthetic effect while at the same time transporting the garden into the palace interior. The spatial effect is further promoted by the many chandeliers that can also be rediscovered in the mirrors. They underline the king's splendor and glory. It was Louis XIV, the "Sun King," who desired such a display of his power in all its facets; the absolutist ruler was considered to be the style-setter regarding the staging of his position, pomp and circumstance of his court at Versailles. Louis XIV took absolutism to the extremes, as was clearly expressed in his motto: "L'État c'est moi" ("I am the state").

Even after the palace was abandoned in the French Revolution of 1789, the Hall of Mirrors remained the venue for historic events such as the Proclamation of the German Empire in 1871 and the signing of the Peace Treat of Versailles in 1919. It is one of the largest and certainly one of the most famous palace rooms anywhere in the world. Along with the mirrors themselves, the extensive ceiling frescoes underline the spatial effect in glorification of the Sun King.

The Gate of Heavenly Peace

The squares and courts between the halls in the Imperial Palace are very spacious.

Imperial audiences once took place on the forecourt of the "Hall of Supreme Harmony." Inside, ceremonies were held for the coronation of the emperor, festivities on the occasion of the emperor's birthday and the appointment of generals before a campaign. Most recently the rooms were used for the armistice ceremony in 1918. The gilded imperial Dragon Throne also stands here.

FORBIDDEN CITY
Beijing, China
1,614,590 sq ft (150,000 sq m)

The spacious and walled Imperial Palace of Beijing was the heart of China and the focal point of the Middle Kingdom. Today it is one of the most outstanding sights in the country. Its name, Gugong, means literally "Purple Forbidden City"; this refers not only to the color of the buildings and walls — the color purple is also associated with power and rule in China. The complex is a typical example of Chinese palace architecture, which is markedly different from that in Europe: the palaces do not have main tracts and side wings but instead consist of buildings and halls that are arranged one behind the other and often linked by gates and passageways. Individual buildings are horizontally oriented instead of rising upward. They were built mainly from wood, which is why devastating fires were a frequent occurrence in the rooms. It is for this reason that more than 300 huge water containers were set up, which were to help people quickly extinguish the fires. The large halls are the points of reference. The emperor ruled his realm from the "Hall of Supreme Harmony." In the "Hall of Perfect Harmony" the officials were put to the test by the emperor, and the "Hall of Preserving Harmony" was used for receptions and New Year's celebrations. Visitors accessed the inner chambers, where the emperor and his family lived, via the "Gate of Heavenly Purity." It is there that ceremonies and Manchurian shaman rituals were performed. The buildings were often used for different purposes by the different dynasties.

The Victoria Memorial opposite Buckingham Palace is suggestive of Britain's naval power.

The Royal Castle and the Chain Bridge

View of the main nave of the palace church

BUCKINGHAM PALACE
London, Great Britain
828,820 sq ft (77,000 sq m)

Buckingham Palace is the official residence of the royal family, yet only on weekdays and not during the summer vacations. Visitation to the palace is thus limited — only in the months of August and September, when 19 of its rooms are opened to the public. In its core, the splendid palace dates back to the year 1705 and originally belonged to the Duke of Buckingham. In 1837 Queen Victoria decided that St. James's Palace was no longer adequate to meet the majestic needs, and so she moved into Buckingham Palace, which had in the meantime been extended and converted into a veritable palace. Improvements and modernization continued until the beginning of the 20th century. The most recent construction work was the remodeling of the eastern façade in 1913. It is from the balcony on this side that the Windsors gracefully wave to the people on special occasions such as royal weddings. On the square in front of the palace's main façade, the Victoria Memorial was erected in 1911. It measures 82 feet (25 m) tall and was made from 2,536 short tons (2,300 tonnes) of white marble. Behind it, the embellished palace gates mark the entrance.

ROYAL CASTLE
Budapest, Hungary
699,650 sq ft (65,000 sq m)

The immense Royal Castle (or Buda Castle) on Budapest's Castle Hill looks back on a long and turbulent history. The castle was frequently destroyed during the various wars and attacks, but the Hungarians indefatigably rebuilt the palace time and again. After World War II extensive repairs and renovations also became necessary, and it was then that it was given its present appearance. The magnificent building, long the city's main landmark, today houses the National Library and several museums.

ROYAL PALACE
Stockholm, Sweden
658,750 sq ft (61,200 sq m)

At the northeastern end of the Old Town stands the Royal or Stockholm Palace — with its 608 rooms one of the largest in the world. The magnificent building was erected in the first half of the 18th century, on the site of the medieval royal residence that had been destroyed by a fire. It is considered an excellent example of architecture at the transition from baroque to rococo. These days the palace is only rarely used by the Swedish king, and many of its rooms have therefore been opened to the general public.

The Imperial Palace is considered to be of great architectural and historic significance by the international community. It is surrounded by extensive gardens with a stock of mature trees. The public is allowed to visit the palace only twice a year — on New Year's Day

The imperial family lives at the palace.

and for the emperor's birthday. Its Japanese name, "Kokyo," literally translated means "imperial residence," and it is the residence of the Tenno, the Japanese emperor. Originally, the Edo Castle stood on this site, and the Tokugawa Shoguns lived there, who ruled Japan from 1603 to 1867 with great severity. Construction work on the new palace was completed around 1890. During World War II the entire complex sustained heavy damage, but it was rebuilt by the 1960s.

THE LARGEST INHABITED PALACE COMPLEX IN THE WORLD

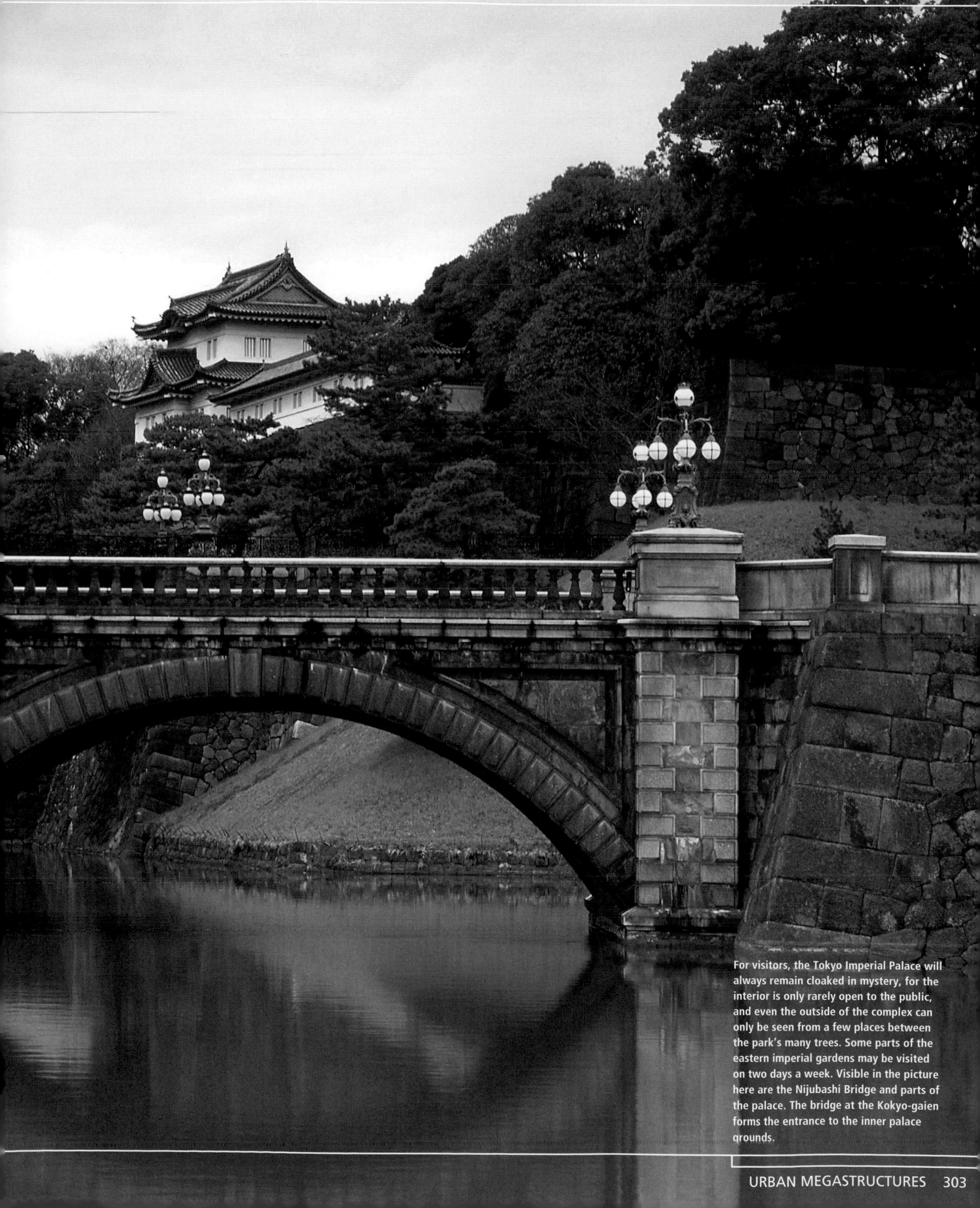

For visitors, the Tokyo Imperial Palace will always remain cloaked in mystery, for the interior is only rarely open to the public, and even the outside of the complex can only be seen from a few places between the park's many trees. Some parts of the eastern imperial gardens may be visited on two days a week. Visible in the picture here are the Nijubashi Bridge and parts of the palace. The bridge at the Kokyo-gaien forms the entrance to the inner palace grounds.

WINDSOR CASTLE

Windsor Castle, from which the royal family take their name, is not only the largest castle in Great Britain but also the longest continuously occupied castle. A castle has stood here to the west of London for almost 1,000 years, built by William the Conqueror as a fortress around 1070 and ever since enlarged, modified, remodeled and occupied by the English kings as well as serving as a fortress, a prison or a garrison. The present palace complex essentially dates back to the 14th century, when Edward III had the state apartments, the mighty Round Tower and

the Norman Gate added. The most recent major remodeling then followed in the early 19th century under George IV. Today it is still one of the three official royal residences, together with Holyrood House in Edinburgh and Buckingham Palace in London, and is also the preferred residence of Queen Elizabeth II. A large fire in 1992 raged for 15 hours before it could be extinguished. By then it had destroyed almost 97,000 sq ft (9,000 sq m), about one-fifth of the entire area. Renovation work, accurate in every detail, took five years to complete.

When the Queen is in residence at Windsor Castle, the Royal Standard flies on the Round Tower.

THE LARGEST STILL OCCUPIED CASTLE COMPLEX IN THE WORLD

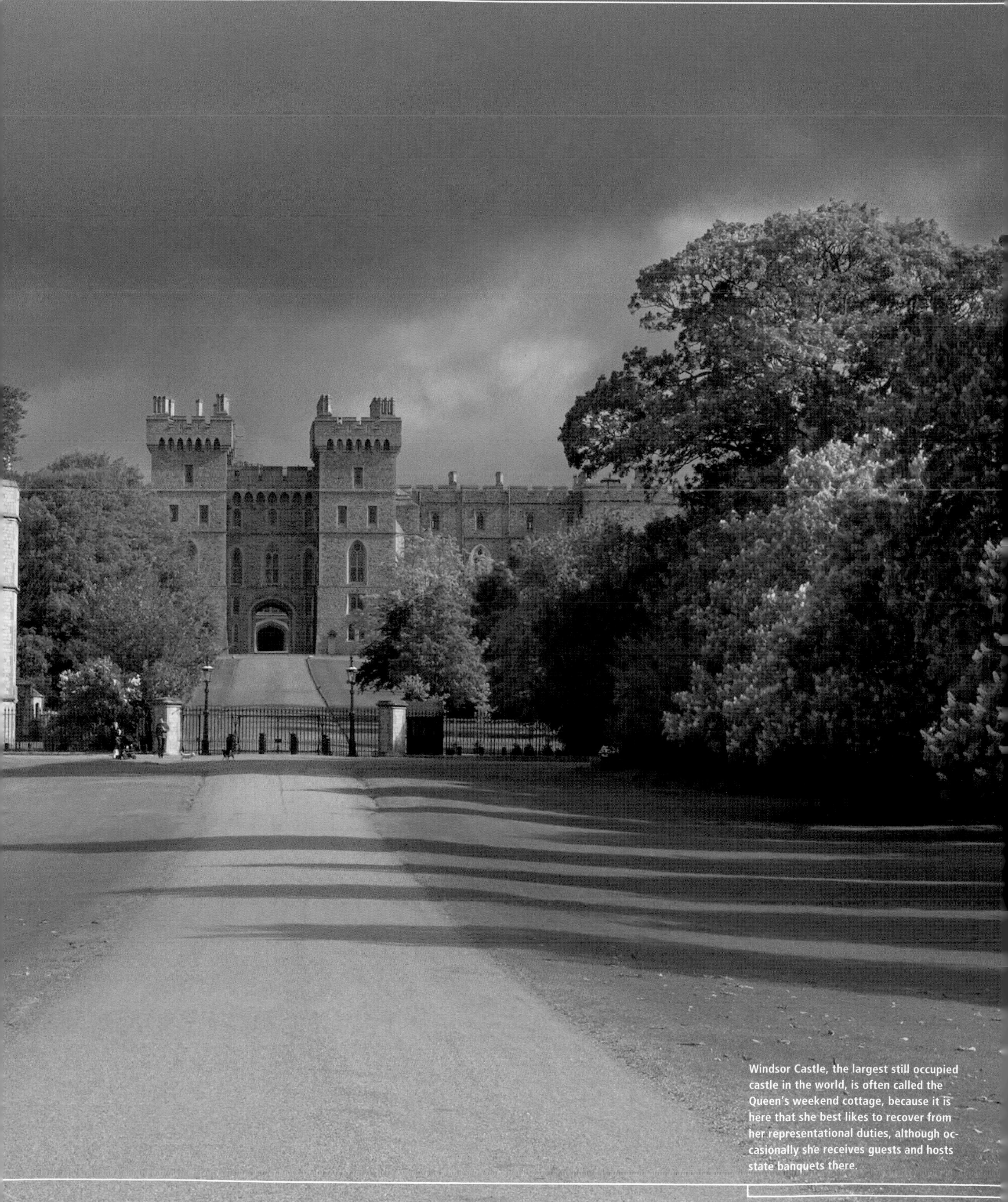

Windsor Castle, the largest still occupied castle in the world, is often called the Queen's weekend cottage, because it is here that she best likes to recover from her representational duties, although occasionally she receives guests and hosts state banquets there.

Not all of the ancient palaces house museums like the Louvre in Paris or the Royal Palace in Madrid. Some are used by heads of state for representative purposes, for example the Royal Palace in Stockholm and Buckingham Palace in London. Some historical palaces today serve as parliamentary buildings or are used for official government business. In countries with a democratic constitution, parliaments, as one part of the legislative branch, are generally separated from the executive power, also in terms of the buildings in which they meet. This is a way of clearly signifying the division of powers to the outside world. On a journey through the world's capitals, parliamentary buildings are found in both historic and more recent structures.

Palace of the Parliament and Unirii Boulevard

Hungary's Parliament on the Danube

Staircase in the Hungarian Parliament

PALACE OF THE PARLIAMENT
Bucharest, Romania
3,928,830 sq ft (365,000 sq m)

After the Pentagon, the Palace of the Romanian Parliament is the second largest administrative building in the world. Built between 1983 and 1989 under the dictator Nicolae Ceauşescu, many historic buildings had to be demolished to make room for it. After Ceauşescu's execution the palace was not destroyed, but the Chamber of Deputies and the Senate moved in instead.

HUNGARIAN PARLIAMENT BUILDING
Budapest, Hungary
376,740 sq ft (35,000 sq m)

The Hungarian House of Parliament was built between 1885 and 1904 in the neogothic style, and was modeled on the Palace of Westminster in London, the seat of the British Parliament. The about 890 foot (270 m) long and 430 foot (130 m) wide building is located directly by the Danube and is the second most important landmark in Budapest after the Royal Castle. Sources report that 40 million blocks of stone were used in its construction, as well as almost 90 lbs (40 kg) of gold. Of its nearly 700 rooms, 200 are used on official occasions. The complex of buildings has 10 inner courtyards and 27 separate entrances, and its distinctive façade is marked by 365 towers and turrets. The interior is adorned with frescoes and murals depicting scenes from Hungarian history.

Main entrance of the Great Hall of the People

The Capitol dominates Washington DC.

George Washington Statue in the rotunda

GREAT HALL OF THE PEOPLE
Beijing, China
1,849,240 sq ft (171,800 sq m)

CAPITOL
Washington, USA
247,570 sq ft (23,000 sq m)

The Great Hall of the People was constructed in 1959. Its main hall is 249 feet (76 m) wide and 197 feet (60 m) long, and accommodates 10,000 people, and a banqueting hall offers room for 5,000 people. In addition it comprises 30 halls, one for each Chinese province or autonomous region. The sessions of the National People's Congress take place in this building.

Both the Senate, which meets in the north wing, and the House of Representatives, which meets in the south wing, are based in the Capitol. George Washington himself laid the foundation stone for its construction in 1793. Up to its completion in 1826, six U.S. American presidents and their architects contributed their ideas to the planning and construction work. Subsequently the building

has been further enlarged time and again and is now a vast complex of buildings. In addition to the parliamentary chambers, the Capitol also holds works of art and collections relating to the history of the United States. The distinctive dome has a diameter of just under 100 feet (30 m) and is almost 180 feet (55 m) tall in its highest spot. Nine presidents of the United States have lain in state there.

Large picture: The central dome hall in the middle of the building is the largest room in the Hungarian Parliament and is covered by a 315 foot (96 m) tall dome; the Holy Crown of Hungary and the imperial regalia are kept here. In the two adjacent wings are conference rooms and premises for state purposes, as well as the offices of the president of the Republic, of the prime minister and for the National Assembly.

The global road network is around 18.6 million miles (30 million km) long. Included in this figure are all the roads, from highways to local roads, as well as unpaved tracks. The leader is the United States, with about 4 million miles (6.5 million km) of roads, followed by China (2.2 million miles/3.6 million km) and India (2 million miles/3.3 million km). France is the top-ranking European country and the No. 7 in the world, with a good 600,000 miles (1 million km). Germany is listed at No. 11, with a road network of about 403,890 miles (650,000 km).

This chapter introduces a small selection of the world's longest road links and highest mountain roads and passes.

On the A-5 in Spain, which forms a part of the E90

THE LONGEST ROADS IN THE WORLD

1. **Pan-American Highway**
   17,240 ml (27,750 km)
2. **Asian Highway 1**
   12,774 ml (20,557 km)
3. **National Highway 1**
   9,010 ml (14,500 km)
4. **Asian Highway 2**
   8,188 ml (13,177 km)
5. **Trans-Siberian Highway**
   6,835 ml (11,000 km)
6. **Trans-African Highway 3**
   6,716 ml (10,808 km)
7. **Asian Highway 6**
   6,509 ml (10,475 km)
8. **Asian Highway 5**
   6,450 ml (10,380 km)
9. **Trans-African Highway 4**
   6,355 ml (10,228 km)
10. **Trans African Highway 1**
    5,366 ml (8,636 km)

Biscayne Bay with Biscayne Bridge and the Miami skyline at dusk. The bridge is part of the General Douglas MacArthur Causeway, on which the Interstate 395 crosses the bay. The six-lane bridge is 3.5 miles (5.6 km) long in total, and the maximum height of the road surface above the water level is 69 feet (21 m). In one place it can be raised for ships' traffic.

PAN-AMERICAN HIGHWAY

The Pan-American Highway extends along the entire American continent — from Alaska to Tierra del Fuego. It consists of a multitude of linked highways — with just a short interruption in Panama.

Altogether, the Pan-American Highway system extends for about 29,800 miles (48,000 km), with the longest north–south section measuring about 17,240 miles (27,750 km). Historically the Pan-American Highway was "born" at an international conference in Buenos Aires. Officially it begins in Laredo (Texas), at the U.S. border with Mexico, and from there runs in the direction of Mexico City. Strictly speaking, Canada and the United States are not part of the Pan-American Highway road network. For tourist reasons however various routes in the United States and Canada have been incorporated into the Pan-American Highway system. You can use either the route via Minneapolis or Denver or drive along the west coast via Los Angeles. The end of the line is always in Prudhoe Bay in Alaska. The section through Central America from Laredo/Texas via Mexico City to the Panama Canal is also known as the Inter-American Highway and is particularly popular with North American tourists.

Between Yaviza in the southeast of Panama and the northwest of Colombia there is a gap of about 62 miles (100 km) length in the Pan-American Highway's

road network, the so-called Darien Gap. Here extends a mountainous, difficult swamp and jungle terrain, where as yet no road has been built. In South America the Pan-American Highway again fans out into a number of different routes. The southernmost one runs via Buenos Aires down to Ushuaia in Tierra del Fuego, right in the south of the continent.

The Pan-American Highway traverses grandiose mountain landscapes north of Lima in Peru (left), but its course along the Californian Pacific coast near Big Sur, where the Bixby Bridge forms a part of the network, is no less spectacular (large picture).

THE LONGEST ROADS IN EUROPE

1. **European Route 40**
   4,970 ml (8,000 km)
2. **European Route 80**
   3,542 ml (5,700 km)
3. **European Route 70**
   3,343 ml (5,380 km)
4. **European Route 22**
   3,306 ml (5,320 km)
5. **European Route 45**
   3,057 ml (4,920 km)
6. **European Route 50**
   3,051 ml (4,910 km)
7. **European Route 90**
   2,964 ml (4,770 km)
8. **European Route 75**
   2,697 ml (4,340 km)

E40 — THE LONGEST ROAD IN EUROPE

European Route 40 is the longest highway road link in Europe that also extends into Asia. The E40 is about 4,970 miles (8,000 km) long; it begins at Calais/France on the English Channel and ends at Ridder in Kazakhstan near the Chinese border,

The European Route 40 in Kiev

traversing many countries: France, Belgium, Germany, Poland, Ukraine, Russia, Kazakhstan, Uzbekistan, Turkmenistan and Kirgizstan. In Atyrau the E40 crosses the bridge over the Ural River that forms the border between Europe and Asia. In Kazakhstan the E40 is not continuously paved in all sections — between the Caspian Sea and the Aral Sea there is a roughly 250 mile (400 km) long stretch that only has the status of a dirt track.

THE LONGEST ROADS IN ASIA

1. **Asian Highway 1**
   12,774 ml (20,557 km)
2. **Asian Highway 2**
   8,188 ml (13,177 km)
3. **Trans-Siberian Highway**
   6,835 ml (11,000 km)
4. **Asian Highway 6**
   6,509 ml (10,475 km)
5. **Asian Highway 5**
   6,450 ml (10,380 km)
6. **Asian Highway 3**
   4,555 ml (7,331 km)
7. **North South and East-West Corridor**
   4,536 ml (7,300 km)
8. **Asian Highway 4**
   3,743 ml (6,024 km)

AH1 — THE LONGEST ROAD IN ASIA

The AH1 (Asian Highway 1) is one of eight long-distance routes that are part of the Asian trunk road project. At a length of 12,774 miles (20,557 km) it is the longest road in Asia. The AH1 runs from Tokyo/Japan via Korea, South-East Asia, India and Iran into Turkey. There it crosses the Bosporus and connects

Bosporus Bridge in Istanbul

The AH 1 near the Khyber Pass in Pakistan

with the E80, which continues via Bulgaria to Portugal. The states that have joined in the project have committed themselves to develop the roads as highways.

THE LONGEST ROADS IN AUSTRALIA

❶ **National Highway 1**
9,010 ml (14,500 km)
❷ **Great Northern Highway**
1,991 ml (3,204 km)
❸ **Stuart Highway**
1,761 ml (2,834 km)
❹ **Outback Highway**
1,740 ml (2,800 km)

THE LONGEST ROADS IN AFRICA

❶ **Trans-African Highway 3**
6,716 ml (10,808 km)
❷ **Trans-African Highway 4**
6,355 ml (10,228 km)
❸ **Trans-African Highway 1**
5,366 ml (8,636 km)
❹ **Trans-African Highway 8**
3,912 ml (6,295 km)

THE LONGEST ROADS IN NORTH AMERICA

❶ **Trans-Canada Highway** (Canada)
4,990 ml (8,030 km)
❷ **U.S. Highway 20**
3,365 ml (5,415 km)
❸ **U.S. Highway 6**
3,205 ml (5,158 km)
❹ **Interstate 90** (USA)
3,101 ml (4,991 km)

Lasseter Highway in Australia

Mountain road in South Africa

Interstate 90 in Montana.

NATIONAL HIGHWAY 1 — THE LONGEST ROAD IN AUSTRALIA

With a total length of about 9,010 miles (14,500 km) Highway 1 is the third longest road link of its kind in the world. The highway runs mostly along the coast, thus circling the entire country. It also links the most important Australian cities with each other.

TRANS-AFRICAN HIGHWAY 3 — THE LONGEST ROAD IN AFRICA

Also known as the Tripoli–Windhoek–Highway or the Tripoli–Cape Town–Highway, the Trans-African Highway 3 runs from north to south through the entire length of the African continent. Its total length is 6,716 miles (10,808 km). Among all the Trans-African Highways, however, this is the one with the most sections missing and the greatest need for repairs.

TRANS-CANADA HIGHWAY AND U.S. HIGHWAY 20 — THE LONGEST ROADS IN NORTH AMERICA

The Trans-Canada Highway Is the only long-distance highway In Canada, linking the country's east and west coasts (total length 4,990 miles/8,030 km).

At a length of 3,365 miles (5,415 km), U.S. Highway 20 is the longest of its kind in the United States. It begins in Newport, Oregon, on the west coast and ends in Boston on the east coast.

THE LONGEST ROADS IN SOUTH AMERICA

❶ **Ruta Nacional 40**
Argentina   3,247 ml (5,225 km)
❷ **Transamazonica**
Brazil   3,231 ml (5,200 km)
❸ **BR-101**
Brazil   2,983 ml (4,800 km)
❹ **BR-116**
Brazil   2,725 ml (4,385 km)
❺ **Ruta Nacional 3**
Argentina   1,892 ml (3,045 km)

TRANSAMAZONICA AND RUTA NACIONAL 40 — THE LONGEST ROADS IN SOUTH AMERICA

The Transamazonica is a road construction project that will connect the Pacific with the Atlantic coasts at the equator and will be 3,231 miles (5,200 km) long. However, as of today the highway is only about half completed.

The Ruta Nacional 40 traverses the entire western side of Argentina, from south to north, with the exception of Tierra del Fuego. At 3,247 miles (5,225 km) it is the longest national route in the country.

On the Ruta Nacional 40

The Asian Highway 1 (AH1), the longest such highway In Asia, crosses this bridge in Shimonoseki. The city of Shimonoseki has 300,000 inhabitants and belongs to the Yamaguchi Prefecture, located in the far southwest of Honshu, the main Japanese island.

The world's highest passes are located in the Himalayas and in the Karakoram mountain range in Asia. The highest pass that is currently open to traffic is the Marsimik La (18,500 feet/5,640 m) in the Indian state of Jammu and Kashmir, followed by the Semo La (18,275 feet/5,570 m) in Tibet. But there are also some very high mountain roads and passes in South America, like for example the Chacaltaya at an altitude of 17,060 feet (5,200 m). Also in South America, on the Ojos del Salado volcano (22,615 feet/ 6,893 m) at an altitude of 21,940 feet (6,688 m), is the highest point ever reached by car anywhere in the world. Generally these very high passes are difficult to drive on — often they only consist of gravel tracks, are very steep and are also at great risk of landslides and rock falls in some areas.

THE HIGHEST MOUNTAIN PASSES IN THE WORLD
(height of pass)

1. **Marsimik La**
   India — 18,500 ft (5,640 m)
2. **Semo La**
   China/Tibet — 18,275 ft (5,570 m)
3. **Karakoram-Pass**
   India — 18,175 ft (5,540 m)
4. **Suge La**
   China/Tibet — 17,815 ft (5,430 m)
5. **Qieshan La (Nat. Highway 219)**
   China/Tibet — 17,720 ft (5,400 m)
6. **Ayi La**
   China/Tibet — 17,650 ft (5,380 m)
7. **Khardung La**
   India — 17,585 ft (5,360 m)
8. **Chang La**
   India — 17,585 ft (5,360 m)
9. **Taglang La**
   China/Tibet — 17,470 ft (5,325 m)
10. **Tanggu La**
    China/Tibet — 17,160 ft (5,231 m)

THE "HIGHEST" CAR JOURNEY IN THE WORLD, ON THE WORLD'S HIGHEST VOLCANO (21,940 feet/6,688 m)

The highest volcano in the world: Ojos del Salado

In April 2007 the Chileans Gonzalo Bravo and Eduardo Canales drove their converted Suzuki Samurai up to an altitude of 21,940 feet (6,688 m) on the slopes of the world's highest volcano, the Ojos del Salado (22,615 feet/6,893 m). However, about 660 feet (200 m) below the summit they had to surrender to this, the second highest mountain in the Americas. The reward for their daredevil enterprise was a mention in the Guinness Book of Records.

THE "HIGHEST" ROAD IN THE WORLD TO THE HIGHEST MINE IN THE WORLD (c. 19,700 feet/6,000 m)

Ruins of a closed sulfur mine on the Aucanquilcha

There has been a sulfur mine near the peak of the Aucanquilcha volcano (20,260 feet/6,176 m) in the north of Chile since 1913. Access to the mine was provided by a road that could be used by trucks weighing up to 22 short tons (20 tonnes). The road went up to an altitude of about 19,700 feet (6,000 m). When the mine was closed in 1992, the road also fell into disrepair. Due to landslides it is today no longer motorable on its entire length.

An empty and badly degraded road near the Khardung-La Pass in the Indian state of Jammu and Kashmir. Many of the passes in the Himalayas look like this. Caution and an all-terrain vehicle are absolutely indispensable here.

THE HIGHEST MOUNTAIN ROADS AND PASSES IN EUROPE

The highest mountain road in Europe that is usable by a normal vehicle or a bicycle is not located in the Alps or the Caucasus, but in the Sierra Nevada, a relatively small mountain range in the south of Spain.

THE HIGHEST MOUNTAIN ROADS AND PASSES IN THE ALPS

❶ **Ötztal Glacier Road**
Austria   9,281 ft (2,829 m)
❷ **Cime de la Bonette**
France   9,193 ft (2,802 m)
❸ **Col de l'Iseran**
France   9,088 ft (2,770 m)
❹ **Stelvio Pass**
Italy   9,045 ft (2,757 m)
❺ **Kaunertal Glacier Road**
Austria   9,022 ft (2,750 m)
❻ **Col d'Agnel**
France/Italy   9,003 ft (2,744 m)
❼ **Col de la Bonette**
France   8,907 ft (2,715 m)
❽ **Col du Galibier**
France   8,678 ft (2,645 m)
❾ **Gavia Pass**
Italy   8,589 ft (2,618 m)

Col de la Bonette

Col de l'Iseran

The highest paved mountain roads in the Alps are not mountain passes but spur roads, like the Ötztal Glacier Road, which leads to the foot of the Rettenbach Glacier as well as the Tiefenbach Glacier. The Cime de la Bonette is a circular road around the mountain peak of the same name. The highest alpine pass roads are the Col de l'Iseran and the Stelvio Pass.

MOUNTAIN ROAD ONTO THE SIERRA NEVADA
Spain   c. 11,150 ft (3,400 m)

The high mountain road leads to the summit of the Sierra Nevada's second highest mountain, the Pico del Veleta (11,142 feet/3,396 m), only about 37 miles (60 km) from the town of Granada. The actual mountain road begins at the village of Cenes de la Vega, leads past the information and administration center of the Sierra Nevada National Park and Nature Reserve, and up to the winter sports resort of Sol y Nieve. As a rule, the journey ends here for motorized vehicles, at a good 8,200 feet (2,500 m) altitude, by the highest hotel in Spain. Driving further is only possible with a special permit or by bicycle. The road ends just a few yards below the top, at an altitude of 11,102 feet (3,384 m). Although its final mile is not paved, it is quite easy to ride it on a normal bicycle. The gradient of the mountain road is altogether not very extreme, so that even ambitious hobby cyclists can master it. The summit road, with its almost

complete 360-degree panoramic views, is a popular test track for new car prototypes and is well known in advertising. Some stretches of the mountain are designated as nature reserves, into which it is forbidden to enter. One attraction are the Iberian ibexes at the higher reaches in the mountains.

Hairpin bends in the road to the Montes de Granada in the Sierra Nevada National Park in Andalusia (left)

GROSSGLOCKNER HIGH ALPINE ROAD — THE MOST FAMOUS MOUNTAIN PASS IN THE ALPS

Near the Kaiser Franz Josefs Höhe

The high alpine road on the Grossglockner (12,461 feet/3,798 m), Austria's highest mountain, is probably the best-known mountain road in the Alps. It goes over two passes, the Fuscher Törl (Fusch Gate) at 7,966 feet (2,428 m) and the Hochtor (High Gate) at 8,215 feet (2,504 m) altitude, linking the Austrian federal lands of Salzburg and Carinthia. Near the Fusch Gate, a short panoramic road branches off to the Edelweiss Peak, which also leads to the highest viewpoint (8,435 feet/2,571 m) on the Grossglockner High Alpine Road. Also here is the "Bikers Point," a place popular with motorbikers. Another highlight is the Kaiser Franz Josefs Höhe (7,772 feet/2,369 m), from which spectacular views of the Pasterze Glacier and the Grossglockner can be enjoyed.

The road climbs in many switchbacks up to the peak of the Pico del Veleta (11,142 feet/3,396 m). In the summer, the pass is free of snow and can easily be traversed by bike.

THE HIGHEST MOUNTAIN PASSES

❶ **Roki Pass**
South Ossetia (Georgia)
9,826 ft (2,995 m)
❷ **Mamison Pass**
Georgia/Russia
9,252 ft (2,820 m)
❸ **Klukhor Pass**
Abkhazia (Georgia)
9,140 ft (2,786 m)

IN THE CAUCASUS

For centuries the so-called Georgian Military Highway has been the most important link road between north and south across the Caucasus high mountain

Jvari Pass in Georgia

region. It runs from Vladikavkaz in Russian North Ossetia via the 7,815 feet (2,382 m) high Jvari Pass to Tbilisi in Georgia. Currently none of the pass roads can be used without major difficulties due to the dispute over South Ossetia.

THE HIGHEST MOUNTAIN PASSES IN THE CARPATHIANS

The highest road in the Carpathians is the Transfaqaras High Road, which crosses the Transylvanian Alps in the Romanian Southern Carpathians in a south–north direction. The road links the Arges Valley into the Wallachia and the Olt Valley in Transylvania. Its highest point is the Balea Pass (6,699 feet/2,042 m).

The Transfagaras High Road in winter

MARSIMIK LA

The highest motorable pass in the world from Leh via the Chang Chemno Range to the Chinese Border
Top of the pass   18,504 ft (5,640 m)

The altitude readings for this pass vary between 18,314 and 18,635 feet (5,582 and 5,680 m). Satellite readings come to an altitude of 18,504 feet (5,640 m) at the zenith, which makes it the highest motorable pass in the world. The track is, however, very sandy and so the pass road can only be tackled by all-terrain vehicles. Additionally, the pass is situated right on the ceasefire line between India and China, and a special permit from the local authorities is therefore required to drive on it. Currently, however, such a permit is not issued to tourists.

KARAKORAM PASS

Pass road from Leh via the Depsang Plains into the Tarim Basin
Top of the pass   18,176 ft (5,540 m)

The height of this pass is officially given as 18,291 feet (5,575 m). Independent readings, however, only come up with an altitude of 18,176 feet (5,540 m). The pass road goes from the Indian city of Leh to Yarkant in the Tarim Basin, which is controlled by China, and the pass itself is on the border between India and China. In its immediate vicinity is the Siachen

Road into the Nubra Valley

Glacier, which is being fought over by Pakistan and India. The pass is therefore closed to normal traffic and is only used by military vehicles.

An Indian truck on the road from Leh to Manali at the Taglang La, one of the highest passes in the world that can be used by trucks. It is located in the Ladakh region of northern India.

CHANG LA

**Pass road from Leh
to the Pangong Lake**

Top of the pass   c. 17,585 ft (5,360 m)

This pass route is located in the Ladakh region of the Indian Himalayas. It links the Indus Valley with the Pangong Lake, which is on the Indian border with Tibet and China, and it was once an important route between the Indian city of Leh and Tibetan Lhasa. The official pass altitude has been declared as 17,585 feet (5,360 m). Because

Pangong Lake in Ladakh

of border disputes between India and China, the pass is controlled by the military, and tourists will need an official authorization before driving on it.

KHARDUNG LA

**Pass road from Leh into the Shyok
and Nubra valleys**

Top of the pass   17,585 ft (5,360 m)

This pass, located in the Ladakh mountain range in the northwest of India, links the Indus Valley with the Nubra Valley. The road winds along from Leh (11,483 feet/3,500 m)

Tibetan prayer flags at the Khardung La

for just under 25 miles (40 km) and up to the pass, which according to official records is 18,379 feet (5,602 m) above sea level — so says a sign at the top of the pass. A whole series of independent measurements, however, have only attested to a height of 17,585 feet (5,360 m). Due to the persisting border conflicts

between India, Pakistan and China, the strategically important pass is cleared and kept open all year round. Similarly to many other passes in this highly militarized zone, a travel permit for driving on the Khardung La is needed; it is available in Leh for around 100 rupees.

Motorbikers in the Nubra Valley

Mountain road in the Nubra Valley

TAGLANG LA

Leh–Manali Highway

Top of the pass   17,470 ft (5,325 m)

This pass in Ladakh Province in northwestern India is part of the Leh–Manali Highway, which over a distance of just under 310 miles (500 km) leads from the Indian city of Leh in the state of Jammu and Kashmir to Manali, in the state of Himachal Pradesh, its southern neighbor. The Leh–Manali Highway is of strategic importance for the Indian military. On a noticeboard, the Indian road authorities state the pass altitude as 17,582 feet (5,359 m), but according to independent sources it is only about 17,470 feet (5,325 m).

Mountain panorama in Ladakh

Baralacha Pass in Ladakh

SUGE LA

Third highest motorable pass in the world on the Friendship Highway between Shigatse and Lhasa

Top of the pass   17,815 ft (5,430 m)

Satellite measurements have found an altitude of 17,815 feet (5,430 m) for this pass route, about 62 miles (100 km) northwest of Lhasa. This makes it the third highest motorable pass in the world. It is located on the northern section of the Friendship Highway, which links Tibetan Lhasa with Kathmandu in Nepal.

SEMO LA

Second highest motorable pass in the world from Raka to Coquen

Top of the pass   18,274 ft (5,570 m)

Near Gerze, Tibet

This pass road runs through central Tibet, and the pass is located between Raka and Coquen. At 18,274 feet (5,570 m) above sea level, the Semo La is considered the second highest motorable pass in the world. The road is not paved, but it may be used by trucks nevertheless.

Mountain road from Lhasa to Shigatse

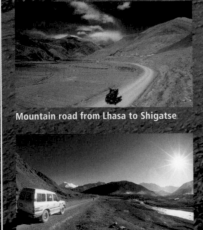

The toll road from Lhasa to Shigatse

NATIONAL HIGHWAY 219

The longest high mountain road in the world from Kashgar to Kathmandu   (Qieshan La Pass)

Top of the pass   17,717 ft (5,400 m)

The China National Highway 219 runs 1,455 miles (2,342 km) from northwest to southwest. The road begins at Yecheng (Karghilik) in the autonomous area of Xinjiang and continues via Rutog, Gar and Ngamring to Lhatse in Tibet; from there travelers continue on the Friendship Highway to Kathmandu. Highway 219 runs mostly at an altitude of 13,120 feet (4,000 m) and more than 16,400 feet (5,000 m). The highest elevation is the Qieshan La Pass; according to satellite measurements this pass is supposed to be at 17,717 feet (5,400 m) altitude. Highway 219 also passes the Kailash holy mountain.

National Highway 219

The Tonh La Pass

AYI LA

Pass road from Namru to Zhada (turn-off from National Highway 219)

Top of the pass   17,650 ft (5,380 m)

The ancient kingdom of Guge

On a side road off the National Highway 219 from Namru to Zhada one crosses the 17,650 feet (5,380 m) high Ayi La Pass. The altitude measurements were determined by independent surveys. Near Zhada in Guge stands an old royal palace in ruins; it is visited by many tourists traveling on the 219 in the direction of Lhasa or Khatmandu.

TANGGU LA

Pass road on the Qinghai Tibet Highway

Top of the pass   17,162 ft (5,231 m)

This pass road on the northern border with Tibet climbs, according to official figures, to a height of 17,162 feet (5,231 m). Since 2006 the Qinghai Tibet Railway, the line between Golmud and Lhasa, also runs along here. The top of the pass for the trains is officially set at 16,640 feet (5,072 m), making it the highest in the world. Quite near the top of the pass is also the highest rail station in the world (16,627 feet/5,068 m).

Top of the Tanqqu La Pass

GYATSO LA

Highest pass on the Friendship Highway

Top of the pass   17,126 ft (5,220 m)

According to satellite readings, the top of the pass is at 17,126 feet (5,220 m) above sea level. The

The Friendship Highway from above

Friendship Highway continues via the pass from Lhasa in Tibet to Kathmandu in Nepal. Also at the Gyatso La begins the Qomolangma National Nature Reserve, a nature protection area on the Tibetan side of the Mount Everest region.

The Friendship Highway between Tingry and Nyalam. This road is the only land connection between Lhasa in Tibet and Kathmandu in Nepal

The highest mountain road in Australia is the Great Alpine Road in the state of Victoria. This tourist overland highway goes from Wangaratta in the north via the Australian Alps to Bairnsdale in the south. It is the highest road in Australia that is passable all year round. At its peak by Mount Hotham (6,106 feet/1,861 m) it reaches a height of 6,037 feet (1,840 m) above sea level. The Mount Hotham resort is located on the pass road at an altitude of 5,741 feet (1,750 m). In the event of heavy snowfalls it is quite possible that the road will be closed for traffic. Also on Mount Hotham is one of only a few skiing resorts in Australia, with a total of 22 miles (35 km)

THE HIGHEST ROADS IN OCEANIA
(Top of the pass)

① Great Alpine Road
Australia — 6,037 ft (1,840 m)
② Crown Range Road
New Zealand — 3,530 ft (1,076 m)
③ Desert Road
New Zealand — 3,524 ft (1,074 m)
④ Arthur's Pass
New Zealand — 3,018 ft (920 m)
⑤ Lewis Pass
New Zealand — 2,835 ft (864 m)

On the Crown Range Road in New Zealand

of ski slopes and 13 ski lifts. In New Zealand, the highest mountain road is the Crown Range Road between Queenstown and Wanaka on South Island, reaching 3,530 feet (1,076 m) above sea level. The road leads across the Southern Alps past Mount Cook (12,316 feet/3,754 m). The second highest road is the State Highway 1 on North Island. Also known as Desert Road, it reaches a height of 3,524 feet (1,074 m). An important pass is the Arthur's Pass (3,018 feet/ 920 m), on which the State Highway 73 crosses the Alps of New Zealand's South Island.

Via many switchbacks, the pass road climbs to the Sani Pass in Lesotho. With an average gradient of about 20 percent the pass is one of the steepest in Africa, which is why it may only be used in all-terrain vehicles. Located at the top of the pass (9,252 feet/2,820 m) is the allegedly highest bar in Africa.

TIZI N'TICHKA

Highest pass road in the Atlas Mountains in Morocco

Top of the pass   7,415 ft (2,260 m)

The top of this pass is at 7,415 feet (2,260 m) above sea level. It is one of two important passes crossing the main ridge of the High Atlas and is a part of the

road connecting Marrakech and Ouarzazate. The road is continuously paved and in good condition. Another pass on this section is the Tich n'Test (6,867 feet/2,093 m). Both pass roads go from the Atlantic toward the Sahara.

Pass road at the Tizi n'Tichka

Landscape impressions in the Atlas Mountains

WOLKEFIT PASS

The most famous pass road in Ethiopia's Simien Mountains

Top of the pass   10,335 ft (3,150 m)

The Wolkefit Pass is on the road leading through the Simien Mountains from Aksum to Gondar. Also in its immediate vicinity is

A bus traveling across the Ethiopian highlands

MAHLASELA PASS

The highest pass road in Lesotho

Top of the pass   10,571 ft (3,222 m)

SANI PASS

The highest pass road in South Africa

Top of the pass   9,252 ft (2,820 m)

MOTENG PASS

The second highest pass road in Lesotho

Top of the pass   9,252 ft (2,820 m)

The Sani Pass in Lesotho

Ethiopia's highest mountain, the Ras Dashen (14,928 feet/4,550 m). The top of the pass is situated at 10,335 feet (3,150 m) altitude. The pass road is currently in a very bad condition, however — permanent roadworks are the order of the day here.

The region is an ancient settlement area. The palace of the legendary Queen of Sheba is said to have stood at Aksum. Her son, Menelik, allegedly brought the Old Testament Ark of the Covenant containing the Ten Commandments to Aksum, where it is still being guarded by a monk. The emperors of Ethiopia called themselves the descendants of the Queen of Sheba right up to the 20th century.

The two mountain passes, Mahlasela and Moteng, are in the Maloti Mountains, on the road between Butha-Buthe and Mokhotlong in Lesotho. By the Mahlasela Pass is also one of only a few skiing areas in southern Africa, with a total of two ski slopes and a lift for each one. The Sani Pass links Lesotho with South African Underberg. On the South African side, the pass road, which is unpaved in this section, winds its way via many switchbacks down into the valley. Along a stretch of just under 4.3 miles (7 km) it decends some 4,265 feet (1,300 m) in altitude.

The highest passes and mountain roads in North America are concentrated in the United States, in the state of Colorado. The highest mountain road that can be used by a normal passenger car leads up to Mount Evans (14,265 feet/4,348 m), to a height of 14,130 feet (4,307 m), just short of the summit. Some pass roads are unpaved and can only be driven on with all-terrain cars — for example the Black Bear Pass (12,841 feet/3,914 m) and the Mosquito Pass (13,186 feet/4,019 m). An important and well-developed pass road is the Colorado State Route 82, with the Independence Pass (12,093 feet/3,686 m).

THE HIGHEST PASS ROADS IN NORTH AMERICA

1. **Mount Evans Byway**
   USA/Colorado
   14,130 ft (4,307 m)
2. **Mosquito Pass**
   USA/Colorado
   13,186 ft (4,019 m)
3. **Imogene Pass**
   USA/Colorado
   13,114 ft (3,997 m)
4. **Black Bear Pass**
   USA/Colorado
   12,841 ft (3,914 m)
5. **Engineer Pass**
   USA/Colorado
   12,779 ft (3,895 m)
6. **Cinnamon Pass**
   USA/Colorado
   12,618 ft (3,846 m)
7. **Trail Ridge Road**
   USA/Colorado
   12,182 ft (3,713 m)
8. **Independence Pass**
   USA/Colorado
   12,093 ft (3,686 m)
9. **Loverland Pass**
   USA/Colorado
   11,991 ft (3,655 m)
10. **Hagerman Pass**
    USA/Colorado
    11,939 ft (3,639 m)

MOUNT EVANS BYWAY

The highest mountain road in North America

Top of the pass   14,130 feet (4,307 m)

The Mount Evans Scenic Byway is a panoramic road climbing up to Mount Evans (12,265 feet/4,348 m), but ending just short of the summit, at a height of 14,130 feet (4,307 m). This makes the Scenic Byway the highest paved mountain road in North America. The road begins at Idaho Springs, about 25 miles (40 km) west of Denver. From there it runs about 28 miles (45 km) along and about 6,890 feet (2,100 m) up to the summit of Mount Evans. About 12 miles (20 km) before the summit there is a toll station. The road, which is in good condition, is only open to traffic from the end of May to the beginning of September, however.

Mountain lake at Mount Evans

BLACK BEAR ROAD
Black Bear Pass
Top of the pass   12,841 ft (3,914 m)

The Black Bear Road is an unpaved mountain road, which branches off the U.S. Highway 550 at the Red Mountain Pass (11,017 feet/3,358 m) and ends at Telluride in Colorado, once a gold-mining town and today winter sports resort. The road runs across the Black Bear Pass past the Bridal Veil Falls, the highest waterfalls in the Rocky Mountains. The road may only be used by all-terrain vehicles.

Alpine meadow at the Black Bear Pass

ALPINE LOOP NATIONAL BACK COUNTRY BYWAY
Engineer Pass
Top of the pass   12,779 ft (3,895 m)
Cinnamon Pass
Top of the pass   12,618 ft (3,846 m)

The 52 mile (84 km) long circuit of this panoramic road starts in Lake City (Colorado). The largely unpaved mountain road continues via the Engineer Pass (12,779 feet/3,895 m) and the Cinnamon Pass (12,618 feet/ 3,846 m), past some ghost towns in ruins and the remains of abandoned gold mines as well as through a largely treeless alpine tundra landscape. Due to dangerous road conditions and sections with extremely steep gradients, a four-wheel drive all-terrain vehicle is imperative.

Engineer Pass at the Alpine Loop

TRAIL RIDGE ROAD
Top of the pass   12,182 ft (3,713 m)

The Trail Ridge Road is a 48 mile (77 km) long section of U.S. Highway 34, which runs between Estes Park and Grand Lake (Colorado) in the Rocky Mountain National Park. The road is the

Sunset on the pass road

highest highway in the United States, a roughly 12 mile (20 km) long section being located above the treeline. The highest point of the road is in the proximity of the Alpine Visitor Center, at an altitude of 12,182 feet (3,713 m). The road is well developed and can be used by normal vehicles.

Landscape impressions from the Cinnamon Pass on the panoramic Alpine Loop Byway in the San Juan Mountains (Colorado). The unpaved pass road is open only during the summer months

The highest pass in South America open to traffic is the Abra Huayraccasa in Peru. At just over 16,400 feet (5,000 m) altitude it occupies the No. 1 rank in the list of real pass roads (which descend again on the other side of the pass) on the continent. Even heavy rigs can use this unpaved road. The Paso de San Francisco is one of the most important passes in South America, linking the Argentinian province of Catamarca with the Atacama region in Chile. The pass is 15,577 feet (4,748 m) high. The highest motorable mountain road (which is simply a spur road to high ground) is the road to the former skiing area on the Chacaltaya in Bolivia.

THE HIGHEST PASS ROADS IN SOUTH AMERICA
(Top of the pass)

1. **Chacaltaya**
   Bolivia
   17,060 ft (5,200 m)
2. **Abra Huayraccasa**
   Peru
   16,598 ft (5,059 m)
3. **Sol de Mañana**
   Bolivia
   16,240 ft (4,950 m)
4. **Abra del Acay**
   Argentina
   16,076 ft (4,900 m)
5. **Punta Olimpica**
   Peru
   16,043 ft (4,890 m)
6. **Pata Pampa**
   Peru
   15,912 ft (4,850 m)
7. **Abra de Anticona**
   Peru
   15,807 ft (4,818 m)
8. **Punta Huarapasca,**
   Peru
   15,748 ft (4,800 m)
9. **Paso Portachuelo**
   Peru
   15,640 ft (4,767 m)
10. **Abra Apacheta**
    Peru
    15,583 ft (4,750 m)
11. **Paso de San Francisco**
    Chile/Argentina
    15,577 ft (4,748 m)
12. **Paso del Condor**
    Bolivia
    15,535 ft (4,735 m)

View from the Peruvian Portachuelo Pass into the valley. The pass is located at 15,640 feet (4,767 m) altitude. The pass road is not paved, but it can be used by normal vehicles and trucks. The route is an important gateway to the Huascarán National Park in the Cordillera Blanca in Peru.

CHACALTAYA ROAD – THE HIGHEST MOTORABLE MOUNTAIN ROAD IN SOUTH AMERICA 17,060 ft (5,200 m)

The Chacaltaya (17,785 feet/5,421 m) is located about 19 miles (30 km) east of Bolivia's capital La Paz. An unpaved gravel track runs in switchbacks over a length of 9 miles (15 km) from the suburb of El Alto (14,108 feet/4,300 m) to a mountain refuge and observatory, which both stand at a height of about 17,060 feet (5,200 m). The road can be mastered by normal vehicles. The Chacaltaya once boasted the highest skiing area in the world. The glacier with the slopes was, however, completely gone by 2009, and the ski run had to be closed down.

The Chacaltaya observatory

Paso Tambo Quemado (15,289 feet/4,660 m, Chile)

Paso Condor (15,535 feet/4,735 m, Bolivia)

Road to the Sol de Mañana (16,240 feet/4,950 m)

Past the Laguna Verde to the 15,577 feet (4,748 m) high Paso San Francisco (Chile/Peru)

TOYOTA COROLLA — THE MOST PRODUCED CAR IN THE WORLD

The Toyota Corolla occupies the No. 1 rank, even ahead of the Volkswagen Golf and the Ford F-Series, in the list of the most sold cars in the world. Toyota has now (2012) built around 39 million compact cars. They have been sold under this brand name around the world, and the Corolla still ranks as one of the most popular models in the product range. Toyota launched the Corolla in 1966, and it was the first car to have a dedicated plant

A Toyota Corolla at the Chicago Auto Show in 2010

built solely for its production. In the ten model generations developed up to 2006, some radical alterations were made to the design, for example a change from rear- to front-wheel drive, so that a Corolla today has precious little in common with the original model of 1966. The reasons for the success of the car, which so far has been built in 15 countries and sold in 116, are likely to be its high reliability on the one hand and the enormous model diversity on the other hand: there are specially adapted versions for every possible market.

Historic VW Beetle in the ZeitHaus Automobile Museum in Wolfsburg. The first cars in civilian production after World War II were delivered to the British occupying forces. The four-cylinder boxer engines of the CCG version of the beetle (Control Commission for Germany) achieved 18 kW.

VW BEETLE — THE CAR WITH THE LONGEST PRODUCTION RUN

Ferdinand Porsche designed the VW Beetle prototype as early as the 1930s. Before the car could go into production, however, World War II began, and the project was stopped. But as early as December 1945, mass production began of the car that was initially called Volkswagen Type 1. By August 5, 1955, more than one million Beetles had been produced. Production at the VW works in Emden/Germany ended on January 19, 1978; and it was finally terminated altogether, after nearly 57 years and 21,529,464 cars, on July 30, 2003, when the very last Beetle rolled off the production line in the Puebla Volkswagen de Mexico works.

A VW Beetle in the heart of Cairo, Egypt

The VW Beetle used as a police car in Veracruz, Mexico

The Bugatti Veyron Super Sport accelerates from 0 to 62 mph (100 km/h) in 2.5 seconds, to 124 mph (200 km/h) in 6.7 seconds, exceeds 186 mph (300 km/h) after just less than 15 seconds, and shortly after reaches its top speed of

At a car show in Los Angeles

268 mph (431 km/h). The versions on sale are blocked at 258 mph (415 km/h) because of the tires; nevertheless the Bugatti Veyron Super Sport is the fastest series-produced street-legal car. The powerful 16-cylinder engine has a 488 CID (7,993 cc) cylinder capacity and at 6,400 rpm produces 882 kW; the maximum torque of 1,100 lbf ft (1,500 Nm) is reached at 3,000 to 5,000 rpm. These figures too are record values for the Bugatti Veyron Super Sport, and so is its fuel consumption: according to company figures it does on average 3 miles per U.S. gallon Super Unleaded (burns 23.1 l per 100 km).

THE FASTEST STREET-LEGAL SERIES-PRODUCED CAR IN THE WORLD

In 2008 a duel took place between a Bugatti Veyron and a fighter jet. On a runway the Bugatti Veyron drove one mile, then returned to the start/finish line. The fighter jet started at the same time right beside it, climbed a mile vertically into the air, turned and came back down. The fighter jet won only narrowly in this race organized by the English TV program "Top Gear."

TURBINATOR

Don Vesco, 2001   458.4 mph (737.8 km/h)
Bonneville Salt Flats, Utah

The Turbinator, built by the brothers Don and Rick Vesco, has been the fastest vehicle with powered wheels since October 18, 2001. The engine is a cargo helicopter's T-55 gas turbine built in 1967, which achieves 2,758 kW. Weighing 1.65 short tons (1.5 tonnes), the Turbinator is 31 feet (9.5 m) long, but only 3 feet (0.91 m) wide and 2.7 feet (0.81 m) tall.

BLUE FLAME

Gary Gablich, 1970   622.4 mph (1,001.7 km/h)
Bonneville Salt Flats, Utah

On October 23, 1970, the "Blue Flame" was the first wheeled vehicle to break the 621 mph (1,000 km/h) barrier. Its engine was a rocket burning a mix of liquefied natural gas and hydrogen peroxide (which generates the eponymous blue flame), achieving a thrust of 15,980 lbf (7,248 kg/42,658 kW).

Don Vesco drives the Turbinator across the Bonneville Salt Flats

The "Blue Flame" on the Bonneville Salt Flats

MERCEDES BENZ W 125

Rudolf Caracciola, 1938   268.9 mph (432.7 km/h)
Frankfurt—Darmstadt expressway

On January 28, 1938, Rudolf Caracciola reached the highest speed ever driven on a public road, at 268.9 mph (432.7 km/h). For his record drive, a Grand Prix car of the model W125 had been modified — one of the legendary "silver arrows" that allowed Mercedes Benz to dominate the car races of the 1930s. Instead of the normal eight-cylinder engine, the record-breaking car had a V12 supercharged engine (340 CID/5,577 cc, 541 kW).

Mercedes Benz driver Hermann Lang demonstrated the potential of the W 125 in 1986 on the Laguna Seca race track in Monterey, California. It was one of the most powerful racing cars into the 1980s.

As early as April 29, 1899, Camille Jenatzy exceeded 62 mph (100 km/h) with his electric car "Jamais Contente" (Never Satisfied One). The record of 65.8 mph (105.9 km/h) established at the Concours de Vitesse near Paris only lasted until April 13, 1902, however, when Léon Serpollet achieved 75.1 mph (120.8 km/h) with his steam car "Œuf de Pâques" (Easter Egg). The race toward greater speeds has not stopped since. Ever more powerful engines allow for ever-greater speeds to be achieved. Into the middle of the 20th century combustion engines dominated, but in the 1960s aircraft engines began to be installed. Since a large, completely level surface is needed to set a new record, attempts are held on the salt lakes, such as the Bonneville Salt Flats in Utah.

THE FASTEST LAND VEHICLES IN THE WORLD

❶ Thrust SSC
1997
763.033 mph (1,227.985 km/h)

❷ Thrust2
1983
633.47 mph (1,019.47 km/h)

❸ Blue Flame
1970
622.41 mph (1,001.67 km/h)

❹ Spirit of America Sonic 1
1965
600.841 mph (966.961 km/h)

❺ Green Monster
1965
576.552 mph (927.872 km/h)

❻ Spirit of America
1965
526.214 mph (846.861 km/h)

❼ Wingfoot Express
1964
415.092 mph (668.027 km/h)

❽ Blue Bird CN7
1964
400.76 mph (644.96 km/h)

❾ Railton Mobil Special
1947
394.19 mph (634.39 km/h)

❿ Railton Special
1939
369.74 mph (595.04 km/h)h

THRUST SSC

Andy Green, 1997   763.033 mph (1,227.985 km/h)
Black Rock Desert, Nevada

On October 15, 1997, the Thrust Supersonic Car was the first land vehicle to break the sound barrier. The car is 54 feet (16.5 m) long, 12 feet (3.7 m) wide, 7 feet (2.14 m) high and weighs 11.6 short tons (10.5 tonnes), giving it the proportions of a fighter jet on wheels. The car is also powered by the same turbofan engines with afterburners that are used in fighter jets. The twin Rolls Royce Spey 202 engines have a thrust of 12,140 lbf (9,299 kgf) each, which is the equivalent of about 54,729 kW. Appropriately, the record-setting driver, Andy Green, is a fighter pilot in the British Air Force.

The Thrust SSC during a test drive on September 13, 1997

Two jet engines on wheels seen from the front: the Thrust SSC

TRANSPORTATION AND TRAF

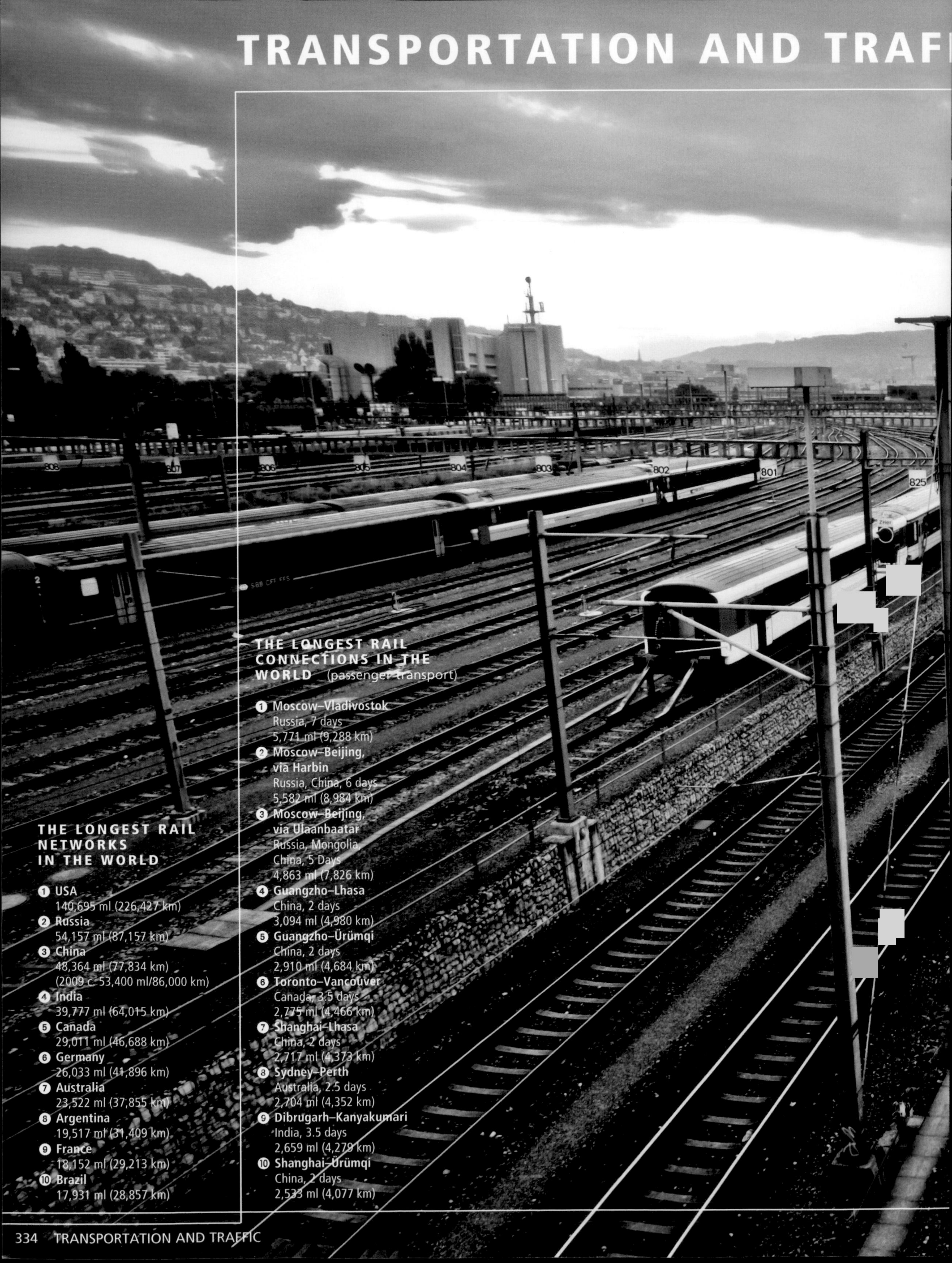

THE LONGEST RAIL NETWORKS IN THE WORLD

1. **USA**
   140,695 ml (226,427 km)
2. **Russia**
   54,157 ml (87,157 km)
3. **China**
   48,364 ml (77,834 km)
   (2009 c. 53,400 ml/86,000 km)
4. **India**
   39,777 ml (64,015 km)
5. **Canada**
   29,011 ml (46,688 km)
6. **Germany**
   26,033 ml (41,896 km)
7. **Australia**
   23,522 ml (37,855 km)
8. **Argentina**
   19,517 ml (31,409 km)
9. **France**
   18,152 ml (29,213 km)
10. **Brazil**
    17,931 ml (28,857 km)

THE LONGEST RAIL CONNECTIONS IN THE WORLD (passenger transport)

1. **Moscow–Vladivostok**
   Russia, 7 days
   5,771 ml (9,288 km)
2. **Moscow–Beijing, via Harbin**
   Russia, China, 6 days
   5,582 ml (8,984 km)
3. **Moscow–Beijing, via Ulaanbaatar**
   Russia, Mongolia, China, 5 Days
   4,863 ml (7,826 km)
4. **Guangzho–Lhasa**
   China, 2 days
   3,094 ml (4,980 km)
5. **Guangzho–Ürümqi**
   China, 2 days
   2,910 ml (4,684 km)
6. **Toronto–Vancouver**
   Canada, 3.5 days
   2,775 ml (4,466 km)
7. **Shanghai–Lhasa**
   China, 2 days
   2,717 ml (4,373 km)
8. **Sydney–Perth**
   Australia, 2.5 days
   2,704 ml (4,352 km)
9. **Dibrugarh–Kanyakumari**
   India, 3.5 days
   2,659 ml (4,279 km)
10. **Shanghai–Ürümqi**
    China, 2 days
    2,533 ml (4,077 km)

The first tracks for transporting heavy goods in carriages and carts were laid as early as the Late Middle Ages. In the mining industry especially, wooden tracks were used at first, and from the middle of the 18th century tracks were made from cast iron. The carts that ran on these tracks were improved by human muscle

power, later with the help of horses. The first official horse-drawn railroad ran in England from 1801. During the course of the industrial revolution the horse trams were soon replaced by steam-powered railroads. In 1825 the first rail line in the world was opened between Stockton and Darlington in England. The

first railroad in Germany ran from 1835 between Nuremberg and Fürth. The boom was unstoppable: widely branched networks were being created in the United States, Russia and Europe. Today all the railroad tracks in the world are about 540,590 miles (870,000 km) long when laid end to end.

A modern traffic system without a rail network is today unthinkable. In Germany alone, one-fourth of all goods are transported by rail, and more than five million people take the railroad every day for both local and long-distance travel — the environmentally friendliest way to travel.

The longest continuous railroad line in the world, the Trans-Siberian Railway, or for short Trans-Sib, measures exactly 5,771.4 miles (9,288.2 km).

Electric loco of the WL 80 series

Construction of the line from European Moscow to Asian Vladivostok began in 1891. At times more than 90,000 workers slaved away for 25 years, in the extreme cold of winter and fighting against heat, mud and mosquito plagues in the summer. Thousands lost their lives during its construction. When in 1916 the bridge over the Amur River at Chabarovsk was opened, the line was finally completed. The Trans-Siberian Railway was enormously influential in opening up and settling the Far Eastern regions of Russia.

It brought the raw materials of Siberia within reach, and numerous new settlements sprang up along the line. Thus, for example, Novosibirsk was founded in West Siberia during the construction of a rail bridge across the Ob River in 1893, Russia's third largest city with just under 1.5 million inhabitants today. From 2002 the Trans-Siberian Railway, which is a broad-gauge line with a gauge of 4 ft 11⅚ in (1,520 mm), like almost all rail lines in Russia, was continuously electrified. Along its route are 396 stations and 89 towns, including Yekaterinburg, Krasnoyarsk and Irkutsk on Lake Baikal. A journey on the Trans-Sib from the Yaroslavl Station in Moscow to Vladivostok on the Sea of Japan takes almost seven days and passes through seven time zones — truly an adventure on rails.

The Trans-Sib at its final destination: Vladivostok

THE LONGEST RAIL CONNECTION IN THE WORLD

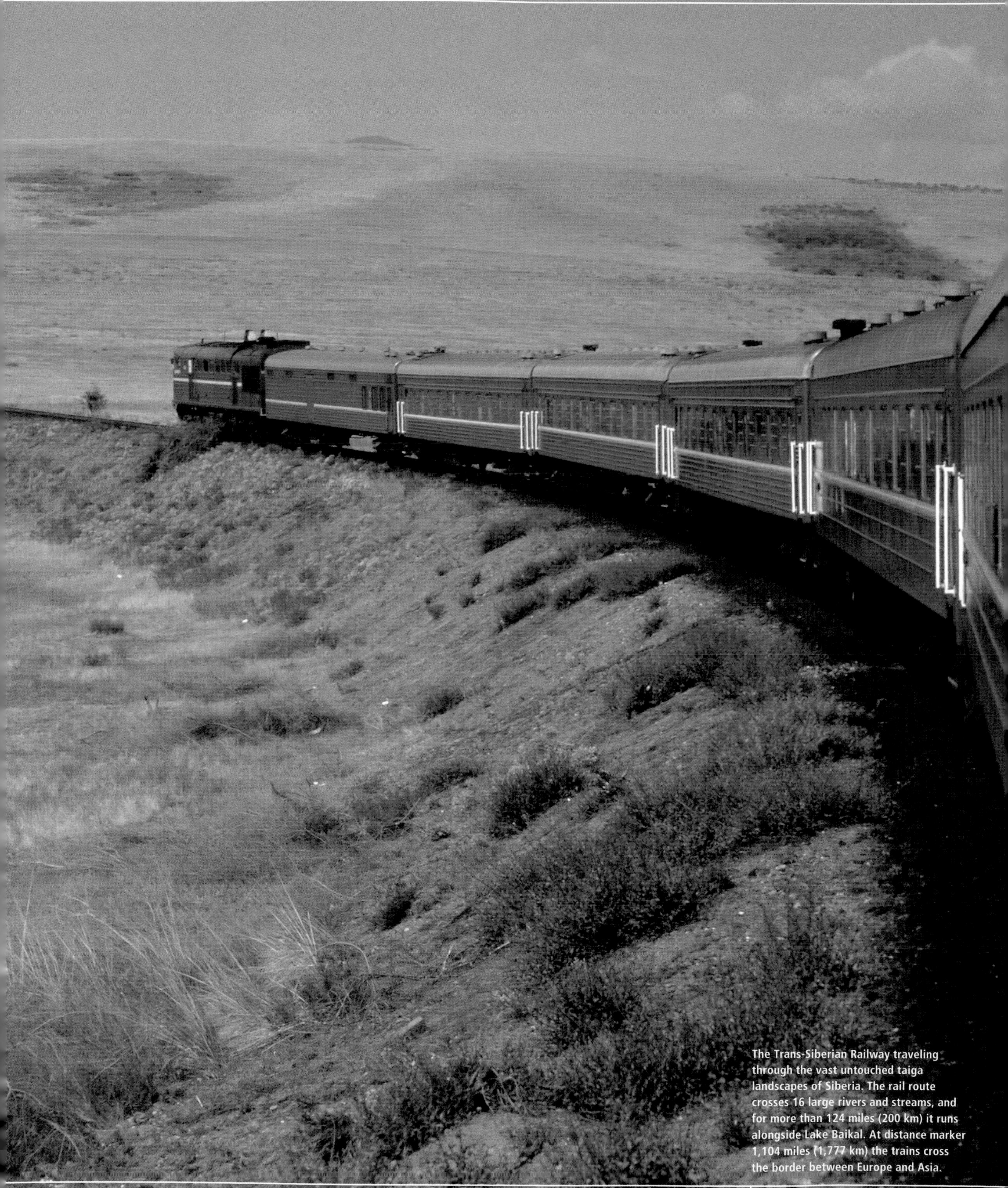

The Trans-Siberian Railway traveling through the vast untouched taiga landscapes of Siberia. The rail route crosses 16 large rivers and streams, and for more than 124 miles (200 km) it runs alongside Lake Baikal. At distance marker 1,104 miles (1,777 km) the trains cross the border between Europe and Asia.

QINGHAI RAILROAD
China   16,640 ft (5,072 m)

When the 1,215 mile (1,956 km) long rail route from Xining to Lhasa was completed in the summer of 2006, the People's Republic of China celebrated its transport links with Tibet — and the world marveled at a technological masterstroke

A train on the Qinghai–Tibet high plains

of superlatives. With a highest point of 16,640 feet (5,072 m), the section between Golmud and Lhasa is the highest rail connection in the world. Tanggula Station (16,627 feet/ 5,068 m) is the world's highest station. The mammoth project posed great challenges for engineers and construction workers alike: 597 miles (960 km) of the route run at an elevation of at least 13,120 feet (4,000 m) above sea level. Permafrost ground, extreme cold and lack of oxygen had to be overcome during building and at the same time, a highly sensitive ecosystem needed to be protected.

The Qinghai–Tibet-Railroad is the longest and highest high-elevation railroad in the world. The first section, between Xining and Golmud (506 miles/814 km), was completed in 1984. The second section, from Gol-mud to Lhasa (710 miles/1,142 km), has been operational since 2006.

FERROCARRIL CENTRAL ANDINO
Peru   15,686 ft (4,781 m)

One of the most spectacular mountain railroads runs between Lima and Huancayo. The route was built from 1870 to 1908, on the initiative of the American pioneer

The Peruvian central railroad

and businessman Henry Meiggs. The Andes stretch, operated today by the Peruvian railroad company, Ferrocarril Central Andino S. A., is the highest standard-track railroad line in the Americas and the second highest anywhere in the world. Over a distance of 206 miles (332 km), the trains pass 58 bridges, 69 tunnels as well as six hairpin bends. The Galera summit tunnel is located at an altitude of 15,686 feet (4,781 m) above sea level — only about 330 feet (100 m) below the Ticlio Pass (15,889 feet/4,843 m).

PIKES PEAK COG TRAIN
USA   **14,111 ft (4,301 m)**

In 1891 the first passenger train of the Pikes Peak Cog Railway went on its maiden journey to the 14,111 foot (4,301 m) high summit of the Pikes Peak in the Rocky Mountains Front Range. This Swiss-type mountain railroad still runs today from Manitou Springs in the state of Colorado, on an 8.7 mile (14 km) long track. It is the highest cog railroad in the world and runs at the highest elevation of any train in the United States.

En route to the Pikes Peak

JUNGFRAU RAILROAD
Highest railroad in Europe   **11,332 ft (3,454 m)**

One hundred years ago, the Jungfrau Railroad in the Bernese Oberland was the highest railroad to be taken into operation in Europe. Starting from the Kleine Scheidegg (6,762 feet/2,061 m), it traverses the mountain ranges of the Eiger and the Mönch up to the Jungfraujoch, where it stops at Europe's highest railroad station, at 11,332 feet (3,454 m) above sea level. Over a distance of 5.8 miles (9.34 km) the cog railroad rises about 4,600 feet (1,400 m) in altitude, and more than 4.3 miles (7 km) are in a tunnel. The Jungfau Railroad has been electrified since the startup of its first section in 1898.

Start of the railroad at Kleine Scheidegg

Tunnel station of the Jungfrau Railroad

THE HIGHEST STATIONS IN THE WORLD

1 Tanggula
China   16,627 ft (5,068 m)
2 Tanggula North/South
China   16,240 ft (4,950 m)

At 16,627 ft (5,068 m) the Tanggula Pass Station is the highest station in the world.

3 Tuoju
China   16,403 ft (4,890 m)
4 Zhajiazangbu
China   16,030 ft (4,886 m)
5 Ticlio
Peru   15,843 ft (4,829 m)

At one time, stations were the focal points of the technological revolution. In contemporary writing the monumental buildings in the big cities were often described as "cathedrals of progress." When the first steam-powered train started up in England in 1825, the new means of transportation soon became a catalyst for industrialization. In the early days, stations functioned as transshipment points for the goods that had been transported there by rail and as a gathering point for travelers and traders. From the 1950s however, in parallel with the triumphal march of the automobile, the importance of rail traffic began to wane, lines were shut down, stations closed. The opposite trend could be observed in the cities: here stations were often developed as grand shopping malls.

GRAND CENTRAL STATION
New York, USA   67 tracks

In 1968 it was all set to be demolished to make room for an office complex — after years of dispute, a decision by the American Supreme Court in 1978 was able to stop this, and subsequently New York's main station was comprehensively renovated. The cathedral-like building on the corner of 42nd Street and Park Avenue in Manhattan, built in the Beaux-Arts style, was first opened in 1913. It is now one of New York's most famous landmarks. With its 41 aboveground and 26 underground tracks Grand Central Terminal is the largest passenger railroad station in the world.

THE LARGEST STATIONS IN THE WORLD

(number of tracks)

1. **Grand Central Terminal**
   New York, USA   67
2. **Paris Gare du Nord**
   Paris, France   44
3. **Munich Central Station**
   Munich, Germany   40
4. **Frankfurt Central Station**
   Frankfurt, Germany   33
5. **Shinjuku Station**
   Tokyo, Japan   33
6. **Naples Central Station**
   Naples, Italy   30
7. **Tokyo Station**
   Tokyo, Japan   30
8. **Paris Gare de l'Est**
   Paris, France   29
9. **Pennsylvania Station**
   New York, USA   29
10. **Roma Termini railway station**
    Rome, Italy   29

GARE DU NORD
Paris, France   44 tracks

Gare du Nord, in Paris's 10th Arrondissement on Place Napoléon III, is the busiest station in Europe — every year it is used by around 190 million travelers. Opened in 1864 after three and a half years of construction, the station has since been repeatedly modified and enlarged, most recently on the occasion of building the high-speed TGV Nord line that linked Paris with the Belgian border and the Eurotunnel from 1993.

Inside view of the Gare du Nord

NEW HAVEN LINE DEPARTURES

K	DESTINATION	REMARKS
	NEW HAVEN	GREENWICH - 1ST STOP
	NEW HAVEN	CONNECTION TO NEW CANAAN - WATERBURY
	NEW HAVEN	1ST STOP
	HARRISON	MOUNT VERNON - 1ST STOP
	NEW HAVEN	SOUTH NORWALK - 1ST STOP

MTA METRO-NORTH TICKETS

Inside view of the Grand Central Terminal. The main hall with its 75 feet (23 m) tall arched windows does indeed remind one of a cathedral. The impressively vaulted ceiling is painted with a night sky and the constellations. Originally built as a major overland station, today it only serves local traffic. With about 500,000 visitors (including c. 100,000 travelers) each day, the New York's main station is the most-visited structure in the city.

MUNICH CENTRAL STATION

Munich, Germany   **40 tracks**

Measured by the number tracks, Munich Central Station is the largest passenger station in Germany. Its surface area is equally impressive: 8,180,570 sq ft (760,000 sq m). Every day about 350,000 travelers pass through, a number that in Germany is only surpassed by Hamburg Central Station.

Munich Central Station, in the background the steeples of the Frauenkirche (Cathedral of Our Dear Lady)

Frankfurt Central Station

FRANKFURT CENTRAL STATION

Frankfurt, Germany   **33 tracks**

With its 25 mainline tracks, four subway lines and four suburban lines Frankfurt Central Station is the fourth largest station in the world. Thanks to its central location it is also Germany's most important rail traffic hub. Its roughly 350,000 passengers a day make it one of the busiest stations in the country.

DHANGHAI HONGQIAO
Shanghai, China
14,000,000 sq ft (1,300,000 sq m)

With an area of 14 million sq ft (1.3 million sq m) Hongqiao railroad station in Shanghai is the largest in the world. Located in Shanghai's Minhang district, it is also located right next to Shanghai's Hongqiao

Beijing West Railroad Station, northern entrance

Departure hall featuring clear lines

International Airport. The central station (Shanghai has three others) is served by subway lines 2 and 10. The station was opened on July 1, 2010, after only two years of construction. The total building costs were 15 billion yuan (2.4

billion U.S. dollar). To build the station, which has four levels and 30 tracks, most of which are laid out for high-speed trains, 88,200 short tons (80,000 tonnes) of steel were used. The main building measures 1,378 feet (420 m) in length and 656 feet (200 m) in width, and is 230 feet (70 m) high (incl. subterranean levels), and 10,000 passengers can be checked through at the same time.

BEIJING WEST RAILROAD STATION
Beijing, China
5,490,000 sq ft (510,000 sq m)

Beijing West Railroad Station, located in the Fengtai district in the western half of the city, is the second largest station in the world, covering a total area of 5,490,000 sq ft (510,000 sq m). It was taken into operation in early 1996, after three years of construction work. The distinctive main building, which is shaped like a Chinese character, measures 295 feet (90 m) tall. Some 180,000 passengers use the station every day to travel, for example, to Hong Kong, Guangzhou, Wuhan, Xi'an, Lhasa or other cities in the south and east of China.

Hongqiao High-Speed Railway Center

The way down to the trains

NANJING SOUTH RAILROAD STATION
Nanjing, China
4,930,000 sq ft (458,000 sq m)

Nanjing, the capital of the Chinese province of Jiangsu, is one of the most important railroad junctions in Asia. Until 2010 Nanjing Central Station was the largest hub for long-distance travel, but since the opening of Nanjing South Railroad Station, which is about five times as large, the picture has fundamentally changed. Now most of the high-speed trains that pass through the city are diverted here. The station, featuring 28 rail tracks and 128 moving stairways, is the fourth largest in the world by area (4,930,000 sq ft/458,000 sq m). The impressive main roof, most of which is covered with solar panels measures 1,060,000 sq ft (98,500 sq m). Its steel frame weighs more than 8,820 short tons (8,000 tonnes).

Atrium of Nanjing South Railroad Station

NAGOYA STATION
Nagoya, Japan
4,413,000 sq ft (410,000 sq m)

Nagoya Station in the Japanese metropolis of Nagoya owes its rank as the world's fourth largest station its 804 foot (245 m) high twin towers. The JR Central Towers, comprising a hotel tower (59 stories) and an office tower (56 stories), immediately adjoin the platforms. First opened in 1886, the current station compound on an area of 4,413,000 sq ft (410,000 sq m) was completed in December 1999.

The atrium of the Guangzhou South Railroad Station with its dramatic roof: the roof span measures between 164 and 328 feet (50 and 100 m). With its surface area of 3,444,000 sq ft (320,000 sq m) and 26 tracks on three levels, the station, opened in 2010, is the fifth largest in the world.

SHINJUKU STATION TOKYO

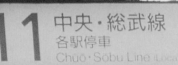

11 中央・総武線 千駄ヶ谷・千葉方
各駅停車　Chūō・Sōbu Line (Local)

Shinjuku Station in Tokyo

Commuters in the rush hour

Train of the East Japan Railway Company

The largest station in the world by passenger numbers is Shinjuku Station in the west of Tokyo. An estimated three million people a day and more than 1.3 billion travelers a year jostle here. The above ground station buildings are comparatively plain, but underground extends a gigantic network of tunnels and shopping malls on several levels, with more than 200 exits. The station, which is served by only a few long-distance lines, reaches its high passenger volume mainly thanks to the countless numbers of Shinjuku commuters. The district is an important business center in the Japanese capital, home to the headquarters of numerous banks, hotels and the seat of the Tokyo government. It is also very popular as a shopping and nighttime entertainment district. In the morning and evening rush hours the station is incredibly crowded. It is only quiet here when the last train has left Shinjuku at midnight — for a few hours, until the next morning's rush hour begins.

渋谷・品川方面
for Shibuya & Shinagawa

山手線
Yamanote Line **12**

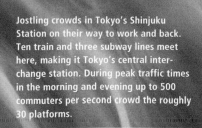

Jostling crowds in Tokyo's Shinjuku Station on their way to work and back. Ten train and three subway lines meet here, making it Tokyo's central interchange station. During peak traffic times in the morning and evening up to 500 commuters per second crowd the roughly 30 platforms.

Classification yards, also known as switchyards or marshaling yards, are the power centers of goods traffic by rail. It is here that the railroad cars that have been loaded for transportation are assembled into trains, and also separated out again. Such yards are mostly located in industrial regions as well as near major industries and mining areas, port facilities and urban agglomerations — wherever there is a high volume of cargo to be transported. Central Europe has the greatest number and density of classification yards.

BAILEY YARD
Nebraska, USA
124,146,000 sq ft (11,533,541 sq m)

The world's largest railroad classification yard is located in the United States, west of the small town of North Platte in the state of Nebraska. It owes its name to Edd H. Bailey, the one-time president of the Union Pacific Railroad. Located in the middle of the country, halfway between Chicago and Salt Lake City as well as between Denver and Omaha, Bailey Yard enjoys an outstanding economic importance. On a vast expanse of 4.44 sq miles (11.5 sq km) and using two humps, about 14,000 cargo cars are serviced every day. The track network comprising 315 miles (507 km) in total also has 17 receiving and 16 departure tracks as well as 114 "bowl" tracks.

The classification yard in North Platte, Nebraska

Every day some 14,000 freight cars are serviced.

MASCHEN MARSHALING YARD
Hamburg, Germany
30,139,000 sq ft (2,800,000 sq m)

The largest classification yard in Europe is located in Maschen, southeast of Hamburg. With an overall expanse of 1.08 sq miles (2.8 sq km) it is trumped in size only by the Bailey Yard in the United States. On July 7, 1977, it was ceremoniously inaugurated as a "miracle of technology" (start up: May 27, 1979, north–south system; September 28, 1980, entire yard). Today the classification yard has lost none of its fascinating appeal, even if parts of the cargo traffic are increasingly being transferred from rail to road. Currently, up to 4,000 cargo cars a day are serviced in Maschen.

View of the track system

Maschen Marshaling Yard at night. It is the central hub for the rail cargo services from and to Scandinavia as well as for the hinterland traffic of the ports of Hamburg, Bremerhaven and Lübeck. The double-sided classification yard has two train-formation yards, which have sets of 16 and 17 reception sidings respectively, and a set of 48 departure sidings.

The CRH2 train is based on Shinkansen E2-1000 series technology, developed by the Japanese company of Kawasaki Heavy Industries. In total 60 trains of this design have been produced for China's high-speed tracks since 2006, most of these in China by technology transfer. On April 22, 2008, a CRH2-061C reached a top speed of 230 mph (370 km/h) on the Beijing–Tianjin route.

THE FASTEST RAIL TRACK SYSTEM IN THE WORLD

THE FASTEST CRUISE SPEEDS ON RAIL

❶ **CRH 380A**
China
236 mph (380 km/h)

❷ **CRH3 (Velaro CN)**
China
217 mph (350 km/h)

❸ **AVE S-103 (Velaro E)**
Spain
217 mph (350 km/h)

❹ **KTX-II**
South Korea
205 mph (330 km/h)

❺ **AVE S-102 (Talgo 350)**
Spain
205 mph (330 km/h)

❻ **ICE 3 (BR 403/406)**
Germany, Belgium,
Netherlands, France
205 mph (330 km/h)

❼ **TGV POS**
France, Germany
199 mph (320 km/h)

❽ **TGV Duplex**
France
199 mph (320 km/h)

❾ **Shinkansen E6**
Japan
199 mph (320 km/h)

❿ **Shinkansen E5**
Japan
199 mph (320 km/h)

Maintenance center in Shanghai

CRH3 traveling toward Hangzhou

CRH 380A in front of Hongqiao Station

The latest generation CRH 380A

December 3, 2010, was a memorable day for China's ambitious "China Railway High-Speed" prestige project in the development of its high-speed network: on the Shanghai–Hangzhou line, at 302 mph (486.1 km/h), a train of the CRH 380A series reached the fastest speed ever measured in a series production multiple-unit train. Today China boasts not only the longest high-speed rail network in the world (2012: 8,080 miles/13,000 km; planned by the end of 2015: about 24,860 miles/40,000 km), but also an impressive fleet of high-speed trains. Currently five different production series with standard operating speeds of over 124 mph (200 km/h) are in use. Four of these are based on technology transfer: the CRH1 by Bombardier (up to 155 mph/250 km/h), the CRH2 by Kawasaki technology (Shinkansen; up to 155 mph/250 km/h), the CRH3 by Siemens (up to 217 mph/350 km/h) and the CRH5 by Alstom (up to 155 mph/250 km/h). The latest generation of super-high-speed trains of the CRH 380A series with the distinctive streamlined head is a Chinese development and designed for a top speed of 236 mph (380 km/h). The train of the future is even planned to hit 311 mph (500 km/h). A prototype of the appropriate innovative CRH 500 series was introduced in December 2011 by the Chinese producer Sifang.

December 3, 2010, was a memorable day for China's ambitious "China Railway High-Speed" prestige project in the development of its high-speed network: on the Shanghai–Hangzhou line, at 302 mph (486.1 km/h), a train of the CRH 380A series reached the fastest speed ever measured in a series production multiple-unit train. Today China boasts not only the longest high-speed rail network in the world (2012: 8,080 miles/13,000 km; planned by the end of 2015: about 24,860 miles/40,000 km), but also an impressive fleet of high-speed trains. Currently five different production series with standard operating speeds of over 124 mph (200 km/h) are in use. Four of

these are based on technology transfer: the CRH1 by Bombardier (up to 155 mph/250 km/h), the CRH2 by Kawasaki technology (Shinkansen; up to 155 mph/250 km/h), the CRH3 by Siemens (up to 217 mph/350 km/h) and the CRH5 by Alstom (up to 155 mph/250 km/h).

The latest generation of super-high-speed trains of the CRH 380A series with the distinctive streamlined head is a Chinese development and designed for a top speed of 236 mph (380 km/h). The train of the future is even planned to hit 311 mph (500 km/h). A prototype of the appropriate innovative CRH 500 series was introduced in December 2011 by the Chinese producer Sifang.

TGV V150 — THE FASTEST TRAIN IN THE WORLD
France

AThe record-breaking journey of the world's fastest railed train began on April 3, 2007, at 1:01 p.m. A TGV V150 — the figure in V150 stands for "150 meter per second" — started on the high-speed line between Strasbourg and Paris. The train with its three Duplex cars with powered bogies between two power cars weighed 258 short tons (234 tonnes) and had a maximum power output of 19,600 kW. After a journey of twelve minutes, at exactly 1:13 p.m., the train set a new world record with a speed of 357.16 mph (574,79 km/h). The journey ended after only 29 minutes, at 1:30 p.m. The effort undertaken for this trial run by the producer Alstom, the network operator RFF and the French railroad company SNCF had been gigantic: some 500 workers participated, and tracks and catenaries were specially prepared. The new world record cost about 39 million dollars.

The TGV V150's record run

The TGV V150 with the record displayed

A TGV-PSE train on the TGV Méditerranée route. Since 2001 trains have run from Paris via Avignon and Aix-en-Provence to Marseilles, 487 miles (783 km) away. At top speeds of up to 186 mph (300 km/h) the entire journey today only takes three hours.

The "Adler" steam engine ran on Germany's first railroad track between Nuremberg and Fürth and reached a top speed of 25 mph (40 km/h). Up until the 1960s the average speed of passenger trains rarely went above 75 mph (120 km/h). With the construction of high-speed rail networks in Japan (and since 1981 in France) began a new era of high-speed trains. Today countless new lines have been built and countless more planned in Europe, America and especially in China. Speed improvements to the trains, which already reach cruise speeds of 217 mph (350 km/h), are strongly sought.

ICE
Germany   max. 205 mph (330 km/h)

The ICE is the long-haul travel flagship of Germany's railroad, Deutsche Bahn. Since its introduction in 1991 all ICE trains together have covered more than 930 million miles (1.5 billion km). Nearly 80 million passengers use the ICE every year, which in its third generation today achieves a standard operating speed of 205 mph (330 km/h). The ICE brand is one of the most popular in Germany, with a recognition rating of virtually 100 percent.

Italo type AGV

NTV ITALO
Italy   max. 224 mph (360 km/h)

A "Ferrari on rails" is what the latest high-speed train in Italy is also called, not only because of its fire-engine red color or its possible top speed of 224 mph (360 km/h) — in Italy, however, the maximum speed is limited to only 186 mph (300 km/h) —, but also because the Italo is operated by a private group chaired by the Ferrari boss, di Montezemolo. The very comfortable trains are designed for up to 460 passengers and run on Italy's most important north–south route, from Milan via Rome to Naples.

AVE
Spain   217 mph (350 km/h)

AVE, meaning "bird," is the brand name of the Spanish high-speed network. Its construction began in 1992, and with a total length of 1,656 miles (2,665 km) it is today the longest in Europe. The latest AVE trains run at speeds of up to 205 mph (330 km/h) and take only 95 minutes for the 217 miles (350 km) between Madrid and Valencia on the Mediterranean, for example.

A third-generation ICE

The Spanish AVE — a great brand

A Japanese Shinkansen "bullet" train on a bridge across the Tama River in Tokyo. The trains have underfloor drive units and some also have a tilting system. The extremely aerodynamic design features a very long, slowly rising nose that not only looks good but also counteracts tunnel boom.

CRH
China   max. 236 mph (380 km/h)

For its ambitious CRH high-speed program, China bought trains around the world and then modified these for use in China. Thus the CRH1 is from Bombardier, the CRH2 from the Japanese Shinkansen series, the CRH3 from Siemens and the CRH5 from Bombardier. The CRH 380A, however, which is used on the line between Beijing and Shanghai among others, was entirely

The streamlined CRH 380A

developed and built in China. On a test run it achieved a record speed for non-modified, conventional trains, at 302 mph (486.1 km/h).

Shinkansen type JR 500

SHINKANSEN
Japan   max. 224 mph (360 km/h)

Japan is thought of as the mother country of high-speed trains. The first Shinkansens of the Japanese national railroad ran at a standard operating speed of 124 mph (200 km/h) as early as 1964. Since the privatization of the JNR state railroad in 1987, the Shinkansen network has been operated by a number of companies, who all use different series. The Shinkansen trains are legendary, especially because to their average speeds of up to 128 mph (206 km/h) and their punctuality. The average delay on the line between Tokyo and Ōsaka is just 0.3 minutes!

Hard to beat in terms of aerodynamics: CRH3 and CHR 380A

December 2, 2003, was a significant date in railroad history: a manned train of the Japanese JR-Maglev magnetic levitation system reached a speed of 361 mph (581 km/h), which today is still the highest speed ever measured for a railed vehicle. Comparable

The JR-Maglev being tested

The JR-Maglev uses an electro-dynamic suspension system (EDS).

record times have so far only been achieved by the TGV (2007: 357.2 mph/574.8 km/h), but with a wheel/rail system. Success came as no surprise: the innovative magnetic levitation technology has been intensively researched in Japan since 1962. Billions have been invested with the prospect of trains with low noise levels as well as high speeds, (up to

2000: 5.85 billion U.S. dollars). A large part of the funds went into the 11.4 mile (18.4 km) long Yamanashi test track. Since being put into operation in 1997, speed records have repeatedly been set here (October 3, 1997: 280 mph/451 km/h; December 12, 1997: 330 mph/531 km/h; April 14, 1999: 343 mph/552 km/h). Within the framework of the "Chuo Shinkansen" project, the

construction of a commercial line from Tokyo to Osaka is planned that will cost around 104 billion U.S. dollars. Construction is set to begin in April 2014 and to be completed by 2045. The Japanese supertrain will probably only take 67 minutes to cover the distance of 342 miles (550 km).

THE FASTEST MAGNETIC LEVITATION TRAIN IN THE WORLD

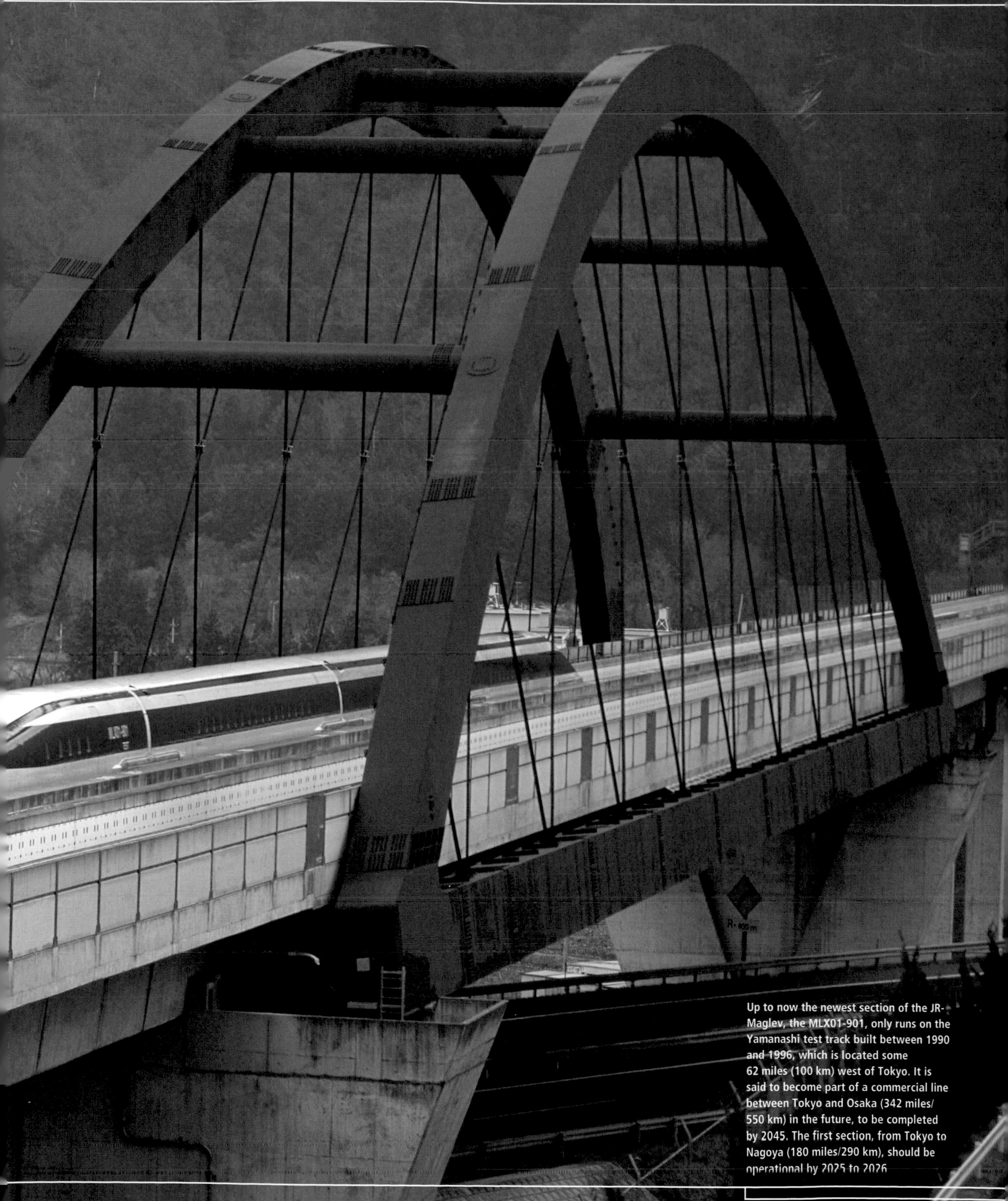

Up to now the newest section of the JR-Maglev, the MLX01-901, only runs on the Yamanashi test track built between 1990 and 1996, which is located some 62 miles (100 km) west of Tokyo. It is said to become part of a commercial line between Tokyo and Osaka (342 miles/550 km) in the future, to be completed by 2045. The first section, from Tokyo to Nagoya (180 miles/290 km), should be operational by 2025 to 2026.

Subway, underground train, metro, MRT — these are the most widely used terms to describe the electric track railroads that transport passengers around large cities. As well as in tunnels, subway trains also run overground in many places, on separate tracks or elevated on supports above the city's streets. The subways, which today operate in almost all of the world's metropolitan regions, owe their success to their great efficiency: they can transport up to 50,000 passengers per hour and direction, with a train succession interval of only 90 seconds.

THE LONGEST SUBWAY SYSTEMS IN THE WORLD

① **Shanghai** China	264 ml (425 km)	
② **London** Great Britain	248 ml (402 km)	
③ **New York** USA	229 ml (368 km)	
④ **Beijing** China	209 ml (337 km)	
⑤ **Seoul** South Korea	196 ml (316 km)	
⑥ **Moscow** Russia	190 ml (306 km)	
⑦ **Tokyo** Japan	189 ml (304 km)	
⑧ **Madrid** Spain	178 ml (286 km)	
⑨ **Guangzhou** China	144 ml (232 km)	
⑩ **Paris** France	134 ml (215 km)	

NEW YORK CITY SUBWAY
New York City, USA
229 ml (368 km)

The New York Subway is one of the oldest subways in the world. It was opened as early as 1904, and the essential sections of the network were built by three different companies until 1940. Since 1953 it has been run by the New York City Transit Authority (NYCTA). After problems in the 1970s and 1980s, when the reputation of the Subway was tainted by vandalism, crime and numerous accidents, it experienced a revival since the 1990s thanks to major investment programs. With 1.5 billion passengers a year it is one of the most-used subways in the world.

METRO SHANGHAI
Shanghai, China   264 ml (425 km)

Although construction of the Shanghai Metro did not begin until 1990, today it already has the longest route network, and is considered the fastest growing metro in the world. Since the opening of Line No. 1 in 1995, ten further lines have been added. By 2020 another 22 lines are planned as well as an extension of the network to 603 miles (970 km).

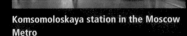

Komsomoloskaya station in the Moscow Metro

METRO MOSCOW
Moscow, Russia   190 ml (306 km)

At 2.4 billion users a year the subway in the Russian capital is one of the busiest in the world. It is particularly famous for its magnificent architecture. The stations especially, built in the 1930s and 1940s, feature impressive marble cladding, stucco ceilings and chandeliers. Its depth is also extraordinary: Park Pobedy station lies 276 feet (84 m) underground and boasts the longest uninterrupted moving stairway in the world (413 feet/126 m).

Very busy from the start: the old Subway station at Whitehall Street in New York, built in the year 1918. Since a conversion in 2009, the station, which is located in the banking district of Manhattan, has been linked up with the South Ferry Station. It is used by more than nine million passengers a year.

LONDON UNDERGROUND
London, Great Britain   250 ml (402 km)

Baker Street station

Mornington Crescent station, reopened in 1998 after renovation

The London subway, then an underground steam-driven railroad line, was opened on January 10, 1863. Its first line, the Metropolitan Line, gave its name to many similar systems around the world. The London subway, however, is known as the "Underground" or the "Tube." For the most part the subway runs aboveground, only 45 percent of all lines are actually in tunnels. Further lines were built by various companies until 1907, and were taken over by a public body in 1933. During World War II some stations served as air-raid shelters, and Prime Minister Churchill and his Cabinet met in the now-abandoned Down Street station. In 1999 an extension of the most recent line, the Jubilee Line, was opened. In 2008 Terminals 4 and 5 of Heathrow Airport were also linked into the system. Today 1.1 million passengers use the London Underground each year.

Against a superb backdrop the stairs goes down to Piccadilly Circus station, which is located right underneath the eponymous square. During the days of the British Empire, Piccadilly Circus in London's West End was also known as the "center of the world." The unmistakable London Underground logo was designed as early as 1908.

The six longest bridge structures in the world are currently railroad bridges on the Beijing–Shanghai high-speed line in China. The longest, at 102.4 miles (164.8 km), is the Danyang–Kunshan Grand Bridge. The first road bridge does not appear until

The China Railway Express

rank No. 7: the Thai Bang Na Expressway with an overall length of 33.6 miles (54 km). It is followed by further bridges in China and in the United States ranking eighth to twelfth.

THE LONGEST BRIDGES IN THE WORLD

1. **Danyang–Kunshan Grand Bridge**
   China
   102.4 ml (164.8 km)
2. **Tianjin Grand Bridge**
   China
   70.6 ml (113.7 km)
3. **Cangzhou–Dezhou Grand Bridge**
   China
   65.8 ml (105.9 km)
4. **Huaihe River Bridge**
   China
   65 8 ml (105.9 km)
5. **Weinan Weihe Grand Bridge**
   China
   49.5 ml (79.7 km)
6. **Sui River Grand Bridge**
   China
   40.8 ml (65.6 km)
7. **Bang Na Expressway**
   Thailand
   33.6 ml (54.0 km)
8. **Beijing Grand Bridge**
   China
   30.0 ml (48.2 km)
9. **Jiaozhou Bay Bridge**
   China
   25.8 ml (41.6 km)
10. **Lake Pontchartrain Causeway**
    USA
    23.9 ml (38.4 km)

THE LONGEST TUNNELS IN THE WORLD

1. **Seikan-Tunnel**
   Japan
   33.5 ml (53.9 km)
2. **Channel Tunnel**
   France/Great Britain
   31.0 ml (49.9 km)
3. **Lötschberg Base Tunnel**
   Switzerland
   20.3 ml (32.6 km)
4. **Guadarrama Tunnel**
   Spain
   17.6 ml (28.3 km)
5. **Hakkoda Tunnel**
   Japan
   16.4 ml (26.4 km)
6. **Iwate-Ichinohe Tunnel**
   Japan
   16.0 ml (25.8 km)
7. **Lærsdal Tunnel**
   Norway
   15.2 ml (24.5 km)
8. **Dai-Shimizu Tunnel**
   Japan
   13.8 ml (22.2 km)
9. **Simplon Tunnel**
   Switzerland
   12.3 ml (19.8 km)   29.8 km
10. **Vereina Tunnel**
    Switzerland
    11.9 ml (19.1 km)

The Chesapeake Bay Bridge in the U.S. state of Maryland has an attractive filigree outline. The parallel suspension bridge of 4.3 mile (6.9 km) length spans Chesapeake Bay, linking the comparatively rural eastern part of Maryland with the urban western areas of the state.

CHINA RAILWAY EXPRESS LINE BEIJING–SHANGHAI — THE LONGEST BRIDGE STRUCTURES AND RAIL BRIDGES IN THE WORLD

The trains on the Beijing to Shanghai line travel at up to 186 mph (300 km/h).

① Danyang–Kunshan Grand Bridge
China   102.4 ml (164.8 km)
② Tianjin Grand Bridge
China   70.6 ml (113.7 km)
③ Cangzhou-Dezhou Grand Bridge
China   65.8 ml (105.9 km)

The longest bridge structures are railroad bridges or viaducts that were built for the 819 mile (1,318 km) long Beijing–Shanghai high-speed rail line. The longest bridge is the Danyang–Kunshan Grand Bridge, its 102.4 mile (164.8 km) overall length making it the longest bridge structure anywhere in the world. The bridge consists largely of precast components, 105 foot (32 m) long box girders that are predominantly used to elevate the bridge. Only some sections of the bridge, where it goes over railroad lines, roads or water, are a little longer. There are four further bridges on the Beijing–Shanghai high-speed line that also rank among the world's ten longest bridge structures: the Tianjin Grand Bridge (70.6 miles/113.7 km), the Cangzhou–Dezhou Grand Bridge (65.8 miles /105.9 km), the Huaihe River Bridge (65.8 miles/105.9 km) and the Sui River Grand Bridge (40.8 miles/65.6 km). All were built using the same construction method.

JIAOZHOU BAY BRIDGE — THE LONGEST BRIDGE OVER WATER

China   25.8 ml (41.6 km)

The road project to which the Jiaozhou Bay Bridge belongs has an overall length of 25.8 miles (41.6 km). The six-lane highway bridge itself crosses the bay in

The Jiaozhou Bay Bridge

a straight line for 16.6 miles (26.7 km), and then there is also a nearly 1.2 mile (2 km) long turn-off to Hongdao peninsula as well as just under 4.3 miles (7 km) of bridge sections above land. Altogether some 22.7 miles (36.5 km) of the bridge are said to extend over water. It is a box girder bridge made from prestressed concrete; altogether 496,000 short tons (450,000 tonnes) of steel and 2.5 million short tons (2.3 million tonnes) of concrete were used in its construction. The road bridge links the two cities of Quindao and Huangdao. In the Guinness Book of Records, the bridge is listed as the longest bridge structure above water.

The Jiaozhou Bay Bridge has three larger navigable sections, the Cangzhou Channel Bridge being largest with a span of about 1,970 feet (600 m). The bridge structure is designed to withstand earthquakes of a magnitude of 8.0, as well as typhoons and ship collisions. On the picture a section of the bridge can be seen cloaked in mist.

BANG NA EXPRESSWAY – THE LONGEST ROAD BRIDGE IN THE WORLD

Thailand   33.6 ml (54.0 km)

This six-lane highway bridge is 33.6 miles (54 km) long, making it the longest road bridge in the world. Architecturally the bridge structure is more a sort of elevated highway, and in static terms it is a box girder bridge. The beams have an average span of 144 feet (44 m) and a width of 17 feet (27.2 m). The highway runs from Bangkok's Bang Na district past the international airport and in a southeasterly direction into Chonburi Province.

Bhumibol Bridge lit up at night

THE LONGEST BRIDGES
IN EUROPE

The two longest bridge structures in Europe stand in Portugal and in Russia. The Portuguese bridge, named after the navigator Vasco da Gama, spans the Tagus River at a length of over 10 miles (17 km). The Russian bridge crosses the Kama River, a major tributary of the Volga. It measures 8.7 miles (14 km) in length. The third place is taken by the Wuppertal Suspension Railroad, about 8 miles (13 km) in length. This is not actually a bridge but a steel lattice structure for an elevated railroad. The next-longest bridge structures are in Russia, Portugal and Denmark, for example the Øresund Bridge and the Great Belt Fixed Link.

The Vasco da Gama Bridge was erected between 1995 and 1998 for Expo '98, the World Exposition in Lisbon. It was to alleviate congestion in Lisbon and divert the north–south traffic away from the city center —the bridge gives direct access to both Lisbon airport and the exhibition grounds. The picture shows the bridge across the Tagus River in the evening.

THE LONGEST
BRIDGES IN EUROPE

① Vasco da Gama Bridge
Portugal
10.6 ml (17.2 km)

② Kama Bridge
Russia
8.7 ml (14.0 km)

③ Wuppertal Suspension Railroad
Germany
8.3 ml (13.3 km)

④ Ulyanovsk Bridge
Russia
8.0 ml (13.0 km)

⑤ Saratov Bridge
Russia
8.0 ml (12.8 km)

⑥ Leziria Bridge
Portugal
7.3 ml (11.7 km)

⑦ Øresund Bridge
Denmark/Sweden
4.8 ml (7.8 km)

⑧ Volgograd Bridge
Russia
4.4 ml (7.1 km)

⑨ Storebælt Bridge (eastern section)
Denmark
4.2 ml (6.8 km)

⑩ Storebælt Bridge (western section)
Denmark
4.1 ml (6.6 km)

VASCO DA GAMA
BRIDGE

Portugal   10.6 ml (17.2 km)

The bridge, named after the Portuguese navigator Vasco da Gama, is the longest in Europe, at 10.6 miles (17.2 km). Structurally it is a cable-stayed bridge to the main opening, spanning the Tagus River. The six-lane highway bridge links Lisbon with the south of the country. The pylons are 509 feet (155 m) tall.

LEZIRIA BRIDGE
Portugal   7.3 ml (11.7 km)

This box girder bridge spans the rivers Tagus and Sorraia over a total length of 7.3 miles (11.7 km). The main structure of the bridge has a length of 3,189 feet (972 m). It offers a route for the north–south traffic bypassing the urban area of Lisbon.

The Leziria Bridge elegantly soars above the sandy riverbed

ØRESUND BRIDGE
Denmark/Sweden   4.8 ml (7.8 km)

The Øresund Bridge is the longest combined road and rail cable-stayed bridge in the world. Its total length is 4,875 miles (7,845 km). Two ramp bridges lead to the central high bridge, which is 3,583 feet (1,092 m) long and has a span of 1,608 feet (490 m).

The Øresund Bridge with its distinctive (676 feet/206 m) high central pylons

KAMA BRIDGE
Russia   8.7 ml (14.0 km)

This bridge link is just under 8.7 miles (14 km) long. The main bridge crossing the Kama River in the autonomous Republic of Tatarstan has a length of 5,276 feet (1,608 m). The box girder bridge carries a highway and also crosses two other rivers.

ULYANOVSK BRIDGE
Russia   8.0 ml (13.0 km)

This bridge, crossing the Volga River at Ulyanovsk, is 8 miles (13 km) long. The bridge was opened in 2009 after 23 years of construction. Used by some 40,000 vehicles each day, it is an important link between Russia's European and Asian regions.

SARATOV BRIDGE
Russia   8.0 ml (12.8 km)

The 8.0 mile (12.8 km) long Saratov Bridge stretches across the Volga River south of Saratov. It is currently the third longest bridge in Russia. The old bridge at Saratov, only 1.7 miles (2.8 km) long, was the longest bridge in the Soviet Union until 1965.

THE LONGEST BRIDGES IN ASIA

1. **Danyang–Kunshan Grand Bridge**
   China
   102.4 ml (164.8 km)
2. **Tianjin Grand Bridge**
   China
   70.6 ml (113.7 km)
3. **Cangzhou–Dezhou Grand Bridge**
   China
   65.8 ml (105.9 km)
4. **Huaihe River Bridge**
   China
   65 8 ml (105.9 km)
5. **Weinan Weihe Grand Bridge**
   China
   49.5 ml (79.7 km)
6. **Sui River Grand Bridge**
   China
   40.8 ml (65.6 km)
7. **Bang Na Expressway**
   Thailand
   33.6 ml (54.0 km)
8. **Beijing Grand Bridge**
   China
   30.0 ml (48.2 km)
9. **Jiaozhou Bay Bridge**
   China
   25.8 ml (41.6 km)
10. **Hangzhou Bay Bridge**
    China
    22.4 ml (36 km)

HANGZHOU BAY BRIDGE
China   22.4 ml (36 km)

At its inauguration in 2008, this attractive bridge across Hangzhou Bay was the largest transoceanic bridge in the world,

The pylons of the Hangzhou Bay Bridge

with a total length of 22.4 miles (36 km). Integrated into the box girder structure are two cable-stayed sections with 1,470 and 1,043 feet (448 and 318 m) spans respectively. The two pylons with the tension cables are almost 328 feet (100 m) tall. The bridge is designed to withstand wind speeds of up to 143 mph (230 km/h).

DONGHAI BRIDGE (EAST SEA GRAND BRIDGE)
China   20.2 ml (32.5 km)

The 20.2 mile (32.5 km) long box girder structure with a central cable-stayed section connects Luchao Port in Nanhui New City in the Pudong New Area of Shanghai with the deep-sea port of Yangshan in Zhejiang Province. The bridge, completed in 2005, stands on average 130 feet (40 m) above sea level. The highest passable section of the bridge allows even relatively large ships with a capacity of about 11,025 short tons (10,000 tonnes) to pass underneath. The bridge carries a six-lane highway.

The two pylons of the Donghai Bridge

View of the cable-stayed construction

The Incheon Bridge in South Korea, beautifully illuminated at night: the picture shows the sweeping ascent to the cable-stayed bridge with its tall pylons. The clear height between the pylons in the middle of the bridge is 243 feet (74 m), allowing even large ships to pass easily underneath the bridge.

KING FAHD CAUSEWAY

Saudi-Arabia/Bahrain   16.2 ml (26 km)

The King Fahd Causeway is a 16.2 mile (26 km) long series of bridges and causeways between Saudi Arabia and Bahrain. The bridge structure was erected between the years 1982 and 1986, has four traffic lanes and is 82 feet (25 m) wide. In total there are five bridges linked by causeways and islands, with the bridges built from box girders. The bridge-causeway link is the only road connection between the island state of Bahrain and the mainland. A 163 acre (66 ha) large artificial island was built at about the halfway mark — one half of it now belongs to Saudi Arabia, the other half to Bahrain. Every year, some three million vehicles drive across the King Fahd Causeway. The structure was financed entirely by Saudi Arabia — it cost 1.2 billion U.S. dollars.

Bridge on the King Fahd Causeway

SHANGHAI YANGTZE BRIDGE

China   10.3 ml (16.5 km)

The bridge, a combination of box girder and cable-stayed bridges plus a tunnel, connects Shanghai with Chongming Island. The bridge section is 10.3 miles (16.6 km) long in total, the tunnel 5.5 miles (8.9 km). The longest span on the cable-stayed section is 2,461 feet (750 m). The bridge is part of the Chinese highway network. In combination with two other bridges, it is possible to cross the river by car here.

The Shanghai Yangtze Bridge with its filigree twin pylons

INCHEON BRIDGE

South Korea   7.6 ml (12.3 km)

The Incheon Bridge has a total length of 7.6 miles (12.3 km). The impressive structure is a combination of box girder and cable-stayed bridges. The maximum span of the cable-stayed bridge is 2,625 feet (800 m), and its pylons are almost 150 feet (240 m) tall. The bridge spans a mudflat bay in the Yellow Sea, connecting New Songdo City with Incheon Airport. South Korea's longest bridge, it was opened in October 2009, after four years of construction.

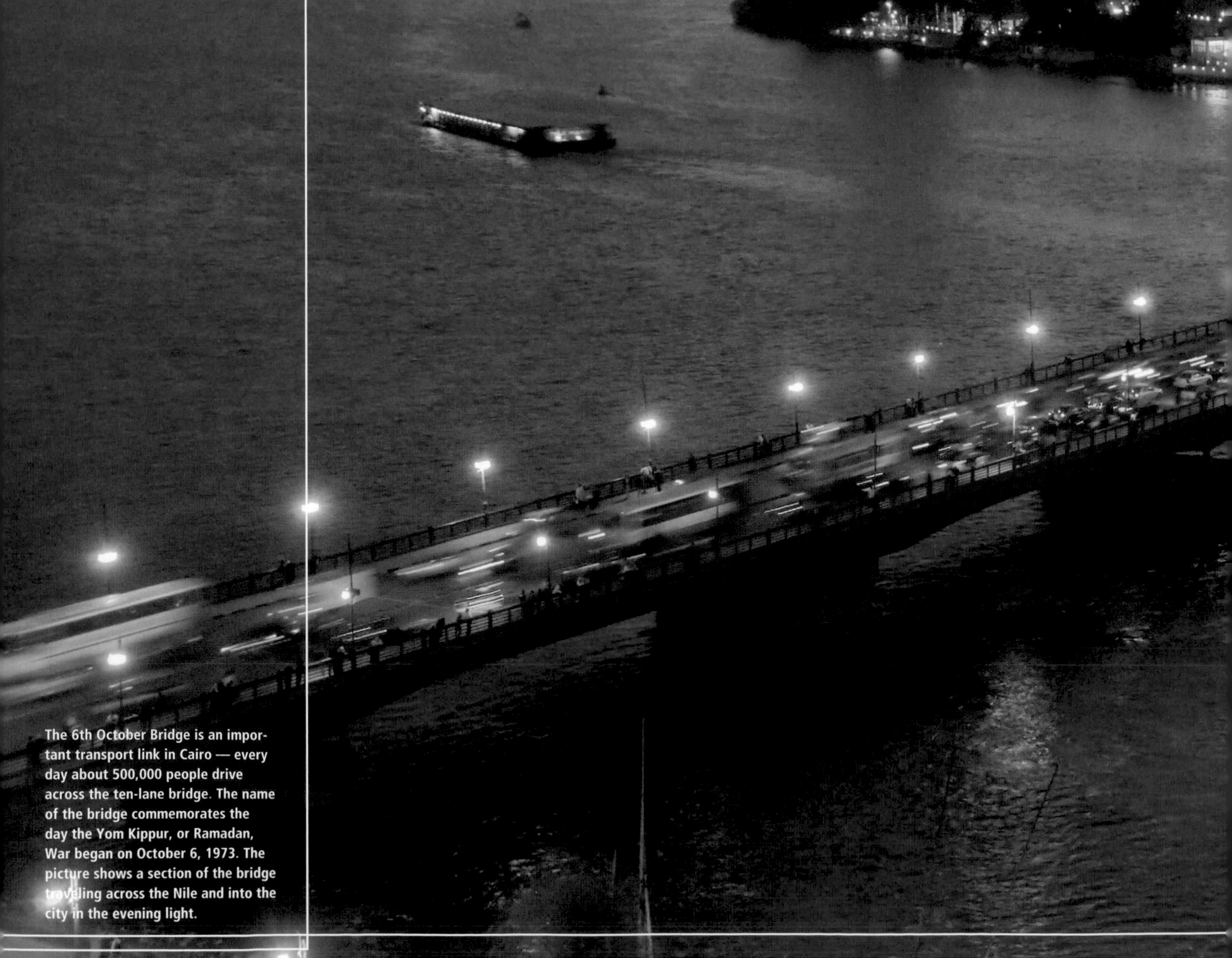

THE LONGEST BRIDGES IN AUSTRALIA AND AFRICA

THE LONGEST BRIDGES IN AUSTRALIA

1. **Houghton Highway**
   Brisbane, Queensland
   8,990 ft (2,740 m)
2. **Ted Smout Memorial Bridge**
   Brisbane, Queensland
   8,990 ft (2,740 m)
3. **West Gate Bridge**
   Melbourne, Victoria
   8,471 ft (2,582 m)
4. **Tasman Bridge**
   Hobart, Tasmania
   4,577 ft (1,395 m)
5. **Sydney Harbour Bridge**
   New South Wales
   3,770 ft (1,149 m)

The Houghton Highway and the Ted Smout Memorial Bridge are two reinforced concrete structures that stand in close proximity to each other (about 100 feet/30 m apart), spanning the shallow waters of Bramble Bay at a low altitude. Both are 8,990 feet (2,740 m) long. The West Gate Bridge in Melbourne spans the Yarra River shortly before it flows into Port Phillip. The bridge is a cable-stayed structure with a maximum span of 1,102 feet (336 m) and a total length of 8,471 feet (2,582 m), making it the third longest on the continent. Almost 170,000 vehicles a day drive across the eight-lane bridge.

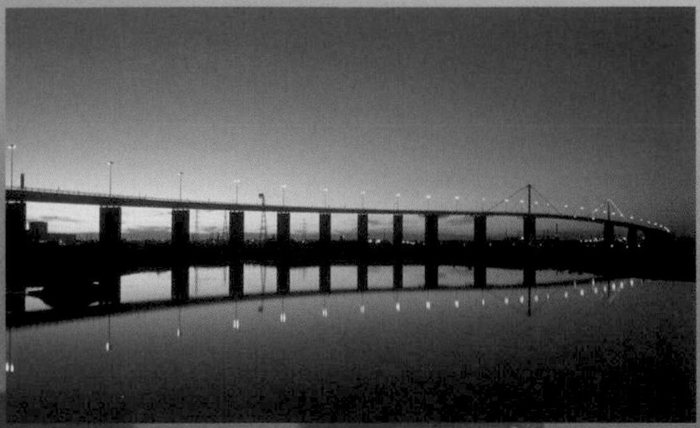

West Gate Bridge and Yarra River at dusk

The 6th October Bridge is an important transport link in Cairo — every day about 500,000 people drive across the ten-lane bridge. The name of the bridge commemorates the day the Yom Kippur, or Ramadan, War began on October 6, 1973. The picture shows a section of the bridge traveling across the Nile and into the city in the evening light.

THE LONGEST
BRIDGES IN AFRICA

1 **6th October Bridge**
Cairo, Egypt
41,010 ft (12,500 m)
2 **Third Mainland Bridge**
Lagos, Nigeria
34,449 ft (10,500 m)
3 **Mubarak Peace Bridge**
El Qantara, Egypt
12,795 ft (3,900 m)
4 **Mozambique Island Bridge**
Sofala–Sambesia, Mozambique
12,467 ft (3,800 m)
5 **Dona Ana Bridge**
Mutarara, Mozambique
12,139 ft (3,700 m)

The Mubarak Peace Bridge spans the Suez Canal.

The highway-like 6th October Bridge, also known as Suez Canal Bridge, in Egypt's capital Cairo is, at a total length of 7.8 miles (12.5 km), Africa's longest bridge. However, apart from the bridge sections across the Nile River, it mostly has the character of an elevated highway.

The bridge links the center of Cairo with its airport, located some 12.4 miles (20 km) out of town. The second longest bridge in Africa is the Third Mainland Bridge in the Nigerian city of Lagos, with an overall length of 6.5 miles (10.5 km). The bridge leads from the international airport via Lagos Lagoon to the north. It was built in 1990, in order to alleviate the chronic congestion in the overloaded traffic network of the large city.

LAKE PONTCHARTRAIN CAUSEWAY
USA   23.9 ml (38.4 km)

The Lake Pontchartrain Causeway, located in the north of New Orleans, is the second longest bridge in the world that extends only across water, with a total length of 23.9 miles (38.4 km). The elevated box girder bridge crosses Lake Pontchartrain, connecting Metairie, a suburb of New Orleans, with the city of Mandeville. The crossing consists of two parallel two-lane bridges, with the carriageways protected by up to 20 foot (6 m) levees.

Two roads, one bridge

MANCHAC SWAMP BRIDGE
USA   22.8 ml (36.7 km)

With a length of 22.8 miles (36.7 km), Manchac Swamp Bridge is the second longest bridge in North America. Interstate 55 crosses the Manchac Swamp on this prestressed concrete bridge. The mammoth structure stands on 246 feet (75 m) long concrete piers that were driven into the swamp.

ATCHAFALAYA BASIN BRIDGE
USA   18.2 ml (29.3 km)

This prestressed concrete bridge runs in two sections across the largest swamp area in the United States, between Baton Rouge and Lafayette in Louisiana. The Atchafalaya Basin is a unique wetland rich in fish and plant species.

Atchafalaya Bridge in the swamp

CHESAPEAKE BAY BRIDGE-TUNNEL
USA   17.6 ml (28.4 km)

The bridge and tunnel combination, officially known as Lucius J. Kellam Jr. Bridge-Tunnel, is 17.6 miles (28.4 km) long in total, of which 2.0 miles (3.2 km) are made up of two tunnels and a further 2.0 miles (3.2 km) of causeways. In addition there are two parallel bridge structures that take U.S. Highway 13 across the bay.

BONNET CARRÉ SPILLWAY
USA   11.0 ml (17.7 km)

Interstate 10 runs across the Bonnet Carré Spillway Bridge. The Spillway is a type of weir system that controls the Mississippi flood waters — the water can drain into Lake Pontchartrain at New Orleans and from there into the Gulf of Mexico.

CONFEDERATION BRIDGE
Canada   8.0 ml (12.9 km)

Opened in 1997, the bridge (Pont de la Confédération) crosses the narrowest stretch of the Northumberland Strait (Atlantic) in the east of Canada. It links Prince Edward Island, Canada's smallest province, with the Canadian mainland in the province of New Brunswick. The box girder bridge is the longest bridge structure in Canada.

SAN MATEO-HAYWARD BRIDGE
USA   7.0 ml (11.3 km)

The San Mateo Bridge crosses San Francisco Bay, linking Hayward and Forster City. It is the longest bridge in the bay as well as the longest in all of California. About 100,000 vehicles cross San Francisco Bay each day via this bridge.

SEVEN MILE BRIDGE
USA   6.8 ml (10.9 km)

Seven Mile Bridge is the longest transoceanic bridge on the Overseas Highway. It links Vaca Key (Marathon) with Bahia Honda via Pigeon Key. The bridge was opened in 1982 and replaced several older structures in the Florida Keys.

Seven Mile Bridge in the Florida Keys

Chesapeake Bay and the bridge-tunnel

Cape Jourimain, New Brunswick

Historic Seven Mile Bridge

The western section of Confederation Bridge. Because of the difficult climate — the strait is often covered with ocean ice in the winter — most bridge components were prefabricated on land and towed with floating cranes to the site where they were then assembled.

THE LONGEST BRIDGES IN SOUTH AMERICA

① **Rio–Niteroi Bridge**
Brazil   8.3 ml (13.3 km)

② **Maracaibo Bridge**
Venezuela   5.4 ml (8.7 km)

③ **Rosario–Victoria Bridge**
Argentina   2.5 ml (4.1 km)

④ **Rodoferroviária Bridge**
(road-rail bridge)
Brazil   2.4 ml (3.8 km)

⑤ **Ayrto Bridge**
Brazil   2.2 ml (3.6 km)

RIO–NITEROI BRIDGE
Brazil   8.3 ml (13.3 km)

This bridge, officially called Ponte Presidente Costa e Silva,

crosses Guanabara Bay,

Carriageways of the Rio–Niteroi Bridge

The bridge in the Guanabara Bay

connecting Rio de Janeiro with its easterly neighbor, Niteroi. The prestressed concrete box girder bridge is 8.3 miles (13.3 km) long in total, with a 5.5 mile (8.8 km) section above water. At its highest point, the carriageway is 236 feet (72 m) above the water level. Every day about 150,000 vehicles cross the bridge, which forms a part of the BR-101 federal highway between Rio de Janeiro and Victoria.

MARACAIBO BRIDGE (PONTE RAFAEL URDANETA)
Venezuela   **5.4 ml (8.7 km)**

The Maracaibo Bridge crosses Lake Maracaibo in the federal state of Zulia in western Venezuela. The combined multispan and cable-stayed bridge is made from pre-stressed concrete and is 5.4 miles (8.7 km) long. At its highest point the carriageway is about 165 feet (50 m) above the lake's water level; the clear height, which is important for the passage of larger ships, is approximately 150 feet (45 m). The frame-style pylons rise about 300 feet (90 m) above the water. The bridge was completed in 1962, after only three years of construction. It is considered a milestone in combining cable-stayed bridges with viaducts using prestressed concrete components.

The pylons of the Maracaibo Bridge

ROSARIO-VICTORIA BRIDGE
Argentina   **2.5 ml (4.1 km)**

This graceful bridge links the towns of Rosario and Victoria, crossing the estuary of the Parana River on the way. A combination of prestressed bridge sections and a cable-stayed structure with a maximum span of 1,083 feet (330 m), the bridge link measures 2.5 miles (4.1 km) in overall length.

Cable-stayed bridge with four pylons

The Rio–Niteroi Bridge in Guanabara Bay is an important traffic link for the metropolis and its environs. Construction of the Rio–Niteroi Bridge was begun in the presence of Queen Elizabeth II on August 23, 1968, and it was opened on March 4, 1974. The completion of the bridge brought about the dynamic development of the Costa do Sol tourist area lying to its east.

THE HIGHEST BRIDGES IN THE WORLD

The Sidu River Bridge travels high above the valley.

Highest cable-stayed bridge across the Baluarte Gorge

SIDU RIVER BRIDGE
China   1,549 ft (472 m)

This bridge is a 0.7 mile (1.1 km) long suspension bridge spanning the deeply carved valley of the Sidu River near Yesanguan in Badong County, in the southwest of China's Hubei Province. The elevation measurements fluctuate depending on the points used between 1,549 and 1,804 feet (472 and 550 m) — generally one calculates the distance between carriageway and riverbed. Even the most conservative figures, however, currently make this bridge the highest motorable bridge structure in the world.

BALUARTE BRIDGE
Mexiko   1,322 ft (403 m)

The Baluarte Bridge is a 0.7 mile (1.1 km) long cable-stayed bridge across a gorge in the north of Mexico. Underneath it flows the Baluarte River. The four-lane bridge connects the coastal town of Mazatlan on the Pacific Ocean with the Mexican federal state of Durango. The bridge found its place in the *Guinness Book of Records* in January 2012 as the officially highest cable-stayed bridge in the world; this is based on the difference in height between the carriageway and the valley floor, at 1,322 feet (403 m). It is still unsurpassed.

BALING RIVER BRIDGE
China   1,214 ft (370 m)

This suspension bridge is 1.4 miles (2.2 km) long and crosses the valley of the Baling River near Guanling in the southwestern Chinese province of Guizhou. The central span has a width of about 0.7 miles (1.1 km), the height above the river is 1,214 feet (370 m). The highway bridge was opened to traffic in December 2009.

A vertiginous view into the depth

THE HIGHEST BRIDGE IN THE WORLD

1. **Sidu River Bridge**
   China   1,549 ft (472 m)
2. **Baluarte Bridge**
   Mexico   1,322 ft (403 m)
3. **Baling River Bridge**
   China   1,214 ft (370 m)
4. **Beipan–Jiana Bridge**
   China (2003)   1,201 ft (366 m)

Gloriously dignified and free from traffic: the Royal Gorge Bridge

ROYAL GORGE BRIDGE
USA   1,053 ft (321 m)

This suspension bridge near Cañon City, about 93 miles (150 km) south of Denver is one of the highest bridge structures in the world. After its completion in 1929, it held the title of "highest bridge in the world" for more than 70 years. The bridge spans the canyon of the Arkansas River at a height of 1,053 feet (321 m). Today, however, it no longer serves as a road traffic bridge, but is a mere tourist attraction. Once built as a single-lane toll bridge, it is today part of a theme park covering an area of 0.56 sq mls (1.45 sq km).

⑤ **Aizhai Bridge**
China   1,148 ft (350 m)
⑥ **Beipanjiang River Railway Bridge**
China (2009)   1,083 ft (330 m)
⑦ **Royal Gorge Bridge**
USA   1,053 ft (321 m)
⑧ **Liuguanghe Bridge**
China   974 ft (297 m)

The Royal Gorge Bridge stretches across the Arkansas River canyon. One of the highest suspension bridges in the world, it has an overall length of 1,260 feet (384 m), and the main span is 938 feet (286 m). The carriageway is only 16 feet (5 m) wide and consists of a steel frame with about 1,300 wooden planks. The lattice steel pylons are 151 feet (46 m) tall.

THE LONGEST TRUSS BRIDGES IN THE WORLD

Truss bridges are one of the oldest construction types among modern steel bridges. Relatively little material is required for the lattice-like load-bearing structure, which made them lighter in weight than solid bridges and allowed for wider spans as well as shorter construction times, and thus enabled the construction of ever-longer bridges. The disadvantage is that bridges with very wide spans are also very high; however, this also makes them look impressive. Truss bridges had a first heyday around the end of the 19th century. The increasingly heavy trains demanded stable bridges and the technology of suspension bridges at the time was not yet capable of coping with such loads at the necessary spans.

THE LONGEST TRUSS BRIDGES IN THE WORLD

1. **Pulaski Skyway**
   Newark, USA
   16,010 ft (4,880 m)
2. **Commodore Barry Bridge**
   Chester, USA
   13,911 ft (4,240 m)
3. **Champlain Bridge**
   Montreal, Canada
   13,724 ft (4,183 m)
4. **Crescent City Connection**
   (formerly Greater New Orleans Bridges 1 & 2)
   New Orleans, USA
   13,428 ft (4,093 m)
5. **Bay Bridge (East)**
   San Francisco, USA
   10,177 ft (3,102 m)

PULASKI SKYWAY
USA   16,010 ft (4.880 m)

The centerpiece of the Pulaski Skyway between Newark and Jersey City is formed by two truss bridges, each 1,250 feet (381 m) long, on which the elevated highway crosses the rivers Hackensack and Passaic at an elevation of 131 feet (40 m). It was built between 1930 and 1932 as part of the Lincoln Highway, one of the first "superhighways" in the United States. Since 2005 it has been listed in the federal and state registers of historic places.

COMMODORE BARRY BRIDGE
Canada   13,911 ft (4.240 m)

Built from 1969 to 1974 for 115 million U.S. dollars, the Commodore Barry Bridge is not only one of the longest truss bridge structures in the world, but with a main span of 1,644 feet (501 m) the bridge across the Delaware River also boasts the fourth longest span of all truss bridges.

Commodore Barry Bridge at the stadium

CHAMPLAIN BRIDGE
Canada   13,724 ft (4.183 m)

The bridge stretches across the Saint Lawrence River at a height of 121 feet (37 m), connecting the two Montreal boroughs of Verdun and Brossard. At about 49 million vehicles a year, the Champlain Bridge, built between 1957 and 1962, has the most traffic of any bridge in Canada. The centrally located cantilever truss bridge has a total length of 2,507 feet (764 m), and its span is 705 feet (215 m).

Boul. Ville-Marie ES
Av. Viger
Aut. Ville-Marie ouest

Stretching across the Saint Lawrence River between Montreal and Longueuil in eastern Canada, the 8,816 feet (2,687 m) long Jacques Cartier Bridge has to be one of the most beautiful truss bridges. The bridge's main span of 1,096 feet (334 m) is also remarkable.

THE LONGEST STEEL TRUSS BRIDGES IN THE WORLD (SPAN)

THE LONGEST STEEL TRUSS BRIDGES IN THE WORLD (span)

1. **Quebec Bridge**
   Quebec, Canada
   1,801 ft (549 m)
2. **Forth Bridge**
   Edinburgh, Scotland
   1,709 ft (521 m)
3. **Minato Bridge**
   Osaka, Japan
   1,673 ft (510 m)
4. **Commodore Barry Bridge**
   Chester, USA
   1,644 ft (501 m)
5. **Crescent City Connection (formerly Greater New Orleans Bridge 2)**
   New Orleans, USA
   1,594 ft (486 m)
6. **Crescent City Connection (formerly Greater New Orleans Bridge 1)**
   New Orleans, USA
   1,575 ft (480 m)
7. **Rabindra Setu (Haora Bridge)**
   Kolkata, India
   1,503 ft (458 m)
8. **Veterans Memorial Bridge**
   Gramercy, USA
   1,460 ft (445 m)
9. **Bay Bridge (East)**
   San Francisco, USA
   1,401 ft (427 m)
10. **Pulaski Skyway**
    Newark, USA
    1,250 ft (381 m)

QUEBEC BRIDGE

Quebec, Canada　　　　　　　　**1,801 ft (549 m)**

With a 1,801 foot (549 m) central span width, the "Pont de Québec," as it is known in the French-speaking part of the country, is the largest truss bridge in the world. A first bridge, begun in 1904, collapsed in 1907 before it was completed, due to mistakes in the statics calculations, sweeping 75 workers to their death. The second bridge looks exactly the same and was completed in 1917.

The Quebec Bridge across the Saint Lawrence River

FORTH BRIDGE
Firth of Forth, Great Britain   1,709 ft (521 m)

The 1.6 mile (2.5 km) long rail bridge across the
Firth of Forth was at the time of its completion in
1889 the bridge with the widest span globally and
a model for many other cantilever truss bridges.
The trusses between the three 130 feet (100.6 m)
tall towers each have a span of 1,709 feet (521
m). In total 56,183 short tons (50,958 tonnes) of
steel were used in its construction. The bridge
clearance height is 150 feet (45.7 m). Shortly after
construction was begun, the rail suspension bridge
across the Firth of Tay collapsed during a storm.
Construction of the suspension bridge as it was
originally planned was duly stopped, and the bridge
was redesigned. The result was a massive bridge
that was built with a five-fold static safety factor —
today a factor of 2.5 is commonly used.

The mighty rail bridge stretching across the Firth of Forth

Still one of the most impressive bridge
structures in the world today: the gigantic
Forth Bridge heaves itself across the Forth
estuary like a prehistoric monster. Even
after 120 years it is still so stable that
130 trains a day can cross it without any
problems, even though their weight has
increased enormously during this time.
During construction, 63 (out of over 4,000
total) workers hailing from all over
Europe lost their lives.

THE LONGEST ARCH BRIDGES IN THE WORLD

(span)

1. **Chaotianmen Bridge**
   Congqing, China
   1,811 ft (552 m)
2. **Lupu Bridge**
   Shanghai, China
   1,804 ft (550 m)
3. **Banghwa Bridge**
   Gangseo-gu–Goyang, South Korea
   1,772 ft (540 m)
4. **New River Gorge Bridge**
   West Virginia, USA
   1,699 ft (518 m)
5. **Bayonne Bridge**
   Bayonne–Staten Island, USA
   1,673 ft (510 m)
6. **Sydney Harbour Bridge**
   Sydney, Australia
   1,650 ft (503 m)
7. **Wushan Bridge**
   Wushan, China
   1,509 ft (460 m)
8. **Mingzhou Bridge**
   Mingzhou, China
   1,476 ft (450 m)
9. **Zhijinghe Bridge**
   Dazhipingzhen, China
   1,411 ft (430 m)
10. **Xinguang Bridge**
    Guangzhou, China
    1,404 ft (428 m)

CHAOTIANMEN BRIDGE

Chongqing, China   1,811 ft (552 m)

On April 29, 2009, the longest arch bridge in the world, crossing the Yangtze River, was opened near Chongqing in central China. The main span of the steel truss arch is 1,811 feet (552 m), and the length of the main bridge, together with the cantilevers, spans 3,058 feet (932 m). North and south of the bridge there are also two ramp approach bridges, and with these the structure has a total length of 5,712 feet (1,741 m).

THE NEW RIVER GORGE BRIDGE
NEAR FAYETTEVILLE

The arch bridge is one of the oldest types of bridge structures in the world. Even the ancient Romans had already perfected this technology and built gigantic bridges, some of which are still in use today. One such example is the about 590 feet (180 m) long and 165 feet (50 m) high Alcantara Bridge in Spain. For centuries, arch bridges were built in stone, with the bridge deck and carriageway resting on stone arches. Modern arch bridges in the industrial age, however, are mostly made from steel. Unlike stone, steel has the advantage that it can withstand not only compression but also absorb tensile forces. Thus arches can be built above the bridge deck and with the larger arches considerably larger spans can also be obtained. A further advantage is the markedly lower weight of the steel arches, which are usually built as trusses.

LUPU BRIDGE
Shanghai, China   1,804 ft (550 m)

The steel arches of this 12,795 feet (3,900 m) long bridge have a span of 1,804 feet (550 m). The 95 foot (29 m) wide carriageway is suspended from these. There is a viewing platform at the apex (328 feet/100 m). The bridge was completed in 2003 and received the Outstanding Structure Award in 2008.

NEW RIVER GORGE BRIDGE
West Virginia, USA   1,699 ft (518 m)

The 3,031 feet (924 m) long highway bridge across the New River Gorge in West Virginia was opened on October 22, 1977. To build the 1,699 foot (518 m) span arch, 10,535 short tons (9,555 tonnes) of steel were used, and for the entire bridge 22,004 short tons (19,958 tonnes). At 876 feet (267 m) above the valley floor, it is the second highest arch bridge in the world.

The Lupu Bridge across the Huangpu River in Shanghai

The New River Gorge Bridge near Fayetteville

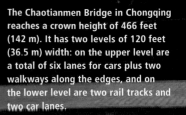

The Chaotianmen Bridge in Chongqing reaches a crown height of 466 feet (142 m). It has two levels of 120 feet (36.5 m) width: on the upper level are a total of six lanes for cars plus two walkways along the edges, and on the lower level are two rail tracks and two car lanes.

SYDNEY HARBOUR BRIDGE

In the middle of the city, the Sydney Harbour Bridge stretches across Port Jackson, which cuts deeply into the countryside. Like the Sydney Opera House (at the bottom left) the bridge is one of Australia's iconic landmarks. Also nicknamed "old coat hanger", because of its shape, it has been an official national monument since 2007. Thrill-seekers may join a guided tour over the steel arches.

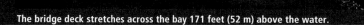

The bridge deck stretches across the bay 171 feet (52 m) above the water.

Sydney Harbour Bridge is one of Australia's most-visited sights. The span of the two 440 foot (134 m) high steel arches is 1,650 feet (503 m), the total length of the bridge 3,770 feet (1,149 m). To build the arches alone, 42,325 short tons (38,390 tonnes) of steel were required, and for the whole bridge 58,215 short tons (52,800 tonnes). When the bridge was completed in 1932, its load capacity was tested by placing 76 steam locomotives on the bridge. Eight road traffic lanes and two rail tracks, as well as sidewalks and a cycle path, go across the 161 foot (49 m) wide carriageway, which is suspended from the two steel arches. This makes it one of the widest bridges in the world.

The first suspension bridges were built hundreds of years ago, in Asia and South America. In Europe this method of construction did not take root until modern times, and the first projects were not realized until wrought iron had been developed as a suitably tensile and at the same time elastic material. Like no other bridge construction method, the technology of the modern suspension bridge makes it possible to achieve large spans, especially when wire cables serve as supports for the bridge deck. The first suspension bridge in an industrial country was built by James Finley in the United States in 1801, with a span of just 69 feet (21 m). But as soon as the year 1820, the Union Bridge with a 449 foot (137 m) span was built in northern England, the oldest suspension bridge still in use today, and in 1883 the Brooklyn Bridge in New York attained a span of 1,594 feet (486 m). Less than 50 years later, in 1931, the 3,281 foot (1,000 m) barrier was broken by the George Washington Bridge (New York), with a 3,501 foot (1,067 m) span between the two pylons.

THE LONGEST SUSPENSION BRIDGES IN THE WORLD (Span)

① Akashi-Kaikyo Bridge
Akashi Kaikyo Bridge
Kobe, Japan
6,532 ft (1,991 m)

② Xihoumen Bridge
Zhoushan, China
5,413 ft (1,650 m)

③ Great Belt Fixed Link
Great Belt, Denmark
5,328 ft (1,624 m)

④ Nancha Bridge
Zhenjiang, China
4,888 ft (1,490 m)

⑤ Humber Bridge
Barton-upon-Humber,
Great Britain
4,626 ft (1,410 m)

⑥ Jiangyin Bridge
Jiangyin, China
4,544 ft (1,385 m)

⑦ Tsing Ma Bridge
Hong Kong, China
4,518 ft (1,377 m)

⑧ Verrazano–Narrows Bridge
New York City, USA
4,259 ft (1,298 m)

⑨ Golden Gate Bridge
San Francisco, USA
4,199 ft (1,280 m)

⑩ Yangluo Bridge
Wuhan, China
4,199 ft (1,280 m)

The Akashi Kaikyo Bridge, or Pearl Bridge, is not only the longest suspension bridge in the world, it is also the bridge with the largest span. Crossing the Akashi Strait near the Japanese city of Kobe, the bridge stands in a zone that is at severe risk of earthquakes and typhoons. The structure was therefore designed to withstand earthquakes up to a magnitude of 8.5 on the Richter scale and wind speeds up to 180 mph (290 km/h).

AKASHI KAIKYO BRIDGE —
THE LONGEST SUSPENSION BRIDGE IN THE WORLD

The foundations of the twin steel pylons each weigh 407,940 short tons (370,000 tonnes), and the pylons themselves about 25,360 short tons (23,000 tonnes) each. Suspended from them is the bridge deck with the carriageway, which comes to a weight of 154,360 short tons (140,000 tonnes).

The Akashi Kaikyo Bridge connects the city of Kobe on Honshu, the main Japanese island, with the city of Awaji on Awaji-shima Island. When the suspension bridge was opened to traffic on April 5, 1998, the originally planned 6,529 foot (1,990 m) span between the pylons had lengthened to 6,532 feet (1,991 m) — the seismic movements after the Kobe earthquake of January 17, 1995, had not only moved the two islands further apart but also the 928 foot (283 m) tall bridge pylons. Thus the dampers that had been built into the pylons to counter the vibrations caused by earthquakes and typhoons had passed their first endurance test. The pylons survived the earthquake without any damage. Since the bridge deck and the carriageway had not yet been built, the plans could also be adapted accordingly. The bridge deck was fabricated from braced steel truss supports. In strong winds it can flex up to 89 feet (27 m) sideways in the middle. The two 2.5 mile (4 km) long suspension cables of the bridge deck have a diameter of 44.2 inches (112.2 cm). They each consist of 36,830 individual wires, of which groups of 127 at

a time are made into 290 braids. Altogether the six-lane highway is 12,831 feet (3,911 m) long, 116 feet (35.5 m) wide and has a clearance height of 213 feet (65 m) for the busy traffic in the Akashi Strait. Construction costs ran to about 7.5 billion dollars.

The steel bridge deck built as a truss resists even the strongest gale-force winds and gives the bridge a filigree appearance.

GREAT BELT FIXED LINK
Denmark   5,328 ft (1.624 m)

Since 1998, two bridges and a tunnel have formed an 11 mile (18 km) long fixed road and rail connection across the Great Belt between the Danish islands of Funen and Zealand. The western section of the Storebælt, or Great Belt, Bridge extends 21,690 feet (6,611 m) between Funen and the island of Sprogø, as a prestressed concrete box girder bridge. The more spectacular East Bridge is 22,277 feet (6,790 m) long in total and links Sprogø with Zealand. This section

The Danish Great Belt Bridge

also includes the longest suspension bridge in Europe. In total it has a length of 8,839 feet (2,694 m) and a central span of 5,328 feet (1,624 m), making it the third longest suspension bridge in the world.

HUMBER BRIDGE
Great Britain   4,626 ft (1,410 m)

When the Humber Bridge was completed in 1981, it was the longest single-span suspension bridge in the world, with a main span of 4,626 feet (1,410 m). Today it ranks as No. 5, yet it is still the longest bridge in the world that can be crossed on foot. The structure spans the Humber estuary on England's

The bridge across the Humber

east coast at a height of 98 feet (30 m). The foundations of its 509 foot (155 m) tall piers reach 118 feet (36 m) into the ground, and its suspension cables measure 44,120 miles (71,000 km) in total length. Combined as mighty cables, they hold the carriageway, which moves up to 9.8 feet (3 m) in force 12 winds.

HÖGA KUSTEN BRIDGE (HIGH COAST BRIDGE)
Sweden   3,970 ft (1.210 m)

The High Coast Bridge has stretched across the Ångermanälven River since 1997, with a clear height of 131 feet (40 m). Located in the High Coast World Natural Heritage Site on Sweden's central east coast near

Sweden's most beautiful bridge

Kramfors, the bridge carrying European Route E4 has an overall length of 6,125 feet (1,867 m) and a maximum span of 3,970 feet (1,210 m), making it one of the longest suspension bridges in the world and the second longest bridge in Sweden. Its pylons soar 610 feet (186 m) into the sky — and thus the High Coast Bridge is also the second tallest structure in the country.

FATIH SULTAN-MEHMET BRIDGE
Turkey   3,576 ft (1.090 m)

The Fatih Sultan Mehmet Bridge, or Second Bosporus Bridge, is a route from Europe to Asia in Istanbul. It is 128 feet (39 m) wide and 4,954 feet (1,510 m) long, and the carriageway is 210 feet (64 m) high above the Bosporus — high enough even

The bridge by the eponymous mosque

for cruise ships. Two mighty twin pylons carry the bridge. With a span of 3,576 feet (1,090 m), the Fatih Sultan Mehmet Bridge occupies the 15th place worldwide.

25TH OF APRIL BRIDGE

Portugal   3,323 ft (1.013 m)

The 2.0 mile (3.2 km) long 25th of April Bridge (Ponte 25 de Abril) travels from Portugal's capital Lisbon to the neighboring city of Almada. The mighty structure was built between 1962 and 1966, in about 2.2 million man-hours. The section across the Tagus is

The 25th of April Bridge across the Tagus

covered by a 7,474 foot (2,278 m) long suspension bridge. With a 3,323 foot (1,013 m) long span it is the second longest combined road and rail traffic suspension bridge worldwide.

FORTH ROAD BRIDGE

Great Britain   3,301 ft (1,006 m)

On the east coast of Scotland the 1.6 mile (2.5 km) long Forth Road Bridge spans the Firth of

The Forth Road Bridge in evening light

Forth. At its completion in 1964, with a span of 3,301 feet (1,006 m), the highway bridge was the longest suspension bridge outside the United States and the fourth longest in the world. For its construction, 43,000 short tons (39,000 tonnes) of steel and 4,414,300 cu ft (125,000 cu m) of concrete were used.

BOSPORUS BRIDGE

Turkey   3,524 ft (1,074 m)

Istanbul's First Bosporus Bridge has linked the European and Asian parts of the city since 1973. With a total length of 5,118 feet (1,560 m) and a main span of 3,524 feet (1,074 m), this technological masterpiece ranks 17th place worldwide. The impressive suspension bridge is dominated by a pair of imposing twin pylons soaring 344 feet (105 m) above the carriageway, to which pedestrians only have access during the Istanbul Marathon. With a clear height of 210 feet (64 m) the bridge is no obstacle for the busy ship traffic on the Bosporus.

The Forth Road suspension bridge looks particularly impressive when it is illuminated by the light of the setting sun. Its pylons rise about 512 feet (156 m) above the waters of the Scottish Firth of Forth. The main cables, which run over the steel towers, were spun from more than 11,600 individual steel wires and measure about 24 inches (60 cm) in diameter. They each carry a load of 15,325 short tons (13,900 tonnes). If all of the wires were to be stretched out around the globe, they would trace its circumference 1.25 times.

THE LONGEST SUSPENSION BRIDGES IN ASIA

XIHOUMEN BRIDGE
China   5,413 ft (1.650 m)

With a span of 5,413 feet (1,650 m) the Xihoumen Bridge is the longest suspension bridge in China. On the world stage it is surpassed only by the Akashi Kaikyo Bridge in Japan. The 8,901 foot (2,713 m) long road bridge is part of a 3.3 mile (5.3 km) traffic link, which travels from the Zhoushan Archipelago to the islands of Jintang and Cezi. Together with four other bridges it forms the connection between this group of islands in the East China Sea and the mainland. So that the Xihoumen Bridge would be able to withstand the typhoons, its two parallel carriageway strips are linked with each other by cross braces — this makes the structure more "wind slippery." At high tide the carriageways have a clear height of 162 feet (49.5 m); they are carried by steel cables on 692 foot (211 m) tall pylons.

RUNYANG BRIDGE
China   4,888 ft (1.490 m)

The Beijing to Shanghai expressway crosses the Yangtze in the eastern Chinese province of Jiangsu via the 21.7 mile (35 km) long Runyang Bridge. Part of this link is China's second longest suspension bridge — with a span of 4,888 feet (1,490 m) the Runyang suspension bridge ranks in fourth place worldwide.

The Runyang Bridge over the Yangtze

JIANGYIN BRIDGE
China   4,544 ft (1.385 m)

At its completion, the Jiangyin highway bridge was China's first steel suspension bridge whose span was longer than 0.6 miles (1 km). In addition, at the time no other bridge crossed the Yangtze nearer the sea — today there are two more crossings between this six-lane highway bridge and the coast. With a span of 4,544 feet (1,385 m) it is today the third longest suspension bridge in the People's Republic. It links the cities of Jing-jiang on the north bank and Jiangyin on the river's south bank in Jiangsu Province. Its concrete pylons are 623 feet (190 m) tall, as tall as a 60-story skyscraper.

TSING MA BRIDGE

China   4,518 ft (1.377 m)

A bridge of superlatives: with its span of 4,518 feet (1,377 m) Hong Kong's Tsing Ma Bridge is the longest suspension bridge in the world with one deck each for road and rail traffic. There is no other rail traffic bridge in the world with a greater central span — and only six suspension bridges are longer. Altogether about 54,000 short tons (49,000 tonnes) of steel were used in its construction.

The most important link between Hong Kong and the airport on Lantau Island

Brightly illuminated the Tsing Ma Bridge across the Ma-Wan Canal soars into Hong Kong's evening sky. The bridge between the islands of Tsing Yi and Ma Wan is 1.4 miles (2.2 km) long in total and 135 feet (41 m) wide. Its giant, 676 foot (206 m) tall pylons carry the mighty steel cables from which the double deck for rail and road traffic is suspended. In strong winds, only the two-lane carriageway on the lower rail deck is open to traffic,

GOLDEN GATE BRIDGE

San Francisco, USA

4,199 ft. (1.280 m)

Between San Francisco and Marin County one of the most famous bridges in the world spans the Golden Gate Strait: the Golden Gate Bridge is the symbol of San Francisco, an architectural icon and — at least for the American Engineering Association – one of the seven modern wonders of the world. With a span of 4,199 ft (1,280 m) it was the longest suspension bridge on the globe at its completion in 1937, a record it held onto until the construction of the Verrazano Narrows Bridge in 1964. Today the mighty suspension bridge ranks second in America and ninth place worldwide. Its technological specifications are still impressive today: for the two 745 foot (227 m) tall main pylons alone 44,300 short tons (40,200 tonnes) of steel and around 1.2 million rivets were used. The total weight of the steel cables is 23,900 short tons (21,700 tonnes). They carry the roughly 154,360 short tons (140,000 tonnes) heavy bridge superstructure.

The view from one of the two pylons soaring 499 feet (152 m) above the carriageway of the Golden Gate Bridge is breathtaking; 220 feet (67 m) below the cars roars the Pacific Ocean. The "international orange" color of the steel structure is particularly visible in fog and it also underlines the bridge's Art Deco beauty very well. The structure counters the strong winds in the strait with its flexibility: the bridge can flex up and down as well as up to 27.6 feet (8.4 m) sideways.

VERRAZANO NARROWS BRIDGE
New York City, USA

4,199 ft (1.298 m)

This two-level road bridge spans the strait known as the Narrows between the New York boroughs

Between Staten Island and Brooklyn

of Brooklyn and Staten Island. With a span of 4,259 feet (1,298 m) it was from its completion in 1964 to the year 1981 the longest suspension bridge in the world. It is today still the record-holder in America and globally occupies eighth place at the moment. The Verrazano Narrows Bridge is 228 feet (69.5 m) high in the middle.

MACKINAC BRIDGE
Mackinac, USA   3,799 ft (1.158 m)

This 26,370 foot (8,038 m) long highway bridge has a span of 3,799 feet (1,158 m), making it the third longest suspension bridge in the United States. Since 1957 it has crossed the Straits of Mackinac, the strait between

"Big Mac" between two of the Great Lakes

Lake Michigan and Lake Huron in the U.S. state of Michigan. The "Big Mac" is just under 70 feet (21 m) wide, weighs more than 1.1 million short tons (1 million tonnes) and at 8,615 feet (2,626 m) held the world record between two anchorages until 1998. This is now held by the Japanese Akashi Kaikyo Bridge.

GEORGE WASHINGTON BRIDGE
New York City, USA

3,501 ft (1.067 m)

The George Washington Bridge with its 3,501 feet (1,067 m) span was the longest suspension bridge in the world from its completion in 1931 to 1937. Today it still ranks as No. 4 in the United States. In total 4,695 feet (1,431 m) long, the bridge across the Hudson River

Bridge between two states

links the New York borough of Manhattan with the neighboring state, New Jersey. The traffic volume on the twin-storied bridge may also be record-breaking: more than 100 million vehicles a year!

MILLAU VIADUCT

The highway goes through the split pylons of the Millau Viaduct like a thread through the eye of a needle. The longest cable-stayed bridge in the world, it extends between two plateaus of different heights across the hilly landscape of the Tarn Valley in southwestern France.

Bridge-builders in southwestern France began the new millennium with a fabulous technological feat: between 2001 and 2004 the Millau Viaduct, which is also esthetically very attractive, was built there spanning the deeply cut valley of the Tarn River. The longest cable-stayed bridge in the world, it measures 8,071 feet (2,460 m) in length. It is supported by seven pylons, which vary in height between 253 and 804 feet (77 and 245 m) because of the

Conceived by Michel Virlogeux and designed by Sir Norman Foster

hilly terrain and which are anchored by foundations of up to 52 foot (16 m) depth. The carriageway of the bridge floats in a gentle curve above the river, 886 feet (270 m) at its highest point — from up there the view is simply breathtaking. The pylons soar 318 feet (97 m) above, with their slender cables carrying the main weight of 1,650 short tons (1,500 tonnes) of steel in the superstructure, which alone used around 39,690 short tons

(36,000 tonnes) of steel in its construction. As a comparison, for the construction of the Eiffel Tower at the end of the 19th century only one-fifth of this volume was needed. The bridge nevertheless has a filigree appearance thanks to the shape of its reinforced concrete pylons, which split into two supports and are tapered toward the top. In 2006 the viaduct received the "Outstanding Structure Award."

THE HIGHEST BRIDGE PYLONS IN THE WORLD

❶ **Millau Viaduct**
France   1,125 ft (343 m)

❷ **Sutong Bridge**
China   1,004 ft (306 m)

❸ **Akashi Kaikyo Bridge**
Japan   978 ft (298 m)

❹ **Stonecutters Bridge**
Hong Kong   978 ft (298 m)

❺ **Great Belt Fixed Link**
Denmark   833 ft (254 m)

❻ **Golden Gate Bridge**
USA   745 ft (227 m)

❼ **Tatara Bridge**
Japan   722 ft (220 m)

❽ **Normandy Bridge**
France   705 ft (215 m)

❾ **Runyang Bridge**
China   705 ft (215 m)

❿ **Verrazano Narrows Bridge**
USA   692 ft (211 m)

TOWER BRIDGE

A bridge that was not to hinder access to the port facilities of the Pool of London — that was the most important brief for the construction of the Tower Bridge. In 1884, Horace Jones and John Wolfe Barry presented the final draft agenda for the mighty structure across the Thames. Completed in the year 1894, more than 400 workers worked to construct the then-largest bascule bridge in the world to these plans. To do so they sunk two massive piers into the riverbed, which alone carry more than 12,130 short tons (11,000 tonnes) of steel for the framework of the towers and the pedestrian walkways. The mighty structure is 940 feet (286.5 m) long and has a span of 259 feet (79 m). At the lofty height of 141 feet (43 m) pedestrian walkways run between the 213 feet (65 m) towers. A unique technological masterstroke are the hydraulically operated bascules (leaves). The energy required to raise and lower these is supplied by giant pumping accumulators that were originally pressurized by steam power. Today they are raised and lowered with an electro-hydraulic system.

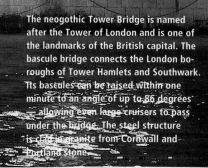

The neogothic Tower Bridge is named after the Tower of London and is one of the landmarks of the British capital. The bascule bridge connects the London boroughs of Tower Hamlets and Southwark. Its bascules can be raised within one minute to an angle of up to 86 degrees allowing even large cruisers to pass under the bridge. The steel structure is clad in granite from Cornwall and Portland stone.

LÆRDAL TUNNEL — THE LONGEST ROAD TUNNEL IN THE WORLD
Norway   80,413 ft (24.510 m)

The about 6.8 mile (11 km) long Mont Blanc Tunnel goes under the Mont Blanc massif, linking Courmayeur in Italy with Chamonix in France. Every year, some two million vehicles drive through the single-gallery tunnel. After a catastrophic fire in 1999, which caused the death of 39 people, the safety and ventilation systems in the vast tunnel were modernized.

Since the opening of the tunnel between Aurland and Lærdal in 2000, travel between Oslo and Bergen has become considerably easier even in winter. To create this, the longest road tunnel in the world, three construction teams cut through the ground for five years. Satellite navigation systems and laser technology ensured that they would meet up almost to the

Miracle of technology underground

dot. The routing was deliberately designed with a small descent and in gentle curves so that drivers would not fall asleep. Three large caves interrupt the monotonous journey. On the advice of lighting experts they are illuminated from floor to ceiling in the colors yellow, green and blue. Anyone arriving in these spaces has the refreshing illusion of a sunrise.

Overcoming obstacles — this is the purpose of the giant tunnel structures that have been cut through mountains and under water. It demands the greatest engineering skills to ensure that the seemingly unspectacular tubes are able to withstand the incredible pressures exerted by the volumes of earth and water that rest on top. Building tunnels is complicated in technological terms as well as dangerous; however, thanks to the huge improvements in technology it no longer causes the deaths of so many people. Thus, the construction at the end of the 19th century of the 9.3 mile (15 km) long Swiss Gotthard Rail Tunnel led to the death of several hundreds of workers; the Italian–Swiss Simplon Tunnel, the longest tunnel in the world between 1906 and 1982, claimed 67 lives. In the 1980s the construction of the Seikan Tunnel still caused 34 fatalities.

THE LONGEST RAIL TUNNELS IN THE WORLD

1 Seikan Tunnel
Japan 176,969 ft (53,940 m)
2 Eurotunnel
France/Great Britain
163,845 ft (40,940 m)
3 Lötschberg Base Tunnel
Switzerland
106,880 ft (32,577 m)
4 Guadarrama Tunnel
Spain 92,848 ft (28,300 m)
5 Hakkoda Tunnel
Japan 86,762 ft (26,445 m)
6 Iwate–Ichinohe Tunnel
Japan 84,678 ft (25,810 m)
7 Dai-Shimizu Tunnel
Japan 72,736 ft (22,170 m)
8 Simplon Tunnel
Switzerland 64,970 ft (19,803 m)

THE LONGEST ROAD TUNNELS IN THE WORLD

1 Lærsdal Tunnel
Norway 80,413 ft)24,510 m)
2 Zhongnanshan Tunnel
China 59,121 ft (18,020 m)
3 St. Gotthard Road Tunnel
Switzerland 55,505 ft (16,918 m)
4 Arlberg Road Tunnel
Austria 45,853 ft (13,976 m)
5 Hsuehshan Tunnel
Taiwan 42,460 ft (12,942 m)
6 Fréjus Road Tunnel
France/Italy 42,224 ft (12,870 m)
7 Mont Blanc Tunnel
France/Italy 38,058 ft (11,600 m)
8 Gudvanga Tunnel
Norway 37,493 ft (11,428 m)

CHANNEL TUNNEL — THE SECOND LONGEST RAIL TUNNEL IN THE WORLD
France/Great Britain 163,845 ft (49.940 m)

It is thanks to 15,000 workers and 11 giant tunnel boring machines, cutting up to 246 feet (75 m) through the ground every day, that from 1994 it became possible again to travel between England and France on land, the first time in 8,500 years. Today the Eurostar railroad whizzes from the island to the continent in only around 20 minutes. Only the Seikan Tunnel surpasses the Channel Tunnel in overall length, and it is the tunnel with the longest section under the seabed in the world. One of the crossover halls for the trains is at 512 by 59 feet (156 by 18 m) the largest cave ever dug under the sea.

SEIKAN TUNNEL — THE LONGEST RAILROAD TUNNEL IN THE WORLD
Japan 176,969 ft (53.940 m)

The Seikan Tunnel has linked the Japanese islands of Hokkaido and Honshu since 1988. Its massive tunnels are up to 787 feet (240 m) underneath the earthquake-prone Tsugaru Strait. The Seikan is the only tunnel on Earth to have two stations built underneath the sea: Yoshioka-kaitei is the deepest station in the world at a depth of 484 feet (147.4 m), and Tappi-kaitei is only marginally less deep.

Although shipping has received stiff competition in the rapid development of air traffic, ships are still the most impor-

A containership at Long Beach

tant means of transportation. They still move people and cargo over distances of thousands of miles. Merchant shipping especially is still expanding. Containerships, freighters and oil tankers transport billions of tons of goods across the world's oceans, thus contributing to the growth of the global economy. The tradition of the large passenger ships that once shuttled between the continents lives on in today's cruise vacations. Although the Cold War is now a part of history, countless warships still travel the seven seas.

The vast bow of the liquefied natural gas carrier "Berge Boston" dwarfs the 46 foot (14 m) long U.S. coastguard control boat. The tugboats on the left and right in the picture are towing the tanker to its berth in the Port of Boston.

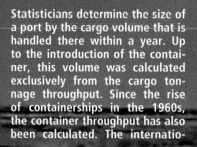

Statisticians determine the size of a port by the cargo volume that is handled there within a year. Up to the introduction of the container, this volume was calculated exclusively from the cargo tonnage throughput. Since the rise of containerships in the 1960s, the container throughput has also been calculated. The internatio-nal unit of measurement for this is the "TEU." The acronym stands for "twenty-foot equivalent unit," and designates a 20-foot container with a length of 20 feet (6.096 m), a width of 8.0 feet (2.438 m) and a height of 8.5 feet (2.591 m). A 40-foot container is the equivalent of 2 TEU.

THE LARGEST PORTS IN THE WORLD
TEU (Container)   (year of reference 2010)

① Shanghai
People's Republic of China
29.9 million

② Singapore
Singapore
28.4 million

③ Hong Kong
People's Republic of China
23.5 million

④ Shenzhen
People's Republic of China
22.5 million

⑤ Busan
South Korea
14.2 million

⑥ Los Angeles
USA
14.0 million

⑦ Ningbo
People's Republic of China
13.0 million

⑧ Guangzhou
People's Republic of China
12.6 million

⑨ Qingdao
People's Republic of China
12.0 million

THE LARGEST PORTS IN THE WORLD
(MMST – million short tons/MMT - million tonnes)   (Bezugsjahr 2010)

① Shanghai
People's Republic of China
716.6 MMST (650.0 MMT)

② Ningbo & Zhoushan
People's Republic of China
691.3 MMST (627.0 MMT)

③ Singapore
Singapore
554.0 MMST (502.5 MMT)

④ Rotterdam
Netherlands
474.0 MMST (429.9 MMT)

⑤ Tianjin
People's Republic of China
449.8 MMST (408.0 MMT)

⑥ Guangzhou
People's Republic of China
441.0 MMST (400.0 MMT)

⑦ Qingdao
People's Republic of China
386.0 MMST (350.1 MMT)

⑧ Dalian
People's Republic of China
331.6 MMST (300.8 MMT)

⑨ Hong Kong
People's Republic of China
295.3 MMST (267.8 MMT)

Since 2010 the Chinese metropolis of Shanghai has led the ranking list of ports with the

Iron conveyor belt and …

… container terminal in Shanghai

greatest throughput volumes in the world. In that year, 29.9 million standard containers were handled in Shanghai. The port area covers a surface area of 8,943 acres (3,619 ha) in total and today consists of five terminals. The two oldest terminals are located in the north of the city, in the area of the Yangtze estuary. In the early 1990s the port facilities were enlarged with the addition of the Waigaoqiao Container Terminal. The Yangshan Deep-Water Port is currently being built on the Zhoushan Islands in Hangzhou Bay south of Shanghai. In addition, a new cruise terminal has been established in the city center.

With the Yangshan Deep-Water Port, which was partially opened in 2005, the Port of Shanghai boasts ultramodern container terminals, where currently more than ten million standard containers are handled every year. The berths were built to accommodate the largest container ships in the world.

SINGAPORE
THE SECOND LARGEST PORT IN THE WORLD

For a long time, the city-state of Singapore, located on a group of islands off the southern tip of the Malay Peninsula, topped the list of the largest commercial ports in the world. In 2010 only Shanghai handled a larger number of standard containers. Singapore owes its top ranking to its geographical location on an extremely busy shipping route, as well as to shrewd commercial and industrial policies. Once it gained independence, Singapore began to build up flourishing light industries. The city-state imported semi-finished products for further processing and then exported the finished products around the world. In addition, Singapore has large oil refineries and a highly developed petrochemical industry. Singapore's port facilities boast more than 1,000 berths and extend over a total length of about 18 miles (30 km). They are operated by two companies: the PSA International administistrates, the Pasir Panjang container port and some smaller plants, while the Jurong Port Pte. Ltd. is responsible for the port of the same name.

Around one-fifth of the globally shipped containers are dispatched in the container terminals of the Port of Singapore. Until 2010 it was the largest container port in the world.

Europe's largest commercial ports are located on the North Sea coast. They are connected with the main urban centers in the hinterland by a well-developed network of road, rail and waterways.

ROTTERDAM
Netherlands

11.6 million containers
474.0 MMST (429.9 MMT) cargo

Within the last decade, the Port of Rotterdam fell way behind Shanghai and Singapore in the ranking of the busiest ports in the world. However, it still leads the list of European commercial ports, a long way ahead of Antwerp and Hamburg. For the industrial agglomerations in the Netherlands, Belgium and Germany, connected with the port by the Rhine River, it is a gateway to the world. In the past Rotterdam has always set new standards in the development of its port. Europoort, which was established between 1958 and 1964 as one part of the port, is still today the world's largest throughput port for oil and the products of the petrochemical industry. Rotterdam was the first European port that a containership called at — on May 5, 1966, the "Fairland" docked here, with its cargo of 400 containers. Rotterdam's container terminals became the largest on the continent.

ANTWERP
Belgien   8.5 million containers
196.3 MMST (178 MMT) cargo

The largest port in Belgium, Antwerp is located 50 miles (80 km) inland on the wide estuary funnel of the Schelde River, which can be used even by large seagoing vessels. In the European port ranking, it is in constant competition for second place with Hamburg. The Port of Antwerp owes its leading position to its proximity with the large European economic centers. Antwerp is the largest port in the world for break bulk cargo, and it is still on course for expansion.

HAMBURG
Deutschland   7,9 Mio. Container
133.4 MMST (121 MMT) cargo

The largest port in Germany is located on the Lower Elbe, roughly 62 miles (100 km) from the coast. Since the river is dredged regularly, seagoing vessels with a draft of up to 49 feet (15 m) can call here. Every year, 10,000 cargo ships dock at one of the four container terminals and 13 port quays. With a cargo flow of 7.9 million standard containers, Hamburg occupied third place in the ranking of European ports in 2010.

BREMEN AND BREMERHAVEN
Germany   4,9 million containers
75 MMST (68 MMT) cargo

The ports of Bremen and Bremerhaven are among the "big five" of European seaports. In 2011 just over 88 million short tons (80 million tonnes) of cargo and six million standard containers were handled here. Nowhere else in the world is there a greater throughput of vehicles than at the Bremerhaven Auto Terminal — 2.1 million in 2010 alone. The storage area at the container terminal extends over 1.16 sq ml (3 sq km), making it the largest in the world.

The Port of Rotterdam (left) has ultra-modern container gantry cranes, just like the Port of Hamburg (below). Every year more than ten million containers are handled here.

THE LARGEST PORTS IN EUROPE   TEU (Container)

❶	**Rotterdam** Netherlands	11.6 million
❷	**Antwerp** Belgium	8.5 million
❸	**Hamburg** Germany	7.9 million
❹	**Bremen** Germany	4.9 million
❺	**Valencia** Spain	4.2 million
❻	**Felixstowe** Great Britain	3.4 million
❼	**Gioia Tauro** Italy	2.8 million

THE LARGEST SEAPORTS IN ASIA

Nine of the ten busiest container ports in the world are located in eastern Asia, six of these in the People's Republic of China alone, the new "export world champion."

HONG KONG

People's Republic of China
23.5 million containers
295.3 MMST (267.8 MMT) cargo

With a throughput of 23 million standard containers in 2010, the Port of Hong Kong, the legendary city on the Pearl River estuary where it flows into the South China Sea, is one of the "big five" of the world's leading commercial ports. Its beginnings go back to the trading post built by British merchants on both sides of the straits between Hong Kong Island and the Kowloon Peninsula after signing the Treaty of Nanjing in 1842. The Crown colony of Hong Kong was founded in 1843 and Victoria Harbour, named after the British Queen Victoria, rapidly became the largest commercial port in eastern Asia. From 1992 to 2004 it was the busiest port in the world. The port facilities were extended in the 1970s and 1980s with the construction of the Kwai Tsing Container Terminals. At these alone 18 million standard containers are handled every year.

THE LARGEST PORTS IN ASIA
TEU (Container)   (year of reference 2010)

1. **Shanghai**
   People's Republic of China
   29.0 million
2. **Singapore**
   Singapore
   28.4 million
3. **Hong Kong**
   People's Republic of China
   23.5 million
4. **Shenzhen**
   People's Republic of China
   22.5 million

5. **Busan**
   South Korea
   14.2 million
6. **Ningbo**
   People's Republic of China
   13.0 million
7. **Guangzhou**
   People's Republic of China
   12.6 million
8. **Qingdao**
   People's Republic of China
   12.0 million

One of the giant container terminals in the Port of Singapore, the largest in the world until 2010

SHENZHEN

China   22.5 million containers
232.6 MMST (211 MMT) cargo

In 2010 the metropolis "only" occupied place No. 4 in the ranking of the world's largest commercial ports, still trailing its neighboring city of Hong Kong. However, Shenzhen has mightily caught up in recent years. Whereas in 2004 it still handled 8.3 million standard containers fewer than Hong Kong, both cities had come virtually neck and neck by 2010 — Hong Kong had a throughput of only one million standard containers more than Shenzhen.

View of the container terminal in Shenzhen

BUSAN

Südkorea   14.2 million containers
289 MMST (262 MMT) cargo

The largest port in South Korea, Busan has been in fifth place in the ranking of the world's largest container ports year after year since 2005. It owes its leading position to its favorable geographic position in the southeast of the Korean peninsula. The products of the country's highly developed industry are shipped from here into the Pacific area and via South-East Asia to Europe. Its quays measure about 16.7 miles (26.8 km) in length, and no fewer than 170 ships can be loaded or unloaded here at the same time.

The Kwai Tsing Container Terminals were built in the west of the Kowloon Peninsula (left).

View of the Busan container terminal

NINGBO

China   **13.0 million containers**
        410 MMST (372 MMT) cargo

The Port of Ningbo, located about 186 miles (300 km) south of Shanghai, is growing at an above-average speed even for China. In 2010, an increase of 25 percent in the cargo it handled was recorded, and with a total volume of 13 million standard containers Ningbo ranks as No. 7 among the world's ports. If one adds in the throughput of the Port of Zhoushan, which was merged with Ningbo in 2006, then its 691 million short tons (627 million tonnes) even propel it to second place.

THE LARGEST SEAPORTS
IN AUSTRALIA AND AFRICA

MELBOURNE
**Australia   2.5 million containers
99 MMST (90 MMT) cargo**

Measured by total volume of cargo handled, the Port of Melbourne is Australia's largest and at the same time the most important container port on the continent. The Port Authority reported a new record for 2011: in that year, the two container terminals had a throughput of more than 2.5 million standard containers. This makes Melbourne one of the five largest container ports in the southern hemisphere. The port takes a leading position also in the clearance of bulk and break bulk cargo. In 2010, 90 million tonnes of cargo were dispatched at 34 berths.

THE LARGEST
SEAPORTS IN OCEANIA
TEU (container)

(year of reference 2010)

1 **Melbourne**
   Australia   2.5 million
2 **Sydney**
   Australia   2.0 million
3 **Brisbane**
   Australia   0.9 million
4 **Auckland**
   New Zealand   0.8 million

The Port of Melbourne on Australia's south coast is the largest on the continent. In the ranking of the world's leading container ports it occupies place No. 54.

THE LARGEST PORTS IN
AFRICA
TEU (container) (year of reference 2010)

1 **Port Said**
   Egypt   3.5 Million
2 **Durban**
   South Africa   2.6 Million
3 **Tangiers**
   Morocco   2.0 Million
4 **Damietta**
   Egypt   1.1 million
5 **Cape Town**
   South Africa   0.7 million
6 **Casablanca**
   Morocco   0.7 million

PORT SAID

Egypt　　3.5 million containers
93.8 MMST (85.1 MMT) cargo

DURBAN

South Africa 2.6 million containers
46.0 MMST (41.7 MMT) cargo

The Egyptian city of Port Said on the Mediterranean Sea was founded in 1859, at the beginning of the construction of the Suez Canal. Since then the waterway has formed the backbone of its economy. The port's main source of income is transshipment — the transfer of cargo from larger to smaller vessels. In 2004 the Suez Canal Container Terminal opened, providing Port Said with an ultramodern container terminal. The port has developed as Africa's largest container hub: in 2010 the throughput was 3.5 million standard containers. In the coming years, the port operators want to double its capacity.

The South African port on the Indian Ocean has become the largest universal port in Africa, not least because of its favorable position at the intersection of important shipping routes. In 2010 the throughput was 2.6 million standard containers as well as 46.0 million short tons (41.7 million tonnes) of bulk and break-bulk cargo. The Port of Durban has more than 57 berths, and on average around 4,000 ships call here every year. The port operator, the state-run Transnet National Ports Authority, is continuing its program of expansion. The port is set to be modernized and its facilities extended.

A fully loaded containership heading for the Port of Durban

THE LARGEST SEAPORTS
IN THE AMERICAS

THE LARGEST PORTS IN NORTH AND CENTRAL AMERICA

TEU (container)
(year of reference 2010)

1 Los Angeles
USA 7.8 million

2 Long Beach
USA 6.3 million

3 New York
USA 5.3 million

4 Savannah
USA 2.8 million

5 Vancouver
Canada 2.5 million

6 Oakland
USA 2.3 million

L. A. / LONG BEACH

USA 14.1 million containers
519 MMST (471 MMT) cargo

In 2010 the largest port in the Americas occupied place No. 16 in the global ranking of largest ports — in that year, the throughput of the Port of Los Angeles was 7.8 million standard containers and 174.0 million short tons (157.8 million tonnes) of cargo. When taking account of the results of the neighboring port of Long Beach, then the Los Angeles throughput was 14.1 million standard containers and 260.2 million short tons (236.0 million tonnes) of cargo.

NEW YORK / NEW JERSEY

USA 5.3 million containers
206 MMST (187 MMT) cargo

The port facilities of New York Harbor comprise not only those located in the area of the metropolis of the same name but also those in New Jersey. Mostly situated in Upper New York Bay, they have been operated by the Port Authority of New York and New Jersey since 1921. After the Port of Los Angeles, this is the largest container port in the United States. Its throughput in 2010 was 5.3 million standard containers.

SAVANNAH

USA 2.8 million containers
139 MMST (126 MMT) cargo

Rich in tradition, this port in the U.S. state of Georgia extends on both banks of the Savannah River, about 18 miles (29 km) inland from the coast. When measuring the standard container throughput, it is the fourth largest in the United States. The container terminal is equipped with 15 ultramodern gantry cranes for post-Panamax ships and has at its disposal a storage area of about 1,2912,000 sq ft (120,000 sq m).

SANTOS

Brazil **2.7 million containers**
146 MMST (132 MMT) cargo

The Port of Santos is located only 50 miles (80 km) from the metropolitan region of São Paulo. Here raw materials for the region's rapidly growing industry are imported and almost one-fourth of Brazilian exports are shipped out. Cargo of all kinds is handled at the 62 berths. Santos is one of the engines of the Brazilian economy and has recorded double-figure growth rates in recent years.

THE LARGEST SEAPORTS IN SOUTH AMERICA

TEU (container)   (year of reference 2010)

❶	Santos	
	Brazil	2.7 million
❷	Buenos Aires	
	Argentina	1.7 million
❸	Cartagena	
	Colombia	1.6 million
❹	Callao	
	Peru	1.3 million

Containerships are discharged with the help of container gantry cranes — like here at the Port of Los Angeles.

THE LARGEST INLAND PORTS IN THE WORLD

Inland waterway shipping still plays an important role in both the regional and the continental transportation of cargo. All sorts of goods are transported on inland waterways. In Germany, for example, the proportion of the total volume of goods transported on inland waterways is around ten percent. The network of rivers and canals running through the country and Europe connects the large economic hubs of the continent and the seaports with their hinterland. Ports such as that of Duisburg (Ruhrort) are hubs where cargo is transshipped for onward transportation by other traffic systems. Most ports are directly linked into the road and rail systems. Large volumes of cargo are transported on rivers and canals not only in western Europe, but also in the United States, Russia and China.

THE LARGEST INLAND PORTS IN THE WORLD
(Cargo)   (year of reference 2010)

1. **Duisburg-Ruhrort**
   Germany
   126 MMST (114 MMT)
2. **Nanjing**
   China
   117 MMST (106 MMT)
3. **Huntington-Tristate**
   USA
   88 MMST (80 MMT)
4. **Pittsburgh**
   USA
   42 MMST (38 MMT)
5. **Montreal**
   Canada
   29 MMST (26 MMT)

The Port of Duisburg is busy around the clock.

DUISBURG (RUHRORT)
Germany   126 MMST
                       (114 MMT) cargo

The Port of Duisburg (Ruhrort) is still the most important inland port in Europe and the largest in the world. Up until the 1980s predominantly iron ore and coal were unloaded here for the steelworks of the Ruhr area. Today, a gigantic logistics operation has developed in Duisburg, which supports the carrier and truckage enterprises. The Duisport Group offers transportation facilities and storage halls. A packaging center also forms part of the service. A company affiliated with Duisport takes care of the smooth transfer of cargo to other transportation systems.

NANJING
China   117 MMST
                    (106 MMT) cargo

With a throughput of 117 million short tons (106 million tonnes) of cargo in 2010, the port of the old imperial Chinese city of Nanjing is the largest inland port in the country and the second largest in the world. Nanjing is located in the Yangtze estuary and is connected with the open seas by the vast river. Even deep-sea tankers can berth at the oil port here. Ships with a gross tonnage of more than 10,000 GRT can berth at one of a total of 64 quays in the river port. The Longtan Container Port, opened recently in 2004, has a storage capacity of one million containers.

For a long time, the inland port of Duisburg, an artificially created sidearm of the Rhine River, was in decline. Since the 1980s it has been transformed into an attractive residential, commercial and leisure district with a varied program of cultural activities.

Canals are artificially created waterways that link rivers, lakes and oceans with each other. Construction of the Suez Canal significantly shortened the sea route between Europe and Asia; the Panama Canal facilitated traffic between the North American Atlantic and Pacific coasts; the Kiel Canal in Germany saves many ships from having to take the long detour around Denmark through the Skagerrak strait. Modern inland shipping is also unimaginable without the network of canals covering large parts of Europe, Asia and North America. They connect rivers and seaports with their hinterland and shorten transportation routes. Obstructive differences in height are overcome by locks and canal lifts.

THE LONGEST INTER-OCEANIC CANALS IN THE WORLD

1. **Suez Canal**
   Egypt — 120.1 ml (193.3 km)
2. **Kiel Canal**
   Germany — 61.1 ml (98.3 km)
3. **Panama Canal**
   Panama — 50.7 ml (81.6 km)
4. **Corinth Canal**
   Greece — 3.9 ml (6.3 km)

THE LONGEST INLAND CANALS IN THE WORLD

1. **Grand Canal**
   China — c. 1,118 ml (1,800 km)
2. **Tennessee–Tombigbee Waterway**
   USA — 234 ml (377 km)
3. **Nantes–Brest Canal**
   France — 225 ml (362 km)
4. **Mittelland Canal**
   Germany — 203 ml (326 km)
5. **Marne–Rhine Canal**
   France — 180 ml (289 km)
6. **Burgundy Canal**
   France — 150 ml (242 km)

The Gatun Locks are the largest of three lock systems on the world-famous Panama Canal; its construction shortened the sea route between the Atlantic and the Pacific coasts of North America by around 6,215 miles (10,000 km).

SUEZ CANAL

The longest artificial inter-oceanic canal in the world connects the Mediterranean with the Red Sea over a distance of 120.1 miles (193.3 km), thus shortening the sea route between the North Atlantic and the Indian Ocean by almost 3,110 miles (5,000 km). The Suez Canal was opened in 1869, after ten years of construction,

The Suez Canal in 1860 …

… and in 1880

and has been open to ships of all nations since the Convention of Constantinople of 1888. Up to its nationalization by Gamal Abdel Nasser in 1956, the canal was controlled by Great Britain and the Suez Canal Company founded by Ferdinand de Lesseps, who had built the canal. After the Six Days' War of 1967, the canal remained closed for eight years.

The canal at Suez on the Red Sea. Unlike the Panama Canal, it is being continuously expanded, allowing the passage of ships of almost any size. The Suez Canal is a single-lane waterway and therefore has three passing zones.

THE LONGEST INTER-OCEANIC CANAL IN THE WORLD

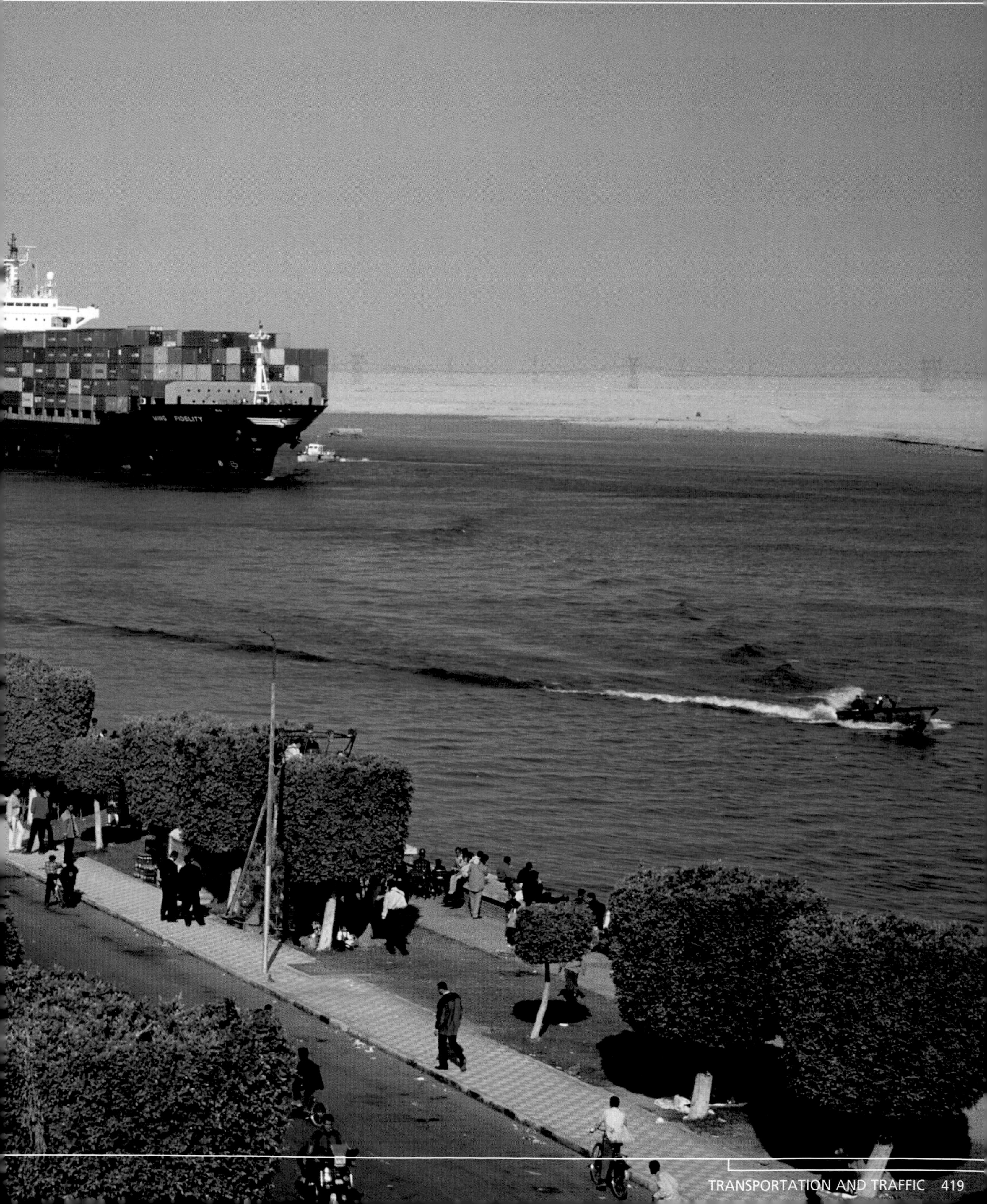

KIEL CANAL

This German waterway connects the North Sea with the Baltic Sea over a distance of almost 62 miles (100 km), and is the busiest inter-oceanic canal in the world. In 2011 a total of 35,522 ships passed through, almost twice as many as through the Suez Canal.

A cruise liner in the Kiel Canal

There are locks both at its start in Brunsbüttel on the Elbe estuary and at its finish in Kiel-Holtenau; these balance out the tidal differences in the water levels of the North and Baltic Seas. After eight years of construction, the canal was opened in 1895 by Kaiser Wilhelm II and initially named after his grandfather. After World War I the Versailles Treaty stipulated that it be opened to international ships' traffic; however, the National Socialists temporarily reversed this "internationalization" in 1936. In 1948 the canal was renamed Nord-Ostsee-Canal, literally North Sea–Baltic Sea Canal.

Containerships on the Kiel Canal. The waterway has a width of between 335 and 531 feet (102 and 162 m) and a depth of 36 feet (11 m). It can be navigated by ships with a length of 770 feet (235 m), a width of 106.6 feet (32.5 m) and a draft of 31 feet (9.5 m).

The Panama Canal cuts through the narrowest section of the Central American isthmus. The shortest connection between Atlantic and Pacific, it is one of the busiest waterways in the world. Every year on average 14,000 ships passages are counted here. The Panama Canal runs from northwest to southeast, and comprises excavated canals as well as a total of three gigantic lock systems that allow ships to negotiate a difference in height of 85 feet (26 m). Two sections of the canal run through artificial lakes: the section through the Gatun Lake, which measures 164 sq mls (425 sq km) and starts only a few miles off the Caribbean coast, is 20.5 miles (33 km) long and is reached via the first large lock system. Another 1.1

The Panama Canal's Pedro Miguel Lock

mile (1.7 km) long section goes through the small Miraflores Lake between the Pedro Miguel Lock and the Miraflores Locks, at 8.2

miles (13.2 km) distance from the Pacific. The Panama Canal was opened in 1914, and it is currently being expanded for large ships.

20.5 miles (33 km) of the Panama Canal traverse the Gatun Lake. The artificial lake was dammed between 1907 and 1913, flooding large rainforests in the process. Some higher areas now rise from the lake as wooded islands. Barro Colorado Island is one of the most heavily researched tropical areas in the world.

GRAND CANAL (IMPERIAL CANAL)

Over a distance of 1,118 miles (1,800 km) this inland canal connects the Chinese capital of Beijing with Hangzhou on the East China Sea. More than a single waterway, the Grand Canal designates an entire system of canals that has been repeatedly modified and extended since its beginnings, which probably date back to the Sui Dynasty (581–618 AD). Until the first locks were built — invented by Qiao Weiyue in the 10th century — the ships had to be pulled onto land in some places in order to overcome a total difference in height of 138 feet (42 m). After the foundation of Peking in the 13th century the canal was rebuilt. It developed as the most important transportation route in China, but the canal became less important from the middle of the 19th century.

The Grand Canal in the east of China now only has regional importance as a shipping route; however, it has become all the more attractive as a tourist destination. The structure is considered a masterpiece of ancient Chinese engineering and is often compared with the Great Wall.

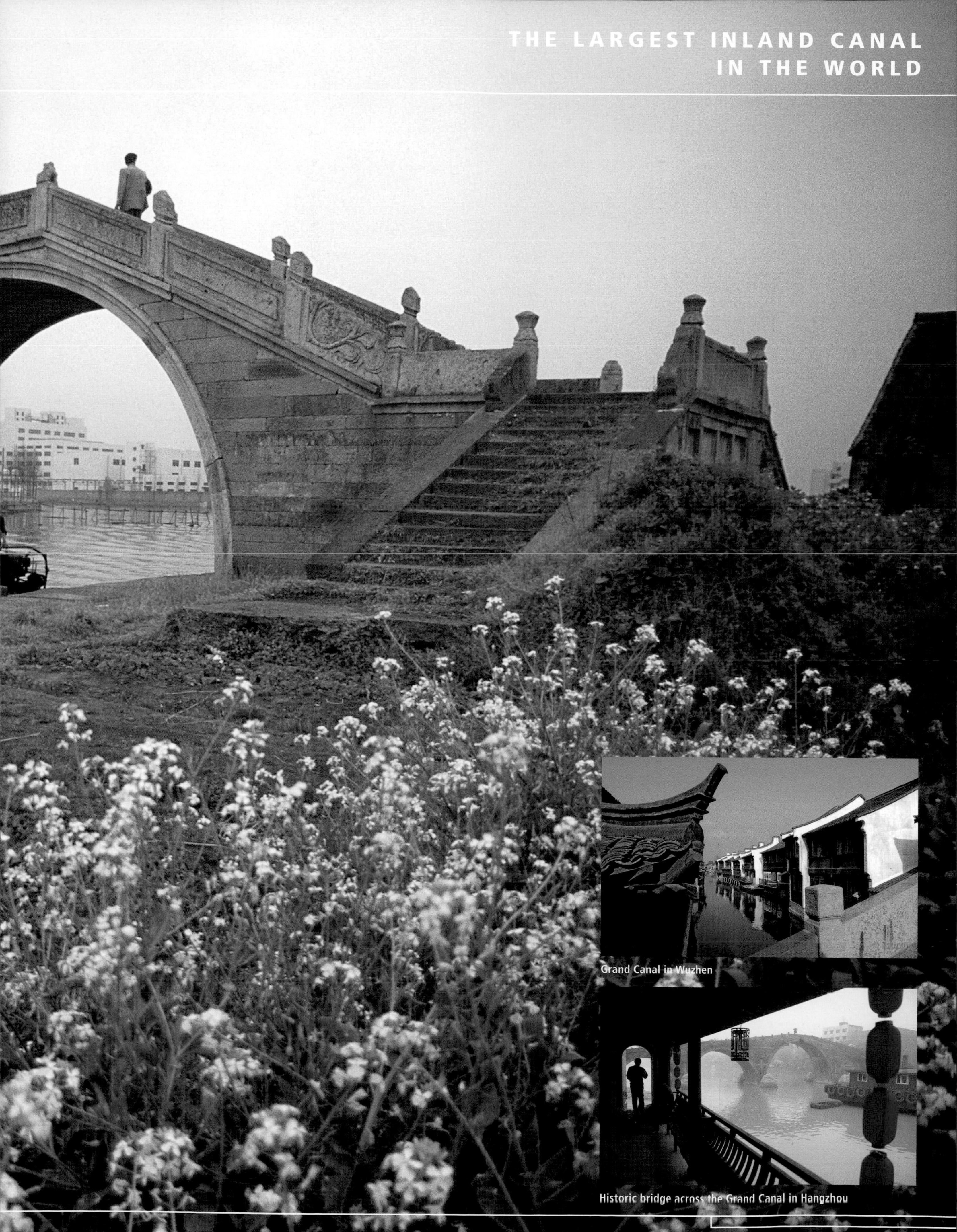

Grand Canal in Wuzhen

Historic bridge across the Grand Canal in Hangzhou

MAGDEBURG WATER BRIDGE — THE LONGEST CANAL BRIDGE IN THE WORLD

The Magdeburg Water Bridge takes the Mittelland Canal across the Elbe River near Magdeburg, over a distance of 3,012 feet (918 m). Completion of the navigable aqueduct in 2003 extended the Mittelland Canal as far as the Elbe–Havel Canal, at last creating a connection between the waterway networks of western and eastern Europe. The first stages of construction were begun as early as 1934, but shelved again in 1942. Only with German reunification did it become possible to revive the project.

Ships crossing over the Elbe Rover ...   ... via the water bridge near Magdeburg.

The Mittelland Canal near Mehrum

A cargo vessel on the canal

The longest canal in Germany connects, over a distance of 203 miles (326 km), the western European waterway network with the Elbe River, the rivers of the federal state of Brandenburg as well as the Oder River, thus making it probably the busiest artificial inland waterway on the continent today. It begins in the west as a branch off the Dortmund–Ems Canal, and then continues eastward across northern Germany up to the Hohenwarte Locks, where it merges with the Elbe–Havel Canal. Through a number of branch canals it is linked with cities like Osnabrück, Hannover, Hildesheim, Salzgitter, Brunswick and Wolfsburg. Via navigable aqueducts the Mittelland Canal crosses several smaller rivers as well as the Weser River near Minden and — since 2003 — the Elbe River at Magdeburg. Junction canals branch off to the rivers at these waterway intersections.

Part of the Mittelland Canal's lock system is the double lock in Hannover's Anderten district. Around 22,000 ships are raised or lowered here every year by about 48 feet (14.7 m). The lock was inaugurated in 1928 and named after the then President of the Reich, Hindenburg. Today it is known as Anderten Lock.

Sea locks offset the difference in water level between tidal and non-tidal waters, thus facilitating tide-independent port operations. Like all locks, sea locks consist of lock chambers with gates at both narrow ends through which ships enter or leave the lock. If a ship is to be taken from tidal waters into a port, then the water level inside the chamber is adjusted to that in the port once the ship has entered the locks and the gates have been closed. Then the portside gate is opened and the ship can continue its journey. Conversely, the water level in the lock is adjusted to that of the tidal waters as the ship leaves the port again.

A containership is maneuvered into the Berendrecht Lock by tugboats.

BERENDRECHT LOCK, ANTWERP
THE LARGEST LOCK IN THE WORLD

This lock complex is 1,640 feet (500 m) long, 223 feet (68 m) wide and 44 feet (13.5 m) deep. Together with the adjacent and only marginally smaller Zandvliet Lock it connects the estuary funnel of the Schelde with the port facilities on the right bank of the river. The Berendrecht Lock was opened in 1989. It makes it possible to maneuver cargo ships of almost any size independently of the tides, thus contributing to the expansion of the Port of Antwerp. An even larger system is currently being built on the left bank of the Schelde.

ENTRANCE 4 WILHELMSHAVEN
THE SECOND LARGEST LOCK IN THE WORLD

This two-chambered sea lock connects the inner terminal and

The Port of Wilhelmshaven

the new offshore terminal at Wilhelmshaven. It belongs to the German Navy, but is operated by the Waterways and Shipping Office in Wilhelmshaven. Entrance 4 was inaugurated in 1964, after the Allied forces had dismantled an earlier lock begun in 1936 and partly completed by the end of World War II. Each of its chambers is 1,280 feet (390 m) long.

A German navy ship is maneuvered out of the Wilhelmshaven sea lock by a tug

The Three Gorges Dam on the lower reaches of the Yangtze River, opened in 2006, is one of the most controversial major construction projects of the present day. It was built in the easternmost of the "Three Gorges," is 6,506 feet (1,983 m) long, 607 feet (185 m) high and dams China's longest river right up to the

Five-step ship lock at the dam

city of Chonqqing, situated more than 410 miles (660 km) farther west. Damming the river caused the water level of the Yangtze to rise by 62 feet (19 m). Thirteen villages and several hundred factories were submerged by the waters. Millions of people had to be resettled. Since the

start of construction in 1993, critics have stressed that the mammoth project would destroy one of the most scenic landscapes in the country and upset the ecological balance in the region. Its proponents, however, point to the benefits of floodwater protection and power generation. The hydroelectric power plant on the wall of the dam produces

as much energy as 20 medium-sized nuclear power stations. Navigability of the Yangtze has improved due to the fact that the river is wider and deeper. These days, ships with a carrying capacity of 11,025 short tons (10,000 tonnes) can travel as far as Chonqqing, thanks also to the two-way five-step ship locks at the dam face.

A ship enters the lock.

Two ships wait for the lock action.

The two five-step ship locks at the dam wall of the Three Gorges Dam are the largest in the world. Each lock chamber has a length of 919 feet (280 m) and a width of 98 feet (30 m). Transit takes about two and a half hours.

Ships passing through the Panama Canal have to surmount a total of 85 feet (26 m) difference in height with the help of three lock systems. The Gatun, Pedro Miguel and Miraflores Locks are today still regarded as masterpieces of engineering. Each of the three systems consists of two

The Miraflores Locks

A cargo ship at the Gatun Locks

locks working in parallel, so that while one ship is being raised another can be lowered. The largest system, the Gatun Locks, has three lock chambers, transporting ships that arrive from the Caribbean Sea to the Gatun Lake, which is 85 feet (26 m) higher. About 28 miles (45 km) farther along, the descent begins with the help of the Pedro Miguel Locks, comprising one chamber each. With the passage through the Miraflores Locks, situated 8.2 miles (13.2 km) inland from the Pacific entrance to the canal, the ships will again arrive at sea level height.

A chamber in the Gatun Locks. In the locks of the Panama Canal, most ships are pulled into the chambers with steel ropes from rack and pinion locomotives. Only smaller ships may enter the locks under their own steam. Each lock chamber is 1,000 feet (305 m) long and 109 feet (33.3 m) wide.

KNOCK NEVIS
(PREVIOUSLY JAHRE VIKING)

With a load capacity of 622,671 short tons (564,763 tonnes) this supertanker was scrapped in 2010 but today still leads the list of the largest ships ever built. During its years in active service it changed owners and name several times. Built in the early 1970s, the ship transported

On the deck of the "Knock Nevis"

crude oil from the Gulf region on behalf of a Hong Kong ship-owner between 1979 and 1988, and was then known as "Seawise Giant." Severely damaged during an air raid in the First Gulf War in 1988, the tanker was completely refurbished during the early 1990s at a shipyard in Singapore. The Norwegian shipping company that had bought it in the meantime renamed the ship "Jahre Viking." From 2004 to 2009, the tanker served in Qatar as an FSO, or crude oil storage tank, known as "Knock Nevis." The supertanker made its final journey under the name "Mont."

Supertankers like the scrapped "Knock Nevis" were built in the 1970s. After the accident of the "Exxon Valdez" in 1989, which caused a huge oil spill, oil corporations started to take note and built smaller ships. Today giant tankers are once more in operation; however, they have been fabricated with double-hulled tanks.

Until the 1990s cruise vacations were a luxury diversion that only few people could afford, but today operators are offering journeys for every taste and every budget. Special expeditions, adventure, fun and family cruises have all joined the classic cruises. The number of those interested in cruises grows steadily. The

The "Oasis of the Seas" at Nassau

Dining room on the "Freedom of the Seas"

market booms. Every year new and larger ships are being built. They offer room for many thousands of passengers and are often compared to floating cities. In terms of their lengths, widths and gross tonnage, cruise giants such as the "Allure of the Seas" and its sister ship, the "Oasis of the Seas," compete with the largest containerships and aircraft carriers.

THE LARGEST CRUISE
SHIPS IN THE WORLD
(gross tonnage, GT)

❶ Oasis class
Royal Caribbean   200,000
❷ Norwegian Epic
Norwegian Cruise Line   155,873
❸ Freedom class
Royal Caribbean   154,407
❹ Queen Mary
Cunard Line   148,873
❺ MSC Splendida
MSC Crociere   137,936

The "Queen Victoria," a cruise ship of the Cunard Line, is escorted by numerous boats and ships as it leaves the Port of Sydney in 2008.

THE LARGEST CRUISE SHIPS IN THE WORLD

Despite growing competition it is still two ships of the Royal Caribbean Cruise Line that lead the list of the largest cruise ships. The U.S.–Norwegian enterprise has banked on megaliners that can accommodate many thousands of people and that are equipped with giant lifestyle areas since the 1980s. Other

The "Disney Dream" leaving the harbor in Port Canaveral on its maiden voyage in 2011

ship owners have begun to copy the concept. Thus the ships of the Disney Cruise Line (founded in 1995) boast grass play areas, clubrooms and theaters for the whole family. Lifestyle areas can also be found on board the "Norwegian Epic," the second largest cruise liner in the world by passenger capacity.

ALLURE OF THE SEAS
OASIS OF THE SEAS
Tonnage: 220,000 GT
Length: 1,180 ft (360 m)

When the "Oasis of the Seas" and its sister ship, the "Allure of the Seas," were put into service in 2009 and 2010 respectively, a new era of cruise shipping began. The giants of the sea resemble not so much the classic ocean liners but floating cities that are able to provide their guests with every possible amusement and entertainment. On seven of the two giants' 18 decks each, experience worlds have been created, where passengers

can choose among a multitude of leisure activities. There are several swimming pools, spa and entertainment areas with theaters, jazz club and dance

lounge, as well as an ice rink, a crazy golf course, a climbing wall and a volleyball court. Spread over the ship are 24 restaurants and cafés, which ensure that

guests won't go hungry. For kids there is a Youth Zone. The ships each accommodate up to 6,300 passengers, and 2,165 crew ensure a smooth operation.

The "Allure of the Seas" is a ship of the Royal Caribbean Cruiseline

The atrium of the "Allure of the Seas"

The "Norwegian Epic" cruise line giant leaving the Port of Palma de Mallorca. The ships of the Norwegian Cruise Line are easy to recognize thanks to the striking decoration of their bows. The main Balearic island of Mallorca is one of the most popular destinations for cruises in the western Mediterranean.

NORWEGIAN EPIC

Tonnage: 155,873 GT
Length: 1,079 ft (329 m)

Since 2010, the flagship of the Norwegian Cruise Line has been traveling through the Caribbean in winter and the Mediterranean in summer. With a length of 1,079 feet (329 m) and a width of 131 feet (40 m) as well as a passenger capacity of 4,200 people, the "Norwegian Epic" is one of the megaliners. Construction of the ship as the lead ship for a new class of cruise liners began in 2006 at the French shipyard Chantiers de l'Atlantique. When NCL canceled its order for two more ships, it remained the only ship in its class.

FREEDOM OF THE SEAS
LIBERTY OF THE SEAS
INDEPENDENCE OF THE SEAS

Tonnage: 15,407 GT
Length: 1,112 ft (339 m)

Until the inauguration of the "Oasis of the Seas," the "Freedom of the Seas," launched in 2005, and its two sister ships were the largest cruise ships ever built. The Royal Caribbean Cruise Line set completely new standards in the cruise business and at the same time it continued a tradition within the enterprise. The shipping line advertises the giant size of its ships and the diverse range of indoor and outdoor activities on offer for its passengers like no other operator. The "Freedom of the Seas" was the first ship in the world to be fitted with an ice rink, a climbing wall, a surf simulator and a volleyball court.

The "Freedom of the Seas" in the Port of Hamburg

The "Independence of the Seas" in Southampton

QUEEN MARY 2
THE LARGEST OCEAN LINER IN THE WORLD

The "Queen Mary 2" is the only cruise ship that regularly crosses the Atlantic, thus continuing the tradition of the great ocean liners. Also included in its program are journeys around the world.

The flagship of the Cunard Line, the "Queen Mary 2" was built at the French shipyard Chantiers de L'Atlantique and taken into service in January 2004, after only two years of construction. With this ship, the venerable shipping line recalls the great era of the ocean liners that connected Europe with the New World with regular services into

the 1960s. Like its predecessor, the legendary "Queen Elizabeth 2," the "Queen Mary 2" is predominantly employed on transatlantic cruises and regularly serves the Southampton–New York line. The black rump and the white superstructure as well as the distinctive, elegant shape recall the design of the classic transatlantic liners, and the luxurious interior of the

ship also relives the glamor that once surrounded these ocean giants. Wood paneling, plate glass and stucco in the lobby, restaurants and stairways create a nostalgic atmosphere, while the modern works of art adorning the walls create an interesting contrast. The "Queen Mary 2" offers its guests every imaginable comfort: there are several pools on board, as well as

spas, restaurants, bars and luxury shops. There is a casino, a library, a theater and even a planetarium. Up to the completion of the "Freedom of the Seas," the "Queen Mary 2" was the longest passenger ship ever built.

The "Queen Mary 2" is easy to recognize by its distinctive bow (left). The ship is regularly maintained by Blohm + Voss in Hamburg (large picture).

EMMA MÆRSK
THE LARGEST CONTAINERSHIP IN THE WORLD

Thanks to the steadily increasing number of containerships, the world's commercial fleet grows continuously year on year. The leading container shipping company in the world, the Danish Mærsk Line, currently has 550 cargo ships.

The series of eight identical sister carriers in the Emma Mærsk class are able to load 15,000 standard containers and thus boast a capacity more than 30 times that of earlier containerships. With a length of 1,302 feet (397 m) and a width of 185 feet (56.4 m) they can pass through the Suez Canal, but not through the only 98 feet (30 m) wide Panama Canal.

Thanks to its 81 MW (109,000 hp) ships' diesel engine, burning 3,600 U.S. gallons (14,000 l) of heavy fuel oil per hour, the ships can reach a speed of 27 knots per hour. They need a crew of only 13 people. All eight cargo ships were built between 2006 and 2008 by the Odense Staalskibsværft shipyard, on the orders of the Danish shipping company Mærsk Line, which

– like the shipyard – belongs to the A. P. Moller-Mærsk group of companies. They travel a route from Gdansk through the Suez Canal to Shanghai, with one round trip taking about ten weeks. In February 2011 the shipping line commissioned the construction of a total of 20 mega-containerships with carrying loads of 18,000 standard containers each.

On its route from Gdansk to the Far East, the "Emma Mærsk" regularly calls at the Port of Rotterdam to load containers (left).

Although the proportion of container traffic in the total global maritime trade is currently only about 14 percent, it can nevertheless boast above-average growth rates. Containers can be handled and transferred to other means of transport faster, more easily and at a lower cost than bulk or break bulk cargo. Since the start of the container revolution in the mid-1960s, almost every year has seen larger ships taken into service. Whereas the cargo ships that were launched until 1968 had a transport capacity of only 500 to 800 standard containers, the ships of the Emma Maersk class that were built between 2006 and 2008 can load 14,770 standard containers. These large carriers can only call at ports that are equipped with gantry cranes for the loading and unloading of the ships.

THE LARGEST CONTAINERSHIPS IN THE WORLD
(by capacity in standard containers, TEU)

❶ Emma-Mærsk class		
Mærsk Line	14,770 TEU	
❷ MSC Daniela class		
MSC	13,296 TEU	
❸ MSC Danit		
MSC	13,200 TEU	
❹ Hyundai Tenacity		
Danaos Shipping	13,100 TEU	
❺ Mærsk Eindhoven		
Mærsk Line	13,092 TEU	
❻ MSC Fabiola		
MSC	12,562 TEU	
❼ MSC Luciana		
MSC	11,660 TEU	
❽ MSC Francesca		
MSC	11,312 TEU	
❾ CMA CGM Thalassa		
NSB Niederelbe	10,980 TEU	
❿ Gudrun-Mærsk-Klasse		
Mærsk Line	10,150 TEU	

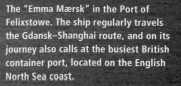

The "Emma Mærsk" in the Port of Felixstowe. The ship regularly travels the Gdansk–Shanghai route, and on its journey also calls at the busiest British container port, located on the English North Sea coast.

THE LARGEST ORE CARRIERS IN THE WORLD

Aside from giant machines and machine components, break bulk cargo is today transported almost exclusively on containerships. Loose, firm general goods, such as coal and ore, but also cereals and other foodstuffs, are transported by ore or bulk carriers respectively. These are built as

Ore carrier in Qingdao, China

simply as possible yet also in a way that allows for the loading of the various goods without incurring any risks. In order to stop the ship listing if the load slides, the cargo holds have been equipped with high-level ballast tanks.

VALE BRASIL – THE LARGEST ORE CARRIER IN THE WORLD

The ore carrier "Vale Brasil" on its journey

THE LARGEST ORE CARRIERS IN THE WORLD
(by length)

❶ **Vale Brasil**
Vale Shipping Holding
1,188 ft (362 m)

❷ **Berge Everest**
Berge Bulk
1,181 ft (360 m)

❸ **Berge Stahl**
BW Bulk
1,125 ft (343 m)

❹ **Berge Fjord**
BW Fjord
1,086 ft (331 m)

A cargo ship at the bulk-loading terminal in Maasvlakte, an artificial island in the Maas estuary, which is a part of the Port of Rotterdam

The "Vale Brasil" was the first of 35 ore carriers with a loading capacity of 441,010 short tons (400,000 tonnes) commissioned by the Brazilian mining company Vale in 2008 from two Korean and two Chinese shipyards, and to be delivered in 2013. The Very Large Ore Carrier (VLOC) was taken into service in March 30, 2011, and has since transported Brazilian iron ore across the Atlantic and the Indian Ocean to Asia. Vale, one of the largest mining companies in the world, and which is being criticized for its environmentally destructive activities, boasts to have reduced the CO_2 emissions with the building of the Valemax ships by 35 percent per ton of transported ore.

THE LARGEST OIL TANKERS AND LNG CARRIERS IN THE WORLD

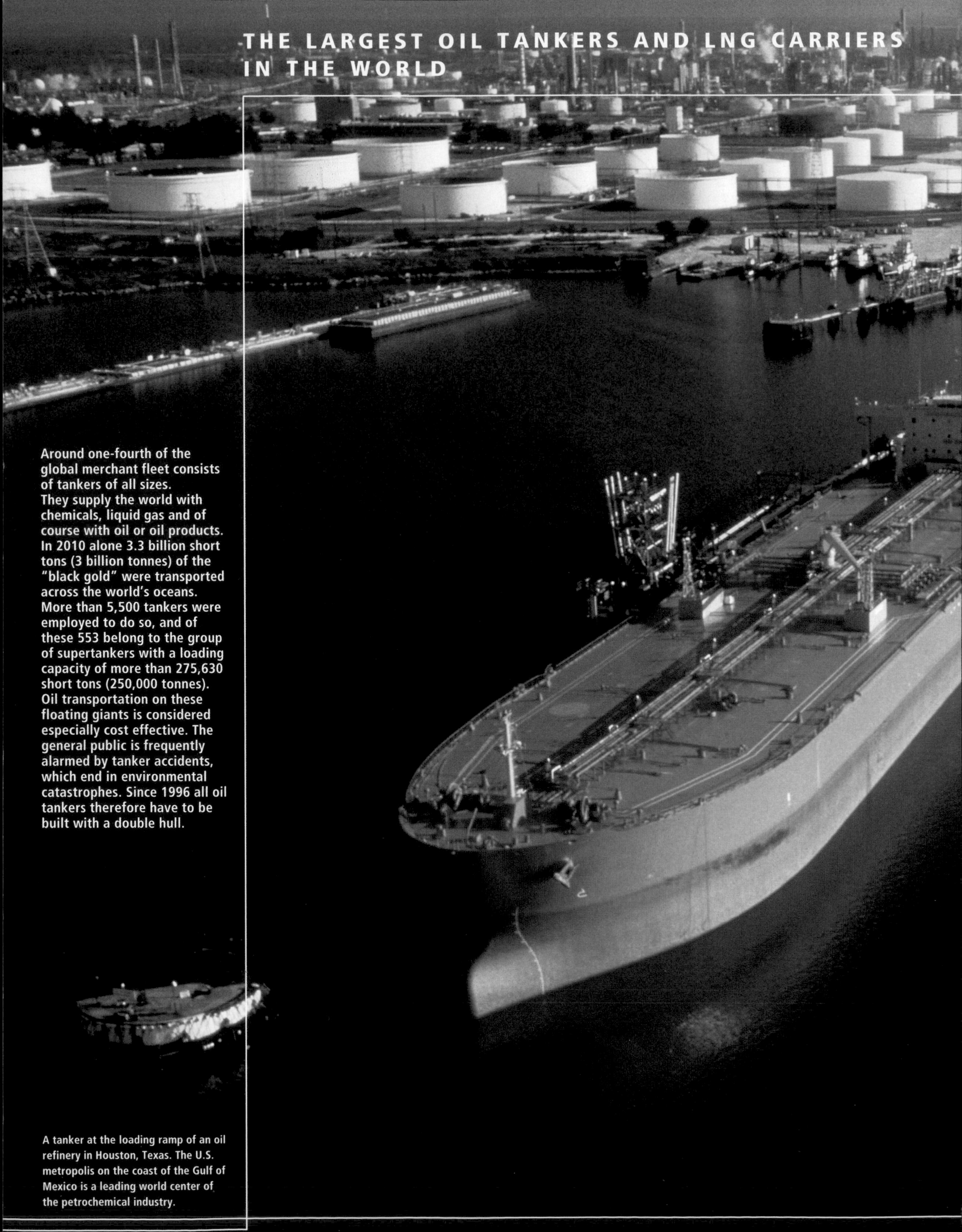

Around one-fourth of the global merchant fleet consists of tankers of all sizes. They supply the world with chemicals, liquid gas and of course with oil or oil products. In 2010 alone 3.3 billion short tons (3 billion tonnes) of the "black gold" were transported across the world's oceans. More than 5,500 tankers were employed to do so, and of these 553 belong to the group of supertankers with a loading capacity of more than 275,630 short tons (250,000 tonnes). Oil transportation on these floating giants is considered especially cost effective. The general public is frequently alarmed by tanker accidents, which end in environmental catastrophes. Since 1996 all oil tankers therefore have to be built with a double hull.

A tanker at the loading ramp of an oil refinery in Houston, Texas. The U.S. metropolis on the coast of the Gulf of Mexico is a leading world center of the petrochemical industry.

THE LARGEST OIL TANKERS IN THE WORLD

The ships of the Alhambra class are double-hulled oil tankers.

After an interruption of 20 years, for the first time supertankers with a loading capacity of more than 441,010 short tons (400,000 tonnes) were launched again in 2002 and 2003. The four ships of the Hellespont Alhambra class, built by the Daewoo shipyard on the orders of the Greek shipping company Hellespont, have a load capacity of 487,320 short tons (442,000 tonnes). The lead ship of the class has since been converted into an FSO, or "floating storage and offloading" vessel. The tankers of the Alhambra class are ULCCs or "ultra large crude carriers," with a loading capacity of more than 352,810 short tons (320,000 tonnes). Only a few of these giants are currently in service. They can only pass through the Suez Canal without cargo and are therefore pumped empty before every passage. The oil is sent through pipelines alongside the canal and then loaded back onto the ship once it has passed through the canal. Tankers with a carrying capacity of between 220,510 and 352,810 short tons (200,000 and 320,000 tonnes) are known as VLCCs or "very large crude carriers."

THE LARGEST LIQUID GAS CARRIERS IN THE WORLD

A liquid gas carrier of the Q-Max class

With a carrying capacity of 9,393,700 cu ft (266,000 cu m) each, the 14 ships of the Q-Max class owned by the Qatar Gas Transport Company are currently the largest liquid gas carriers in the world. They deliver natural gas that has been liquefied for transportation from the emirate on the Persian Gulf to the rest of the world. As LNG (Liquefied Natural Gas) carriers they have heavily insulated tanks, in which the gas can be kept liquid over long periods of time at temperatures down to -256 °F (− 160 °C). Unlike the LNG tankers, LPG (Liquefied Petroleum Gas) carriers transport gases that can be kept liquid even at room temperature.

THE MOST POWERFUL TUGS AND CRANES IN THE WORLD

Tugs are usually small and maneuverable ships that can push or pull ocean giants thanks to their enormous engine power. A distinction is made between harbor tugs, which take ships to their berths in the port, and ocean-going tugs, which are used for the transportation of oilrigs and damaged ships. Inland ships, too, often have to rely on tugboats. The performance of a tug depends on its traction capacity. The widely applied measurement for this is the bollard pull value, which is usually given in tonnes. Whereas harbor tugs have a max bollard pull of up to 66 short tons (60 tonnes), some ocean-going tugs achieve a max bollard pull of more than 386 short tons (350 tonnes). Thanks to special means of propulsion the ships are extremely maneuverable.

KL SANDEFJORD — THE MOST POWERFUL TUG IN THE WORLD

The ocean-going tug "KL Sandefjord"

The "KL Sandefjord," currently the most powerful tug in the world with a max bollard pull of more than 386 short tons (350 tonnes), has been in service since 2011. It tows oilrigs into position and lays pipelines on the ocean floor. It is also equipped with remote-controlled underwater vehicles. Like its sister ship, the "KL Saltfjord," the "KL Sandefjord" also operates in the North Sea and the Atlantic off the Brazilian coast, on behalf of the KL Line oil service company, a joint venture of a Norwegian and a Japanese enterprise.

THIALF — THE MOST POWERFUL CRANE VESSEL IN THE WORLD

"Thialf" on the way to deployment

Built at the Japanese Mitsui shipyard and taken into service in 1985, the "SSCV Thialf" is today still the most powerful floating crane in the world. Its two 659 feet (201 m) tall main cranes have a capacity of 7,828 short tons (7,100 tonnes) each and thus would be able to lift the Eiffel Tower in Paris. The "Thialf" is a semi-submersible vessel and has a max speed of six knots. It is often deployed for work on oil platforms, but also in the salvage of vessels. It is well known for its use in the decommissioning of the "Brent Spar" oil storage and tanker-loading buoy.

Four ocean-going tugs pull a floating oilrig to its final destination. Powerful tugs are also needed in the course of the exploitation of undersea oil and gas fields.

THE LARGEST AIRCRAFT CARRIERS IN THE WORLD

Aircraft carriers, the largest of all warships, are mobile air bases that allow the air force to intervene quickly and flexibly in conflict areas anywhere in the world.

The "John F. Kennedy" in action

Currently 37 of these floating monsters are traveling the world's oceans, 20 of which are a part of the United States' armed forces. The remaining 17 ships are kept by 11 different nations. Since they do not carry any weapons of their own, aircraft carriers are always escorted by destroyers and frigates. Such a flotilla is also known as a carrier strike group (CSG) or a carrier battle group (CVBG). Whereas a classic aircraft carrier serves exclusively as a starting and landing base for fighter jets, amphibian assault craft and helicopter carriers are also used during landing operations. Aircraft carriers are equipped not only with aircraft and helicopters, but also with landing craft.

THE LARGEST AIRCRAFT CARRIERS IN THE WORLD
(displacement in standard tons, ts)

❶	Nimitz class USA	97,000 ts
❷	USS Enterprise USA	93,000 ts
❸	Admiral Kusnezow Russia	61,390 ts
❹	Wasp class USA	41,000 ts
❺	Charles de Gaulle France	40,500 ts

USS ENTERPRISE
USS NIMITZ

With a displacement of just under 100,000 standard tons, the "Nimitz" and its now ten identical sister ships are currently

The "Nimitz" on the high seas ...

the largest aircraft supercarriers in the world. Their vast flight decks have one runway extending beyond the bow and a second one angled in relation to the ship's longitudinal axis by nine degrees. Aircraft catapults are set within the floor and ensure that jets have the necessary speed for launching, and arrester wires recover jets when landing. In total, the carriers of the Nimitz class can hold up to

85 aircraft. The 682 feet (208 m) long hangar extending over three decks in the hull of the ships has room for 60 fighter jets that are brought up to the flight deck with the help of an elevator. All these

... and at full speed

carriers are nuclear-powered and produce a maximum speed of over 30 knots. Of the 5,680 crew, 2,480 are responsible for the flight operations. The name-giving lead ship of the class was taken into service in 1975, replacing the "USS Enterprise" as the largest warship In the world.

The "Kitty Hawk," the lead ship of the class named after it, traveling the world's oceans. The 1,063 foot (324 m) long and 253 foot (77 m) wide aircraft carrier was deployed in several military interventions – for example in Vietnam and in the Persian Gulf. Launched in 1960, the still conventionally powered carrier was decommissioned in 2009, after almost 50 years in active service.

THE LARGEST SUBMARINES IN THE WORLD

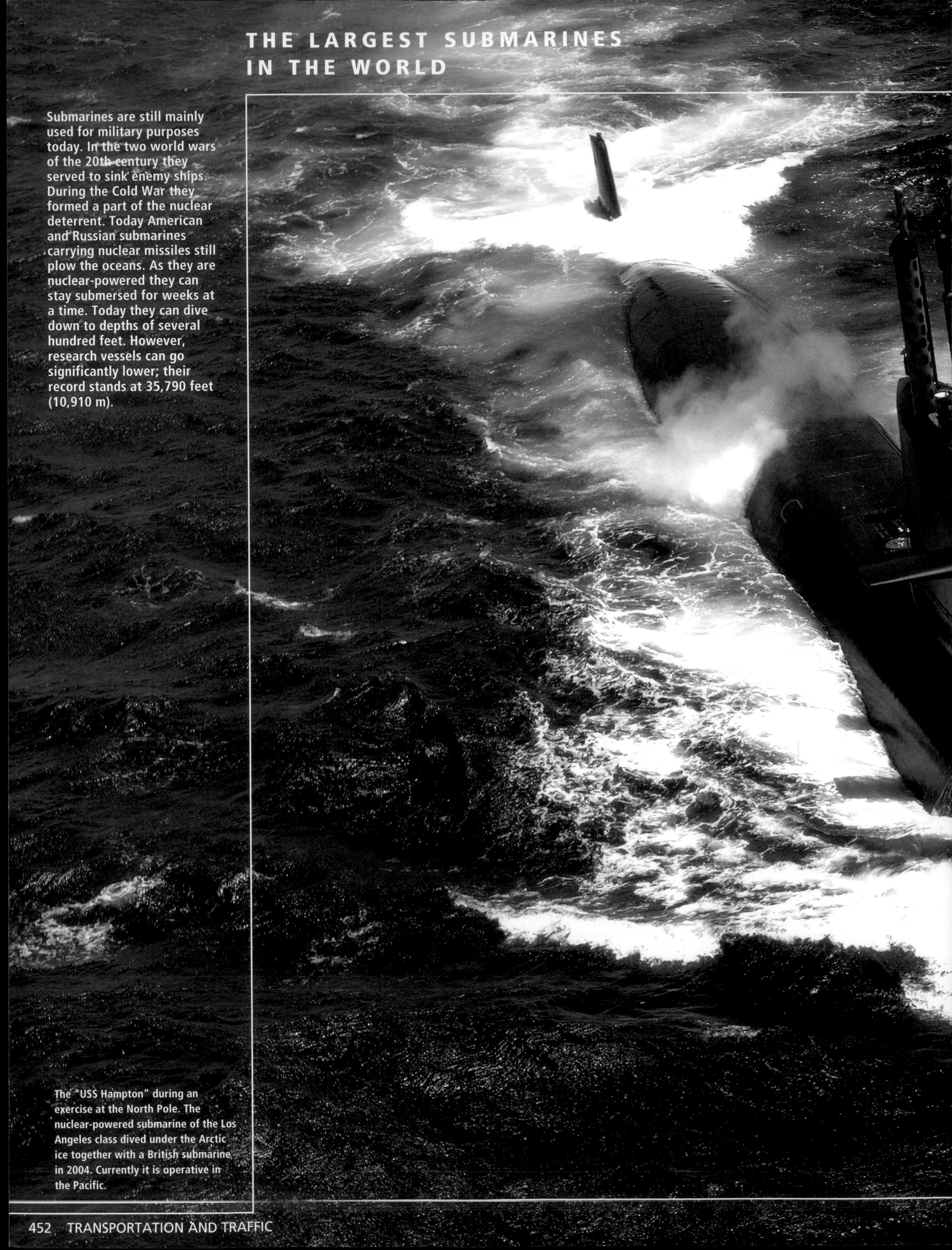

Submarines are still mainly used for military purposes today. In the two world wars of the 20th century they served to sink enemy ships. During the Cold War they formed a part of the nuclear deterrent. Today American and Russian submarines carrying nuclear missiles still plow the oceans. As they are nuclear-powered they can stay submersed for weeks at a time. Today they can dive down to depths of several hundred feet. However, research vessels can go significantly lower; their record stands at 35,790 feet (10,910 m).

The "USS Hampton" during an exercise at the North Pole. The nuclear-powered submarine of the Los Angeles class dived under the Arctic ice together with a British submarine in 2004. Currently it is operative in the Pacific.

TYPHOON-CLASS SUBMARINES

Typhoon-class submarines …

"Typhoon class" is the NATO term for a series of submarines carrying nuclear missiles that were built for the Soviet navy after 1976. Of the altogether seven ships that had been launched by 1989, half have been broken up, and three are still in use by the Russian navy. They

… are mighty colossuses.

THE LARGEST SUBMARINES IN THE WORLD
(by displacement in standard tons, ts)

❶ Project 941 class
Russia   48,000 ts
❷ Ohio class
USA   18,750 ts
❸ Project 667BDRM class
Russia   18,200 ts
❺ Projekt 955 class
Russia   17,000 ts
❻ Vanguard class
Great Britain   15,900 ts

are 584 feet (178 m) long and have a displacement of 52,920 short tons (48,000 tonnes). In the Soviet Union the submarines were known as "Project 941."

THE LARGEST AND MOST POWERFUL ICEBREAKERS IN THE WORLD

Ships that can break through ice that is several feet thick are needed for a variety of reasons. In the Arctic regions they keep navigational channels free from ice for merchant ships. During very

An icebreaker on a polar cruise

hard winters when waters freeze that are normally free from ice, they cut channels into the ice, "paving" the way for the ships that follow them. Some are in use as research vessels; others have been converted into cruise liners, offering adventure trips in the Arctic and Antarctic regions. The "Arctic Sunrise" icebreaker is operated by Greenpeace for protest action. So that they can fulfill their role, icebreakers are equipped with extra-strong engines and a much more solid hull than other ships. Its bow is shaped so that it pushes itself across the ice and crushes it underneath. Modern icebreakers have devices that enhance this effect and are capable of crushing even thick pack ice. Thus some ships can be made to rock back and forth, increasing the pressure on the ice by moving a large volume of water between bow and stern. Various Russian nuclear-powered icebreakers are equipped with a system for generating steam, which allows the ice in front of the bow to be slightly "thawed." This method is efficient, however it is not considered environmentally safe.

THE LARGEST ICEBREAKERS IN THE WORLD
(displacement in short tons/tonnes, t)

① **Manhattan**
USA
168,029 short tons (152,402 t)

② **50 Let Pobedy**
Russia
28,490 short tons (25,840 t)

③ **Arktika**
Russia
28,070 short tons (25,460 t)

④ **Yamal**
Russia
25,860 short tons (23,455 t)

⑤ **Rossiya**
Russia
25,270 short tons (22,920 t)

⑥ **Sovetsky Soyuz**
Russia
24,390 short tons (22,120 t)

⑦ **USCGC Healy**
USA
24,390 short tons (22,120 t)

⑧ **Oden**
Schweden
12,130 short tons (11,000 t)

50 LET POBEDY – THE MOST POWERFUL ICEBREAKER IN THE WORLD

Russia   23,439 GT

The nuclear-powered Russian giants of the Arktika class are the only icebreakers that can crush ice up to several feet thick. The "50 Let Pobedy," the largest ship in its class with a displacement of 28,490 short tons (25,840 tonnes), was taken into service on April 7, 2007. It operates in the Arctic Ocean, also offering cruise trips to that area. Equipped with two nuclear reactors and two steam turbines, the colossus reaches a max speed of up to 21.4 knots. Like all icebreakers it is disproportionately wide in shape.

The "50 Let Pobedy" in the harbor of Murmansk

SS MANHATTAN — OIL TANKER AND ICEBREAKER

The "SS Manhattan" in permanent ice

With a length of 1,007 feet (307 m) and a width of 131 feet (40 m), the "SS Manhattan" is today still the largest icebreaker ever built. Built in the United States in 1962, it was fitted with a spoon-like icebreaker bow several years later. On a transit through the Northwest Passage, which the ship undertook as the first tanker ever in 1969, those responsible wanted to test whether the transport of oil from northern Alaska would be possible via this sea route. The "SS Manhattan" was able to master the Passage on its first journey; however, it failed on the second trip in April 1970. The project was thus put on ice, so to speak. The "SS Manhattan" served as a tanker until 1987 and was then scrapped.

A nuclear-powered icebreaker of the Russian Arktika class plows through the permanent ice on its way to the North Pole. These colossuses are also used for cruise vacations in the North Pole region.

THE LARGEST POWERED TALL SHIPS AND SAILING SHIPS IN THE WORLD

For more than 3,000 years, sailing ships ruled the seas. It was only during the course of the 19th century that they were gradually replaced by steamships and in the 20th century by motor vessels. The largest sailing ships today either belong to cruise operators or are used as training ships, like the German navy's "Gorch Fock." In the modern world sailing is a recreational activity or a sport. Circumnavigations of the globe, especially if done single-handed, still cause a stir internationally. Sailing regattas like the America's Cup, a race that has been held since 1851, are still considered major sporting events. Since 1900 sailing has been an Olympic discipline.

THE LARGEST SAILING SHIP IN THE WORLD
(by length)

1. **Royal Clipper**
   Malta   433.7 ft (132.2 m)
2. **Sedow**
   Russia   385.5 ft (117.5 m)
3. **Star Clipper**
   Malta   378.9 ft (115.5 m)
4. **Kruzenshtern**
   Russia   375.7 ft (114.5 m)
5. **Juan Sebastián Elcano**
   Spain   370.7 ft (113 m)
6. **Esmeralda**
   Chile   370.7 ft (113 m)
7. **Dar Mlodziezy**
   Poland   357.6 ft (109 m)
8. **Mir**
   Russia   354.3 ft (108 m)

ROYAL CLIPPER – THE LARGEST SAILING SHIP IN THE WORLD

"Royal Clipper" under full sails

The dream ship of the Monegasque Star Clippers line has been traveling as a luxury cruise ship since 2000. It is a reproduction of the legendary "Preussen" – a tall ship of the Hamburg-based F. Laeisz shipping line that was launched in 1910 and was wrecked on the white cliffs of Dover in 1913. When it was taken into service, the "Royal Clipper" was the first five-masted full-rigged ship to have been built in 100 years. It was assembled at the Dutch Merwede Shipyard BV, where the hull of a Polish cruise liner was fitted with clipper bow and stern. The sailing ship is 440 feet (134 m) long and boasts 42 sails with an impressive total area of about 56,000 sq ft (5,202 sq m). When they are all set, the ship, which is fitted with the latest in navigation systems, can reach a top speed of 18 knots. In a lull, two diesel engines stand in. The "Royal Clipper" offers all the creature comforts of a modern cruise ship: it has three swimming pools, a fitness center as well as a restaurant, bar and disco. The stern gate can be opened out and used for a swim in the sea. The 114 cabins of the tall ship accommodate up to 227 guests.

WIND SURF – THE LARGEST MOTORIZED SAILING SHIP IN THE WORLD

The "Wind Surf" off Bequia Island, one of the islands in the St. Vincent and the Grenadines group

The five-masted sailing yacht was in service as "Club Med I" until 1998. Today it cruises for the U.S. sailing cruise operator Windstar Cruises — in winter in the Caribbean and in summer in the Mediterranean and the Baltic Seas. Modern computer technology is used for the ship's navigation as well as for remotely controlling the electronic raising and lowering of the seven sails, which have an impressive combined area of about 28,000 sq ft (2,600 sq m). The "Wind Surf" has two electric engines so that it can sail at a speed of up to 12 knots even during a lull in the wind.

The "Royal Clipper" travels as a cruise ship in the Mediterranean and in the Caribbean Seas. It combines the tradition of the tall ship with the comforts of a modern cruise liner.

Founded in 1972, it took Hyundai Heavy Industries only 40 years to overtake the European shipbuilders and to rise to the top as largest shipyard in the world. Today they feel the pressure from the Chinese competition.

Although the enterprise, which has its headquarters in the metropolis of Ulsan in the southeast of Korea, has begun to feel the strong competition from the expanding Chinese shipyard industry in recent years, it is today still the largest shipbuilder in the world, with a market share of 15 percent. Since Hyundai Heavy Industries was founded in 1972, a total of 1,686 ships have left the now nine graving docks of the giant shipyard, including 345 break bulk cargo ships, 503 containerships and 353 supertankers. The ships were supplied to 268 different shipping lines in 48 countries. The shipyard in Ulsan covers an area of no less than 27 sq ml (70 sq km). In 2010 the roughly 20,000 employees of the enterprise generated a turnover of around nine billion U.S. dollars. Hyundai Heavy Industries is specialized in merchant ships of all kinds, but it also handles the construction of warships like destroyers and submarines. The shipyard is a subsidiary of the Hyundai group of companies. Hyundai Heavy Industries Europe, with its headquarters in Belgium, produces construction machinery.

Around 20,000 people work around the clock at the Hyundai shipyard in Ulsan, assembling giant cargo ships and tankers (left and below).

Dry docks, or graving docks, are up to 2,133 feet (650 m) long basins where ships can be built and floated into the water, or rested within the dry platform and repaired. They have been around since antiquity and shipbuilding is unthinkable without them. All dry docks have an entrance caisson and can be flooded. For repairs or maintenance, tugboats pull the ships into the basin that is flooded with water and position them exactly on top of the keel blocks – concrete or wooden struts running across the center of the dock floor. Once the caisson is closed, the dock is pumped dry, gradually lowering the ship onto the keel blocks. Once it has been secured by additional struts on both sides it can now be repaired. When the work has been completed, the dock is flooded again and the ship can once more be launched into the water.

HYUNDAI — THE LARGEST DRY DOCK IN THE WORLD

Two ships can be constructed at the same time at Dock No. 3 in the Hyundai shipyard.

With the 2,205 feet (672 m) long Dock No. 3 in Ulsan and the 2,297 feet (700 m) long Dock No. 10 at the Gunsan shipyard, Hyundai Heavy Industries, the world's leading shipbuilder, has at its disposal the two largest dry docks on the planet. Ships with a displacement of more than 1 million tonnes can be built there. The foundation stone for the shipyard at Gunsan on the west coast of the Korean peninsula was laid as recently as 2008.

HARLAND & WOLFF — THE LARGEST DRY DOCK IN EUROPE

This venerable Belfast shipyard boasts a 1,824 feet (556 m) long and 305 feet (93 m) wide graving dock – the largest plant of its kind in Europe. Erected between 1968 and 1970 for the construction of supertankers, its capacity was however never fully exploited due to the decline of the European shipbuilding industry. The last newly built ship was launched in 2003. Today Harland & Wolff are specialized in ship repair and the construction of offshore wind turbines. In the heyday of passenger ocean liner transport the enterprise was one of the largest shipyards in the world.

Harland & Wolff around 1910 and ...

The "Titanic" was built at this shipyard.

... in the year 2007

The workers seem tiny when seen against the vast ship's hull in the dry dock of the Waigaoqiao shipyard in Shanghai, the largest shipbuilder in China.

The largest roofed dry dock in the world, with a length of 1,654 feet (504 m) and a width of 148 feet (45 m), belongs to the Meyer Werft in Papenburg on the Ems River. The traditional family firm is known around the world as a builder of cruise liners. Ship operators like Aida Cruises, Royal Caribbean and most recently Disney Cruise Line have all had their megaliners built here. The transfer of the ocean giants on the Ems River from the shipyard, located 22 miles (36 km) upcountry, to the North Sea regularly becomes a major spectacle attracting thousands of curious onlookers. The shipbuilder's second graving dock is similarly impressive in terms of its size: it is 1,175 feet (358 m) long and 128 feet (39 m) wide. The Meyer shipyard builds not only ocean liners, but also gas tankers, ferries, river cruise ships and containerships as well as livestock carriers.

A cruise ship under construction

Tugs pull a ship out of the dock

THE LARGEST ROOFED DRY DOCK IN THE WORLD

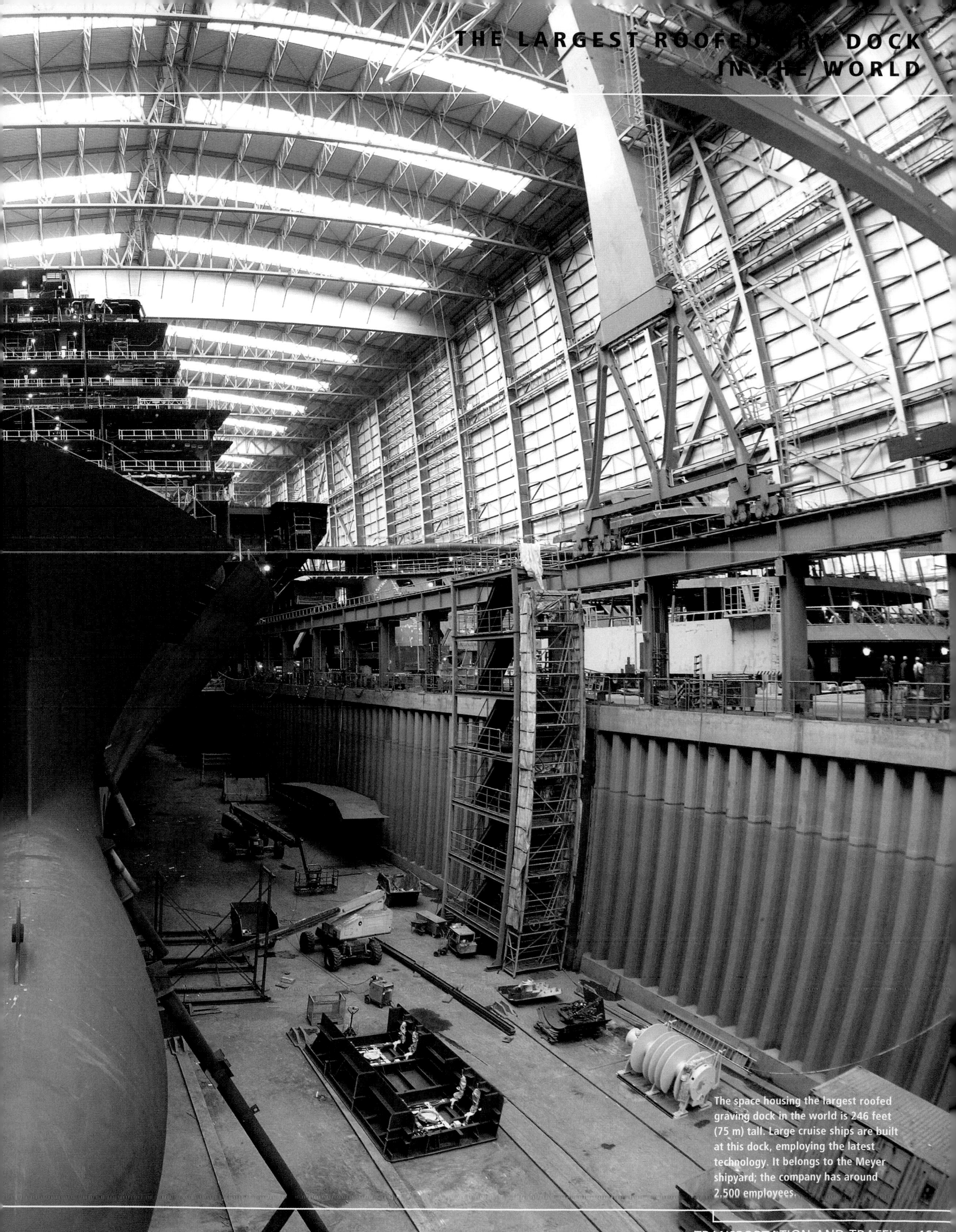

The space housing the largest roofed graving dock in the world is 246 feet (75 m) tall. Large cruise ships are built at this dock, employing the latest technology. It belongs to the Meyer shipyard; the company has around 2,500 employees.

THE LARGEST DRILLING RIGS AND PRODUCTION PLATFORMS IN THE WORLD

Oil and gas are still the most important energy sources on our planet, and a steadily increasing demand necessitates the development of still more wells today. Since a major part of the global oil and gas reserves exists under the ocean floor, offshore production technology is continually being further developed. Drilling can now take place in ultra-deep water at more than 3,280 feet (1,000 m) depth, thus permitting the exploitation of oil wells or gas fields

Oil engineers at work

that are situated many tens of thousands of feet under the ocean floor. Explorative drilling is undertaken by specially equipped offshore oil rigs or drilling barges. After this reconnaissance phase, they are replaced by working platforms, which have pumps, separators and tanks for the interim storage. Often the oil is transported away via pipelines on the ocean floor. Offshore production is considered very prone to accidents. Most recently damage on the "Deepwater Horizon" drilling rig led to worldwide protests.

AKER H-6E — THE LARGEST DRILLING RIG IN THE WORLD

The "*Transocean* Spitsbergen"

The Norwegian *Transocean Norway Drilling SA* drilling rigs of the type Aker H-6E are currently the largest and most powerful exploration platforms in the world. They were designed to operate in harsh conditions

such as Arctic waters and permit drilling down to a depth of up to 9,840 feet (3,000 m) – its derricks can penetrate up to 32,800 feet (10,000 m) deep rock strata. Today two of the 39,690 short ton (36,000 tonnes) colossuses, the "Transocean Barents" and the "Transocean Spitsbergen," have been assembled and delivered. They are deployed above the continental shelf in the northern Norwegian Sea. The Aker H-6E rigs are dynamically positioned semi-submersible drill barges. Their working decks can be raised or lowered by flooding or pumping dry the pontoons respectively. Mooring anchors hold them in place above the drill hole. Both drill rigs can travel at speeds of up to eight knots per hour.

SEA TROLL – THE LARGEST OFFSHORE GAS PLATFORM IN THE WORLD

The 118 feet (36 m) high concrete base of the gas production platform has been anchored in the ocean floor 62 miles (100 km) off the Norwegian coast at a depth of 994 feet (303 m). The four legs that are fixed to the base and carry the platform reach a height of 1,125 feet (343 m) yet rise only 98 feet (30 m) from the sea. The individual components of the "Sea Troll" were assembled in the Norwegian Vats fjord. During construction, legs and base were initially flooded and sunk in the fjord. Then the working deck was towed by tugboats onto the legs and connected with these. Base and legs were then pumped dry, raising the platform more than 656 feet (200 m), and transferred to their operational site.

A ship leaving the enormous platform

Humankind's ravenous appetite for energy demands the exploitation of ever deeper undersea oil wells and gas fields. The Troll gas platforms positioned in the North Sea are expected to supply Europe with gas for the next 70 years.

Humankind has always been inspired by the great dream of being able to fly, but it was not until the late 19th century that pioneers succeeded in gliding for short distances. A milestone was set by the first motorized flight undertaken by the Wright brothers in 1904. Soon, alongside powered aircraft, the first helicopters, flying boats, gliders, bombers and zeppelins appeared. With the coming into service of the first jet aircraft in the 1950s the plane became a means of intercontinental mass transportation. Today modern airports are often as extensive as medium-sized cities, their infrastructures including terminals, cargo centers, shopping malls and so on. The development of aircraft construction has often been propelled by military research – many speed and altitude records were achieved by military aircraft, such as the stealth reconnaissance aircraft of the U.S. Air Force.

Space travel also owes its progress to military needs. The development of rocket propulsion since the end of World War II was the precondition for the manned and unmanned space race that Americans and Soviets soon embarked on from giant space centers. It culminated in the Apollo 11 moon-landing mission of 1969. After that, the focus shifted to the exploration and exploitation of space with the help of space stations visited by space shuttles, as well as with satellites, space probes and space telescopes.

THE LARGEST AIRPORTS IN THE WORLD
(by passenger numbers, 2011)

1. **Atlanta Hartsfield-Jackson International Airport**
   USA   92.4 million
2. **Beijing Capital International Airport**, China   77.4 million
3. **London Heathrow Airport**
   Great Britain   69.4 million
4. **Chicago O'Hare International Airport**, USA   66.6 million
5. **Tokyo Haneda International Airport**, Japan   62.3 million
6. **Los Angeles International Airport**, USA   61.8 million
7. **Chicago Charles de Gaulle Airport**, France   61.0 million
8. **Dallas/Fort Worth International Airport**, USA   57.8 million
9. **Frankfurt Airport**
   Germany   56.4 million
10. **Hong Kong Chek Lap Kok International Airport**
    China   53.3 million

THE LARGEST AIRPORTS IN THE WORLD
(by cargo in short tons/tonnes, 2011)

1. **Hong Kong Chek Lap Kok International Airport**, China
   4.38 million (3.97 million)
2. **Memphis International Airport**
   USA   4.32 million (3.92 million)
3. **Shanghai Pudong International Airport**, China
   3.42 million (3.10 million)
4. **Ted Stevens Anchorage International Airport**, USA
   2.90 million (2.63 million)
5. **Incheon International Airport**
   Seoul, South Korea
   2.80 million (2.54 million)
6. **Dubai International Airport**
   UAE   2.50 million (2.27 million)
7. **Frankfurt Airport**
   Germany
   2.45 million (2.22 million)
8. **Louisville International Airport**
   USA   2.41 million (2.19 million)
9. **Charles de Gaulle Airport**
   Paris, France
   2.32 million (2.10 million)
10. **Narita International Airport**
    Tokyo, Japan
    2.15 million (1.95 million)

The X-shaped Theme Building with the famous Encounter Restaurant is the main tourist attraction at Los Angeles International Airport. Looking like a flying saucer that got stranded on all fours, the building was erected in 1961 in the futurist Googie Style. It marks the site where according to the original plans a giant glass dome was to be built that would enclose all the airport terminals and parking lots.

ATLANTA INTERNATIONAL AIRPORT
THE LARGEST AIRPORT IN THE WORLD (PASSENGERS)

The airport with the largest number of passengers worldwide (since 1998) is not found in the great metropolises of New York or Los Angeles, but in the internationally rather less well-known city of Atlanta, Georgia.

Along with the greatest passenger numbers (2011: more than 92 million, checked through at about 200 gates), Hartsfield Jackson Atlanta International Airport also holds the world record as regards the number of aircraft movements (around one million per year including cargo traffic). Hartsfield Jackson Atlanta International Airport owes its records mainly to its role as a major aviation hub for domestic flights. Initially known as Candler Field, then as Atlanta Municipal Airport, before it was given its present name in 2003 after two former mayors, the airport has grown continually since its opening in 1926. In 1948 it already recorded one million, and in 1957 more than two million passengers. Bit by bit the infrastructure was developed, most recently in 2006 with completion of the fifth runway and the construction of a 397 foot (121 m) tall control tower, the tallest in the United States and the third tallest in the world. Atlanta's significance for air traffic is also reflected in the fact that the largest airline in the world, Delta Airlines, has its base and headquarters here.

Left: home airport of Delta Airlines, the largest airline in the world with 750 commercial aircraft: Hartsfield Jackson Airport in Atlanta

Bird's-eye view of Hartsfield Jackson Atlanta International Airport: a giant network of takeoff and landing runways as well as taxiways, separated by the terminal area, with dozens of aircraft docking at its boarding bridges.

THE LARGEST AIRPORTS IN EUROPE

For many years London's Heathrow Airport, with just under 70 million passengers, has occupied the No. 1 rank in the list of busiest airports in Europe. Together with the other airports of the British capital (Gatwick, Stansted, Luton, City Airport), this is also where more passengers in the greater area of a single city are checked through than anywhere else in the world (in total just under 130 million). Also among the leaders in Europe are Charles de Gaulle Airport in Paris, Frankfurt Airport, Schiphol Airport in Amsterdam and Barajas Airport in Madrid, all with passenger numbers of at least 50 million. With 2.43 million short tons (2.20 million tonnes) Frankfurt is also the largest cargo airport in Europe (rank No. 7 in the world), followed by Paris Charles de Gaulle and London Heathrow.

THE LARGEST AIRPORTS IN EUROPE (BY PASSENGER NUMBERS, 2011)

1. London Heathrow Airport
   Great Britain   69.4 million
2. Paris Charles de Gaulle Airport
   France   61.0 million
3. Frankfurt Airport
   Germany   56.4 million
4. Amsterdam Schiphol Airport
   Netherlands   49.8 million
5. Madrid Barajas Airport
   Spain   49.6 million
6. Munich F. J. Strauss Airport
   Germany   37.8 million
7. Rome Leonardo da Vinci / Fiumicino Airport
   Italy   37.6 million
8. Istanbul Atatürk International Airport
   Turkey   37.4 million
9. Barcelona El Prat Airport
   Spain   34.4 million
10. London Gatwick Airport
    Great Britain   33.7 million

One of the two takeoff and landing strips at London Heathrow. Due to lack of available space no further runways can be built, and its capacity is therefore almost impossible to increase.

LONDON HEATHROW
Great Britain   69.4 million

At Europe's largest airport around 70 million passengers are checked through in five terminals, and cargo runs at a volume of around 1.65 million short tons (1.50 million tonnes) (worldwide rank No. 15), which adds up to a total of around 500,000 aircraft movements. Together with the airports Paris Charles de Gaulle and Frank-

Approach to landing above residential housing

furt, Heathrow also employs the most airport staff (about 75,000 each). At Terminal 5, designed by star architect Richard Rogers, one of the worldwide largest baggage systems handles around 12,000 pieces of baggage per hour on 11 miles (18 km) of conveyor belts.

PARIS CHARLES DE GAULLE
France   61.0 million

Inaugurated in 1974, Paris Charles de Gaulle Airport is the second largest airport in Europe by passenger numbers (60 million), cargo

Aerial view of Terminal 1

The glass structure of Terminals 2F

volume (about two million tons) and area (8,650 acres/3,500 ha). Over half a million aircraft movements are handled on four parallel takeoff and landing strips. Three terminals with several satellites are available for passenger check-through, and a fourth is being planned.

FRANKFURT ON THE MAIN
Germany   56.4 million

The largest German and third largest European airport (the largest in terms of its cargo volume), Frankfurt has two main terminals, a Lufthansa First Class Terminal, two cargo centers as well as four takeoff and landing strips. More than 100 airlines depart from there to 275 destinations. Other superlatives are the

AMSTERDAM SCHIPHOL
Netherlands   49.8 million

In the European ranking, Schiphol stands at fourth place for both its 50 million passengers and 1.65 million short tons (1.5 million tonnes) cargo volume (globally Nos. 14 and 17 respectively). However, it does hold one absolute record: at

Parade of Lufthansa aircraft at Frankfurt airport

A KLM aircraft docking at a boarding bridge

1,115 x 459 x 148 foot (340 x 140 x 45 m) A-380 maintenance hangar and Germany's largest office building ("The Squaire") with a surface area of about 1,507,000 sq ft (140,000 sq m) above the airport's long-distance railroad station.

10 feet (3 m) under sea level it is the lowest lying hub airport in the world. From a total of six takeoff and landing strips, many flights of the national KLM airline leave for destinations around the world from this civilian airport, opened in 1920.

Check-in desk at Tokyo Haneda

A giant arched steel and glass structure allows plenty of light into the new Terminal 3 at Beijing Airport.

The economic growth of Asia is also reflected in an increasing shift of international air traffic to that region. Whereas in 2000 Asia was represented by only three airports among the 20 largest in the world (by passenger numbers), in 2010 it already occupied nine places. Alongside the old "top dogs" of Tokyo, Hong Kong and Singapore, the emerging metropolises of Beijing, Shanghai, Jakarta, Dubai and others are now sharply rising in importance – the trend is ever upward. The situation regarding cargo traffic, where Hong Kong is the world leader, is similar.

THE LARGEST
AIRPORTS IN ASIA
(by passenger numbers, 2011)

❶ Beijing Capital International
Airport, China   77.4 million
❷ Tokyo Haneda International
Airport, Japan   62.3 million
❸ Hong Kong Chek Lap Kok
International Airport
China   53.3 million
❹ Jakarta Soekarno Hatta
International Airport
Indonesia   52.4 million
❺ Dubai International Airport
United Arab Emirates 51.0 million
❻ Bangkok Suvarnabhumi Airport
Thailand   47.9 million

**BEIJING CAPITAL
INTERNATIONAL AIRPORT**
Beijing, China   77.4 million

Beijing Capital International Airport (BCIA), represented for the first time in 2002 among the top 30 largest airports in the world (by passenger numbers), advanced to rank No. 2 in the global list by 2010 (2011: 77 million passengers). The heart of the previously chronically congested airport is Terminal 3, completed in 2008 to the plans of Sir Norman Foster and the longest freestanding building in the world. The baggage system also features impressive superlatives: on about 42 miles (68 km) of baggage belts 20,000 pieces of baggage can be moved per hour.

TOKYO HANEDA
Tokyo, Japan 62.3 million

Opened in 1931, this airport has 62 million passengers (2011), placing it at the fifth rank internationally, although for a long time it was used only for domestic flights (international air traffic was predominant-

Terminal 2 at Tokyo Haneda

ly handled at Narita; both airports together form the third largest airport system of a single city in the world). Since the extension of the airport in 2010 with the addition of a further terminal (now three) and another runway (now four), it now has more international air routes in its schedule.

HONG KONG CHEK LAP KOK
Hong Kong, China 53.3 million

Hong Kong's Chek Lap Kok Airport, built in the 1990s, has one of the most attractive airport approaches (along the coast). The passenger terminal with the spectacular roof structure (architect: Sir Norman

The departure hall at Chek Lap Kok

Foster) is at 4,170 feet (1,270 m) the second longest building in the world (2011: 53 million passengers). In terms of cargo handling, in 2010 Chek Lap Kok replaced Memphis International Airport, which had been the world leader until then (2011: 4.41 million short tons/4.00 million tonnes).

DUBAI INTERNATIONAL AIRPORT
Dubai, UAE 51.0 million

Founded in 1960 and for a long time no more than a transit stop on the way to South or South-East Asia, Dubai International Airport is today a much-frequented flight destination in its own right and

Moving walkway and artificial palm trees

boasts one of the largest duty-free shops in the world. More than 50 million passengers get on or off planes here every year (rank No. 13 worldwide). Its growth became possible with the completion of Terminal 3 in 2008, one of the largest buildings in the world. In terms of cargo handling Dubai occupies place No. 6 in the world.

SOEKARNO-HATTA AIRPORT
Jakarta, Indonesia 52.4 million

Built to the plans of the architect Paul Andreus, the airport integrates in its design elements of indigenous architecture: red roof tiles, gable façades in the form

Far Eastern designs in Jakarta

of row houses, pavilions, tropical gardens. Despite its village-like character, however, over 52 million passengers (rank No. 12 worldwide) crowded here in 2011. The terminal that was opened in 2009, and a further, fourth terminal, are planned to increase capacity in the future.

Aircraft take off and land at minute-intervals in the airports of the emerging metropolises of Asia. The rapidly growing passenger numbers and cargo volume can only be accommodated by extensive expansion and new building.

THE LARGEST AIRPORTS
IN AUSTRALIA / OCEANIA AND AFRICA

In Australia the largest cities in the country also have the busiest airports, and the ranking according to the number of inhabitants accords with the passenger numbers: Sydney, Melbourne, Brisbane, Perth, Adelaide. Kingsford Smith International Airport in Sydney, where national, continental and intercontinental (especially to Asia) flights all take off from three runways, is one of the 30 largest airports in the world, at 35 million checked-through passengers. In New Zealand, Auckland has by far the greatest number of passengers, but is still left behind in the continental league by the five Australian cities.

Ready for takeoff: the Australian Qantas fleet

THE LARGEST AIRPORTS IN OCEANIA
(by passenger numbers, 2006)

① **Sydney Kingsford Smith International Airport**
Australia   31.0 million
② **Melbourne Airport**
Australia   22.2 million
③ **Brisbane International Airport**
Australia   17.4 million
④ **Auckland International Airport**
New Zealand   11.2 million
⑤ **Perth International Airport**
Australia   8.0 million
⑥ **Adelaide Airport**
Australia   6.2 million

A Boeing 747 and a Boeing 767 of the Australian market leader Qantas Airways meet at the continent's largest airport, Sydney's Kingsford Smith International Airport.

THE LARGEST AIRPORTS IN AFRICA
(by passenger numbers, 2011)

1. **Johannesburg OR Tambo International Airport**
   South Africa   18.9 million
2. **Cairo International Airport**
   Egypt   13.0 million
3. **Cape Town International Airport**
   South Africa   8.4 million
4. **Casablanca Mohammed V International Airport**
   Morocco   7.3 million
5. **Hurghada International Airport**
   Egypt   5.9 million
6. **Nairobi Jomo Kenyatta International Airport**
   Kenya   5.8 million

In Africa the largest airports are concentrated in the far north and the south of the continent. The ranking is led by Johannesburg, where OR Tambo International Airport is the main gateway for intercontinental connections to and from South Africa. It is also an important hub for domestic flights. With Cape Town and Durban, the country has two more airports among the continent's top ten. Egypt is also represented with three airports (Cairo, Sharm el-Sheikh, Hurghada); however the unstable political situation in the country since the "Arab Spring" has led to a collapse of passenger numbers in 2011 by up to 25 percent.

OR Tambo Airport, Johannesburg

THE LARGEST AIRPORTS IN THE AMERICAS

In the United States, the country where the first motorized flights took place, flying is as normal as driving is elsewhere because of the country's enormous size. In 2000, thirteen of the world's

Inside Chicago O'Hare Airport

20 largest airports (by passenger numbers) were located in the United States. The Asian airports may now have broken through U.S. dominance, yet Hartsfield Jackson Atlanta International Airport with its over 92 million passengers still claims the leading slot. Other important airports are Chicago O'Hare, Los Angeles, Dallas-Fort Worth, Denver and New York John F. Kennedy. Many of the busiest U.S. airports are not final destinations but aviation hubs for the large U.S. airlines, where passengers simply change planes (as for example in Atlanta, Chicago, Dallas-Fort Worth). In terms of cargo volumes, Memphis (alternating with Hong Kong) leads the world's ranking list, with 4.41 million short tons (4.00 million tonnes) of cargo handled.

THE LARGEST AIRPORTS IN THE AMERICAS
(by passenger numbers, 2011)

1. **Atlanta Hartsfield-Jackson International Airport**
   USA   92.4 million
2. **Chicago O'Hare International Airport**
   USA   66.6 million
3. **Los Angeles International Airport**
   USA   61.8 million
4. **Dallas/Fort Worth International Airport**
   USA   57.8 million
5. **Denver International Airport**
   USA   52.7 million
6. **New York John F. Kennedy International Airport,**
   USA   47.9 million
7. **Las Vegas McCarran International Airport**
   USA   41.5 million
8. **San Francisco International Airport**
   USA   40.9 million

O'HARE INTERNATIONAL AIRPORT CHICAGO
Chicago, USA   66.6 million

Connecting tunnel in Terminal 1

The airport, built in the grounds of a Douglas production airport, was the busiest in the world between 1961 and 1997. It was only then that the main aviation hub for United Airlines had reached the limits of its capacity. With 67 million passengers (2011), at whose disposal are four terminals and seven takeoff and landing strips, it is today the second largest U.S. airport and the fourth largest in the world.

LOS ANGELES INTER-NATIONAL AIRPORT
Los Angeles, USA   61.8 million

The IATA code for the "City of Angels"

At the third largest airport in the United States (by passengers number; the fifth largest by cargo volume) about 600 domestic flights depart every day for over 90 U.S. cities from the nine terminals. International air traffic contributes around one-fourth to the annual passenger numbers (61 million). The Theme Building, constructed in the Googie Style, is its architectural landmark.

DALLAS-FORT WORTH INTERNATIONAL AIRPORT
Dallas-Fort Worth, USA   57.8 million

Peak time at dusk

Although it is located in provincial Texas, the Dallas-Fort Worth Airport is a domestic hub (connecting with 130 U.S. destinations), and with about 58 million passengers it is the fourth largest in the United States (No. 8 in the world). Globally it occupies fourth rank in terms of the number of aircraft movements (2011: 656,000) and second rank in terms of surface area (about 27 sq ml/70 sq km).

DENVER INTER-NATIONAL AIRPORT
Denver, USA   52.7 million

Terminal with a Teflon glass fiber canopy roof

With regard to its passengers volume (2011: 52.7 million) ranked only as No. 5 (USA) and No. 11 (worldwide), Denver Airport, opened in 1995, nevertheless holds two world records: with a surface area of 54 sq ml (140 sq km) it is the most extensive airport in the world, and it also boasts the world's longest takeoff strip at (15,980 feet/4,870 m), allowing fully loaded Boeings 747 and Airbuses A380 to take off at an altitude of 5,250 feet (1,600 m) above sea level.

Road and air traffic side by side: Texas Highway 97 runs right through the center of Dallas–Fort Worth International Airport, dividing the airport into approximately symmetric halves.

DUBAI INTERNATIONAL AIRPORT — TERMINAL 3
BEIJING INTERNATIONAL AIRPORT — TERMINAL 3

With its shapes and colors, Terminal 3 pays homage to Chinese traditions.

Boldly sweeping curves characterize the appearance of Terminal 3.

BEIJING CAPITAL INTERNATIONAL AIRPORT TERMINAL 3 — THE LONGEST AIRPORT BUILDING IN THE WORLD

Beijing International Airport owes its rapid growth in recent times to its Terminal 3, built in 2008 on the occasion of the Olympic Games to the plans of Sir Norman Foster. With a length of 9,840 feet (3,000 m) the vast steel–aluminum–glass structure — which, by the way, conforms with Feng Shui princip-les — is the longest building in the world, and at 14.0 million sq ft (1.3 million sq m) it also has the second largest floor surface. Seen from a bird's-eye perspective, the giant structure with its vaulted roof and Y-shaped cantilevered ends resembles a flying dragon.

DUBAI INTERNATIONAL AIRPORT TERMINAL 3 — THE LARGEST AIRPORT BUILDING IN THE WORLD BY AREA

Construction of Terminal 3 at Dubai International Airport, at a cost of 4.5 billion U.S. dollars, increased the airport's capacity to about 60 million passengers. With a total floor area of around 12.9 million sq ft (1.2 million sq m) it is — after the Abraj Al Bait Towers in Mecca — the second largest building in the world altogether and the largest airport building in this category. Designed by the renowned architect Paul Andreu, the terminal is dominated by curved transparent elements, reflecting shapes that are typical in aircraft construction.

Despite its vast dimensions – as can be clearly seen here – Terminal 3 of Beijing Capital International Airport appears light and transparent.

TEMPELHOF — THE LARGEST AIRPORT BUILDING IN EUROPE

The "mother of all airports" (according to Sir Norman Foster), built between 1936 and 1941 to the plans of Ernst Sagebiel, was conceived to check through six million passengers a year at its monumental curved airport terminal (length: 4,035 feet/1,230 m) — thirty times the actual passenger volume at the time. With a gross floor area of 3,304,500 sq ft (307,000 sq m), the airport building, which comprised gates and hangars, was for several years the largest building in the world by area. External and internal façades reflect an ambivalence between National Socialist Monumentalism and

Almost 66 feet (20 m) tall: the check-in hall. Above it there was once a "ballroom."

New Sobriety. The subterranean connections with the road and rail network were pioneering, as was the architectural guidance of traffic flow by the functional segregation of the various levels and wings of the building, with separate areas serving visitors, departure, arrival, cargo etc. Under the canopy jutting out toward the airport ramp by about 164 feet (50 m) and over a length of 1,247 feet (380 m), passengers were able to stay dry while boarding and getting off planes. After 1945 the airport, which had served as a concentration camp for the Nazi regime, was in military (U.S. Army) and civilian use until the cessation of operations in 2008.

THE BERLIN AIRLIFT

Eagerly expected by the Berliners: a "raisin bomber" on its approach to Tempelhof

After the introduction of the deutschmark in West Berlin, on June 24, 1948, the Soviet head of state Stalin ordered all transit routes to Berlin, all of which ran through the Soviet occupation zone, to be blocked. In response the Americans decided to organize an airlift and to supply the sealed-off city by air. Thus, within just under a year, 280,000 flights arrived at Tempelhof Airport carrying around 2.3 million aid shipments. Before landing, the pilots threw down packs of candy for the children of Berlin – hence the nickname "raisin bombers." In the end, West Berlin won: Stalin lifted the blockade on May 12, 1949.

Historical symbol of National Socialist megalomania, but also of advanced engineering skills: the giant curved airport building of Berlin Tempelhof. On the roof, reachable via staircase towers, the National Socialists wanted to erect stands for about 100,000 spectators so they could enjoy the air shows of the Reich – but this never happened.

The presently largest operational aircraft in the world appears like an enormous "primordial monster" crawling along the ground as it rolls along the runway on its 32 wheels. The Antonov AN-225 cargo aircraft was originally designed for the regular piggyback transport of the

The AN-225 colossus lifts off …

"Buran" spacecraft. It was developed from the smaller Antonov AN-224 model. Both planes have the same fuselage diameter (131 feet/40 m), but fuselage and wingspan sizes were increased by 49 to 279 or 289 feet (by 15 to 85 or 88 m) respectively, and the four turbofan engines were complemented by two more. For the transportation of loads outside the aircraft, a giant bizarre-looking vertical and horizontal stabilizer structure was fitted at the rear.

The hold size of 43,080 cu ft

(1,220 cu m) and the maximum load capacity of 276 short tons (250 tonnes) considerably surpass the figures for all other cargo aircraft and make the operation of even a single aircraft within its class profitable (only a single aircraft, fabricated in 1988 and intermittently

… and amazingly remains airborne.

inoperative, is in service; a second one is kept at the Kiev works).

The AN-225 holds a whole string of world records for cargo aircraft in terms of weight, track and altitude (heaviest total cargo transported: 272 short tons/247 tonnes; heaviest individual cargo piece: 209 short tons/190 tonnes). The flying giant is licensed for a takeoff weight of around 662 short tons (600 tonnes). Loading is possible without any elaborate infrastructure, in fact via a ramp: the aircraft simply opens and lowers its nose.

The Antonov AN-225 travels the whole world for special operations. Here it is shown just after landing at Frankfurt Hahn Airport on August 11, 2009, where it took on board the largest and heaviest individual piece of cargo ever transported by air: a power plant generator weighing 209 short tons (190 tonnes) and destined for Armenia. No other aircraft would have been able to transport this record cargo.

With its maiden flight in 2005, Airbus A380 replaced the then record-holder Boeing 747 as the largest passenger aircraft in the world. With a fuselage length of 236 feet (72 m) the Airbus is shorter than its rival, however it wins with regard to

The A380 with cabins on two levels

all other measurements. Due to its wingspan of 262 feet (80 m) and its height of 79 feet (24 m), the A380 can only land and be processed at a few specially adapted airports. Depending on the model, between 525 and 850 passengers are accommodated. They are seated on two continuous passenger decks – recognizable from the outside by the double rows of windows on both sides. Thanks to the use of new, lighter composite materials in structure and components, it was possible to restrict the unladen weight to 303 short tons (275 tonnes); a maximum of 617 short tons (560 tonnes) is permitted as takeoff weight. Four engines with a thrust of 69,690 to 71,940 lbf (310 to 320 kN) each allow the A380 to reach a cruising speed of 572 mph (920 km/h). Its range is around 9,320 miles (15,000 km).

Operates the largest fleet of A380: Emirates airlines

One of several Lufthansa A380s on the runway

An Airbus A380 of the Emirates airline based in Dubai high up in the sky. Emirates received the second series-produced aircraft of this type in 2008 and by 2012 it had more than 20 aircraft in use; it has ordered 90 planes in total. In first and business class, passengers have shower cabins, onboard lounges, private suites and flatbed seats at their disposal.

Boeing no longer builds the largest commercial aircraft in the world, yet the U.S. aircraft manufacturer can still claim one superlative for itself: at its premises in Everett, around 31 miles (50 km) north of Seattle, stands the largest hangar in the world, with an enclosed area of 459

Final assembly of the Boeing 787 "Dreamliner"

million cu ft (13 million cu m). It was erected in 1967 for the production of the then brand-new Jumbo 747; in 1993 it was enlarged again by about half for the introduction of the Boeing 777. Today, the final assembly of more than 60 aircraft of the types 747, 767, 777 and 787 (Dreamliner) happens here, in an area of 43 million sq ft (4 million sq m) in total. On the "Future of Flight Aviation Center and Boeing Tour" visitors have the opportunity to watch some of the workforce of 25,000 employees during final assembly, amidst a spectacular tangle of giant conveyor belts, scaffolds and cranes.

The Boeing 747, for many years the world's largest commercial aircraft, has been in production since 1967/68, and there is no end in sight for its production run. The production hangar in Everett near Seattle, which was specially built for its assembly, is of exactly the same age. Here we see several Jumbo Jets together, all awaiting final assembly.

THE LARGEST HANGAR IN THE WORLD

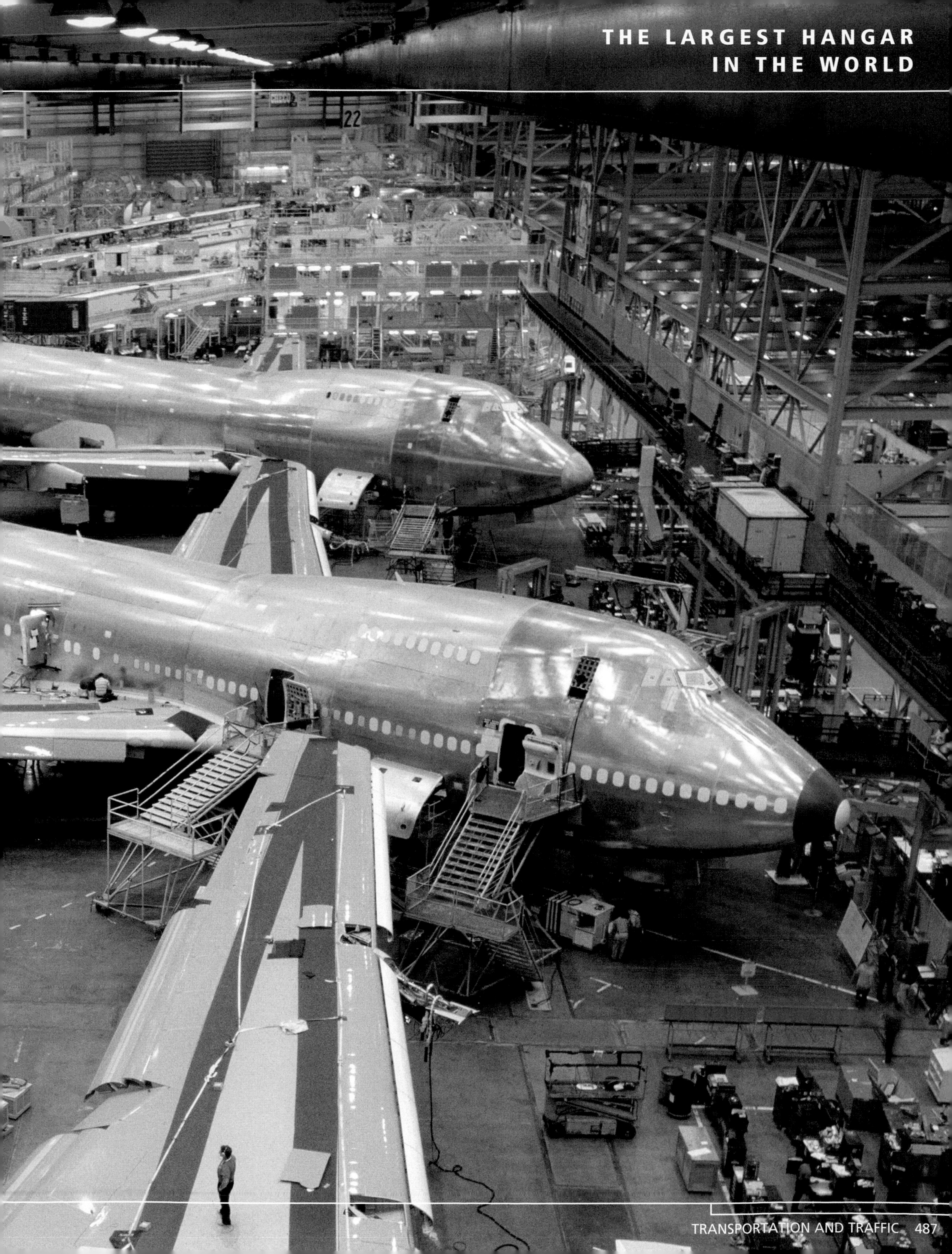

In the Port of Long Beach

Interior view of the big bird

Tail unit of the "Spruce Goose"

Four of the eight 28-cylinder radial engines

Gigantic and unique – its wingspan of 318 feet (97 m) and height of 82 feet (25 m) are still world records today — the Hughes H-4 flying boat can be visited at the Evergreen Aviation Museum in McMinnville near Portland (Oregon). It owes its nickname of "Spruce Goose" to its timber construction – built from 1942, the use of materials that would be needed was not permitted during wartime rationing. The monster was financed and co-developed by billionaire Howard Hughes, who had it completed in 1947 despite a lack of interest from the U.S. Navy. But the wooden flying giant was too heavy and remained a floating giant: Hughes himself flew the plane on its maiden journey on November 2, 1947; however despite its eight 28-cylinder engines the H-4 was not able to lift more than 66 feet (20 m) out of the water.

After its "maiden flight" the Hughes H-4 Hercules stayed for many decades in the Port of Long Beach (California). Eventually, in 1992, it was taken to the Evergreen Aviation Museum in McMinnville (Oregon), where today it is a magnet and the main attraction for visitors.

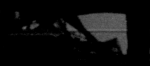

ANTONOV AN-22 – THE LARGEST PROPELLER PLANE IN THE WORLD

An Antonov AN-22 at the Turin Air Show 1968

Once the largest production aircraft in the world, the Antonov AN-22, built between 1965 and 1975, is today only the largest propeller plane. In its 108 x 14.4 x 14.4 foot (33 x 4.4 x 4.4 m) large cargo hold, the flying giant can transport up to 88 short tons (80 tonnes) of cargo.

On the outside it has high-mounted wings with two pairs of contra-rotating propellers fitted one behind the other and four turboprops as well as two rudders piercing the tail plane. The aircraft is still in use today and can take off and land from grass airstrips.

THE FASTEST MANNED AIRCRAFT IN THE WORLD

X-15 – THE FASTEST MANNED AIRCRAFT IN THE WORLD

A pilot-controlled plane that flies at nearly seven times the speed of sound and reaches altitudes of more than 62 miles (100 km)? Yes, it really does exist! In 1959 one of the three experimental planes of the "North American Aviation X-15" type took off for the first flight. These extreme planes

Presentation of the X-15

were launched at an altitude of 49,200 feet (15,000 m) from a B-52. During 199 flights (up to 1968), it reached records of 4,520 mph (7,274 km/h) and 354,200 feet (107,960 m) of altitude. In order to resist extreme forces and temperatures, new materials were being deployed.

X-43A – THE FASTEST UNMANNED AIRCRAFT IN THE WORLD

Painting of an X-43-Scramjet

A speed of almost ten times the speed of sound (7,546 mph/12,144 km/h) was achieved in 2004 by the unmanned experimental aircraft X-43A developed by Boeing and NASA. A B-52 (its airborne launch pad) and a Pegasus rocket reached a flight altitude of 98,425 feet (30,000 m). Only then did it start its independent flight with its scramjet (a supersonic ramjet), but only for a few seconds.

A X-15 at great altitude as it detaches itself from its flying launch pad, a B-52, in order to attempt new altitude and speed records

HEINKEL HE 178 – THE FIRST JET AIRCRAFT IN THE WORLD

On August 27, 1939, in the grounds of the Rostock-based Heinkel aircraft manufacturing company, an aircraft started on its maiden voyage, ringing in a new technological era with a deafening noise: the Heinkel He 178 was fitted not with the propellers and piston engines in use until then, but instead it had a jet engine

Heinkel He 178, photographed in 1942

that compressed air, injected and ignited fuel and then drove a turbine and compressor with the exhaust expelled via jets. Thanks to this principle, revolutionary in its day, speeds could be significantly increased: test pilot Erich Warsitz thundered across the airfield at 373 mph (600 km/h). When World War II broke out only a few days later, any further development of the He 178 and preparation for serial production was halted. In 1942 a Messerschmitt Me 262 took off for the first time, the first series-produced jet aircraft.

BELL X-1 –
THE FIRST SUPERSONIC JET IN THE WORLD

The record-breaking "Glorious Glennis" (1947)

On October 14, 1947, at an altitude of 22,970 feet (7,000 m), a special aircraft started on a very special mission from the bomb recess of a B-29. Charles "Chuck" Yeager, the pilot of the Bell X-1, known as a "bullet with wings" because of its projectile-like shape, ignited the combustion chambers of the rocket engine operated with methanol and oxygen, and for the first time in aviation history, at an altitude of 42,650 feet (13,000 m), he broke through the sound barrier 700 mph (1,127 km/h = Mach 1.06). The advanced X-1a version surpassed Mach 2 for the first time in 1953.

Even with its appearance, the strategic long-range bomber aircraft taken into service in 1993 caused a sensation: it is a flying wing plane, in which fuselage and wings form a unit, without any horizontal or vertical stabilizers. This construction type has very good "camouflaging" or stealth properties, that is, the aircraft is difficult to detect by radar. It is also for this purpose that carbon fiber reinforced plastic and radar-absorbing materials as well as zigzag and saw tooth shapes were used. All this does not come cheap: the development and acquisition costs per aircraft run at about two billion and one billion U.S. dollars respectively (due to the limited number of only 21 aircraft built).

At the Andersen Air Force base, Guam

A B-2 dropping precision-guided munitions

Stealth bomber lit by lightning.

A B-2 Spirit Stealth during aerial refueling by a Boeing KC-135. Thanks to such maneuvers a B-2 was able to complete, at 44 hours, the longest combat mission in military aviation history during the Afghanistan War in 2001: from the air base in Missouri to Afghanistan, onward for refueling and rearming in Guam, and from there via Afghanistan back to the United States.

U-2

When a U-2 was shot down over the Soviet Union in 1960, the entire world found out about its

A U-2 during a reconnaissance mission

mission. The spy plane can climb to an altitude of 84,970 feet (25,900 m) and for a long time it remained unreachable for enemy air defenses.

MIG-25

Various versions of the Russian interceptor and reconnaissance aircraft MiG-25 established a

A Libyan MiG-25 (1981)

whole series of world records. Still standing today is the altitude record for non-rocket powered aircraft: 123,520 feet (37,650 m) – however, only in parabolic flight.

LOCKHEED SR-71A BLACKBIRD

From its appearance alone it is easy to make out that this strategic reconnaissance aircraft, taken into service from 1966, is an outstanding plane: flowing, undulating shapes, a lack of right angles, black paint finish, two vertical stabilizers slanted inward – these are all stealth features that make detection difficult. And its aerial performance is also amazing: the "Blackbird" is the fastest non-rocket powered plane in the world, both with and without payload — its absolute speed record is 2,193 mph (3,529 km/h). And all this in almost unattainable altitudes: in horizontal flight, the "high-flyer" reached 86,000 feet (26,213 m) – and that is a world record too.

Blackbirds at the Edwards Air Force Base

Too fast and too invisible to be shot down: a Lockheed SR-71-A high above the clouds. From 1966 until 1968, 32 high-performance reconnaissance aircraft of this type were built. Although not a classic stealth aircraft, stealth technology was already in use. The deployment of undulating shapes and the avoidance of right angles significantly reduced the plane's radar signature. In 1998 the program was discontinued, and remaining aircraft were passed to museums.

THE MOST IMPORTANT SPACEPORTS
IN THE WORLD

Spaceports are rocket-launching sites from which spacecraft can be sent into orbit. They have launch pads for carrier rockets of such enormous thrust that they can take satellites, space probes or manned command modules into orbit around Earth at a speed of at least 17,400 mph (28,000 km/h). Since it is always possible that a rocket could misfire, most of the space centers that are currently operating on Earth are located in sparsely populated regions and on a coast where possible. Today the veteran space-exploring nations of America, Russia and China are not the only ones with spaceports, rather countries like Brazil, India and Japan now also do, and – just like the establishments of the big space powers – these are probably also used for military purposes. Operating a space center is also a lucrative business. The launching of commercial satellites brings in many millions of dollars for the owner. In October 2011 a privately operated space center for tourist excursions into space was inaugurated in the U.S. state of New Mexico.

On July 8, 2011, "Atlantis" took off from the Kennedy Space Center at Cape Canaveral for a 13-day flight to the International Space Station. It was the very last flight of a space shuttle. The legendary fleet was decommissioned 20 years after their first mission.

CAPE CANAVERAL AIR FORCE STATION
USA, Florida   US Air Force

Beginning with the flight of Alan Shepard, the first American to be sent into space on May 1961, right up to the Apollo 7 mission of October 1968, all the United States manned space flights started from this spaceport. Of the 47 launch pads that were built at the center since it came into service in 1949, only four are today used for satellite launches. In January 1967 the Air Force Station was the site of a tragedy: fire claimed the lives of three astronauts during a routine exercise.

KENNEDY SPACE CENTER
USA, Florida   NASA

Located in the immediate proximity of the Cape Canaveral Air Force Station, this spaceport was the starting point for many manned space flights. The Apollo missions started from here between 1968 and 1972 for their spectacular lunar landing missions. The launch pads and landing strips for the space shuttles, which took astronauts into space and to the ISS from 1981 to 2011, are also located here. The visitor center of the Kennedy Space Center provides information on all the fascinating aspects of space travel.

THE MOST IMPORTANT SPACEPORTS IN THE WORLD

BAIKONUR

Kazakhstan   Roscosmos

This space center, located in the independent republic of Kazakhstan since the dissolution of the Soviet Union, was leased by Russia in 1994 and is used by

Preparations for the launch of a rocket in Baikonur

the Russian space agency. Numerous satellites are launched into space from the Cosmodrome, and all the manned Russian space flights also started from here. In April 1961 Yuri Gagarin was the first person to start on a 106-minute excursion into space from Baikonur.

SATISH DHAWAN SPACE CENTER

India, Andhra Pradesh   ISRO

Located on the southeastern coast of India, this space center was brought into operation in 1971. Although not every launch was successful, some satellites have been taken into Earth's orbit. Until 1980 Indian satellites were launched into space with Soviet carrier rockets. The first successful rocket launch was in 1980, and the first lunar probe in 2008. By 2015 at the latest the spaceport is set to be the liftoff point for a manned space flight.

Launch of the Chandrayaan-1 lunar probe

TANEGASHIMA UCHU SENTA

Japan, Tanegashima   JAXA

Japan's largest space center was built on the island of Tanegashima to the south of Kyushu and came into service in 1969. From there weather and research satellites are launched into orbit. Observation of the Earth's surface is one of the main tasks of the Japanese space agency, but its space probes also make important contributions to research of the moon and of the planetary system. Kibo, the largest component of the ISS, comes from Japan.

Launch of the Akatsuki Venus probe

GUIANA SPACE CENTER
French Guiana, Kourou   ESA

This spaceport is operated jointly by the French National Center for Space Studies, the European Space Agency and the commercial venture Arianespace. Until 2011 it was used exclusively for the launch of Ariane rockets. In October 2011 the first Soyuz rocket took off from Guiana with two satellites for the Galileo European satellite navigation system, the basis for which was a Russian–European cooperation agreement. The first of the new European Vega rockets started into space in February 2012, carrying nine small research satellites.

Launch of a Delta 2 rocket at the Vandenberg Air Force Base

VANDENBERG AIR FORCE BASE
USA, California   USAF

This U.S. Air Force base boasts 50 launch pads, which are for the most part set up underground and were built for the launch of intercontinental missiles. Being in an advantageous location on the Pacific coast, it permits the launch of satellites that are to circle Earth in a polar orbit, but it is also used for civilian purposes. Originally space shuttles were also planned to be launched into space from Vandenberg. But after the "Challenger" disaster of 1986, which led to a re-examination of the entire shuttle program, the plan was abandoned.

Launch of an Ariane rocket on Kourou

On May 12, 2012, a Soyuz rocket with a Soyuz command module at its nose lifted off from the Cosmodrome in Baikonur, in order to transport three new crewmembers to the International Space Station. The ISS crew is replaced every six months. Since the shutdown of the space shuttles the space station crew start exclusively from the spaceport operated by Russia.

JIUQUAN WEIXING
FASHE ZHONGXIN

P.R. China, Jiuquan, Gansu

This rocket launch pad founded in 1958 is located in Inner Mongolia, around 124 miles (200 km) from the city of Jiuquan. It is the

"Shenzhou 9" on the launch pad

Liu Yang, China's first spacewoman

oldest and still the largest of four spaceports currently operated by the People's Republic of China. In 1970 the first Chinese satellite was launched into orbit from there, and in 2003 the "Shenzhou 5," China's first manned spaceship, lifted off from there into space. The "Tiangong 1," the first Chinese space station, which has been orbiting Earth since September 2011, was also launched from the Jiuquan Space Center. At the station astronauts are prepared for longer stays in space.

The "Shenzhou 9" spaceship is being fitted to the "Long March 2F" carrier rocket in the assembly hall of the Jiuquan Cosmodrome. The "Shenzhou 9" was launched on June 16, 2012, for a flight to the "Tiangong 1" space station. Onboard were Jing Haipeng, Liu Wang and Liu Yang, the first female astronaut from the People's Republic. The crew put the space station into service and returned safely to Earth after eight days in space.

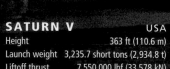

SATURN V
USA

Height	363 ft (110.6 m)
Launch weight	3,235.7 short tons (2,934.8 t)
Liftoff thrust	7,550,000 lbf (33,578 kN)
Max payload	146.6 short tons (133 t)

The rockets in this series made a major contribution to the success of the United States' lunar landing program. All the spaceships in the project, from Apollo 8 to Apollo 17, were launched with these rockets. The final Saturn V took a Skylab into space in 1973.

Third stage of a Saturn V

Second stage of a Saturn V

SATURN V – THE ROCKET TO THE MOON

To this day the Saturn V, developed for NASA's lunar landing program, is still the most powerful rocket ever built. The three-staged giants of the series transported the Apollo spaceships together with their landing craft into a high Earth orbit, from which a trajectory toward the moon was possible. The five first stage engines were ignited at launch to lift the rocket to an altitude of 38 miles (61 km) within only two and a half minutes. They burned 2,205 short tons (2,000 tonnes) of fuel and after that were burned out. After separation of the first stage, the second stage was ignited which then lifted the rocket to an altitude of 115 miles (185 km, at a speed of 15,285 mph/24,600 km/h). Twelve minutes after liftoff this stage was also separated, and the third stage was ignited, which took the spaceship into or-

The launch of Apollo 11 on July 16, 1969

The "Columbia" Command Module at liftoff

bit. Before it could set course for the moon it orbited Earth several times. During this phase the engine of the third stage was shut down. It was reignited to propel the spacecraft into its translunar trajectory. After this the third stage was separated and discarded.

During the course of the "race to the moon" that started in 1960, the Soviet Union also worked on plans for a manned lunar mission. At the time, Soviet space technology was highly developed and appeared far more advanced than that of the United States. After all, the Soviets had launched the first satellite in the world in 1957, sent a space probe to the moon in 1959 and were the first to send a human being, Yuri Gagarin, into space in 1961.

N1	Soviet Union
Height	345 ft (105.3 m)
Launch weight	3,030 short tons (2,750 t)
Liftoff thrust	9,734,230 lbf (43,300 kN)
Max payload	77 short tons (70 t)

However, their lunar landing program was not realized and was abandoned in 1974. Experts believe that the lack of a suitable carrier rocket may have been one of the reasons for the failure. All the test flights of the N1, which had been built for this purpose, remained unsuccessful.

The "Saturn V" erected at the Johnson Space Flight Center in Houston in 1977 was assembled from the stages of different rockets of this type. The five powerful F-1 engines of the first stage have a diameter of 10 feet (3 m). The Space Flight Center houses the Mission Control Center, which oversaw the Apollo missions and still controls the flights to the ISS today.

THE LARGEST SPACECRAFT IN THE WORLD

SPACESHUTTLE USA

Height 160 feet (48.9 m)
Launch weight 2,256 short tons (2,046 t)
Liftoff thrust 6,780,240 lbf (30,160 kN)
Max payload 27 short tons (24.5 t)

The space shuttles were the first reusable spacecraft. The shuttles could be used

The "Discovery" shuttle

repeatedly and so could the two solid-fuel rockets, which supplied about 83 percent of the thrust during a shuttle's liftoff. The rockets were fixed to the giant external tank that supplied the shuttle with fuel and were already burned out two minutes after liftoff. After their separation

they drifted back to Earth on parachutes and fell into the Atlantic where they could be recovered. The shuttle continued with its main engine and within only six minutes accelerated to 16,980 mph (27,328 km/h). Once it had reached orbit, the large main engines were shut down and the non-reusable external tank was discarded. Landing was begun with a braking maneuver. The shuttles then descended to Earth like gliders. During re-entry into the Earth's atmosphere they had a speed of about 16,030 mph (25,800 km/h), and when touching down on the runway it was still 215 mph (346 km/h). Between 1981 and 2011 five shuttles took off into space a total of 135 times. On these flights, among others, satellites were taken up and astronauts transported to the MIR, later the ISS. In 1986 the "Challenger" exploded shortly after launch; in 2003 the "Columbia" burned up during landing because of a defective thermal protection system.

In September 29, 1988, the "Discovery" started a five-day flight into space. It was the first space shuttle mission after the Challenger disaster of January 28, 1986, during which all seven astronauts had lost their lives. The accident brought about great debates about the United States' space program.

BURAN
Soviet Union

Height	193 ft (58.8 m)
Launch weight	n/a
Liftoff thrust	7,868,310 lbf (35,000 kN)
Max payload	24 short tons (22 t)

This spacecraft was developed in the 1970s and 1980s. Although initially it appeared to be a copy of the space shuttle, it is actually based on a different technology. Whereas the U.S. shuttles possessed built-in main engines, which were supported by solid-fuel rockets only during the first few minutes after liftoff and then took over propulsion, the Soviet spacecraft was propelled into orbit by a giant rocket, the "Energia." The first stage of this rocket consisted of liquid-fuel engines, which were discarded once they had burned out, gliding to Earth

The "Energia" carrier rocket with the "Buran" spacecraft on the launch pad

suspended from parachutes. Only the main stage with the giant tank could not be reused. In 1988 a "Buran" took off on an "Energia" for an unmanned flight that

proved successful. However, the program was stopped anyway for budgetary reasons.

VEHICLE ASSEMBLY BUILDING

The "Discovery" is rolled out of the Vehicle Assembly Building and to the launch pad after fitting the solid-fuel rockets and the external tank. After both the Challenger and the Columbia disasters it was the first shuttle to be back in operation.

Vehicle Assembly Building

The assembly hall of Launch Complex 39 at the Kennedy Space Center built for the assembly of the almost 364 feet (111 m) tall Saturn V rockets was inaugurated in 1966. It covers an area of about 370,688 sq ft (34,438 sq m) and is 526 feet (160.3 m) tall. The building houses four assembly sites, where three Saturn Vs can be simultaneously assembled. Each area has a giant, 456 feet (139 m) tall gate through which the spacecraft are taken to their launch pads. Between 1981 and 2011 the space shuttles had their external tanks and their solid-fuel rockets fitted in the Vehicle Assembly Building and were then moved to their launch pads on a mobile platform. More than 70 cranes, including five gantry cranes, two of which can lift weights of 358 short tons (325 tonnes), are still standing here ready for assembly work.

Discovery

Ares rocket in the assembly hall

Astronaut Robert L. Behnken, who flew to the ISS in March 2008 with the "Endeavour" Space Shuttle, fixes a robot hand at the station. The ISS orbits Earth at an altitude of between 217 and 249 miles (350 and 400 km). One orbit takes 91 minutes.

The ISS is run jointly by NASA, the ESA and the space agencies of Russia, Canada and Japan. Since 1998 it has been systematically assembled from modules that are brought into orbit by Russian carrier rockets, space shuttles and since 2008 also by unmanned spacecraft of the ESA and Japan. The ISS now weighs about 440 short tons (400 tonnes) and has attained a span of 328 feet (100 m). Its construction is planned to be completed by 2015. The space station has been manned since 2000. The crew are replaced every six months. Initially there were only three crewmembers, but since 2009 there have been six. Regular flights by Russian, Japanese and European space transfer vehicles ensure a continuous supply of provisions.

Two Soyuz spacecraft are ready to evacuate the crew in case of emergencies. An extensive research program is being conducted on board the ISS. The nations and organizations participating in the program have set up laboratories to observe the sun's activity, conduct tests with atomic clocks and measure cosmic radiation, for example. The ISS will be operational at least until 2020.

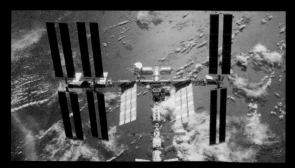

ISS with a transfer vehicle (at the bottom of the picture)

The Japanese "Kibo" experimental module

The lunar landing project set in motion by John F. Kennedy in 1961 posed an enormous challenge, demanding the development of new technologies and years of preparations. Yet everything was ready within only eight years: the Apollo 11 mission

The crew of Apollo 11

lifted off on July 16, 1969, and the astronauts Neil Armstrong, "Buzz" Aldrin and Michael Collins set off onboard the "Columbia" on their journey to the moon. They reached it after a three-day flight. Whereas Collins remained in lunar orbit onboard the "Columbia," Armstrong and Aldrin landed in the Sea of Tranquility with the "Eagle" Lunar Module. After a stay of two and a half hours they returned to the lunar module and made their way back to Earth. On July 24, 1969, the "Columbia" landed safely in the Pacific.

The preparations for docking the "Eagle" Lunar Module to the "Columbia" Command Module were observed and photographed by the astronaut Michael Collins, who had remained in lunar orbit onboard the mother spaceship. After reclaiming the astronauts the Lunar Module was uncoupled from the Command Module and left behind on the moon. The ascent back from the moon's surface to the "Columbia" had taken four hours.

The first time a human being landed on the moon was celebrated as an extraordinary event of global historical significance. Thanks to a camera fixed to the outside of the Lunar Module, whose images could be transmitted via a parabolic aerial at the tip of the craft straight to Earth, millions of people were able to witness live on their TV sets the moment when Neil Armstrong became the first man to step onto the moon's surface. "Buzz" Aldrin left the Lunar Module 20 minutes after Armstrong. During the two and a half hours of their stay on the moon, the two astronauts hoisted the American flag, set up measuring instruments and collected rock samples. They were filmed all the time by the camera that Armstrong had meanwhile fixed to a tripod.

An astronaut of the Apollo 11 lunar mission

ART AND CULTURE

With the emergence of bourgeois society in the 18th century, public institutions sprang up all over Europe that were dedicated to the preservation of the cultural heritage of the past, with an emphasis on making it accessible to the general public. Many of the hitherto private book and art collections owned by secular or

The Clementinum in Prague

religious princes, as well as court theaters, were transformed into public libraries, museums and stages. In the 19th century the middle class's eagerness to learn led to the foundation and construction of ever more museums. The large universal museums like the British Museum and the splendid theater buildings like the Palais Garnier, which appeared all over Europe

during this period, became models for similar institutions around the world. Although the public still has the same interest today and the attraction to cultural institutions is great, many are having to cope with drastic budget cuts by the public authorities.

The famous Trinity College Library in Dublin was originally the private collection of a church dignitary: James Usher, archbishop of Armagh, who bequeathed his library consisting of several thousand books and manuscripts to the Irish university in 1659. Today it holds more than four millions books and has the status of a national library.

The Abbey Library of St. Gall

Palais Bourbon in Paris

The total stock of the Library of Congress currently consists of about 151 million media units, including almost 23 million books. Founded in April 1800 as the research library of the House of Congress, it took on the role of a national library during the course of the 19th century. The collections are housed in three separate buildings that are linked by underground passages and are located on Capitol Hill in Washington. The Thomas Jefferson Building inaugurated in 1897 holds the famous Main Reading Room. The John Adams Building opened in 1938 has several stories with book shelving as well as a reading room, and in the James Madison Memorial Building, opened recently in 1980, administration offices and some special departments are housed.

Only the most precious materials were used for the decoration of the grandiose entrance hall of the Thomas Jefferson Building. Two marble staircases lead up to the gallery on the second floor. They are guarded by bronze torchbearers.

THE LARGEST LIBRARY IN THE WORLD

The Main Reading Room in the Thomas Jefferson Building of the Library of Congress

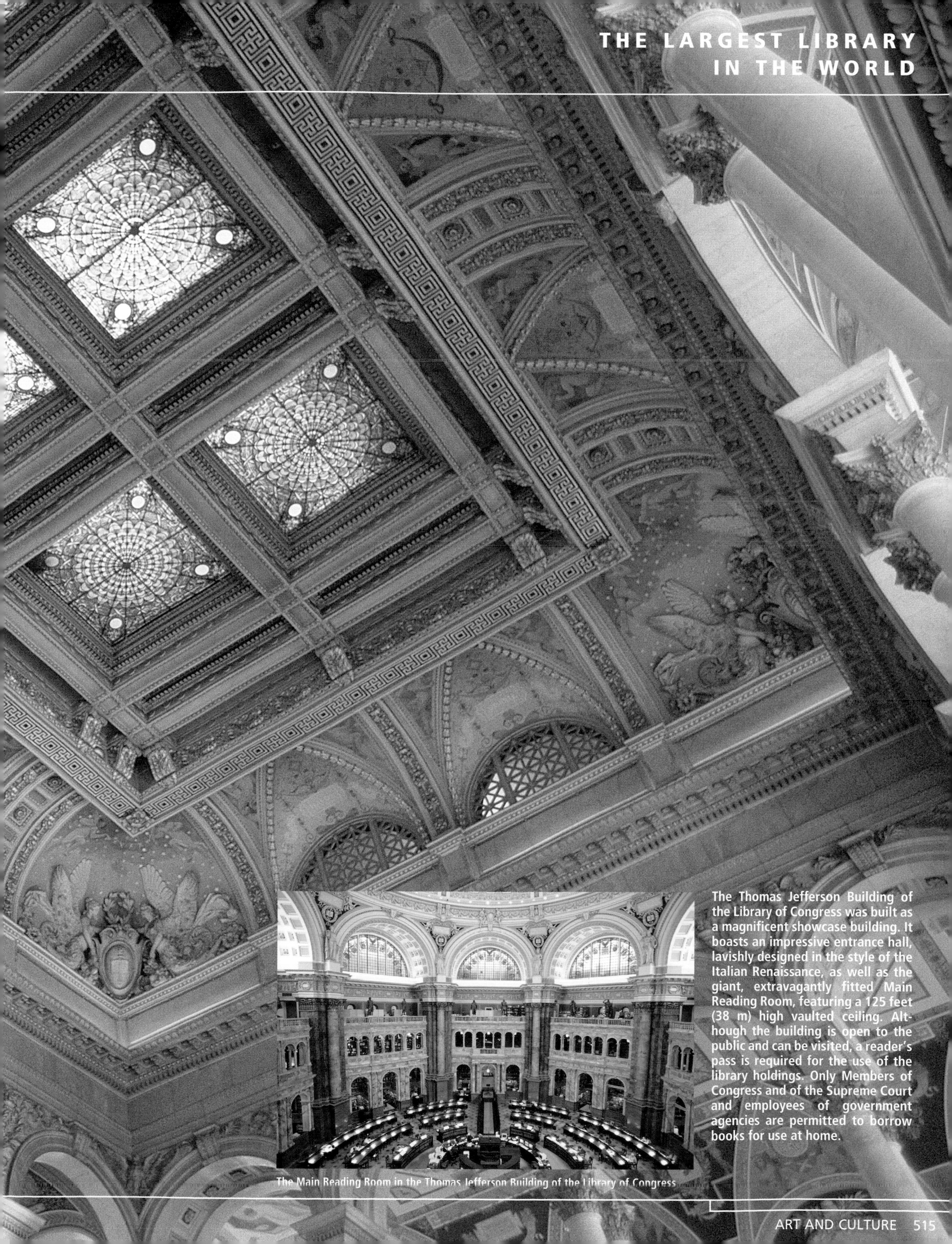

The Thomas Jefferson Building of the Library of Congress was built as a magnificent showcase building. It boasts an impressive entrance hall, lavishly designed in the style of the Italian Renaissance, as well as the giant, extravagantly fitted Main Reading Room, featuring a 125 feet (38 m) high vaulted ceiling. Although the building is open to the public and can be visited, a reader's pass is required for the use of the library holdings. Only Members of Congress and of the Supreme Court and employees of government agencies are permitted to borrow books for use at home.

BRITISH LIBRARY
LONDON

With a current stock of about 150 million media units, including almost 20 million books, the United Kingdom's national library competes with the Library of Congress for the title of "largest library in the world." The British Library was created in 1973 by the merging of what were then the National Library and the British Museum Library with other leading libraries in the country. Since 1998 it has been based in a new building designed by architect Colin St. John Wilson at St. Pancras in London.

RUSSIAN STATE
LIBRARY
MOSCOW

With its holding of about 42 million media units, the Russian State Library is one of the largest libraries in the world. It developed from the Rumyantsev Museum, a collection of written documents, coins and paintings that was founded by Count Nikolai Rumyantsev in the middle of the 19th century and closed in 1925. The museum's art collections went to other Moscow museums, and the library was transformed into a national library. It is housed in a complex of buildings dating from the Soviet era.

NATIONAL LIBRARY
OF FRANCE
PARIS

The collections of the Bibliothèque Nationale de France currently comprise an estimated 30 million media units. Since 1996 a large part of its holdings has been housed in a new building designed by the architect Dominique Perrault. The building comprises four L-shaped glass towers symbolizing opened books. They soar at the corners of

15 acres (6 ha) of grounds, enclosing a park landscape. The futuristic new building was initiated by President François Mitterrand and is named after him. The old library building still holds a large part of the collection.

The statue of Isaac Newton in the entrance hall of the British Library was created by the Scottish sculptor Eduardo Paolozzi (1924–2005).

CHINESE NATIONAL LIBRARY BEIJING

Currently holding more than 30 million print, image and sound documents, the Chinese National Library is the largest library in Asia. It is tasked not only with the collection of all publications in the Chinese language but also with the safekeeping of many thousands of written documents from all eras in the history of China, including many manuscripts from the Magao Caves. Since 2008 the library has resided in a new building designed by the German architectural office Engel.

The reading room in the Chinese National Library's new building

BIBLIOTHECA ALEXANDRIA

The new library of Alexandria was built on the site of and recreated its world-famous ancient predecessor; it was inaugurated in 2002.

The vast reading room has 2,000 places.

The impetus for the new building came from Egyptian professors, who were supported in their quest by UNESCO. The library, which also has museums and several research centers adjoining it, sees itself as a center of scholarship.

ARDO PAOLOZZI · 1995

Although the origins of the Vatican Apostolic Library date back as far as the fourth century, the foundations for the current collection were not laid until about 900 years later: in 1447 Pope Nicholas V combined the collection of the Vatican, which then held only a few works, with

Working places in the library

his private library and systematically continued to enlarge it. In 1455, the year of the pope's death, the library already boasted around 1,500 manuscripts from all corners of Europe among its holdings. In subsequent centuries it grew continually through further acquisitions and bequests. Today the library holds 150,000 manuscripts, as well as around one and a half million books.

The magnificent Sistine Hall in the Vatican Library begun under Pope Sixtus V (r. 1585–1590) was decorated by the painters Giovanni Guerra (1544–1618) and Cesare Nebbia (1536–1614). The frescoes on the hall's columns depict the pioneers of western written culture.

THE LARGEST OPERA HOUSES AND THEATERS IN THE WORLD

Opera outings are still considered major social events today, where the upper crust meet, not only to listen to the music, but also to see and be seen. Although the dress code has long become more casual, tuxedos and evening gowns are still common at such events. The magnificent opera buildings that were erected as meeting places for "high society" in the large

European cities during the 19th century form a suitable backdrop for these events. Houses like the Vienna State Opera, completed in 1869, or the Opera Garnier in Paris, inaugurated in 1875, resemble royal palaces. In the design of the façades, the master-builders reveled in the architecture of earlier styles, with sweeping marble staircases and lavishly decorated corridors leading to the auditoriums. The

large opera houses and theater buildings of the modern day on the other hand impress with the clarity and sobriety of their architectural shape. During the construction of the Sydney Opera House, but also of the National Grand Theatre in Beijing, particular importance was attached to multifunctionality. The futuristic Bastille Opera in Paris was conceived as a counterpoint to the Opera Garnier.

THE LARGEST
OPERA HOUSES AND
THEATERS IN THE
WORLD

(seats)

1 **Sydney Opera House**
Australia, Sydney 5,532
2 **National Grand Theater of China**
China, Beijing 5,452
3 **Bastille Opera**
France, Paris 3,903
4 **Metropolitan Opera**
USA, New York City 3,900
5 **Civic Opera House**
USA, Chicago 3,563
6 **Grand Theater**
Poland, Warsaw 2,705
7 **Shanghai Grand Theatre**
China, Shanghai 2,650

The Sydney Opera House was built at an outstanding location on Bennelong Point, a headland projecting into the city's port. The bold roof structure reminds many of the inflated sails of a five-master. The magnificent building, by the Danish architect Jørn Utzon, hosts not only operas: pop concerts, entertainment shows and fascinating exhibitions take place here throughout the year.

SYDNEY OPERA HOUSE

Australia, Sydney   5,532 seats

Sydney's Opera House accommodates five different theater stages with a total of 5,532 seats. It comprises a large musi-

The opera house is Sydney's best-known landmark.

cal theater with 1,547 seats, as well as three drama stages and a giant concert hall – the latter alone offers seats for 2,669 spectators. The opera is renowned around the world as a cultural center. Every year, more

View of one of the window façades of the opera house

than 1,000 events are hosted there, attracting an audience of millions. Not least because of its daring roof structure, the building is a masterpiece of modern architecture and has been included on the UNESCO World Heritage list since

2007. It was conceived by the Danish architect Jørn Utzon and inaugurated in a festive ceremony by Queen Elizabeth II in 1973, after 24 years of construction.

The concert hall in the Sydney Opera House has excellent acoustics. The Sydney Symphony Orchestra and the Australian Chamber Orchestra regularly hold concerts there, as do many international pop stars.

BASTILLE OPERA
Paris, France   3,903 seats

The glass structure of the new opera house in Paris

Paris' new opera house on the Place de la Bastille comprises four theater stages with nearly 4,000 seats in total. Along with the large opera hall it has two studio theaters and an amphitheater with 500 seats. The initiative for the building of the new opera house came from then-President François Mitterrand. It was to relieve the old Opera Garnier and also to liberate opera as an institution from its elitist image. The Uruguayan–Canadian architect Carlos Ott emerged as the winner in the 1982 competition for the realization of the project. The modern opera house he created enthused the whole world. It was inaugurated in 1989, on the eve of the French National Holiday.

GRAND THEATER
Poland, Warsaw   2,705 seats

Built between 1825 and 1833 to the plans of Antonio Corazzi, this monumental neoclassical building houses Poland's National Opera and the country's most important theater. Also known as Wielki Theater, the building comprises three stages, providing seating for 2,705 spectators. During World War II the theater was almost completely destroyed by the German Army. During the course of its reconstruction the theater was enlarged and fitted with the latest stage technology. At the time of its reopening in 1965 it was the largest and most modern theater in the world.

FESTIVAL THEATER
Baden-Baden, Germany
2,500 seats

Currently the largest opera house in Germany, the Festival Theater did not open until 1998 but is already one of the most frequented in the country. The ultramodern structure was built to the plans of the Viennese architect Wilhelm Holzbauer, on the site of the former Baden-Baden rail station. The building is flooded with light and boasts the very latest in sound and stage technology. The historic station building was restored and integrated into the complex. Today it serves as the entrance hall of the Festival Theater and houses a restaurant.

The magnificent Grand Theater in Warsaw illuminated at night

The latest in technology is employed at the Baden-Baden Festival Theater.

LA SCALA
Milan, Italy   2,200 seats

Milan's Teatro alla Scala is one of the most important opera houses in the world. For many singers, a contract on this stage is a launch pad to an international career. The opera house was built to the designs of Giuseppe Piermarini and opened in 1778. It became the model for many theaters in the 19th century. Almost totally destroyed during World War II, it was rebuilt in record time after 1945. The Scala was completely modernized from 2001 to 2004.

View of the Scala's auditorium, with its 2,200 seats

The new Paris opera house was built in a historic square, on the Place de la Bastille. The storming of the Bastille, which had been used as a prison, on July 14, 1789, is considered to have triggered the French Revolution. The July Column commemorates the Revolution of 1830.

OPERA GARNIER

France, Paris   2,150 seats

Since the opening of the new opera house on the Place de la Bastille in 1989, the Opera Garnier stages almost exclusively classical ballet performances, yet the splendid neobaroque building has nevertheless remained one of Paris' landmarks. Built between 1860 and 1875, its architects wanted it to be a counterpoint to the strict classicism of contemporary architecture. Its façade is abundantly decorated with sculptures and friezes and the interior seems overloaded with luxurious deco, yet it is nonetheless fascinating.

The Opera Garnier at night

View of the opera stage

VIENNA STATE OPERA

Vienna, Austria   **1,700 seats**
560 standing places

Although Vienna has long lost its role as the world's music capital, the opera house of the Austrian capital is still one of most outstanding musical stages today. The theater still grabs attention with its ambitious staging of classical and modern operatic pieces. The ballet troop too enjoys worldwide renown. Well-known conductors have worked at the State Opera. One of the most famous of all orchestras, the Vienna Philharmonic Orchestra, is composed of members of the opera orchestra. The building, in which the opera has resided since 1869, is considered a successful example of historicizing architecture. It was built in the style of the neo-Renaissance and is one of the earliest buildings on the Viennese Ring, a UNESCO World Heritage Site.

Main façade of the State Opera

Auditorium during the Viennese Opera Ball

A view of the luxuriously decorated auditorium of the Opera Garnier, which was the largest theater in Europe at the time of its inauguration and later became a model for other large opera houses, such as the Amazo Theater in Manaus, Brazil.

NATIONAL CENTER FOR THE PERFORMING ARTS

China, Beijing   5,452 seats

Opened in December 2007, construction of the Chinese National Theater is one of the spectacular major projects in

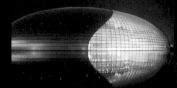

The glass front in the central part of the building

the People's Republic of China. It was designed by the French architect Paul Andreu and is popularly also known as "bird's egg" because of its distinctive semi-spherical shape. The building houses an opera stage, a concert hall and a theater, where the world-famous Peking Opera performs its pieces, among others. The building, which is surrounded by an artificial lake, was clad with a skin of titanium tiles. Glass fronts in the central part of the structure provide a view of the interior.

The vast lobby of the National Center for the Performing Arts in Beijing offers room for many hundreds of visitors. The glass fronts dominating the central section of the new building are tapered toward the top, letting light flood into the building.

SHANGHAI GRAND THEATRE

Shanghai, China   2,650 seats

This theater in the heart of Shanghai, designed by the French architect Jean-Marie Charpentier, combines the shapes of Far Eastern architecture with modern western design in a grand manner. The roof sweeps upward and recalls traditional Chinese ways of building, whereas the glazed base is held in a contemporary style. The building houses three theater auditoriums, all of which are equipped with the latest in stage technology and boast excellent acoustics. Since the opening of the theater in 1998, some ten million people have already visited countless operas, concerts, dramas, lectures and other events.

Gardens have been created on the theater's upward sweeping roof.

THE LARGEST OPERA HOUSES AND THEATERS IN THE AMERICAS

METROPOLITAN OPERA

USA, New York   3,900 seats

New York's opera house is not only one of the largest musical stages in the world, it is also one of the most important. Being called to the "Met" is still an accolade for artists and conductors. Starting with Enrico Caruso, via Maria Callas and Grace Bumbry to Luciano Pavarotti, Placido Domingo and Anna Netrebko: virtually all the stars of the opera world have performed at the "Met" and celebrated fabulous successes. Since September 1966 the ope-

The vast auditorium of the "Met"

ra, founded in 1880, has resided in a modern building that forms a part of the Lincoln Center for the Performing Arts. The repertory includes both classic and avant-garde operas. Every year around 28 different works are performed, including many new productions.

CIVIC OPERA HOUSE

USA, Chicago   3,563 seats

The largest opera house in North America after the New York Metropolitan Opera is part of a complex of buildings that also includes three office towers. It was opened in 1929 and the Chicago Civic Opera initially resided there, before it went bankrupt during the Great Depression. Since 1954 the private Lyric Opera Chicago has performed at the Civic. Maria Callas sang at the opera house in the same year, celebrating her first success in North America. Until 1993 the Lyric Opera only leased the building, then it bought the opera house.

The Civic Opera in Chicago

The new building of the New York Metropolitan Opera was designed by the architect Wallace K. Harrison and inaugurated in September 1966 as a part of the Lincoln Center. The design of the façade with its giant arched windows did not meet with universal approval.

COLUMBUS THEATER
Argentina, Buenos Aires
2,500 seats, 1,000 standing places

Thanks to its outstanding acoustics, South America's largest theater is one of the most popular musical stages in the world. During the course of its history the theater attracted artists like Enrico Caruso and Maria Callas as well as renowned conductors like Arturo Toscanini and Wilhelm Furtwangler. Today international stars of the world of music still pride themselves in performing at the Teatro Colón. The opera house was inaugurated in 1908. It features impressively projecting façades and luxuriously fitted auditoria.

The magnificent Columbus Theater

View of the auditorium's galleries

The new National Museum of China was created by merging the National Museum of Chinese History and the Museum of the Chinese Revolution. It is housed in the same building as its two predecessor institutions. The structure was built in 1958–1959 together with the Great Hall of the People on

The entrance area in the museum

Tiananmen Square in the center of Beijing. It was converted and enlarged to house the new museum under the auspices of the German architectural office Gerkan, Mark and Partner.

The external look of the building remained unchanged due to requirements imposed by the authorities. Inside the museum now has light and airy rooms. In an exhibition area covering a total of 2,152,800 sq ft (200,000 sq m) treasures from the many thousand years of Chinese history are ex-

hibited. The remains of Yuanmou Man, who probably lived in South China some 500,000 years ago, are the oldest exhibits. A flag personally hoisted by Mao Zedong is one of the most recent pieces in the permanent exhibition. Whereas the museum is tasked with preserving the national cultural

heritage of China, the temporary art exhibitions are dedicated to other cultures. Thus, in May 2011, the museum was reopened with the exhibition "The Art of Enlightenment," curated by museum directors from Germany.

The building housing the new National Museum of China was constructed in the "socialist classicist" style in 1959.

A visitor in front of a revolutionary painting

In the Department of Revolutionary Art

Sculptures such as this ancient Buddha in the National Museum in Beijing attest to the great sophistication of sculpture in ancient China. The oldest testimonies of the Buddhist tradition in the Middle Kingdom date from the second century; the religion originated in India and experienced a first heyday during the Tang dynasty (618–907).

The rotunda in the museum's courtyard

Assyrian relief from Nimrud

A Buddha statuette from northern China

BRITISH MUSEUM
Great Britain, London

This museum is one of the largest universal museums in the world. Its collections comprise works of art, articles of daily use and artifacts from all periods of history and all parts of the world. The ancient cultures of Asia Minor, Egypt and Europe are represented here with a wealth of exhibits, and so are the civilizations of Africa, Asia, Oceania and the Americas. Absolute highlights are the Rosetta Stone and parts of the Parthenon Frieze. The museum developed out of the art collection belonging to the physician Hans Sloane. It was founded in 1753, and was the first museum in the world accessible to the general public. The grand building, where it has been housed since 1850, was the largest in the world at the time of its opening. The vast courtyard was redesigned in the late 1990s under the auspices of Sir Norman Foster and was given a glass roof.

Colossal statues from ancient Egypt in the British Museum, which – after the Egyptian Museum in Cairo – possesses the largest collection of art treasures from the realm of the pharaohs. Probably the best-known single item is the Rosetta Stone, which made it possible to decode hieroglyphics.

METROPOLITAN MUSEUM OF ART
USA, New York City

This museum competes with the British Museum for the title of "largest universal museum in the world." Founded in 1870, today it houses an immense wealth of art treasures from all of the world's cultures. The collection of sculptures and craft objects from Europe alone comprises more than 50,000 exhibits of recent European history, from the 15th to the early 20th century. One department is dedicated to modern art. Almost every big-name artist in the art history of the 20th century is represented here with at least one masterpiece.

The impressive entrance hall

The ancient Temple of Dendur

The exhibition with art from Oceania

LOUVRE
France, Paris

The former residence of French kings in the heart of Paris today houses one of the most important and comprehensive collections of works of art from almost all periods of the European and Near Eastern histories of art. The museum owns about 380,000 paintings, sculptures, prints and illustrations. Only 35,000 exhibits are displayed in a total area of 645,800 sq ft (60,000 sq m) of exhibition halls. During the French Revolution the Louvre was transformed into a state-run museum that was to make the royal art collection accessible to the general public. During the 19th century its inventory grew significantly with Napoleon's raids and later by acquisition. The two elongated wings framing the Napoleon Courtyard were built at this time. During the course of the museum's renewal initiated by then-President François Mitterrand in 1981, the exhibition area was extended across the entire complex and the glass pyramid was erected in the Napoleon Courtyard.

The "Salle des États" was integrated into the museum in 1878

Leonardo da Vinci's "Mona Lisa"

The Napoleon Courtyard is framed in the north and south by two wing buildings, which were completely transformed and enlarged in the second half of the 19th century.

The glass pyramid in the Napoleon Courtyard designed by Ieoh Ming Pei forms the new main entrance to the museum.

THE MOST IMPORTANT MUSEUMS IN THE WORLD

HERMITAGE
Russia, St. Petersburg

With a total holding of about three million works of art, of which 60,000 are exhibited, the collections of the Hermitage Museum surpass those of the Louvre in size many times over. Founded by Catherine the Great, who systematically had works of art bought all over western Europe, the collection was further enlarged by her successors. After the October Revolution the art collections of expropriated Russian noblemen were integrated. From Renaissance artists right up to the classics of modernity: the Hermitage represents all those who have made a name for themselves in the European art scene with at least one masterpiece each. Its large prehistoric collection, the department of antiquities and the collection of art from eastern Asia and India are also considered remarkable. The museum is housed in the building of the same name on the banks of the Neva River. The complex of buildings includes the Old, the Small and the New Hermitage, as well as the magnificent Winter Palace, the former residence of the Russian czar.

The Jordan Staircase in the Winter Palace

Ceremonial hall in the Winter Palace

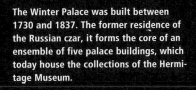

The Winter Palace was built between 1730 and 1837. The former residence of the Russian czar, it forms the core of an ensemble of five palace buildings, which today house the collections of the Hermitage Museum.

The "White Hall" in the Winter Palace

War Gallery of 1812 in the Hermitage's Winter Palace

Situated at the northern tip of an island in the Spree River in the heart of Berlin, this complex of five impressive museums is a unique architectural achievement and a great example of the development of museum construction in the 19th

Nefertiti bust in the New Museum

and early 20th centuries. It has therefore been included on the UNESCO list of World Heritage Sites since 1999. As part of a master plan agreed in 1999 the complex is being fully renovated. The plan provides for subterranean corridors to link all the museums (aside from the Old National Gallery), and for a combined entrance hall.

OLD MUSEUM

The magnificent neoclassical building was a masterpiece of the Prussian state architect Karl Friedrich Schinkel. It houses one of the most important collections of ancient Greek, Etruscan and Roman art in the world. The museum was inaugurated in 1830, the first museum in Prussia to be opened to the general public.

A UNIQUE COMPLEX OF MUSEUMS AND UNESCO WORLD CULTURAL HERITAGE

The splendid Old Museum, a masterpiece of the renowned architect Karl Friedrich Schinkel, is a highlight of the neoclassical style in Germany. The building boasts strict, clear lines both inside and out.

NEW MUSEUM

Constructed between 1843 and 1855 by Schinkel's student Stüler, this building is home to the Museum for Prehistory and Early History as well as the Egyptian Museum's collections, which include the world-famous bust of Nefertiti. The museum was severely damaged during the war and was reopened only in October 2009.

BODE MUSEUM

The splendid neobaroque building erected between 1897 and 1904 occupies the northernmost tip of Museum Island. It houses the Museum of Byzantine Art, a unique collection of older sculptures from all over Europe and the Berlin Coin Cabinet, one of the largest numismatic collections in the world.

PERGAMON MUSEUM

This museum is the most-visited museum in Berlin. Each year, the Pergamon Altar and the Ishtar Gate from Babylon attract millions of visitors. The museum, built from 1910 to 1930, combines three collections in one building: the Middle East Museum, the Islamic Art Museum and parts of the Antiquity Collection.

OLD NATIONAL GALLERY

The grand neoclassical building dating from between 1867 and 1876 displays a rich collection of masterpieces from the 18th and 19th centuries, including many important paintings by Caspar David Friedrich. The museum was reopened in 2001 after comprehensive restoration.

Many major museums have gained fame for their collections of European art from the Middle Ages to the 18th century. They developed out of the private collections of princes, like the Uffizi Gallery in Florence and the Prado in Madrid, or were systematically built up like the National Gallery in London. When the holdings grew continuously during the 19th century through bequests and acquisitions of contemporary works of art, additional departments for modern art were created. From these emerged the great specialist collections of 19th century art like the New Masters Gallery in Dresden, the New Pinakothek in Munich and the collection of Impressionist masterpieces at the Musée d'Orsay in Paris.

PRADO
Spain, Madrid

This museum holds one of the most important collections of old masters globally. Its collection comprises major works by Spanish artists from El Greco to Francisco de Goya as well as outstanding paintings by other European masters, including the "The Garden of Earthly Delights" triptych by Hieronymus Bosch.

UFFIZI
Italy, Florence

The Renaissance palace built between 1559 and 1581 is the home of one of the best-known art collections in the world. Every year it attracts millions of enthusiastic visitors. Exhibited are many masterpieces by Italian and European artists from the 13th to the 18th centuries.

NATIONAL GALLERY
Great Britain, London

Although this art collection was not founded until 1824, it is now one of the greatest in the world, with a holding of 2,300 paintings by European artists from the 13th to the 19th centuries. English artists like Turner and Gainsborough are represented here, as are French masters like Cézanne and Watteau.

ALBERTINA
Austria, Vienna

Based in Duke Albrecht's palace, this museum possesses probably the most comprehensive collection of graphic works in the world, comprising 65,000 illustrations, one million prints and more than 50,000 photographs. Also part of the collection are masterpieces by Durer, Leonardo and Raphael, as well as works by Kokoschka and Gustav Klimt.

ORSAY MUSEUM
France, Paris

Opened in 1986, the museum was founded in 1978 to keep paintings and sculptures from the years between 1848 and 1914. Along with the Impressionism collection of the old Jeu de Paume it also holds works from the Louvre and the Museum of Modern Art. The former trainshed hall of the Orsay Station was restored to house the collections of the Musée d'Orsay.

rulers and estab[lished]
n the hands of the burghers. . It was not [long]
ations, constantly warring with its neighbours. The country gre[w]
ans. In the Dutch Republic, products and raw materials from across
massed fortunes and art and culture flourished.

OLD MASTERS PICTURE GALLERY
Germany, Dresden

Both painting galleries in Dresden present outstanding masterpieces of European art. The Old Masters Picture Gallery is famed for its collection of Italian, Flemish and old German masters. The New Masters Gallery boasts work by Caspar David Friedrich and artists from the "Bridge" expressionist movement, among others.

OLD AND NEW PINAKOTHEK
Germany, Munich

The holdings of the Old Pinakothek comprise more than 1,000 masterpieces of European art from the 14th to 18th centuries. The building, in which the collection is housed, was completed in 1836 to the most modern standards in museum construction. The New Pinakothek, housed in a new building opposite the Old Pinakothek, is dedicated to 19th century art.

TATE BRITAIN
Great Britain, London

This museum is specialized in collecting British art from the 16th century to the present day. Its current holdings are 3,500 paintings, prints and sculptures, including masterpieces by such important artists as William Turner and Francis Bacon. Until the opening of the Tate Modern, the museum also boasted an important collection of modern art.

STATE MUSEUM
Netherlands, Amsterdam

The Rijksmuseum has achieved world fame thanks to its unique collection of Dutch old masters. Almost a million visitors come each year, with the main attraction probably being Rembrandt's painting "The Night Watch." The museum also holds a comprehensive collection of art objects from the former Dutch colonies.

Visitors at the State Museum in Amsterdam admire "Banquet of the Amsterdam Civic Guard in Celebration of the Peace of Munster," a colossal painting by Bartholomeus van der Helst (1613–1670).

The modern art museums of Europe and America provide a comprehensive overview of developments in the fine arts from the 20th century to the present day. They give space to a wealth of artistic forms of expression, some of which are only partially accepted today. The art of

Museum of Modern Art, New York

the 20th century is characterized by a radical departure from figurative imagery. Instead of creating illusory worlds, artists like Kandinsky, Picasso and Mondrian moved colors, lines and areas into the foreground of their creative work, thus forcing a break with tradition. Fine art today also presents itself as original and experimental. It is presented in modern art the museums by innovative light and sound installations, for example.

The great museums of modern art have in their inventories extensive collections of films and photographs. Exhibitions that are devoted to contemporary video and photographic art are constantly gaining in popularity.

MUSEUM OF MODERN ART
USA, Washington D.C.

The MoMA is a paradise for all those who love modern art. The most important Impressionists and leading representatives of classic modernism as well as contemporary art are shown here in an impressive way. Its complete inventory now comprises around 150,000 paintings, sculptures, photographs, prints and films.

GUGGENHEIM MUSEUM
USA, New York

The museum became famous throughout the world thanks to its distinctive architectural shape, designed by Frank Lloyd Wright. Inside, the works of art are exhibited along a ramp spiraling toward the top of the building. Although the collection now also includes works by the Impressionists, its focus is nevertheless on abstract art.

POMPIDOU CENTER
France, Paris

The Musée National d'Art Modern, which has resided in the Pompidou Center since 1977, is one of the most important modern art museums. The museum's collection provides a comprehensive overview of all trends and styles in 20th and 21st century art. Starting with Fauvism and right up to video art, every artistic direction is represented here by famous artists.

TATE MODERN
Great Britain, London

With around 4.7 million visitors a year, this gallery is the most-visited modern art museum in the world. The collections feature a representative selection of masterpieces of classic modern and contemporary art. Since 2000 the Tate Modern has been based in a converted power station in the London borough of Southwark.

PINAKOTHEK OF MODERNITY
Germany, Munich

The museum, opened in 2002, holds a large collection of modern art as well as the graphics collection of Bavaria and a design museum. The modern art collection was begun only after World War II. It comprises classic works of modern and contemporary art as well as video installations.

The great natural history museums of Europe and North America often combine under one roof zoological and botanical, paleontological, anthropological and mineralogical

British Natural History Museum

collections. Since their beginnings, dating well back into the 19th century, these insti-

tutions have been collecting the manifold testimonies of life on our planet, from all periods of its history, making them accessible to a wider public. They still see it as their task today to document the diversity of animate and inanimate nature. In doing so, for a long time, the natural history museums saw their role merely in the display of monstrosities and curiosities. Today, however, they have transformed themselves into centers of research and education. Their scholars contribute to the identification of unknown species, and special exhibitions provide information on the planet's ecosystems.

NATIONAL MUSEUM OF NATURAL HISTORY
USA, Washington D.C.

The largest natural history museum in the world is one of 19 museums in the Smithsonian Institution. In its rooms it displays the diversity of forms in nature, and parts of the exhibition are dedicated to the evolution of humankind and its culture. The documentation in the "Hall of Human Origin," for example, presents a brief outline of the history of the evolution of

A dermoplastic of an elephant

Homo sapiens, detailing the changes in nature caused by human intervention.

Procession of African animals in the Great Gallery of Evolution at the Natural History Museum in Paris. It is the aim of the exhibition to visualize the diversity of the species brought about by evolution.

NATURAL HISTORY MUSEUM
France, Paris

In the 19th century the Natural History Museum founded during the French Revolution was the most important center in the world for research into the manifold forms of life. Georges Cuvier, the founder of comparative anatomy and paleontology, once taught at the Musée d'Histoire Naturelle. Today it still enjoys a worldwide reputation as a scientific center.

NATURAL HISTORY MUSEUM
Great Britain, London

The museum emerged from the natural history collections of the British Museum. It was opened in 1881 and is today the second largest natural history museum in the world after the National Museum of Natural History in Washington. A major part of its exhibition is devoted to the history of evolution and ecological questions.

The museum's Earth and Sky Section

MUSEUM OF NATURAL HISTORY
Austria, Vienna

The Habsburg dynasty's cabinets of curiosities formed the basis of this museum, which today has a holding of 30 million objects, making it one of the largest natural history museums in the world. Also integrated

The museum's collection of lizards

into the museum is a collection of prehistory and early history in Europe, with the prehistoric statuette, "Venus of Willendorf," being the prize exhibit.

THE AMERICAN MUSEUM OF NATURAL HISTORY
USA, New York

This museum is one of the most-visited institutions of its kind anywhere in the world. Its exhibitions show the treasures of nature as well as the development of humankind from the beginnings of Homo sapiens up to the present day, using a wide range of different materials. It is also famous for its dioramas that simulate the ecosystems of the planet.

Skeleton of a dinosaur

Natural history museums and technology museums, like the German Museum in Munich or the Science Museum in London, explain scientific discoveries and technological inventions to a non-specialist public. Up until the middle of the 20th century such exhibitions were focused on the clear presentation of scientific and technological innovations. Pioneering achievements of researchers and engineers, as well as the history of technology and the sciences stood in the foreground. Today however interactive exhibitions inspire the visitors to join in. Even venerable institutions are rapidly transforming themselves into adventure parks, where young and old can gain experience in the handling of technological apparatuses and scientific instruments. In the exhibition, "You! The Experience," at Chicago's Museums of Science and Industry visitors who are interested can relate scientific knowledge to their own lives.

View of Munich's Museum Island

The museum's Space Pavilion

GERMAN MUSEUM
Germany, Munich

Opened in 1925 the museum is today still the largest of its kind in the world. The exhibition shows around 28,000 exhibits from all areas of the natural sciences and technology. Highlights are, among others, a Foucault's pendulum, the computer maker Conrad Zuse's Z4 as well as a submarine of the imperial navy and various aircraft from the early days of aviation. The museum also boasts a planetarium and an observatory. The distinctive main building is located on an island in the Isar River in the heart of Munich, near Ludwig Bridge. The museum operates a traffic center in the old Munich trade fair halls and a hangar in Oberschleissheim. In 1995 a subsidiary was opened in Bonn.

The vast aviation exhibition at the German Museum in Munich provides visitors with a comprehensive overview of the history of flight. More than 50 flying objects, including parts of an Airbus 300, are displayed in the exhibition halls on Museum Island in the heart of Munich, whereas a Starfighter and rockets can be admired at the Oberschleissheim Hangar.

Façade of the Science Museums

Interactive exhibition in the museum

SCIENCE MUSEUM
Great Britain, London

The Science Museum was founded in 1857 as a department of the Victoria & Albert Museum and transformed into an independent institution in 1909. Since 1913 it has been housed in a grand building opposite the Natural History Museum. The museum depicts milestones in the development of the sciences and technology, starting with the steam machines that started the industrial revolution at the end of the 18th century, and continuing right up to a lunar module. Another highlight is the exhibition on the history of medicine.

Lunar Module in the Science Museum

MUSEUM OF SCIENCE AND INDUSTRY
USA, Chicago

The most architecturally impressive museum

Opened in 1933 the museum has no fewer than 75 halls with epoch-making technological innovations and their application in everyday life and industry. Many interactive exhibits invite visitors to gain experience in handling technology. Thus they can go on a simulated flight in a Boeing 727 or study the conditions below ground in a coalmine. Other highlights are the command module of the Apollo-8 mission and the reproduction of a space shuttle.

The museum inspires active learning.

Unlike the great universal museums, such as the British Museum in London or the Louvre in Paris, which present their archeological treasures as a part of a comprehensive overview of the cultural history of humankind, specialist archeological museums usually concern themselves with the preservation of the cultural heritage of a particular region and era. Like the Egyptian Museum in Cairo and the Gold Museum in Bogota, they were often created out of a need to protect the legacy of a perished civilization from a large-scale selloff and to preserve it for the general public. They are therefore still tasked today with the research and conservation of the material relics of the past and with making these accessible to a wider public.

EGYPTIAN MUSEUM
Egypt, Cairo

Exhibition hall in the museum

With around 120,000 objects the museum owns the largest collection of ancient Egyptian artifacts in the world. On display are statues, sarcophagi, papyri and countless burial objects from more than 4,000 years of Egyptian history. The main attraction is Tutankhamen's burial treasure. Of the 3,500 objects found by the British archeologist Howard Carter in the Pharaoh's tomb in 1922, some 1,700 are exhibited here, including Tutankhamen's fa-

The backrest of Tutankhamen's golden throne

Gilded canopic chest

mous death mask and a gilded throne. Another highlight of the collection is the mummy room, where the mortal remains of nine rulers of the New Kingdom are kept.

The first of three nested sarcophagi contained the mummified Tutankhamen, covered with the famous burial mask. It consists of solid gold sheet and is exhibited at the Egyptian Museum in Cairo together with the other treasures found in the Pharaoh's tomb.

NAPLES NATIONAL ARCHEOLOGICAL MUSEUM
Italy, Naples

This museum is one of the most important collections of antiquities in the world. It is home to a comprehensive collection of found objects from Pompeii and Herculaneum, and also holds a large number of Roman copies of Greek sculptures, like the famous Hercules Farnese and the statue of Venus Callipyge.

Fresco of a couple from Pompeii

NATIONAL ARCHEOLOGICAL MUSEUM
Greece, Athens

The museum possesses the world's most important collection of artifacts from Greek antiquity. Starting with early history, via the archaic and the classic period right up to the Hellenistic and Roman periods, the exhibition superbly documents the creative work of all epochs of Greek antiquity.

A drinking vessel with a war scene from Pharsala

IRAKLION ARCHEOLOGICAL MUSEUM
Greece Crete, Iraklion

The archeological museum in the capital of Crete owns probably the most important and most extensive collection of art objects and items of daily use from the Minoan culture. The holdings comprise many of the unique ceramics and frescoes that have been found in Knossos and other Minoan palaces.

Faïence of a snake goddess from Knossos

PETRIE MUSEUM OF EGYPTIAN ARCHAEOLOGY
Great Britain, London

With its inventory of more than 80,000 objects this museum located in the London borough of Bloomsbury has one of the most comprehensive collections of ancient Egyptian art and everyday objects in the world. It is named after Flinders Petrie, one of the founders of modern Egyptology.

COLLECTION OF CLASSICAL ANTIQUITIES
Germany, Berlin

The collection is considered one of the most significant of its kind in the world. After World War II it was divided up between sites in West and East Berlin, but after German reunification the two parts were reunited and the West Berlin collection returned to its earlier home on Museum Island.

PENN MUSEUM
USA, Philadelphia

The collection comprises numerous archeological finds from Egypt, China, Mesopotamia as well as Central and South America. The museum is a part of the University of Pennsylvania and is very active in archeological research. It still undertakes excavations all over the world today.

GOLD MUSEUM
Columbia, Bogota

The famous Museo del Oro displays one of the most comprehensive collections of art and everyday objects from the pre-Columbian period. It was founded in 1939 and has local branches in many Colombian cities. Its collection of finely worked gold objects is considered unique in the world.

Quimbaya golden breastplates

In space research they are our eyes and ears: giant telescopes, which scientists use to discover distant galaxies or to trace the origins of the universe. Perhaps, some hope, these superlative technical structures will even one day create a connection with extraterrestrial life forms. In order to take advantage of this tiniest possibility, the Arecibo Observatory has been broadcasting radio wave messages into space since 1974. So far, no one has replied. On the quest for quarks and such like, however, scientists have stayed on the ground or even gone underground. In order to

The Very Large Array in the USA

Stored data in the SLAC, USA

explore the smallest building blocks of matter, scientists use the largest research facilities in the world. In technological terms these are currently the ultimate in our abilities.

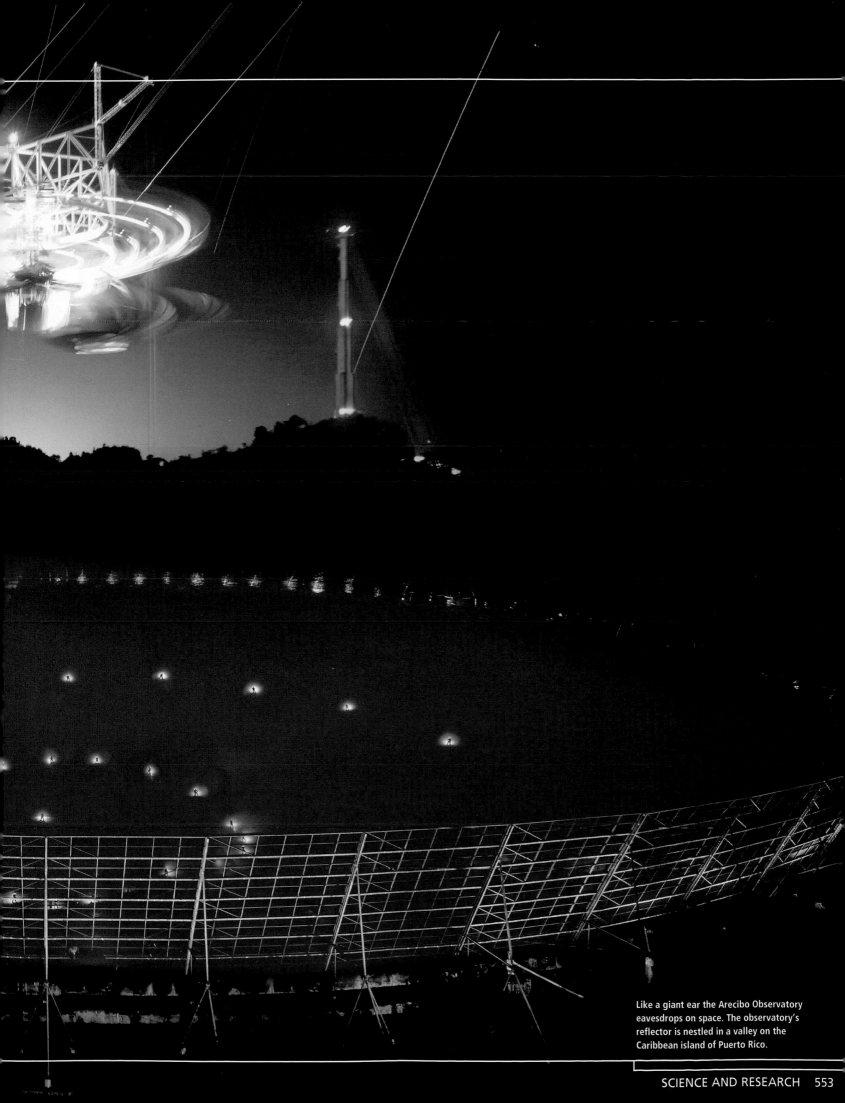

Like a giant ear the Arecibo Observatory eavesdrops on space. The observatory's reflector is nestled in a valley on the Caribbean island of Puerto Rico.

In the Swiss canton of Geneva, near the French border, researchers explore the foundations of the universe. At CERN the elementary particles of matter are the main focus of interest for currently around 7,000 scientists. Since 1954 more than 10,000 scientists from nearly 90 nations have been doing research here, at the largest research center in the world. For their experiments they have at their disposal not only the largest but also the most sophisticated scientific instruments in the world: particle accelerators and particle detectors.

Model of the LHC in CERN's "Microcosm" exhibition

What happens if one accelerates protons, electrons or ions to just less than the speed of light, and then makes them collide? It is just about possible to imagine this: they are "pulverized" as quarks, leptons and other elementary

Explosion of colliding protons

particles. Depending on how these smallest building blocks of matter behave after the collision, scientists draw conclusions on natural laws and the composition of matter in the universe. At the CERN research center they have the Large Hadron Collider (LHC) at their disposal for such fundamental research. The acceleration ring of this largest and most powerful particle accelerator in the world has a diameter of 87,464 feet (26,659 m) and is being cooled by the world's largest cooling plant. Inside the accelerator 9,300 supraconducting magnets create the magnetic fields that bring the particles to such unimaginable speeds. Inside the Large Hadron Collider the protons reach an acceleration voltage of an incredible 7,000 gigaelectronvolts, or 7,000 billion volts. This energy is well over one million times larger than the voltage in an overhead power line. Unbelievable!

The four particle detectors ATLAS, CMS, ALICE and LHCb are installed along the acceleration ring of the Large Hadron Collider (LHC) at CERN, in vast subterranean halls. In this picture the 13,780 short ton (12,500 tonnes) universal detector CMS (Compact Muon Solenoid) can be seen. It records and analyses the countless particles created by the collisions inside the LHC. The magnetic field of the solenoid magnet inside the CMS detector is, at four tesla, around 100,000 times as strong as the Earth's magnetic field.

THE LARGEST OPTICAL TELESCOPES IN THE WORLD

Thanks to the development of new technologies our gaze penetrates ever more distant parts of the universe. What the largest optical telescopes discover today, was still a researcher's utopian dream only a few years ago. The dreams of European researchers now are focused on the European Extremely Large Telescope (E-ELT) that is planned to be built in Chile's Atacama Desert in the 2020s and should become the yardstick of all things astronomical. The 128 foot (39 m) reflector of the planned telescope will be 15 times stronger than all the largest optical telescopes to date — and around 100,000,000 times keener than the human eye.

CANARIES GREAT TELESCOPE
Roque de los Muchachos, La Palma, Spain
Mirror diameter   34.1 ft (10.4 m)

The giant Gran Telescopio on La Palma, the world's second largest reflecting telescope standing at an altitude of 7,861 feet (2,396 m), has gazed into the starry skies since 2007. Some of the objects are so far away that their light has to travel through space for many millions of years before it can be seen on Earth.

THE LARGEST TELESCOPES IN THE WORLD

1. **Large Binocular Telescope (LBT)**
   USA   38.7 ft (11.8 m)
2. **Canaries Great Telescope**
   Spain   34.1 ft (10.4 m)
3. **Keck I**
   USA   32.8 ft (10 m)
4. **Keck II**
   USA   32.8 ft (10 m)
5. **Southern African Large Telescope (SALT)**
   South Africa   max. 32.8 ft (10 m)
6. **Hobby-Ebberly Telescope (HET)**
   USA   30.2 ft (9.2 m)
7. **VLT I–IV**
   Chile   26.9 ft (8.2 m)
8. **Subaru Telescope**
   USA/Hawaii   26.9 ft (8.2 m)
9. **Gemini Northern Telescope**
   Chile   26.6 ft (8.1 m)

Above interfering cloud cover and in a relatively dust-free environment, the conditions on top of the 13,796 feet (4,205 m) high dormant volcano Mauna Kea on Hawaii's Big Island are ideal for astronomers. The Keck I and Keck II telescopes can merge their data and collaborate like a single supertelescope.

KECK I AND KECK II
Mauna Kea Observatory, Hawaii, USA
Mirror diameter   32.8 ft (10 m) each

The third largest optical telescopes in the world weigh 300 short tons (272 tonnes) each and are about as tall as nine-story houses. Their hexagonal mirror segments can be perfectly adjusted.

HOBBY-EBERLY TELESCOPE
McDonald Observatory, Texas, USA
Mirror diameter   30.2 ft (9.2 m)

The mirror of this telescope on Mount Fowlkes at 6,496 feet (1,980 m) altitude consists of 91 segments and is a masterstroke of technical precision. The HET is a leader in the field of spectroscopy.

SOUTHERN AFRICAN LARGE TELESCOPE
Karoo, South Africa
Mirror diameter   32.8 ft (10 m)

SALT has gazed into the depths of the universe from the Karoo semi-desert since 2005. It is the largest optical telescope in the southern hemisphere and the most powerful in the ultraviolet and infrared range.

VLT I–IV
Paranal Observatory, Chile
Mirror diameter   26.9 ft (8.2 m)

The four telescopes of the Very Large Telescope (VLT) look into the sky from the top of the 8,645 foot (2,635 m) high Cerro Paranal in the Atacama Desert. The mountain peak was blown up for the Paranal Observatory.

SUBARU TELESCOPE
Mauna Kea Observatory, Hawaii, USA
Mirror diameter   26.9 ft (8.2 m)

Since 1999 the Subaru Telescope, built by Japan and mainly responsible for discoveries in the visible and infrared areas, has stood right next to the two Keck telescopes. Among other things, the giant telescope permits the exploration of black holes as well as fantastic journeys through time. Thus, for example, it has captured the light from very distant galaxies, which was emitted just under 13 billion years ago — that is, less than a billion years after the "Big Bang."

More than a dozen scientific institutions from the United States, Italy and Germany cooperated in order to get this roughly 129 million U.S. dollar project off the ground. The Large Binocular Telescope (LBT) has stood on the 10,720 foot (3,267 m) high Mount Graham in Arizona since 2008. With

One of the two giant mirrors

its two enormous individual mirrors of 27.6 feet (8.4 m) diameter each it performs a technological quantum leap. In so-called binocular mode, the 18 short ton (16 tonnes) giants together collect as much light as a mirror of 38.7 feet (11.8 m) diameter. This is an as yet unrivaled world record, making the LBT the largest and most powerful single telescope on Earth. With the superlative telescope scientists can look very far into space. The first images it provided showed a spiral galaxy at a distance of 102 million light years from our Milky Way galaxy.

THE LARGEST OPTICAL TELESCOPE IN THE WORLD

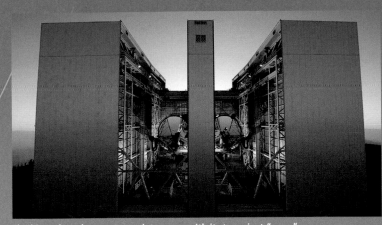

The binocular telescope gazes into space with its two giant "eyes."

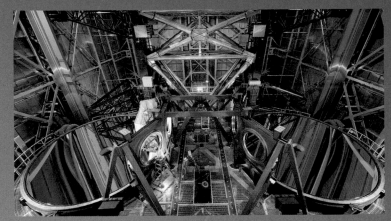

A close-up view of the two mighty main mirrors in the LBT

The gigantic Large Binocular Telescope stands in the U.S. state of Arizona. With the help of this most powerful telescope in the world, scientists explore the history of the universe and the origin of stars and galaxies.

When in 1932 the U.S. physicist Karl Jansky observed that radio waves are emitted from the center of the Milky Way, this meant the start of radio astronomy. This subfield of astronomy concerns itself with the emission of radio waves, X-rays, ultraviolet and infrared radiation from the universe — and giant radio telescopes are needed for the purpose. These mighty installations do not receive the light that can be seen by the human eye but instead undertake a sort of vast "eavesdropping" operation on cosmic radiation. Conveniently this makes them independent of the weather and dark night skies. The technological capabilities of these large supertelescopes are impressive. The Effelsberg 100-m Radio Telescope, for example, a 7,720 short ton (7,000 tonnes) steel giant with hypersensitive technical inner workings, can receive radio waves over a distance of 12 billion light years. Currently it is still a dream, but perhaps at some point it will become a reality: a radio telescope on the dark side of the moon might receive radiation that gets lost in the Earth's "radiation noise."

RATAN 600 – THE LARGEST RADIO TELESCOPE IN THE WORLD
Northern Caucasus, Russia
Reflector dish diameter
1,890 ft (576 m)

Since 1974 the Ratan 600 radio telescope, built in Karachay-Cherkessia in the northern Caucasus, has received signals from deep space. Its reflector consists of 895 adjustable plates that are arranged in a 1,890 foot (576 m) diameter circle. The impressive installation thus holds the world record: Ratan 600 is the largest radio telescope in the world. It is a part of the famous Zelenchuk Observatory. Also belonging to this astrophysical research establishment of the Russian Academy of Science is an optical telescope with a 19.7 foot (6 m) mirror.

ARECIBO OBSERVATORY – THE SECOND LARGEST RADIO TELESCOPE IN THE WORLD
Arecibo, Puerto Rico
Reflector dish diameter
1,000 ft (304.8 m)

The second largest radio telescope in the world is probably the most famous of its kind, for it has served as a backdrop for action and science fiction films. Here signals from space have been received

A vast eavesdropper on outer space

since 1963, and in 1974 the first message in the form of radio waves was emitted to space, in the hope of a response from extraterrestrial life forms.

GREEN BANK – THE LARGEST STEERABLE RADIO TELESCOPE IN THE WORLD
Charlottesville, Virginia, USA
Reflector dish diameter
361 ft (110 m)

The Green Bank Telescope (GBT) was taken into service in 2000. This largest fully steerable radio telescope in the world is also the world's largest terrestrial mobile structure. The installation is about 486 feet (148 m) tall. The plates of the impressive reflector are adjusted with the help of more than 2,000 tiny engines. The giant ear has already detected some pulsars — rapidly spinning neutron stars — and the Ophiuchus superbubble, a giant hydrogen bubble, 23,000 light years away from Earth.

EFFELSBERG – THE SECOND LARGEST STEERABLE RADIO TELESCOPE IN THE WORLD
Eifel, Germany
Reflector dish diameter
328 ft (100 m)

The giant telescope was the largest steerable radio telescope in the world from 1971 until it was superseded by the Green Bank Telescope. The impressive installation in the Ahrgebirge mountains near Bad Münstereifel in Germany stands slightly hidden in a valley and is thus protected from interfering radiation. Already 40 years old, it is still one of the very best radio telescopes in the world. The "white giant" is so powerful that it would even be able to detect a switched-off cellphone

Highly sensitive and revolving

on the moon. The telescope can be rotated with the help of 32 wheels — with a view of the southern Milky Way.

The highly sensitive Green Bank Telescope receives wavelengths between 3 mm and 90 cm. The complex stands in a mountainous region in the heart of the U.S. National Radio Quiet Zone. The area is largely protected from interference by radio waves so that the telescope might detect even the weakest signals from space.

THE LARGEST RADIO TELESCOPE ARRAYS IN THE WORLD

GIANT METREWAVE – THE LARGEST RADIO TELESCOPE ARRAY IN THE WORLD

Maharashtra, India
30 individual telescopes
Reflector dish diameter
148 ft (45 m) each

In western India near Pune, in the federal state of Maharashtra, stands the currently largest radio telescope array in the world. The Giant Metrewave Radio Telescope consists of 30 steerable telescopes, whose reflectors have a diameter of 148 feet (45 m). Fourteen of these mighty aerials are concentrated in an area of roughly 0.39 sq mls (1 sq km); the other 16 are distributed along three arms that radiate out from this core zone; they are each 8.7 miles (14 km) long. The GMRT is currently the most powerful radio telescope in the world for the reception of wavelengths in the meter range. With the help of the GMRT, scientists observe galaxies, pulsars and supernovae. In addition they are searching for neutral cosmic hydrogen, in order to attempt to define the moment when galaxies formed in the universe.

VERY LARGE ARRAY – THE SECOND LARGEST RADIO TELESCOPE ARRAY IN THE WORLD

New Mexico, USA
27 individual telescopes
Reflector dish diameter
82 ft (25 m) each

New Mexico is home to a giant radio telescope installation on a plateau at 6,969 feet (2,124 m) altitude. The Very Large Array

The extremely powerful VLA was inaugurated in 1980.

(VLA) consists of a total of 27 radio telescopes with 82 feet (25 m) diameter each. With the help of three rails that converge in a star shape, these 230 short ton (209 tonnes) colossuses can be arranged in preset positions. A computer merges data from the individual telescopes. As a rule a full cycle of all possible position combinations takes 16 months. After a comprehensive technical upgrade in the last ten years the array currently works with wavelengths in a range of 0.7 cm to 400 cm. The complex additionally serves as a control center for the Very Long Baseline Array (VLBA). It was renamed Karl G. Jansky Very Large Array in 2012 to honor the discoverer of cosmic radio waves.

The sum total is key: thanks to its 27 giant individual aerials the Very Large Array installed on a high plateau in New Mexico can receive even weak signals in a wide band of wavelengths. The huge structures are moved on rails to enable the best possible of numerous position combinations for eavesdropping on space.

SPORTS AND LEISURE

STRAHOV-STADIUM THE LARGEST STADIUM IN EUROPE

Prague, Czech Republic

Seats   220,000

The stadium located in the Prague district of Strahov was built in 1926 and has been

Aerial view of the Strahov Stadium

enlarged and redeveloped several times since. Before the fall of the Iron Curtain it was used for mass gatherings; thereafter rock bands like the Rolling Stones and Pink Floyd performed here. Today it serves as a training center for the AC Sparta Prague soccer club. Its future is currently the subject of debate in the Czech Republic.

THE LARGEST STADIUMS IN THE WORLD

1. **Strahov Stadium**
   Prague, Czech Republic   220,000
2. **May Day Stadium**
   Pyongyang, North Korea   150,000
3. **Salt Lake Stadium**
   Kolkata, India   120,000
4. **Michigan Stadium**
   Ann Arbor, USA   109,901
5. **Beaver Stadium**
   University Park, USA   107,282
6. **Aztec Stadium**
   Mexico City, Mexico   105,064
7. **Neyland Stadium**
   Knoxville, USA   102,455
8. **Ohio Stadium**
   Columbus, USA   102,329

The new Wembley Stadium is easy to recognize by the wide arch that spans across it. At its apex it reaches a height of exactly 436 feet (133 m).

THE LARGEST STADIUMS IN EUROPE

1. **Strahov-Stadion**
   Prague, Czech Republic   220,000
2. **Camp Nou**
   Barcelona, Spain   99,354
3. **Wembley Stadium**
   London, Great Britain   90,000
4. **Luzhniki Olympic Stadium**
   Moscow, Russia   84,745
5. **Rome Olympic Stadium**
   Rome, Italy   82,656
6. **Croke Park**
   Dublin, Ireland   82,500
7. **Twickenham Stadium**
   London, Great Britain   82,000
8. **Atatürk Olympic Stadium**
   Istanbul, Turkey   81.653
9. **Giuseppe Meazza Stadium**
   Milan, Italy   81.389

CAMP NOU – THE SECOND LARGEST STADIUM IN EUROPE

Barcelona, Spain

Seats   99,354

FC Barcelona's home stadium was opened in 1957 and has seen many major soccer matches since. So far, four European Cup finals as well as the opening game for the World Championship in 1982 and the final match of the Olympic tournament of 1992 have all taken place in the "New Field" (Camp Nou, also known as San Siro Stadium). In 1999 Manchester United beat FC Bayern Munich 2–1 here in the UEFA Champions League Final. In November 1982 Pope John Paul II celebrated a mass at the stadium.

The empty stadium at night

The sold-out stadium

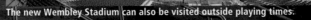
The new Wembley Stadium can also be visited outside playing times.

The British national team during a match

WEMBLEY – THE THIRD LARGEST STADIUM IN EUROPE
London, Great Britain

Seats: 90,000

The legendary venue for the 1966 FIFA World Cup Final was demolished in 2003 and replaced by an arena twice its size. The new stadium built under the auspices of Sir Norman Foster was inaugurated in 2007. To date several European Cup finals and the final of the Olympic tournament in 2012 have taken place here. The arena is operated by the English Football Association.

An Olympic tournament match in 2012

THE LARGEST STADIUMS IN ASIA

1. **May Day Stadium**
   Pyongyang, North Korea 150,000
2. **Salt Lake Stadium**
   Kolkata, India 120,000
3. **Bukit Jalil National Stadium**
   Kuala Lumpur, Malaysia 100,200
4. **Azadi Stadium**
   Tehran, Iran 100,000
5. **Ranji Stadium**
   Kolkata, India 93,000
6. **Beijing National Stadium**
   Beijing, P.R. China 91,000
7. **Gelora Bung Kamo Stadium**
   Jakarta, Indonesia 88,306
8. **Guangdong Olympic Stadium**
   Guangdong, P.R. China 80,012

The exterior of the stadium

An Arirang Festival event

MAY DAY STADIUM — THE LARGEST STADIUM IN ASIA
Pyongyang, North Korea   Seats: 15,000

The stadium was built for the 13th World Festival of Youth and Students, a biennial event organized by the World Federation of Democratic Youth that took place in the North Korean capital in 1989. It is used not only for sports events but also for mass gatherings. More than 100,000 people participate in dance and gymnastic performances during the Arirang Festival that takes place twice a year, for example. Large-scale productions trace the phases of North Korean history and in the process pay homage to the country's communist party and its leaders. The stadium's playing field covers an area of 242,190 sq ft (22,500 sq m), and the spectator ranks rise up to a height of 197 feet (60 m).

THE LARGEST STADIUMS IN AUSTRALIA

1. **Melbourne Cricket Ground**
   Melbourne, Australia 100,000
2. **ANZ Stadium**
   Sydney, Australia 83,500
3. **Eden Park**
   Auckland, New Zealand 60,000

The Melbourne Cricket Ground is perfectly circular.

MELBOURNE CRICKET GROUND – THE LARGEST STADIUM IN AUSTRALIA
Melbourne, Australia   Seats: 100,000

This stadium is not only the largest but also the most traditional "Down Under." A cricket match was played on the same site as early as 1854, and a wooden stand had been built for the members of the Melbourne Cricket Club at the time. Since then the stadium has been continually enlarged and redeveloped as one of the largest sports arenas in the world. The Melbourne Cricket Ground functioned as the Olympic Stadium during the Summer Games of 1956. In 2000 many of the matches in the Olympic soccer tournament were played here and in 2006 the various contests of the Commonwealth Games also took place here. In 1986 Pope John Paul II celebrated a mass in the arena, which also hosts concerts.

THE LARGEST STADIUMS IN AFRICA

1. **First National Bank Stadium**
   Johannesburg, South Africa   94,700
2. **Burj al'Arab Stadium**
   Alexandria, Egypt   80,000
3. **Stadium of the Martyrs**
   Kinshasa, Congo   80,000
4. **Cairo International Stadium**
   Cairo, Egypt   74,100
5. **Moses Mabhida Stadium**
   Durban, South Africa   69,957
6. **5 of July Stadium**
   Algiers, Algeria   66,000
7. **14 January Stadium**
   Tunis, Tunisia   65,000

FNB STADIUM – THE LARGEST STADIUM IN AFRICA
Johannesburg, South Africa   Seats: 94,700

The World Cup 2010 opening and end games as well as six further matches of the tournament were played in this stadium, opened in 1989. Its official name is "First National Bank Stadium," but since FIFA does not permit sponsors to be named it was renamed for the duration of the World Cup to "Soccer City."

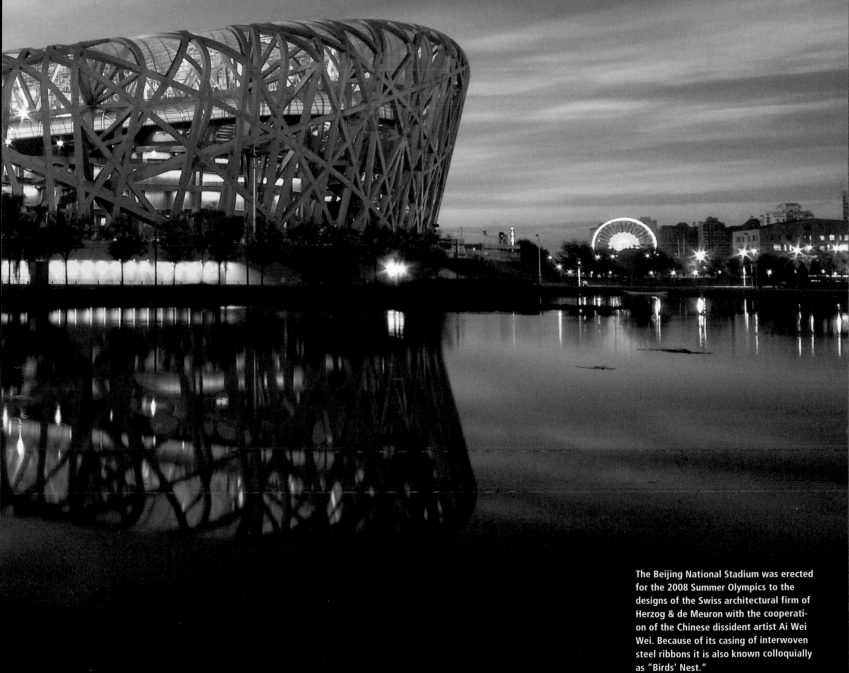

The Beijing National Stadium was erected for the 2008 Summer Olympics to the designs of the Swiss architectural firm of Herzog & de Meuron with the cooperation of the Chinese dissident artist Ai Wei Wei. Because of its casing of interwoven steel ribbons it is also known colloquially as "Birds' Nest."

DALLAS COWBOYS STADIUM

Arlington, Texas, USA
Seats   108,713

Inaugurated in March 2009, this sports arena is a superlative structure in several ways. With its retractable roof structure it is the largest sports arena on the planet as well as boasting the largest column-free interior space in the world. The Dallas Cowboys play home games here. A new spectator record, however, was established during a basketball game, not a football game: the NBA All-Star Game on February 14, 2010, attracted 108,713 spectators and was entered in the Guinness Book of Records as the most visited basketball game of all-time. The Cowboys Stadium is used not only as a sports arena but also as a venue for concerts.

Exterior view of the Dallas Cowboys Stadium

At the Cowboys Stadium spectators can also follow the action on the sports field via huge images transmitted on giant HD screens. The biggest of these measures 151 feet (46 m) long and 72 feet (22 m) wide, making it the largest HD screen in the world.

THE LARGEST STADIUMS
IN THE AMERICAS

THE LARGEST STADIUMS IN NORTH AND CENTRAL AMERICA

1. **Michigan Stadium**
   Ann Arbor, USA   109,901
2. **Beaver Stadium**
   University Park, USA   107,282
3. **Aztec Stadium**
   Mexico City, Mexico   105,064
4. **Neyland Stadium**
   Knoxville, USA   102,455
5. **Ohio Stadium**
   Columbus, USA   102,329
6. **Bryant-Denny Stadium**
   Tuscaloosa, USA   101,821
7. **Texas Memorial Stadium**
   Austin, USA   100,119

THE LARGEST STADIUMS IN SOUTH AMERICA

1. **Maracanã Stadium**
   Rio de Janeiro, Brazil   96,000
2. **Monumental Stadium**
   Lima, Peru   80,093
3. **Mineirão**
   Belo Horizonte, Brazil   75,783
4. **João Castelo Stadium**
   São Luís, Brazil   75,263
5. **Parque do Sabiá Stadium**
   Uberlândia, Brazil   72,000
6. **Fonte Nova Stadium**
   Salvador da Bahia, Brazil   66,080
7. **El Monumental Stadium**
   Buenos Aires, Argentina   65,645

Football is one of the most popular ball games in the United States. The games take place in giant football arenas, with the largest accommodating more than 100,000 spectators. Pictured is a match played at the Beaver Stadium.

MICHIGAN STADIUM
THE LARGEST STADIUM IN NORTH AMERICA
Ann Arbor, Michigan, USA   Seats: 109,901

This sports arena was built in 1927 especially for football games in the grounds of Michigan University, who also manage the arena. The Michigan Wolverines team, which belongs to the National Collegiate Athletic Association, a sports association of American colleges and universities, plays its home games here. The stadium also hosts hockey games and the university's graduation ceremonies. The arena is also known as the "The Big House." A new spectator record was established on September 10, 2011, when 114,804 fans came to watch a Wolverines game.

The Michigan Stadium established ... a new spectator record in 2010.

BEAVER STADIUM –
THE SECOND LARGEST STADIUM IN NORTH AND CENTRAL AMERICA
University Park, Pennsylvania, USA
Seats   107,282

The football arena was built in 1960 in the grounds of Pennsylvania State University and is also managed by the school. The Nittany Lions, the university's football team and a member of the National Collegiate Athletic Association, have their home games here. On September 14, 2002, during a Lions match against the Nebraska University team, a spectator number record was established that is still unbroken today: 110,753 fans came to watch the game.

AZTEC STADIUM – THE LARGEST CLUB STADIUM IN THE WORLD
Mexico City, Mexico   Seats: 105,064

This arena was built in 1966 as a dedicated soccer stadium. It is today the home venue of Club América. In 1968 it was the venue of many matches in the Olympic tournament as well as two World Cup finals. In 1970 Brazil won the coveted Cup in their match against Italy, and in 1986 Argentina won the final against Germany. The quarter final between Argentina and England during the tournament of 1986 was also played in the Estadio Azteca. During the encounter

Diego Maradona scored a goal with his hand, which entered soccer history as the "Hand of God" goal.

The stadium from a bird's eye perspective

MARACANÃ – THE LARGEST SOCCER STADIUM IN SOUTH AMERICA
Rio de Janeiro, Brazil   Seats: 96,000

The Maracanã Stadium and the multipurpose hall in the Maracanã sports complex

The soccer arena was built for the World Cup of 1950. With a capacity of 200,000 spectators it was the largest stadium in the world at its inauguration. Although the number of seats was halved in the course of various modernizations, it still occupies a leading position in the ranking of the world's largest sports venues. The Maracanã Stadium is currently being converted for the football World Cup in 2014. In 2016 the opening and closing ce-

remonies for the Olympic Games are also set to be hosted here.

Soccer fans in the Maracanã Stadium

The giant hangar of the bankrupt Cargolifter AG company was bought by the Malayan Tanjong company in 2003 and transformed into a leisure park with overnight accommodation. A tropical rainforest was planted in the hall, with more than 50,000 different plants, and a tropical village with reproductions of South Sea houses and artificial lagoons were constructed. There are sauna and spa areas, pools and also bars and restaurants. Since its opening in December 2004 this artificial paradise has attracted almost one million visitors annually. Today the enterprise, which in the first few years of its existence had to accept large losses, reaps substantial profits.

LEISURE PARADISE IN THE LARGEST SELF-SUPPORTING HALL IN THE WORLD

CARGOLIFTER HALL — ONCE THE LARGEST HANGAR IN THE WORLD

The vast hall in the grounds of Brand airport, located 22 miles (35 km) south of Berlin, was built in 2002 by the Cargolifter AG company, which then went bankrupt. With a height of 351 feet (107 m), a length of 1,181 feet (360 m) and a width of 689 feet (210 m) it was the largest hangar in the world at the time of its completion in 2000. The Cargolifter AG wanted to develop and build heavy-lift airships here with a transportation capacity of up to 176 short tons (160 tonnes). However, most of the projects could not be realized. Even the company's flagship project, the "Joey" airship, a 1:8 scale model of the planned, larger CL160 heavy-lift airship, did not convince despite its successful test flights, and it was sold in the course of the insolvency proceedings as an only partially airworthy "exhibition showpiece" for about 17,500 U.S. dollars.

In the middle of cold Europe the "Tropical Islands" leisure park created, in an area of 710,420 sq ft (66,000 sq m), a picturesque tropical landscape with rainforest, lagoons, fine sandy beaches and year-round temperatures of 79 °F (26 °C).

CREDITS

Abbreviations: A = alamy, C = corbis, G = Getty,
L = Laif, M = Mauritius

Cover: C/Nomachi (2), C/Souders, G/Nikada, C/NASA, G/NASA, G/Eschcollection, C/Krist, C/Wallich, pp 2/3 H. & D. Zielske, p4 G/Butler, pp4/5 C/Benson, pp6/7 C/Sohm, pp8/9 C/Falzone, pp10/11 G/Taner, p12 G/Newman, pp12/13 M/Alamy, pp14/15 C/Soltan, p15 NASA, pp16/17 C/Kokoshkin, p17 G/Panoramic Images, pp18/19 C/Hardy, p19 G/Baxter, pp20/21 G/Harding, p21 C/SIME, pp22/23 G/Higuchi, p23 G/Greuel, p24 G/stocktrek, pp24/25 C/Zha Chunming, pp26/27 C/U.S. Department of Defense, p27 C/U.S. Navy/Handout, p27 C/Image Source, p27 M/Alamy, pp28/29 G/Simonsen, p29 G/Borkoski, pp30/31 C/Guo Jian She, p31 G/Lawrence, pp32/33 C/Creasource, p33 C/White, p33 C/Friedman, p33 G/Baxter, p34 G/German, pp34/35 G/EschCollection, p35 C/Nir Elias, p35 C/Stringer Shanghai, p35 C/Car Culture (3), p35 C/China Daily, p36 C/O'Rear (2), p36 C/Gail Mooney, pp36/37 G/Hellier, p37 G/Sherman, p37 A/Navin Mistry, p38 C/Mendel, p38 G/Allard, pp38/39 C/Lanting, p40 C/SEGAR, p40 A/Stuwdamdorp, p40 Corbis/Tetra Images, pp40/41 C/Brooks Kraft, p42 M/Alamy, pp42/43 C/Taner, p43 G/Panoramic Images, p44 C/Jetta Productions, p44 M/Heiner Heine, pp44/45 C/Tetra Images, pp46/47 C/Yi Lu, p47 L/Brauer, p47 M/Alamy, pp48/49 A/Seligmann, p49 C/Soltan, p50 C/Mendel, p50 C/Taylor, pp50/51 C/Lee Jae-Won, pp52/53 G/Comstock, p53 C/Sutherland, p53 Chuck Pefley/IPN p53 C/Orti, p53 G/Lonely Planet, p54 A/Gainey, pp54/55 C/Nomachi, p56 C/Sigheti, p56 C/Orsal, p56 A/CTK , pp56/57 C/Lissac, p58 C/Bravo, p58 C/Reuters, pp58/59 G/Gregory, p59 G/Solvain, p59 C/Copson, p59 C/Benedetti, p59 C/Hicks, p59 C/Vidler, p59 G/SuperStock, p59 C/Cristofori, p60 G/Okon, pp60/61 G/Nikada, p62 G, pp62/63 L/Galli, p64 G/Hemis, p64 C/Brynn, p64 G/Travel Ink, pp64/65 C/Vidler, p66 G/Pinto, p66 C/Stringer, pp66/67 C/Taner, p67 G/Thornton, p67 Bildagentur Huber/Ripani Massimo p67 A/GeoTravel, p68 C/Borchi, p68 M/Alamy, p68 G/Baxter, pp68/69 G/Leiva, p70 C/Grand Tour, p70 C/Dickman, p70 A/Pavlenko, pp70/71 C/Fox, p71 C/Grand Tour, p71 C/Stubblemine (2), p71 A/Pegaz, p72 A/Phipp, Spp72/73 C/Demma, p73 A/Frazier, p73 A/Robert Harding, p74 L/Linke, p74 M/Keller, pp74/75 C/Borchi, p75 H & D. Zielske, p75 G/Hemis, p75 A/Goldwater, p75 G/Noble, p75 C/Blythe, p76 A/Torial, pp76/77 A/allOver, p78 A/Henry Brown, pp78/79 A/Bower, p79 G/Shaw, p79 G/Blair, p80 C/Zuckerman, p80 G/Look/Greune, p80 A/imagebroker, pp80/81 C/Damm, p81 A/Monheim, p82 G/Skarzynski, p82 G/isifa, p82 G/Witt, p82 A/Lang, p82 A/Doyle, p82 A/Pereira, pp82/83 C/Antonino, p83 C/Fridman, p84 C/Whiteside, p84 C/Ratner, p84 G/Souders, p84 G/Azouri, pp84/85 C/Hicks, p86 G/Lissac, p86 C/Mooney, pp86/87 C/Bognar, p87 A/Wareham, p87 A/Jenkins, p87 A/Williams, pp88/89 C/Nomachi, p89 C/Abu Turk, pp90/91 C/Nomachi, p91 C/Jadallah, p92 C/Falzone, p92 C/Raga, p92 G/Gray, p92 A/JTB, pp92/93 C/Nomachi, p93 C/Attar, p93 C/Nomachi (2), p93 A/Jon Arnold, p94 A/dbimages, pp94/95 C/Nomachi, p96 G/Turner, p96 C/Nomachi (3), p98 C/Wood, pp98/99 C/Nomachi, p100 M/Alamy, pp100/101 C/Nomachi, p102 C/McQueen, pp102/103 G/Hellier, p103 A/CuboImages, p103 A/Scenics & Science, p103 A/Asia Photopress, p103 C/Zuckerman, p103 C/Horner, pp104 + 104/105 A/Levy, p106 G/Moos, p106 G/Marshall, p106 G/Mack, pp106/107 M/O'Brien, p107 C/Maisant, p108 C/Atlantide Phototravel, pp108/109 C/Ocean, p110 C/Kumar, pp110/111 C/Giansanti, p112 C/Nomachi, p112 C/Soltan, p112 C/Godong (2), pp112/113 C/Nomachi, p113 G/Graham, p113 C/Sutherland, p113 C/Iorio, p113 C/Graham, p113 A/Picture Contact BV, p114 G/Gray, p114 A/Brown, pp114/115 A/Tips Images, p115 C/Soltan, p115 A/Dinodia Photos, pp116/117 C/Lehman, p117 C/Ocean, p118 G/Ombler, pp118/119 G/Allen, p120 C/Soltan, p120 C/Gollings, p120 G/Peter Ptschelinze, p121 G/Panoramic Images, p121 A/Reddy (2), p121 A/imagebroker, pp122/123 G/Panoramic Images (2), p124 G/Allen, p124 A/Madhavan, p124 A/Reddy, pp124/125 C/Jupiterimages, p126 A/Reddy, pp126/127 G/Panoramic Images, p127 C/Tettoni, p127 A/SuperStock, p128 G/Blair, pp128/129 A/Preston, p129 C/Soltan, p129 C/Boisvieux, p130 C/Hicks, pp130/131 C/Hicks, p131 C/Hebberd, p132 A/24BY36, pp132/133 C/Trower, p133 G/Morandi, p134 A/Bagnall, pp134/135 A/Mawson, p135 C/Churchill, p135 C/Sweeney, pp136/137 C/Jupiterimages, p137 M/Alamy, p138 C/Zuckerman, pp138/139 C/Lisle, p139 C/Soltan, p139 C/Borchi (2), p139 A/Hanson, p139 A/Robert Harding, p139 A/Longhurst, p139 C/Baldizzone, pp140/141 A/Aurora Photos, p141 A/Yue, p142 C/Aldo, p142 A/Preston, p142 A/CuboImages, p142 C/Boisvieux, pp142/143 C/Photosindia, p143 A/Aurora Photos, p143 A/Plotkin, p143 A/Muratore, pp144/145 G/Sarkis, p145 G/Delimont, p145 G/Hellier, p145 G/Wakem, p145 G/Allison, p145 G/Hall, p146 G/Martin, p146 G/Harris, pp146/147 G/Ritterbach, p148 C/Howard, pp148/149 C/Horner, p149 C/Yang Liu, p149 C/Howard, p149 C/Boisvieux, p150 C/Bognar, pp150/151 G/Tan, p151 G/Gocher, p152 Imagestate, pp152/153 C/Hicks, p154 A/Indiapicture, p154 A/Lonely Planet Images, pp154/155 C/Nowitz, p155 EyeUbiquitous/Hutchison, p155 C/Soltan (2), pp155 + 156 A/Jon Arnold, pp156/157 A/Horree, p157 L/hemis, p157 A/Picture Contact, p157 C/Boisvieux, p158 G/Delimont, pp158/159 G/Ritterbach, p159 C/Raga, p160 G/Simoni, p160 Calina and Wolfgang Kunth, pp160/161 C/Tettoni, p161 C/Heaton, p161 Calina and Wolfgang Kunth, p162 C/Chesley, p162 G/Tettoni, p162 C/TPX, pp162/163 C/Redlink, pp164 + 164/165 Calina and Wolfgang Kunth, p166 C/Carrasco, p166 C/Mu Xiang Bin, pp166/167 C/Kaehler, p167 C/Forman, p167 C/Colombel, p168 G/Game, p168 C/Liu guoxing, pp168/169 G/Silverman, p169 G/TAO, p169 LOOK/Johaentges, p170 A/Friang, p170 A/Falzone, pp170/171 A/Urbanmyth, p172 A/Cleave, p172 M/Alamy, pp172/173 M/Diversion, p173 A/JTB, p174 A/Deco, pp174/175 C/Bob Krist, p175 Premium, p175 A/Delimont, p175 A/Darby Sawchuk, p175 C/Freeman, p176 G/Hellier, p176 C/Hicks, p176 A/mediacolor's, p176 A/Reddy, pp176/177 G/Travel Ink, p177 G/Thompson, p177 A/Game, p177 A/Lacarbona, p178 G/Gellman, p178 G/Strachan, pp178/179 C/John Stanmeyer, p180 C/Harrington III, pp180/181 C/Falzone, p181 C/Bibikow, p181 C/Pyle, p181 A/Bognar, p181 A/Design Pics, p182 NN, pp182/183 A/Crystite licenced, p183 C/Falzone, p183 C/Zeya, pp184/185 A/Tips Images, p185 A/Wertz, p185 A/Tips Images, p186 A/Vincent, p186 A/Rolf, pp186/187 A/INSADCO, p187 A/Bailey, pp188/189 C/Leynse, p190 C/Woodhouse, pp190/191 C/Hicks, p191 C/Woodhouse, pp192/193 C/Ocean, pp192/193 H. & D. Zielske, p193 C/Borchi, pp194 + 194/195 C/Taner, pp194/195 C/Adams, p195 G/Sheombar, p195 G/Utech, p195 G/Travelpix, p196 Bildagentur Huber/Mirau, p196 G/Oliver, p196 G/Travelpix, p197 G/Slow Images, p197 L/Galli, p197 G/Adams, p197 G/Layda, p198 G/Raga, p198 C/Soltan, p199 C/Bognar, p199 C/Taner, p199 C/asiaimages, pp200/201 C/Atlantide Phototravel, pp200/201 C/Hicks, p201 A/Grant, p202 G/Flickr, pp202/203 G/Dee, pp204/205 C/Ocean, pp204/205 C/Helios Loo, p205 C/Gibb, p206 G/Hemis, pp206/207 G/Baxter, p207 C/Damm, p207 C/Hicks, p207 G/Henning, pp208/209 C/Hardy, pp208/209 G/Driendl, p209 G/Carrasco, p209 C/Woodhouse, p210 C/French, p210 C/Nowitz, p210 G/Panoramic Images, p211 C/Mahovlich, p211 C/Conlan, p211 C/Hardy, p211 C/Krist, p212 C/Fridman, pp212/213 G/Vasconcellos, p213 G/Frerck, p214 G/Simonetti, p214 G/Kittner, p214 C/Damm, p215 C/Lehman, p215 G/Queiriga-Lumiar, p215 A/Wilson, p215 A/dbimages, pp216/217 C/Mu Xiang Bin, pp218/219 G/EschCollection, p219 G/Stoll, pp220/221 G/Cocoroimages.de p221 G/OTHK, p222 G/Barbour, pp222/223 C/Wallis, pp224/225 G/Child, p225 G/Figueres, pp226/227 NN., pp226/227 C/Taner, p228 C/Woodhouse, pp228/229 C/Raga, p230 C/Zumapress, pp230/231 C/Copson, p231 G/Buena Vista, p232 NN., pp232/233 + 233 G/Mordvintsev, p233 G/Bloomberg, p234 C/Harper, p234 A/Raftery, pp234/235 C/Harper, p236 G/MacDougall, pp236/237 G/Baxter, p237 C/Bentley, p238 G/Nureldine, p238 L/Malakawi, pp238/239 C/Top Photo Corporation, p239 M/Alamy, p240 G/Eightfish, pp240/241 C/Leynse, p242 G/Cheong (2), p242 A/Fairweather, pp242/243 G/Vanderelst, p243 G/Bloomberg, p243 C/Trower, p243 A/ITPhoto, p244 C/Metaxas, pp244/245 C/Leynse, p246 C/Sulgan, p246 A/Lattes, p246 M/Bognar, pp246/247 C/Xiaoyang Liu, p248 C/Gollings, p249 G/Jumper, p249 C/Photolibrary, p249 G/Watson, pp250 + 250/251 M/Alamy, p252 C/Blessing, pp252/253 G/Pease, p253 G/Korzekwa, p254 C/Krist, pp254/255 C/Koch, p256 C/Raga, pp256/257 L/Heeb, p258 C/Boesl, p258 L/Tannenbaum, p258 C/Elder, p258 C/Yamashita, pp258/259 C/Tetra Images, p259 C/Develo, p260 G/Pritchard, p260 G/Palmisano, p260 M/Alamy, pp260/261 C/Setboun, p261 C/Andrew, p261 C/Cummins, p261 M/Alamy (2), p262 A/JJM Stock Photography, pp262/263 + 263 (2) C/Hicks, p264 C/Stephens, p264 C/Purcell, pp264/265 C/Stephens, p265 C/Ibrahim, p265 G/Woodhouse, pp266/267 C/Bowater, p267 G/Nureldine, p267 C/Raga, p267 C/lescourret, p267 C/Harrington III (2), p268 C/Frei, pp268/269 C/Koch, pp270/271 G/Latitudestock, p271 C/Lindsay Hebberd, p271 G/Cavalli, p271 A/Prisma, p271 A/Asia Pixels, p271 A/Trower, p271 A/Kober 1, pp272 + 272/273 C/Hicks, p273 C/Copson, pp274/275 C/Atlantide Phototravel, p276 A/Patrick, pp276/277 C/Zumapress, p278 C/Wei Hui, pp278/279 A/View Stock, p279 C/Liao Xueming, p280 C/Trower, p280 A/Chekalov, pp280/281 C/Wallis, p281 G/Gallup Pix, p281 A/Lehne, pp282/283 + 283 C/Simard, p284 G/Wilkes, pp284/285 G/Nikada, p285 China Tourism Press p285 G/T L Chua, p285 C/Nikozbazi, p285 A/Warburton-Lee, p285 A/Robert Harding, p286 C/Axiom Photographic, p286 A/Robert Harding, pp286/287 C/Schlenker, p287 G/Bloomberg, p288 A/Gaertner, pp288/289 G/Vanderelst, p289 C/Stringer, p289 A/Prisma, pp290/291 C/Stulberg, pp292 + 292/293 G/Dee, pp294/295 L/Meyer, pp294/295 C/Ganci, p295 C/Sonnet, pp296/297 G/Flickr RM, pp296/297 C/Gould, p297 A/CuboImages, p298 G/Hemis, p298 C/Listri, pp298/299 C/Listri, p300 C/Atlantide Phototravel, p300 C/Wallis, pp300/301 C/Redlink, p301 C/Sutherland, p301 C/Falzone, p301 C/Listri, p302 G/Min, pp302/303 A/Willson, p304 C/Davies, pp304/305 A/Ivanchenko, p306 C/Pearson, p306 A/Sutherland, p306 A/Kellerman, pp306/307 A/Ammit, p307 G/Flaherty, p307 A/Robert Harding, p307 G/Gridley, p308 C/Dominguez, pp308/309 C/Kiusalaas, pp310/311 G/Everton, p311 G/Sanders, p312 C/Ocean, p312 C/Boisvieux, p312 A/Prisma, pp312/313 A/Amana Images, p313 C/Glubish, p313 C/Ocean, p313 A/Pefley, p313 C/Allofs, pp314/315 M/Alamy, p315 C/Darack, p315 A/Travelfile, p316 C/de Waele, p316 M/Alamy, pp316/317 G/Ghiotti, p317 C/Sweeney, p317 G/Wonish, p317 (2), 318, 318/319 M/Alamy, p319 A/Robert Harding, p319 (5) M/Alamy, p320 A/Giffard, p320 A/Robert Harding, p320 A/imagebroker, pp320 (3) + 320/321 M/Alamy, p321 A/JTB, p321 (3) M/Alamy, pp322/323 G/Compion, p323 G/Baigrie, p323 G/Bibikow, p323 G/Matilde B, p323 A/Buzzard, p324 A/Aurora, pp324/325, 325 (alle), 326/327 M/Alamy, p327 A/Brunker, p327 (4) M/Alamy, p328 C/Car Culture, pp328/329 G/Look, p329 G/Deveson, p329 A/Segre, p330 C/Car Culture, pp330/331 C/Benedict, p332 G/Taylor, p332 C/Bettmann, pp332/333 C/Goddard, p333 C/Nation, p333 C/Skyscan, pp334/335 G/Radler, p336 C/Ocean, p336 C/Kaehler, pp336/337 C/Morandi, p338 C/Hoffmann, p338 A/Bennett, pp338/339 C/Hoffmann, p339 G/Images, p339 C/Huey, p339 A/Bedford, p339 A/TAO Images, p340 C/Simard pp340/341 C/Sciosia, p341 G/Firmhofer, p341 A/imagebroker, p342 C/He Junchang (2), p342 C/Niu Yixin, p342 C/Qilai Shen, pp342/343 C/Hufton & Crow, p343 C/Sun Can, p344 A/Ei Katsumata, p344 A/Isaacson, p344 A/Mixa, pp344/345 A/Ehlers, p346 A/Visions of America (2), pp346/347 C/Behnke, p347 G/EschCollection, pp348/349 C/AStock, p349 C/Wang Dingchang, p349 C/Xinhua Press, p349 C/Chen Ang, p349 C/Niu Yixin, pp350/351 C/Bowater, p351 C/Kessler, p351 C/Platiau, p352 G/Zu Sanchez, p352 G/Cosulich, p352 A/Wareham, pp352/353 G/Slade, p353 C/Sunxin, p353 C/Niu Yixin, p353 G/Panoramic Images, p354 C/Hashimoto, p354 C/Nakao, pp354/355 A/Willson, p356 C/Grand Tour, pp356/357 C/Sciosia, p358 G/Knowles, p358 M/Alamy, pp358/359 G/Yeowell, p360 C/Yuan Ruilun, pp360/361 G/Pease, p362 C/Imaginechina, pp362/363 C/Yan Runbo, p363 C/Xinhua, p363 A/Sarun T., pp364/365 M/Alamy, p365 C/Lagerwall p365 A/Pereira, p366 C/Imaginechina (2), p366 A/Westheim, pp366/367 C/JongBeom Kim, p367 C/Bibikow, p367 C/Imaginechina, p368 C/Shoot, pp368/369 A/Middle East, p369 A/Delimont, p370 C/Barrett & MacKay, p370 G/Theiss (2), p370 A/Goss Images, p370 A/Frazier, p370 C/Fleming, pp370/371 C/Barrett & MacKay, p372 C/Imageplus, p372 A/StockBrazil, pp372/373 M/Alamy, p373 C/Celoria, p373 C/Arthus-Bertrand, p374 C/Liu Jiling, p374 C/Mexico's Presidency p374 NN., pp374/375 A/Foxx, p375 A/Saks, p376 C/Smith, pp376/377 C/Kaminesky, p378 A/Jenny, pp378/379 G/Stockbyte, p379 G/Campbell, pp380/381 C/Imaginechina, p381 C/Jiang ren, p381 M/Alamy, pp382/383 C/Souders, p383 C/Gibb, pp384/385 C/Gyro, pp386/387 C/Taner, p387 G/Mixa, p388 C/Falzone, p388 A/Foster, p388 A/Arco, p388 A/Brooke-Webb, pp388/389 M/Alamy, p389 C/Cornish, pp389 + 390 M/Alamy, pp390/391 C/Trower, p391 M/Alamy, pp392/393 C/Steinmetz, p393 G/Jumper, p393 A/Tetra Images, p393 C/Owaki - Kulla, p394 NN., pp394/395 C/Mills, pp396/397 L/Hemis, p398 A/Robertson, pp398/399 A/Marka, p400 G/Schauer, pp400/401 G/U.S. Coast Guard, pp402/403 C/Pei Xin, p403 C/Shanghai Sanya, p403 C/Qilai Shen, pp404/405 G/Eightfish, pp406/407 G/Schulz, p407 G/Mandel, p408 C/AStock, pp408/409 G/Eightfish, p409 G/Lee Man Yiu, p409 G/JS's favorite things, pp410/411 C/Ocean, p411 G/Woodhouse, pp412/413 C/Richard Cummins, p414 M/Blossey, p414 M/Blossey, pp414/415 A/imagebroker, pp416/417 C/Hicks, p418 C/Hulton-Deutsch (2), pp418/419 G/Scott, p420 Bildagentur Huber /Gräfenhain pp420/421 G/Haug, pp422/423 C/Woodhouse, p423 C/Lehman, pp424/425 C/Liu Liqun, p425 C/Xu Yu, p425 A/Arco, p426 A/Doering, p426 A/LianeM, pp426/427 + 427 G/Johaentges, p427 A/Otto, p428 G/Johaentges, p428 NN. pp428/429 LOOK/Johaentges, p430 C/Tepper, p430 C/Keren Su, p430 C/Zheng Jiayu, pp430/431 A/Keren Su, p432 G/Delimont, p432 C/Orezzoli, pp432/433 C/SPS, p434 G/Vest, pp434/435 G/Kos, p436 C/CSP, p436 A/Strycula, pp436/437 C/Sroczynski, p438 G/Ulander, p438 G/Handout, p438 C/Sandberg, pp438/439 A/Williamson, p439 C/Charisius, p439 A/dbphots, pp440/441 A/Bildagentur Hamburg, p441 C/Domingos, pp442/443 A/Garnham, p443 G/Jannink, p444 C/Imaginechina, p444 NN., pp444/445 A/Picture Contact BV, pp446/447 G/Wood, p447 NN, p447 A/Houghton, p448 argus/Andrews, p448 J.D.C. Plug, pp448/449 A/Transtock Inc., p450 A/Purestock, pp450/451 G/Check Six, p451 C/Langevin, p451 G/Getty Images News, pp452/453 Tokukanaga/Check Six p453 C/Kaufman, p453 C/Kaufman, p454 A/ITAR-TASS, p454 G/Flood, pp454/455 G/Breiehagen, p455 C/Bettmann, p456 A/Lonely Planet, pp456/457 G/Sanger, p457 C/Bartruff, p458 G/Chung Sung-Jun, p458 G/Seokyong Lee, pp458/459 C/Wishnetsky, p459 G/Chung Sung-Jun, p459 G/Macdiarmid, p460 G/UniversalImagesGroup(2), p460 A/Hanley, p460 A/Design Pics, pp460/461 C/Yang Liu, p462 A/Mellmann, p462 C/Bartruff, pp462/463 M/Frey, p464 G/Husmo, p464 NN. pp464/465 Visum/Panos Pictures, p465 G/Ribeiro, pp466/467 C/Steinmetz, pp468/469 A/JRC, p469 G/Williams, p470 C/Raga, p470 C/MacGregor, p470 C/HO, pp470/471 C/Hawkes, p471 C/Johansson, p471 A/Caro, p472 G/TAO Images Limited, p472 G/Tanaka, pp472/473 A/Bamber, p473 C/Borchi, p473 C/Kemp, p473 C/B.S.P.I., p473 A/Kevpix, p474 G/National Geographic, pp474/475 A/Hancock, p475 G/Henning, p476 G/Stulberg, pp476/477 G/Poulides/Thatcher, p477 G/Brown, p477 C/Stulberg, p477 A/Kord, p477 C/Cummins, pp478/479 C/Griffith, p479 C/Hellier, p479 G/Cavalli, p480 Look/Johaentges, p480 C/Bettmann, pp480/481 Look/Johaentges, p482 C/Nogues, p482 G/Niedenthal, pp482/483 A/imagebroker, p484 M/Alamy, pp484/485 M/Alamy, p485 C/Charisius (2), p486 G/Bloomberg, pp486/487 C/Psihoyos, p488 C/Casey (2), p488 C/Bill Nation (2), pp488/489 C/Simonpietri, p489 C/Conger, p490 G/Bridges, p490 G/NASA, p490 G/Apic, pp490/491 G/Conger, p491 C/Smithsonian Institution, pp492/493 G/Stocktrek, p493 C/Air Force, p493 G/Simonsen (2), p494 C/NASA , p494 G/Time Life Pictures, p494 C/Jolly, pp494/495 C/Wallick, pp496/497 C/Cooper, p498 C/Bagla, p498 C/kyodo, p498 C/Oleg, pp498/499 A/NASA, p499 C/Blevins, p499 C/ESA-CNES-Arianespace, p500 C/Imaginechina, p500 C/Wang Jianmin, pp500/501 C/Xu haihan, p502 A/Caldwell, p502 C/Karrass, pp502/503 C/Lehman, p503 A/Roberts, p503 C/Bettmann, pp504 + 504/505 C/NASA, p505 C/Ressmeyer, pp506/507 C/Andrews, p507 C/Theiss, p507 C/Ressmeyer, pp508/509 G/NASA, p509 G/Encyclopaedia Britannica, p509 G/Stocktrek, p510 G/NASA, pp510/511 C/Collins, p511 C/NASA , p512 Schapowalow /Atlantide, pp512/513 C/Barbier, p513 L/Kirchgessner, p513 G/Layma, pp514/515 G/Grant, p515 G/Vogt, p516 C/Simard, pp516/517 C/Lissac, p517 C/Liu Liqun, p517 C/Kennedy, p518 C/Brecelj, pp518/519 A/Kaplan, pp520/521 + 522 C/Chamberlain, p522 C/Harrington III, pp522/523 A/Ball, p524 A/imagebroker, pp524/525 C/Simard, p525 G/Baxter, p525 C/Listri, p525 Visum/Ridder, p526 C/Darbellay, p526 G/Roger Wright, pp526/527 C/Darbellay, p527 C/Foeger, p527 G/Nebesky, p528 C/Alston, pp528/529 C/Astock, p529 G/Gardel, p530 A/Foy, p530 C/Leder, pp530/531 G/Layda, p531 C/Lewis, p531 G/Frerck, p532 C/Kemp, p532 C/Sohm, pp532/533 + 533 (3) C/Kemp, p534 C/Bryant, p534 C/Vidler, p534 C/Harper, pp534/535 C/Sonnet, p535 C/Jon Arnold, p535 C/Krist (2), p536 C/Sonnet, p536 C/B.S.P.I., pp536/537 C/Kamineski, p537 C/Stulberg, p538 C/Clapp, p538 L/Gaasterland, pp538/539 C/Grand Tour, p539 L/Sasse, p539 C/The Gallery Collection, p540 ddp/Michael Gottschalk, p540 Cordia Schlegelmilch, pp540/541 L/Boening, p541 G/Higuchi, p541 L/Adenis (2), p541 L/Galli, p542 G/Hughes, p542 C/Lescourret, p542 C/Sonnet, p542 A/imagebroker, pp542/543 A/Levy, p543 A/Smith, p543 A/Libera, p544 G/Dosfotos, p544 look/age fotostock, p544 C/Amantini, pp544/545 C/Sim Chi Yin, p545 C/Nathan, p545 C/Sonnet, p545 A/imagebroker, p546 C/Simard, p546 C/Edwards, pp546/547 A/Kellerman, p547 L/Sasse, p547 G/Tafreshi, p547 L/Rigaud, p548 G/Look, p548 A/Pearson, p548 A/Gerald, p548 A/Kemp, p548 A/Evans, pp548/549 G/PNC, p549 A/Sadura, p549 A/National Geographic, p550 A/Cox, p550 A/Images of Africa, p550 A/Holt, pp550/551 A/Lemmens, p551 C/Kober, p551 A/Pomortzeff, p551 A/Prisma Archivo, p551 C/Wood, p552 C/Ginter, p552 C/Ressmeyer, pp552/553 C/Psihoyos, p554 A/Pearson, pp554/555 A/Dallaglio p555 G/Coffrini, p556 C/Digfoto, pp556/557 C/Jecan, p557 C/Stocktrek, p557 G/Sven Creutzmann, p557 A/Lemmens, p557 C/Ressmeyer, pp558 + 558/559 A/Smith, p559 G/McNally (2), p560 G/van Ravenswaay, p560 C/Ressmeyer, pp560/561 A/West, p562 A/Visions of America, pp562/563 a/Jim West, p564 A/isifa Image Service s.r.o., p564 M/Alamy, p564 G/Barbour, pp564/565 A/imagebroker, p565 C/Photo Kishmoto, p565 G/Forster, p565 M/Alamy, p566 L/Sinopix, p566 L/Le Figaro Magazine, p566 C/John Gollings, pp566/567 C/Astock, p567 C/Sibeko, pp568/569 A/Lawrence, p569 C/Fox, p570 C/Horwedel, p570 A/Sutton, pp570/571 A/Weidman, p571 G/Pillitz, p571 C/HO, p571 M/Alamy, pp572/573 Rainer Weisflog, p573 C/Derimais. 548 A/Pearson, S. 548 A/Gerald, S. 548 A/Kemp, S. 548 A/Evans, S. 548/549 G/PNC, S. 549 A/Sadura, S. 549 A/National Geographic, S. 550 A/Cox, S. 550 A/Images of Africa, S. 550 A/Holt, S. 550/551 A/Lemmens, S. 551 C/Kober, S. 551 A/Pomortzeff, S. 551 A/Prisma Archivo, S. 551 C/Wood, S. 552 C/Ginter, S. 552 C/Ressmeyer, S. 552/553 C/Psihoyos, S. 554 A/Pearson, S. 554/555 A/Dallaglio S. 555 G/Coffrini, S. 556 C/Digfoto, S. 556/557 C/Jecan, S. 557 C/Stocktrek, S. 557 G/Sven Creutzmann, S. 557 A/Lemmens, S. 557 C/Ressmeyer, S. 558 + 558/559 A/Smith, S. 559 G/McNally (2), S. 560 G/van Ravenswaay, S. 560 C/Ressmeyer, S. 560/561 A/West, S. 562 A/Visions of America, S. 562/563 a/Jim West, S. 564 A/isifa Image Service s.r.o., S. 564 M/Alamy, S. 564 G/Barbour, S. 564/565 A/imagebroker, S. 565 C/Photo Kishmoto, S. 565 G/Forster, S. 565 M/Alamy, S. 566 L/Sinopix, S. 566 L/Le Figaro Magazine, S. 566 C/John Gollings, S. 566/567 C/Astock, S. 567 C/Sibeko, S. 568/569 A/Lawrence, S. 569 C/Fox, S. 570 C/Horwedel, S. 570 A/Sutton, S. 570/571 A/Weidman, S. 571 G/Pillitz, S. 571 C/HO, S. 571 M/Alamy, S. 572/573 Rainer Weisflog, S. 573 C/Derimais.